PLAYING THE BAND

THE MUSICAL LIFE OF JON HISEMAN

MARTYN HANSON

TEMPLE MUSIC

taught how to hold the sticks properly and shown how to do this and that, all in a few days. It took me years to learn what they perhaps learnt in those first few lessons. But the more drummers I watched, the more it seemed to me that there *were* no rules — and that suited me just fine." Growing increasingly headstrong, he often spent months working out one particular idea and being isolated from the world of *real* drumming, he served his own form of apprenticeship, one tailored to his requirements, all of which helped to formulate his unique style.

There was another aspect of playing drums that appealed to John. He was fascinated by the high degree of control that a human being was capable of attaining. Jugglers amazed him...how did they develop the muscle control required to produce such incredible feats of dexterity? He also remembers seeing a film of workers on a production line, putting records into sleeves at high speed and being impressed by the level of control exhibited. Closer to home, his father, who was a member of the *Magic Circle*, used to entertain at birthday parties by making pennies disappear and reappear in unlikely places. Despite lending his son books on how this was done, John didn't read them, preferring to delight in the 'magic'. Was it was this element of mystery that attracted him to the drums?

In the late '50s, BBC radio was the main source of entertainment in the home. It was, by nature, a conservative medium and tried hard to ignore the brash new music that, thanks to the pirate radio stations, became all the rage through the mid '60s. It would be 1967 before Postmaster General, Tony Benn, declared war on the pirates and the BBC launched its own 'pop' station, Radio One. Prior to that, most programmes were tailored to suit adult audiences and Sunday was the most popular day for listening in, as the shops were closed and the cinema was out of bounds. *Housewives' Choice*, *Family Favourites* and the legendary *Billy Cotton Band Show*, were all great shows for John to drum along to on his makeshift drum kit: "I was a dab hand at skiffle —

maybe followed by Mario Lanza or Beethoven's *Fifth* — and you just played through it all..." This wide variety of music helped enable him to tackle anything that came his way later in his professional career. Occasionally he tried tuning into foreign stations, but in those days reception was poor and anything of interest faded as quickly as it came. Still, it gave him a taste of what was out there.

The house in Eltham being semi-detached, John could bash away on the drums without incurring too many complaints from the family or the neighbours, though he *could* still be heard outside on the street. In order to keep noise to a minimum, John had to cover his drums with thick cloth 'sacks', made-to-measure by his mother, which necessitated him having to 'make' each beat, since they prevented the natural rebound from the drumhead. What he didn't realise until much later, was that this constraint served to improve his technique considerably.

John's mother had insisted that both her children attend Sunday school, which was just that — a free afternoon for parents, but *school* for the children and just like school, discipline was strict, with classes divided into age groups. Later, John joined the YPF (Young People's Fellowship) that was attached to a church-run youth club. Noticing his interest in drumming, Tom Bunce, the musical director of a small amateur orchestra that performed every month in the church, persuaded John to join as percussionist. John's first public performance was playing Rossini's *Thieving Magpie* overture, which, as luck would have it, starts with a brief snare drum solo! Tom became a great source of encouragement for John in those early years and they stayed in touch, on and off, until Tom's death some 40 years later.

Rock 'n' roll was taking off fast and many of the kids in the club were showing a keen interest in it. At this time, John met someone with whom he would have a lifelong association. John recalls: "I met Dave Greenslade at the church youth club and he and I took turns to play my homemade drums along to records. At the same church, we met Mike Savage, a drummer in the Boy's Brigade, and he had a military snare drum and a bass drum, which he loaned me while *he* played guitar. Dave was actually a gifted piano player with drum leanings that would serve him well when creating his song demos and TV music later. We formed a skiffle group and the rehearsal day before an inter-church competition made a lasting impression on me. It changed everything. We won — though truth be told, we were playing along to an offstage gramophone record of Lonnie Donegan — but I knew where I was going."

Around this time, John bought a decrepit old snare drum, Zyn cymbals and an Olympic hi-hat stand from Doc Hunt's in Archer Street, Soho. Doc wore an oil-stained white coat and his assistant — a huge, laid-back giant of a man — a grubby white apron. The drum biz, in those days, was still very 'Heath Robinson'![3] Asked how much he had to spend, John said, £6.10s (maybe £75 at today's value). They then asked if he played in a band. John describes their sales pitch: "In well rehearsed banter, the Doc suggested to his assistant that, if they did me a real good deal for my money, I might come back when I was famous — the assistant nodded vigorously. I still don't know whether I got a good deal but, yes, I *did* go back and I *did* get to be treated famously." John also learnt something important that day — something that had been puzzling him and Dave for some time...how to get a particular sound from the hi-hat cymbals. In the film *High Society*, Bing Crosby sings *Now You Has Jazz*, backed by the *Louis Armstrong All-Stars*, with drummer Barrett Deems kicking off the tune on hi-hat, but off camera. By sheer coincidence, Doc Hunt had played this exact figure demonstrating *his* hi-hat cymbals. John noted how he did it and, back home with his new gear, he and Dave quickly learned how to do it too. It was a good day's work all round!

About a year later, John found himself playing a fifteen-minute spot during 'Saturday Morning Pictures' at the Granada cinema in Woolwich. He can't remember much about the band, but when they finished playing, the manager suggested they might like to stay on and enjoy the afternoon film, *The Titfield Thunderbolt*. They were duly shown to the front row of the circle, where an usherette served them tea and biscuits! John never forgot this first taste of 'star treatment'!

Dave Greenslade was born on 18th January 1943 in Woking, Surrey but the family soon moved to Eltham in South-East London. He originally began piano lessons when he was six years old, but gave up after only a few months. Much later, at the age of 14, around the time he met John, he took up the instrument again. Dave told Chris Welch of *Melody Maker*: "I used to play drums when we were kids. John and I used to drum along to Sid Phillips[4] records, played on his old wind-up gramophone. Then one day, John suggested that I get on the piano." Dave probably inherited his musical ability from his father who had played piano in a '30s dance band called *The Melodians*. His mother also played and sang in local choirs. Dave's father was very supportive right from the outset and with his help and advice, Dave quickly developed a desire for perfection, something he had in common with John.

Through a mutual friend, they met a bass player called Darrell Smith-Lyte, who played with *Les Hobeaux Skiffle Group* and had been 'pro' for a while. He joined up with John and Dave and thus the Dave Greenslade Trio was born. Darrell then left, to be replaced by someone who would later play an important part in their musical careers, Tony Reeves. The trio played standards, except for one original composition by Dave, called *Bottle Top*. Even though these were early days, the importance of this meeting cannot be underestimated. Dave now says of the fledgling musical alliance: "I think when we played together all those years ago it was really the start of *Colosseum*." These older friends, who could afford to buy the albums, furthered John's interest in jazz. The Hiseman home didn't have an electric record player until he was 14 and a TV until he was 17!

Tony Reeves was born in South-East London on 18th April 1943. He was educated at Colfe's Grammar School, Lewisham, South London, where he met and befriended Jeff Pritchard who played French horn in the school orchestra and who happened to live at the end of John's road. Tony had always wanted to play the trombone, but fate had other ideas. When the double bass position in the school orchestra became vacant, he quickly applied for the job, planning to switch to trombone when the opportunity arose, but that never happened. To this day he can't remember why he was so keen on the trombone and has no idea where the desire to play *any* instrument came from, since no one else in his family was musical. He took two years classical tuition on the bass, but then realised he wanted to play other kinds of music. The first records that made an impression on him were *Old Rugged Cross*, by Chris Barber and the Glenn Miller EP, *In the Mood*, though he also learned much from the radio: "I accidentally found the *Service Nationale de France*, which offered an hour of jazz, five nights a week. I also listened to Willis Conover's jazz show on the *Voice of America*. These were my early influences."

Jeff, Dave, Tony and John formed a kind of cultural, socio-political clique, which did a lot of sitting around arguing, playing and listening to records — trying to work out who was doing what to whom, why, and how! Soon the four lads sought out live jazz, venturing to Ronnie Scott's Jazz Club and the Royal Festival Hall to hear bands like the *Art Blakey Quintet, Modern Jazz Quartet, Dave Brubeck, Roland Kirk* and the wonderful big bands of *Duke Ellington* and *Count Basie*.

Behind the church elders' backs, aided and abetted by members of the YPF who had duplicated keys to the church hall, they 'broke in' after the Sunday evening service and, for a couple of hours each week, played to an admiring audience in a kind of informal jazz club. Tony brought his double bass from school...they being totally unaware that their precious instrument was regularly being 'schlepped' around on London Transport! Dave played the hall's piano and John his tiny drum kit. Tony Reeves remarked later that, although they were pretty awful to start with, they nevertheless managed to play a few gigs and win a few talent competitions though Tony is convinced they only won because the opposition wasn't up to much. Still, you have to start somewhere!

In 1958, the *Dave Greenslade Trio* made their first recordings, at the church hall, with Mike Savage at the controls of a mono tape recorder. By this time, Mike was already working as a trainee sound engineer for Decca and John remembers actually going to see him there: "I spent a formative time watching him work, recording pro-musicians — that whole process went into my blood as though it had been injected intravenously." Dave recently unearthed three tracks from the trio's fledgling recordings and they make fascinating listening, but the musical standard of the band *was* pretty much as Tony Reeves had described. However, the amount of practice that John was putting in impressed Tony, who recalls that, whenever he walked past John's house, he could hear him. It's obvious that the boy Hiseman was showing a lot of determination for one so young. It was almost as if he already sensed that playing drums would be his career. He was still trying to improve his kit, but money was scarce and progress was slow: "Gradually I built up a set of drums of differing makes...there was no question of buying a drum kit complete and suddenly being able to play it all. I learnt to incorporate each new bit as I added it."

John, though, was still unsure how it all went together in a band context. He clearly recalls the night he saw his first drummer *live*. It was at Goldsmiths College, London: "I was intrigued, because it all seemed quite different to what I thought *I* was doing." John never took his eyes off that drummer all evening. Afterwards he quizzed him and was allowed to sit at the kit, hitting the cymbal and snare drum. It was quite a shock — they sounded terrible close-up, not at all how they sounded from the audience. John remembers being concerned by this: "I've never thought that drums have beautiful sounds at all and never got over how loud they were up close. I used to hear all sorts of extraneous noises as I played — the pedals squeaked, the snares rattled in sympathy with the toms and wing nuts rattled on the cymbal stands. All this worried me greatly...but as soon as you listen to the drums from twenty feet away as part of the music, or on record, it sounds quite different. Looking back, it was a very confusing time for me, but I suppose it was part of realising that what *I thought* I was doing would be perceived quite differently by an audience and for some reason I can't explain, I was *always* worried about the audience..."

Another aspect that interested him was the relationship between the hands and feet, which many young drummers back then thought of as 'independence', though for John it was always more a matter of co-ordination. He remembers Tony Reeves talking about the modern jazz drummer's left hand 'flurging about', while the right kept time on the cymbal. John tried to pin him down — *what exactly is the left hand doing?* Tony demonstrated, but it made no sense to John, who felt instinctively that there had to be a relationship between *all* the elements, *all* the different lines that a drummer played. There's no doubt he gave much more thought to theory than most drummers, but it was his *inability* to imitate others that would play a major part in the development of *his* style. He listened to lots of records, trying to emulate what he heard, but whenever he heard himself on tape recordings, he discovered to his dismay that he didn't sound like his heroes at all. John: "I tried playing in different styles for a couple of years, but gave up in the end. I realised I had no choice but to play like me. It was frustrating, because when you play with bands, they'll often ask you to copy a rhythmical feel from a record, but I could never do that and I felt bad about it. I went through a period thinking I was no good as a result." He eventually came to realise that much of his playing was instinctive and had developed over time — on the road and in the studio. He now feels that this tendency to play semi-consciously, coupled with an inherent unwillingness to analyse his own performances, meant that it wasn't until the late '80s that he began to feel happier with his playing. "From the earliest times, I became aware that when I played, I only heard the band, not the drums — in fact my only advice these days to aspiring young drummers is "Don't play the drums — play the band!"

By 1960, John was playing as many gigs as he could get: "When I was just 16, I was asked, at no notice, to go and play in a pub called The Old Tiger's Head in Lee Green, 'depping' for a drummer who hadn't turned up. Tony Reeves, who played there regularly, collected me in his van and off I went, still in my school blazer. I started setting up my drums and was told by the trumpet player, out of the corner of his mouth, to take the blazer off before Nick, the publican, saw me. There were several jokes later, about not allowing underage drinking in the pub and the crowd was assured that this 'remarkable young drummer' was on orange juice (laughter) — but they couldn't wait to hear what I would do on a double scotch!"

That same year, it was decided that John should stay on at school and study for 'A' levels, at which point he began to be dragged into extra-curricular activities. He remembers one time he was coerced by the English mistress to enter a speaking competition, requiring him to appear in front of the whole Upper School. Almost paralysed with the worst attack of nerves he had yet experienced, then the feeling of enormous relief when it was over, he quite failed to register the fact that he'd won and almost had to be dragged back onstage to reprise it. "Later, I learnt that if I prepared myself properly and knew my stuff, I didn't get nervous." He was also persuaded to give a talk on jazz: "I arrived with my records to find the school library packed. I was about to begin, when the master in charge asked me where my script was. I told him I hadn't got one, which surprised and worried him, but I started talking and they were astonished — after 90 minutes, they had to shut me up. Suddenly, I'd undergone some kind of transformation in their eyes. I wasn't nervous, because I knew I had the goods on me and from that moment, the teachers and pupils attitude to me seemed to change." This experience had certainly boosted the young Hiseman's confidence.

Days later, staff and pupils were still coming up to him and congratulating him for his talk on *History of the Origins of Jazz*. Partly due to this success and some subterfuge by the teachers, he found himself taking part in the school play, *The Winslow Boy* by Terence Rattigan. He had reluctantly accepted a small walk-on part, but it soon became clear that the boy playing the father's role, and who was seldom off-stage, would never make it to the performances and, having got John to the rehearsals, they had him trapped. After a few more run-throughs, he was told the roles would be swapped — John can still see the smirk on the other boy's face. Learning the new part was a massive task, but after playing it for three nights, he was actually quite sorry when the run ended. As he was leaving the theatre, he came face-to-face with Mrs French, the rather frosty deputy headmistress, who had her hands full with a pile of books and commanded John to help her carry them to a room down the corridor: "I remember thinking at the time that this was rather odd, but with *my* hands now full, I managed to push the handle down and went into room backwards. I turned round and suddenly there was the Lord Mayor, some other bigwigs *and* the staff — all applauding me. I stood frozen for a moment then dumped the books on a nearby table, bowed and fled. She'd done it on purpose, of course, and with stealth again — but it was an extraordinary moment. I must say they really learnt how to manage me!" This was John's first real taste of success and it definitely made a lasting impression on him.

At the start of his final year, John was called to the headmaster's study and offered the position of head boy, which he declined on the spot. The somewhat nonplussed headmaster suggested he should talk it over with his parents and he remembers that, while his mother was 'over the moon', his father was much more circumspect. John explains his refusal: "You had to be there on Saturdays *and* for other extra-curricular activities, which would have clashed with my music — my commitment definitely lay outside school. I went back to the headmaster and confirmed that I didn't want the job as I was playing in two bands and didn't have the time. He was incredulous 'You play in two bands!' To my surprise, he then asked me who I thought *should* be head boy!" Fortunately, John's suggestion coincided with the headmaster's second choice.

If John *was* being drawn towards a career in music, he wasn't aware of it — but life is made up of a series of small decisions, small steps and it seemed John had just taken another one.

FOOTNOTES

1. Between 1938 and 1945, as well as appearing in standard 'oaters', Tex Ritter starred in around 40 'singing cowboy' movies, mostly to critical scorn.

2. *Thirteen Women (And Only One Man in Town)*: Bill Haley and His Comets' [1954] *Thirteen Women* is the proto-typical atomic fantasy song that features a working 'stiff' dreaming about being the only male to survive an H-Bomb attack. The creeping beat, the plucked electric guitar chord (that signifies the hydrogen explosion) and the risque lyrics make this tune a landmark 'bomb' tune and the king of its own sub-genre: the Atomic Sex song. Reportedly, Dickie Thompson's original lyrics did not reference the bomb and it was Bill Haley's producer, Milt Gabler, who 'Atomized' the record.

3. 'Heath Robinson' — William Heath Robinson (1872-1944) was an English cartoonist and illustrator. He is best known for his drawings of eccentric machines and 'Heath Robinson' has entered the language (in British usage) as a description of any unnecessarily complex and implausible contraption.

4. Sid Phillips' son went on to become famous in his own right — drummer Simon Phillips has played with many established bands during his career and is widely acknowledged as one of rock's great drummers.

"We always got paid, but I think we were there to drown the screams of the people being tortured out the back!"
Jon's TAKE ON the regular gig at the Kray Twins' club

Chapter 2

APPRENTICESHIP

JOHN FINALLY ESCAPED FROM SCHOOL IN JULY 1962 with three 'A' levels. In his final year he had worked during the holidays, saving up for a new drum kit, eventually choosing a Premier 'Marine Pearl' set-up with Zildjian cymbals. He now came under pressure from his parents, either to go to university, or get a job! His father was keen that his son be exposed to life in the real world, but all John really wanted to do was to play the drums — he just couldn't admit that to anyone, not even to himself. He resisted getting a job for over a year, earning a few pounds gigging here and there, but it never occurred to him or anyone else that, perhaps, he was a 'professional musician'. Thanks to his circle of older friends, he had discovered musicians like Dave Brubeck and his drummer, Joe Morello. As a result, he began listening to a lot more American music, becoming aware of drummers like Gene Krupa and Buddy Rich. Later on, 'Philly' Joe Jones and Roy Haynes became favourites, but ultimately it was Elvin Jones who made the biggest impact on him. The seminal albums were *Screaming the Blues* and *Blues and the Abstract Truth* by Oliver Nelson, *Gretsch Drum Night at Birdland* and most importantly, all the records by the *John Coltrane Quartet*.

John knew he didn't want to go to University, as he'd had enough of formal education. As it turned out, help was at hand. Mike Savage's dad was a director at Unilever and he suggested John apply for a job as a marketing management trainee. He never found out whether any strings were actually pulled, but he still had to undergo a lengthy selection process, culminating in what is now called 'role-playing'. Not taking any of it too seriously, he read his brief on the train. It consisted of newspaper clippings and other documents relating to a small, traditional shirt making company faced with the dilemma of whether to expand by manufacturing cheaper 'own brand' shirts for large chain stores. John takes up the story: "You were the director of a company with decisions to make. They showed you into a real boardroom and let all the applicants argue it out, while real directors of Unilever sat round the edge taking notes on your performance."

He sat it out, listening to several of the other applicants stating, in public school accents, a variety of cases for traditional shirt making. Finally, feeling he would have to make *some* contribution, he outlined the two opposing courses of action, then combined them: "Continue making high price traditional shirts for a shrinking market, while supplying chain stores with own brand ranges and hope to achieve overall economies of scale." He must have impressed them, as he was offered his first full-time job, but secretly John had no idea of *what* he wanted to do. Unilever did, however, play an important part in defining his choices and the experience he gained in their financial, legal and organisational departments would prove to be of crucial value later on.

The time had arrived for the members of the *Dave Greenslade Trio* to branch out. John and Dave joined an R&B band, the *Wes Minster Five*, but circumstances took Tony in other directions. He had left school at 16 to bring some money into the house, as his father had died three years earlier. His first real gig was with the drummer Brian Keeble's band, at the Rising Sun, a large public house in Eltham, which had a big hall with a high stage at the back of the pub. It was really a show band, with two female vocalists and a guitarist (who was heir to the Clark's Bakery business), but it afforded Tony the luxury of rehearsals, something rarely offered later in his career, when, in most cases he would simply turn up and play.

The *Wes Minster Five* was run by Brian Smith, a gigging dance band leader and guitar teacher, who had formed this London based R&B band on the back of the '60s blues boom. Tony Reeves recalls Smith being in his late 20s, but sporting a toupee, which made him seem much older. It was John and Dave's first experience of playing in a *real* group. Tony Reeves was just an occasional member, depping for John Parmenter, but the few gigs he *did* play were quite memorable. They regularly played at American Air Force bases that were dotted around the country and since Britain was still a pretty austere place in the late '50s and early '60s, these bases seemed like paradise to these young lads. There was fast food galore, the atmosphere relaxed and informal and it was the first time they tasted 'lite beers' — Budweiser and Schlitz — all of which came as quite a culture shock, as Tony recalls: "It gave us something to look forward to and it was all very glamorous. We felt privileged."

These weren't the only memorable gigs that the *Wes Minster Five* played. As Dave Greenslade told Chris Welch of *Melody Maker*, things were moving fast: "I used to go to the Flamingo Club in Soho, with Tony and John and listen to Tony Kinsey and Ronnie Ross on a Saturday night...We never dreamt that six months later we would be playing there, sweating away at the all-nighter and dreading every gig." This famous club hosted most of the up-and-coming bands of the day as well as featuring established American jazz stars. Dave also recalls the audition they did for the Flamingo. They walked from their gig at Scene Club in Ham Yard to the Flamingo during their break, with John Parmenter lugging his double bass: "We went on stage and Georgie Fame's Hammond organ was there, which he allowed me to use. It was the first time I had ever played one — he even showed me around the instrument. It was really good of Georgie to do that." They passed the audition and landed a residency at the club, mostly playing R&B numbers such as *Green Onions* and other cover material, similar to the Fame band. Dave sums up the experience: "That band was like a school...and we met many musicians there who would later be part of our careers. At one point, Paul McDowell (who had previously had a big hit singing through a megaphone with the *Temperance Seven*) joined the band and performed a strange kind of monotonic 'camp' blues. It was all unbelievable!"

Around this time, John was 'depping' quite frequently with the Billy Woods Band, which also played the lucrative American bases. Every Saturday morning, rather than undergo the hassle of laundering and pressing their stage wear, they would buy new suits from a West End shop, leaving the old ones behind! The band played almost every night and John remembers their incredibly varied repertoire. He had to get used to playing numbers he didn't know, improvising as the song unfolded. One incident stuck in John's memory: "We were in the van one time and driving past Billy's house, so we went in for a cup of tea. It seemed to be completely furnished from the bases...he had bar stools and everything." So not only were the fees very generous — the perks weren't half bad either!

By early 1963, John was playing every Sunday night with the *Ian Bird Sextet* at The Jazzhouse, a club held upstairs in the Green Man pub in Blackheath, South London alongside Tony Reeves on bass, who had recommended him. Several well-known jazz musicians 'guested' there, including a young man called Graham Bond. The club was run by three jazz enthusiasts, Les Carter, Alan Smith and Colin Richardson, who would later would manage both the *New Jazz Orchestra* and *Colosseum*: Colin describes the set up thus: "The house band was either the *Bird/Burrows Quintet* or *Sextet*, depending on whether or not Frank Powell (who played trumpet with an upturned bell like Dizzy Gillespie), joined the front line. They always played the first set, and then the second half of the evening featured the rhythm section backing a 'name' guest (often referred to as 'the pest'!) usually someone like Tubby Hayes, Ronnie Scott, Joe Harriott, Harry Beckett, Don Rendell or Ian Carr. Clive Burrows and/or Ian Bird would sometimes join in at the end for a 'jam' as the climax of the session." John feels he owes a lot to both Ian and Clive for their confidence in him and for what he learnt while playing with the band...and the pests! Ian Bird felt that 'band sounds' (ensemble playing as opposed to lengthy solos) were important to audiences and in Clive he had a talented arranger who injected fresh elements into the jazz standards they played.

The Jazzhouse also afforded co-manager Colin Richardson the

chance to put together an 'ad hoc' band to play in: "My erstwhile attempts to play bass in a band arose out of my job as agency booker, which gave me the opportunity to get well paid college gigs. I had a ready-made pool of excellent musicians like John Hiseman and Dave Gelly to draw upon. We played jazz gigs as the *New Jazz Quintet* and music for dancing (much better paid!) as *The Cole Richards Combo*."

At the time John was very happy to play as much diverse music as possible maintaining that he just 'played the band,' absorbing the style from those around him. Indeed, on one occasion (actually, the night Cassius Clay beat Sonny Liston for the first time on 25th February, 1964) he played, with little or no rehearsal, for the musical comedy outfit *Dr Crock and his Crackpots*. The 'Maestro' arrived in an enormous Rolls Royce, with lady chauffeur and his succinct brief to John, delivered in ringing tones was just: "When I nod my head...'*it it!*"

Still semi-pro, John continued his management training at Unilever, while Dave Greenslade and Tony Reeves had already been in full-time employment for a couple of years. Dave was in a fairly boring job at a textile company's warehouse and occasionally his friend Dave Silk, who worked at the BBC, would ring him up to play him the latest jazz releases down the phone. Many a lunch hour was whiled away in this manner...at the BBC's expense! In spite of this Dave was eventually promoted from the warehouse to sales rep, but this entailed a lot of travelling which interfered with his gigging. Soon though, Dave's musical career would take him in a very different direction from John and Tony. French singer Teddy Raye saw him at the Flamingo playing with the *Wes Minster Five* and was impressed enough to offer him a job on the spot. The gig was abroad, but by then Dave was already sure that he didn't want to do a day job for the rest of his life and readily accepted. The next day he packed his bags, his Bird Contemporary dual manual organ and left the UK for his first fully professional gig!

Tony Reeves, though, had found a job in the music business straight after leaving school, working in Quality Control for Decca Records at their factory in New Malden, Surrey, where white coats were the order of the day. Tony found it all very interesting to say the least: "I listened to the entire output of Decca. There was Wagner, pop music, Mantovani, Edmundo Ros and African 'high life'." No wonder he described it as: "An incredible gamut of musical tastes and a marvellous musical education." It was the perfect environment in which to balance a day job with life as a semi-pro musician, *and* it would later give him the opportunity to get into record production.

John was still playing with the *Wes Minster Five*, as well as the regular Sunday gig at the Jazzhouse, where Clive Burrows was developing an idea for a larger band. Another important contributor to the local scene was tenor saxophonist Dave Gelly, a teacher by profession, who recalls: "Clive had written a lot of new arrangements for a large line up and thus was born the *Bird/Burrows Big Band*, which had its first rehearsal on November 10th, 1963, followed by its debut gig on December 22nd, both at the Jazzhouse." Colin Richardson outlines the rationale behind the idea: "It was originally formed as a rehearsal band, to give young up-and-coming jazz musicians a chance to gain experience of ensemble playing and reading arrangements, etc."

Apart from 'pro' musicians Ian Carr and John Mumford, the band mainly comprised young semi-pros like John Hiseman, Frank Powell, Tony Reeves, Paul Rutherford, Les Carter plus, of course, Dave Gelly. The average age was around 23, though some of the more experienced players such as Bob Leaper (a musical director at Pye Records) had played in military bands during their national service — Bob had even written arrangements for the Coldstream Guards. Early in 1964, he arranged for the band to be invited by Pye Records to test their new studios at Marble Arch. Sadly, as far as one can ascertain, none of these recordings survive.

Shortly after this promising start, the young band hit turbulence. It began with the departure of Ian Bird, after a bust-up with Clive Burrows. Not long after that, Clive himself announced that he had been offered a 'pro' gig with *Zoot Money's Big Roll Band*, which he had accepted. The nascent big band was suddenly 'sans leader'! "We didn't know what to do when Clive left, as he did everything," Dave Gelly admitted.

The band wasn't left rudderless for very long though, as John explains: "We invited Neil Ardley to come and front us because we needed somebody who could conduct and write for us and he immediately presented some scores. Of course, he was able to use the band to develop his own writing skills, which proved considerable, and before long became our leader." Neil Ardley was born in Carshalton, Surrey, on May 26th, 1937. He learned the piano and played with local jazz groups in his early teens, moving to London after leaving university in 1960. His first major gig was with the *John Williams Big Band*, all the while studying composition and arrangement with Ray Premru and Bill Russo. Ardley's arrival at the Jazzhouse injected a greater sense of purpose into the rehearsals, though as Dave Gelly recalls there was already plenty of discussion going on amongst the musicians and the young Mr. Hiseman was nearly always in the thick of it! "John was always offering opinions as to how things should be played, he was forthright and positive."

It was around this time that a review in *Melody Maker* misspelt John's name and, left uncorrected, John became Jon.

Meanwhile, Jon was developing his style with this new band: "We started off playing big band arrangements of things we had previously played as a small group. For some reason that I can't understand, I largely ignored the big brass phrases, but kept up my small group dialogue with the soloists. It simply never occurred to me to change my style, but everybody thought I was being inventive and modern. I was playing interactive, small group drums with a big band line up and this is what I subsequently did with *Colosseum*. Instead of just keeping time, when there was section work, I'd play around it." Without being aware of it, Jon was making his name and a lot of people got to hear of him, including a certain Graham Bond.

At this stage, gigs were sporadic, but rehearsals were regular...every Sunday morning at the Jazzhouse, until the pub was demolished to make way for a housing development, when they moved to the 100 Club premises in Oxford Street and a pub in New Cross. The departure of Burrows meant a new name had to be found and it was Frank Powell who came up with *New Jazz Orchestra*, as it reflected the youthfulness of the personnel and its innovative approach. Clive Burrows' original vision had been strongly influenced by Gil Evans[1], someone Neil Ardley also greatly admired. Dave Gelly explains the way Evans developed his unique orchestral sound: "His great contribution to jazz came with his recasting of the large ensemble, from the established big band format to the more flexible jazz orchestra. Instead of sticking to the use of sections (trumpets, trombones, saxes) in blocks, he would deploy the instruments in mixed combinations — a practice known as 'cross writing'."

Though big bands were declining in popularity at the time, there was still a hard core of fans who wanted to listen to them. Dave Gelly recalls that after the gigs he was always being asked where and when the next one would be. Wider recognition for the *NJO* came when they won the All England Jazz Competition, the finals of which were held as part of the Guildford Jazz Festival, and were runners-up at the National Amateur Jazz Contest held at the Reading Festival, both in 1964, with Jon's playing receiving special mention. Jazz critic Alun Morgan saw their performance at the Language Tuition Centre in Oxford Street, London, on August 6th, 1964, and wrote: "The sight of seventeen musicians ranged behind music desks is always an impressive one and the *NJO* lives up to its appearance...Whenever the trumpet section makes an entry it is apparent immediately that there are experienced players present." He went on to single out Jon's playing for praise, confirming the progress he had made: "Hiseman is a fine big band drummer and I was interested to see that he read his drum parts, an unusual accomplishment these days!" In fact, Jon *didn't* read his parts well then, or ever, but in some ways this turned out to be to his advantage. He saw musicians go through whole tours reading their parts...*still* be reading them at the end of the tour and *still* playing them the same way! Jon's method was to memorise a piece very rapidly, while playing ambiguously the first few times through, then proceed to develop those parts, sometimes over many years.

In order to end their concerts on a light-hearted note, the *NJO* had a party piece up its sleeve as its final encore. It was still the era when the national anthem was played in cinemas and theatres when the programme ended, so after the closing number, Jon would play a big diminuendo roll on his snare and the band would then come in with the very recognisable opening chords — duping many of the audience into standing up...at which point it would turn into the tango classic *Jealousy*, causing much hilarity — and a few red faces!

Around this time, Jon started playing with the *Mike Taylor Quartet*. Mike Taylor was a brilliantly economical jazz pianist, who was writing his own compositions and creating minimalist arrangements of jazz standards, all played in a very free, improvisational style. The band began as a trio in 1962, with Jack Bruce on bass and Ginger Baker on drums. When Jack and Ginger left to join the *Graham Bond Organisation*, Graham recommended Jon to Mike and Jon in turn, recommended Tony Reeves. The quartet's line-up was completed by Dave Tomlin on soprano sax. Most people who worked with Mike were amazed at just how quietly talented he was and how fearless his very 'avant garde' approach, as he pared the music down to its bare essentials. Jon had to find a way of coping with it: "The nature of much of his improvisation was not chord sequences but modal shifts. That meant piano and bass could be very free and I instinctively responded to this by developing the idea of playing pulse without bar lines and then without regard for the on and off beat. I wasn't sure what I was doing at first, but it was what the music seemed to demand and again, it was seen as innovative. Since much of the music had more to do with intertwined textures than solos, I needed a way to play a continuous tone with my feet, while my hands were free to improvise. So, about this time, I upgraded my drums to a Ludwig Silver Sparkle kit, with two bass drums." Such was the group success that they were invited to open for Ornette Coleman in London the following year. poet (and future *Cream* lyricist) Pete Brown was also involved in that gig, reading some of his poetry within the Mike Taylor set.[2]

Another band that Jon joined at this time, was *Group Sounds Five*...whose varying line-up included Henry Lowther on trumpet, Lyn Dobson on tenor sax, Ron Rubin on bass, and Tony Hymus on piano. Henry had first met Jon when they both played in the *NJO* at the Leofric Hotel, Coventry. He recalls: "I thought Jon was playing very much like Elvin Jones." *Group Sounds Five* became *Group Sounds Four* when they decided to drop the piano from the line-up and Jon remembers Jack Bruce 'depping' on a few dates with them. The band was playing two or three nights a week in the basement of the infamous Kray twins' Regency Club in Stoke Newington, London. Jon confesses he was perplexed by this residency, and still is to this day: "I don't class them as gigs because there was never any audience. We always got paid but I think we were there to drown the screams of the people who were being tortured out the back! On the ground floor of the club there was a restaurant with another band playing dance music, which always seemed to be packed." Later, the band was further reduced to *Group Sounds Three*, when Lyn Dobson left, but this line-up only ever played one gig.

Finally, after much soul searching, Jon left Unilever, following a posting to Leeds for 6 months. This was normal procedure within the company, but Jon had no intention of leaving London. In any case, he knew he had incurred the enmity of a surly Scottish assistant director, when he voiced his opinion on the wonder product of the day — *striped* toothpaste! Unilever's advertising claimed that the red stripe was a mouthwash, but internal papers Jon had seen indicated that it was just red dye. Asked, in passing, for his opinion, he replied that it was clearly a con, one that was unlikely to be tolerated in the future. The Scot, furious at what he considered to be disloyalty, was, nevertheless, quite taken aback at Jon's subsequent resignation. He and another miscreant served out their time in the 'sin bin' for a month as they faded from the company's sight.

Most of the *NJO* musicians were still semi-pro and, though it was never a regular gigging band, it was a magnet for a formidable reservoir of talent. The band members got used to seeing new faces playing in the band, but there was one new face that made more of an impression than most, especially on Jon. A student at the Royal College of Music, she was a pretty useful alto sax player, as well as being young, ambitious and full of confidence. Whilst waiting for a saxophone lesson from Charles Chapman, she had asked fellow student, John Williams, if he knew of any band that needed an alto player. He immediately gave her a contact number for the *NJO*. Jon recalled the impact she made when she first turned up at a rehearsal: "I was sitting in the rhythm section at the front of the room, facing the rest of the band, with the conductor between us. She, of course, came and sat in the front row with the other saxes. She was breathtakingly beautiful — sort of unattainably beautiful. I had to keep tearing my eyes away — trying to be cool about it. All the way through, she was grappling with her parts, but coping very well. I was very impressed with her...er, sight-reading."

Jon wasn't the only one to be transfixed by this talented new arrival, as he explains: "All these guys were playing away, but taking sideways glances at her, trying to work out what this woman was doing and what she was capable of. When it came to the drinks interval, an incredible chatting up process took place, with everybody getting in on the act. It was very funny, yet I felt strangely annoyed, mainly because she didn't appear to notice me!" At the end of that first rehearsal, Barbara was asked to leave the room while they debated whether she was suitable. She'd already proved that she was more than good enough musically and Neil Ardley was certainly in favour, but the discussion wasn't just about her musical ability, but also whether, being a woman, she might have a disruptive effect on the band! This minor concern was quickly overcome — and Barbara was in!

Jon was unquestionably attracted to this beautiful and gifted newcomer but being somewhat shy (he'd hitherto only had one real girlfriend), he held back from approaching her. He patiently watched while others chatted her up, including Dave Gelly, who was the first to ask her out....then she also briefly dated tenor sax player Jimmy Philip...but the next *NJO* member she dated would be her last!

Barbara Gracey Thompson was born in Oxford on 27th July, 1944. Neither of her parents were particularly musical...her father David Richard Thompson, was the Registrar of the Court of Criminal Appeal and her mother was quite involved with politics, once standing as a Labour candidate. She was also pretty handy with a tennis racket...often playing at Wimbledon. The musical influences came from other members of the family...her paternal grandfather William Thompson, was a very able pianist, while her maternal grandmother was an accomplished cellist. Her great uncle on her mother's side was Albert Bosworth who owned Bosworth & Co, the famous music publishers with offices in New York, Cologne, Leipzig, Vienna and London. Her parents divorced acrimoniously when Barbara was just seven, which resulted in the family being split, with her father gaining custody of Barbara and her brother Hugh, while her half-sister, Jane, stayed with her mother: "She took Jane off in a taxi and we thought she would return for us — but she didn't!"

About this time, she started learning the recorder at her primary school, and with the high standard of teaching, it wasn't long before she was playing in front of an audience: "There was a fantastic guy, Mr Yolland, who was really into music. He got us all recorders and gave us lessons. I really loved it — taught myself to read music and played a lot of tunes, so they used to put me on at the school assembly."

When she was about 10, there was a school outing to a concert, where she was enchanted by a most marvellous sound, which she discovered was a clarinet! Her Uncle Ferdy, who ran the London office of Bosworth (the famous music publishers), on hearing that she liked the sound, went out and bought her one! He was good friends with the manager of Boosey & Hawkes, who ensured that it was a good quality instrument...so good that she still plays it to this day!

In 1955, Barbara went to Queen's College in Harley Street, London, where she studied clarinet with Miss Collingwood, but her closest bond was really with her piano teacher, Miss Greenslade. Both of her schools gave her lots of encouragement, something she has never forgotten and in return, she has given much of her time to working with young musicians in jazz workshops. In 1957, she passed her Grade 8 clarinet exam with distinction and was then advised to find a more advanced teacher. There were, however, problems at home over her practising: "While my dad was very supportive, he worked long hours at the Law Courts and was often home late. My stepmother didn't like me practising because of all the nasty noises I made, so in defiance I used to shut myself away in my room and practise an awful lot, which became a real obsession in a way. I also remember playing along to a lot of old 78s and learning the clarinet part to *Bach Goes to Town*."

Also studying at the college was an exceptionally talented cellist by the name of Jacqueline du Pré, who would later gain international renown on her instrument. She was quite shy and rarely attended the lessons, though it transpired she was spending six or seven hours a day practising, a fact duly noted by Barbara![3]

Bright enough to pass five 'O' levels in 1960, Barbara went on to get 'A' levels in Music and English. Unable to bear living with her stepmother, she moved back to live with her mother in Wimbledon, who was far more supportive, even giving Barbara the money for an alto sax when she needed one to play for a fleeting moment in the *London Schools Symphony Orchestra*.[4]

In 1962, Barbara took a course at Queen's Secretarial College, but hated it and left after a year, forging a letter from her mother, giving the reason for her early departure, but making sure she intercepted the reply! She still needed to make a living though and, having few other options, she took a secretarial job anyway!

In 1963 Barbara went to see Duke Ellington in concert and was very impressed, particularly by alto saxophonist Johnny Hodges. She was captivated by his sound and the soulful way he played, deciding then and there, that she would have to learn to play her saxophone properly.[5] Her putative career in classical music now seemed unimportant, as she had become hooked on jazz, buying and listening to many classic jazz records. In May of the following year, (just four months before she joined the *NJO*) she auditioned for the legendary 15-piece all-girl *Ivy Benson Band*. The audition played to her strengths, as she could sight-read her parts and she was duly invited to join. However, it wasn't all plain sailing, as she discovered at her first band rehearsals, held in the Isle of Man. She found that she couldn't make, "head nor tail of what was going on!" They were playing 'swing music' and initially, she didn't understand that though the music notation *looked* the same, the swing phrasing, or rhythmical interpretation, is completely different to that of classical music. Also, being used to a clarinet embouchure, she was having difficulty adapting it to the also sax for any length of time. Ms. Benson was not too impressed with her efforts and initially, it was far from an enjoyable experience, but as time went on, she learned to think on her feet and eventually settled in.

Barbara stayed with the band for four months, including playing through the Old Tyme Dancing World Championships, which was quite a learning curve for her: "Blowing three hours a night, non-stop, was hard work and your 'lip' would just completely go — but I developed my 'chops' and they were as hard as iron when I finished that season!" Barbara didn't really get on with most of the band — they were a tough lot and, ironically, the only one she *did* befriend was the drummer! When she eventually decided it was time to leave, Ivy was, in fact, lining her up to take over the lead alto chair!

After departing the *Ivy Benson Band*, Barbara needed a background income, so she decided to apply for, and won, a grant-aided scholarship to study clarinet, piano and composition at the Royal College of Music, starting in September 1964. Though the Ivy Benson gig had merely been a stop gap, it had put paid to any desire to be a classical musician, as she told *New Musical Express* in 1978: "I got bored — I'd been in classical orchestras as a clarinettist since the age of 12. When I finally got to college, I found there were about 80 clarinettists, all hoping to get into the number one orchestra. I didn't want to know, realising I was more interested in expressing myself in improvised music and feared that a proper classical training would only end up inhibiting me." However, her grounding in classical music from such an early age shouldn't be underestimated and her subsequent training in composition would bear fruit much later on.

Barbara also studied clarinet with Syd Fell and piano with Peter Element, while playing in the student jazz bands led by Alan Cohen, Gordon Rose, Graham Collier and Bill Geldard, all of whom were very encouraging. She soon became a veteran of public performing, living a double life...classical training by day and playing jazz at night. Eventually, her flute teacher, John Francis, stumbled across a review of an *NJO* concert. His response was to applaud 'all the money you must be making!', though it must have been quite a shock for him to realise that one of his students was playing 'the devil's music'! If only he had known that the average *NJO* gig paid just a couple of pounds!

Meanwhile, in November 1964, the *NJO* rehearsals had relocated to the New Cross Inn, where Jon at last got his chance to speak to Barbara, who, as he suspected, hadn't really noticed him. At the break, everybody went to the bar except Jon and Barbara (who was 'on the wagon'!). As it was quite chilly, they moved to the open fire, where they chatted for the first time. During the conversation, it transpired that Barbara, who had just been given an old Ford Anglia, was looking for somebody to teach her to drive. She really needed her own transport, as she was getting fed up with having to fend off the advances of fellow musicians after they'd given her a lift home. As it happened, Jon needed a tape machine to record the Mike Taylor gigs, so a deal was struck...Jon would teach Barbara to drive and she would lend him her stepfather's tape recorder (without his knowledge, it seems!). Jon hadn't yet found the courage ask her out...someone always beat him to it, but those who had, didn't seem to have made much impression. So, the next Saturday morning, Jon drove over to Wimbledon for Barbara's first lesson and to collect the tape recorder: "When I got there, I couldn't get past the gate for this huge collie. On his hind legs, 'Jock' was as tall as me and I guess he was having great fun. I made several attempts to get from the gate to the house, but was beaten back every time. After 20 minutes of this, I was just about to give up when the front door opened and a sleepy Barbara emerged —

wearing a baby-doll nightie...and that was that! We started to see more and more of each other from that moment."

Early in 1965, Colin Richardson, the *NJO* manager, was contacted by Ray Horrocks, a producer at Decca Records, who was keen to record the band. Jazz critic Alun Morgan had already commented that a first album by the band would "represent a major breakthrough in British jazz." That was about to be put to the test. It was decided that, in order to keep costs down, it would be recorded live, in one three-hour session at Decca's West Hampstead studio. So, on Sunday 14th March, after just a few days' rehearsal, they recorded *Western Reunion* in front of a noisily enthusiastic audience. The tracks they recorded were mainly well-known jazz compositions, but with fresh arrangements, giving them a stamp of originality. The band continued recording for a while after the audience had left and Dave Gelly remembers being extremely tired by the end of the session. It had been a long day, but at least they had more material in the can than they would need for the album.

For Jon, though, the day ended in trauma. Isolated from the band in a drum booth, he was wearing headphones for the first time, through which was piped a rough mix of the performance. These headphones were clearly never meant to be worn on the bobbing head of a drummer — as Jon remembers it, they were the same as those used by telephonists and he spent the whole session, trying to keep them on his head. Finally, as the band approached the climax of *Western Reunion*, the headphones could resist the force of gravity no longer, flew off and Jon lost contact with the band. Listening to the subsequent playback, Jon was mortified at the result, but thankfully, the producer understood the situation and was able to splice in another, and better, take. Today such editing is taken for granted, but in those days, especially in the hallowed halls of the Decca Recording Company, it was deemed to be 'cheating.' So Ray Horrocks decided that a couple of lines explaining the edit should be included in the LP sleeve notes. On receiving a copy of this, his first recording, Jon remembers just wanting to crawl away and die!

Western Reunion was released in July and promptly selected as *Melody Maker*'s 'Jazz Album of the Month', ahead of offerings by Wayne Shorter and Lionel Hampton...exalted company indeed! Alun Morgan's prediction had come true...the *New Jazz Orchestra* had put down a solid marker!

Barbara didn't play a solo on the album, mainly because, as she was aware, she wasn't yet fully developed as a jazz musician and had the humility to admit it. As she told *New Musical Express*, in 1978: "In the early days when I couldn't really play, people could have been nasty to me, but they were always encouraging. No one taught me as such, but I learned a lot from working alongside great musicians like Don Rendell and Art Themen. I was lucky, because I suppose if I'd mixed with some of the more elitist musicians, I might have been scared off." Ian Carr observed that the *NJO* was like a university and, as happens in such institutions, people graduate and leave. It often served as a springboard to other endeavours and 'played with the *New Jazz Orchestra*' was a valuable entry to have on your CV. It helped to launch the careers of many young musicians of the day and always retained a special place in their hearts. Many of them remained loyal to the band for years, often foregoing better paid gigs to appear with the band.

Jon had by now been friends with Dave Gelly for some time and it was he who considerably broadened Jon's knowledge of the important jazz figures, past and present. He was great at putting their qualities into words and taught Jon much about the elegance inherent in their playing. Dave, who didn't drive at that time, was always picked up by Jon for the *NJO* rehearsals and gigs. Needless to say, this arrangement now petered out as Jon's attentions became firmly focused elsewhere...

FOOTNOTES

1. Gil Evans was born in Toronto on May 13th, 1912 and later moved to the United States, where he made his mark as a pianist and arranger working with the *Claude Thornhill Orchestra*, winning two successive *Billboard* polls. He had no problem combining such diverse musical styles as Debussy and Charlie Parker and described his sound as: "Everything — melody, harmony, rhythm — was moving at minimum speed. Everything was lowered to create a sound, and nothing was to be used to distract from that sound...the sound hung like a cloud." Evans is mainly remembered for his work with Miles Davis, especially on *Sketches of Spain* and *Birth of the Cool*. There are many who think that Evans didn't get full credit for the work he did with Davis, but it is probably fairer to say that he never promoted himself sufficiently.

2. In the early '60s there was a movement that combined jazz and poetry led by Mike Horowitz. One such project, *New Departures*, included Pete Brown and Dick Heckstall-Smith. Pete recalls: "Ginger Baker and Jack Bruce would sometimes sit in...the jazz scene in those days was quite small." Jon was also involved in the jazz and poetry movement from time to time, until one gig where the poet started throwing raw meat at the audience to emphasise his rhymes. That was OK — until the meat started to come back and Jon, rooted to the spot at his drumkit, became the 'prime' target.

3. When Barbara was 18, she met Jacqueline du Pré again at a party and let her know that, hearing of the amount of time she spent practicing, had made a big impression on her. Acknowledged as one of the greatest cello players of all time, Jacqueline was tragically diagnosed with multiple sclerosis (MS) and gave her last public concerts in New York in February 1973. After a long, slow decline, she died in London on 19 October 1987, aged 42.

4. The following story aptly sums up Barbara's quixotic nature. When playing clarinet with the *London Schools Symphony Orchestra* and rehearsing for a concert at the Royal Festival Hall, she volunteered to play the saxophone solo in an extract from Zoltán Kodály's *Háry János Suite*. What nobody knew was that she didn't actually own a sax at the time, so one had to be hurriedly purchased — with her mother's money! She knew nothing about saxophones and based her choice on price, but after a subsequent overhaul, it turned out to be a particularly fine example of the classic Conn 'Underslung' alto — which she still plays today. Barbara was naturally very nervous as her moment approached, but she must have performed with some distinction, because renowned broadcaster and critic, Peter Clayton, reviewing the concert, commented on her "finely controlled vibrato". Wonderful what nerves can do!

5. Coincidentally, John Coltrane also switched from clarinet to alto saxophone after seeing Hodges play.

> *"Jon joined at very short notice and with no rehearsal, having heard the band and been persuaded to give up his day job by Graham's high pressure sales technique during one long night of rabbit."*
> DICK HECKSTALL-SMITH

Chapter 3

HAVE DRUMS — WILL TRAVEL

ON LEAVING UNILEVER TOWARDS THE END OF 1964, Jon got himself a job with Television Audience Measurement (TAM), a market research company. The company installed fine looking clocks linked to TVs in a 'statistically correct' cross section of homes. They contained a mechanism which burned marks onto paper tape, indicating which channels were being watched and when. The company worked hand in glove with advertising agencies, producing reports enabling them to target campaigns accurately. Jon was hired as a progress chaser, whose main job was to steer these reports through the system, but he was just as unimpressed with TAM as he had been with Unilever. Work was constantly conflicting with his musical activities; although even then he didn't really consider himself good enough to turn professional...not that he had a clear idea of what 'good enough' was. However, he was painfully aware that he was still hearing drummers without understanding what they were doing. Playing, as he was, with several different bands, meant a hectic schedule of one-off gigs. Jon remembers one manic weekend: "I left work at 5pm Friday and went to Brixton Town Hall to rehearse with singer Danny Williams, of *Moon River* fame, for a midnight cabaret. I then drove off to a dance gig, getting back in the nick of time to play Danny's show. When that finished, I went to the Flamingo and played from 1am till 5am with the *Wes Minster Five*, finally getting to bed an hour or so later. Up again at 9am, I drove to central London to do a session for a demo of *My Boy Lollipop* with 'pop' artiste Millie — then it was off to a rehearsal at the Green Man, Blackheath. After a hasty tea at home, I drove to a gig at an American Air Force base, arriving back at 4am on Sunday morning...then up again at 8am for *another* recording session at Island Studios and back for a lunchtime rehearsal at the Green Man with the *Ian Bird Sextet*. I managed to snatch an hour's break, before driving to a gig in Tonbridge that evening, where I arrived minus my cymbals. I didn't make it in to work on Monday morning!"

Jon was also doing occasional stints with Richard Rodney Bennett and Jean Hart at Peter Cook's Establishment Club, as well as 'depping' on the London jazz scene. This manic schedule would continue until mid 1966, though not often at the level of the weekend described.

Around this time, Ian Carr persuaded producer Denis Preston of Lansdowne Studios to record the *Mike Taylor Quartet* album, *Pendulum*, which was made up of half Taylor originals and half standards, with a heavy emphasis on improvisation. For this reason, it was never likely to find a wide audience, something Taylor acknowledges in the sleeve notes, where he also summed up his philosophy: "Our music comes out of the innate character and personality of the musicians who play it.[1]" Tony Reeves[2] recalls: "We made the album in a couple of days. I didn't realise it then, but Mike was a depressive. He was smoking a lot and tried to turn me onto cannabis, but it had no effect." Looking back, Tony thought he worked well with Jon on that album, and indeed, *Pendulum* would later become accepted as a seminal work — possibly the first truly original record by a British jazz artist. Rhythmically and harmonically, it owed almost nothing to the American jazz heritage. His work, like his character, has, with the passage of time, come to be considered unique. Jon recalls depping for Trevor Tomkins in the famous *Don Rendell/Ian Carr Quintet* at the 100 Club, when Ian persuaded Don to let Mike sit in: "An apprehensive Rendell introduced him in the second half, counted in a fast blues and Mike sat at the piano playing nothing through the theme and first solo, then proceeded to play the same single note sporadically throughout his own solo and on to the end of the piece. The crowd applauded wildly...though, looking back, it was probably a case of the 'Emperor's New Clothes'...but to me, that took courage and I thought it showed just how special he was — and of course it *was* the right note!" It's hard to imagine the impact of that contribution now, but one thing is certain, Jon Hiseman never forgot it!

Around this time, Jon played on an album with the *Peter Lemer Quintet*. Peter was another pianist writing his own material and when John Stevens vacated the drum chair, Jon was drafted in. Once again, Tony Reeves was on double bass, Nisar Kahn on tenor sax and John Surman playing baritone, soprano and clarinet. Jon had first worked with this quintet early in 1965 and had been gigging on and off with them for five months, including a weekly spot at Ronnie Scott's Old Place. The album was recorded at a studio owned by Eddie Kramer, who would later become well known for his work with the *Jimi Hendrix Experience* and *Led Zeppelin*, at New York's famous Electric Lady Studios[3], but at this time, like the young musicians who used his studio, he was also serving his apprenticeship. The cuts on the record are quite long and feature some wild playing, with Peter being especially impressed with Jon's performance, as he recalled recently: "He was very smooth and very easy to play with. He was able to play any rhythm and was very sympathetic to what was going on." The album was called *Local Colour* and, as Peter Lemer explained in the liner notes, the musicians were very involved in the creative process: "We take from one another and give willingly, unwillingly, knowingly and unknowingly. Our paid and unpaid performances in clubs, concerts and on the album are a willing, knowing return for all that has been given us." Some time after the album was completed, Peter departed for New York...and the quintet was history! However, Peter and Jon would eventually become lifelong friends, spending much time together, both on the road and in the studio.

Mid 1965, Jon decided to leave TAM...he hated it anyway, but it wasn't long before he found more conducive employment. His old friend Colin Richardson got him a job at the London City Agency as a booker and thought he was pretty good at it. Jon remembers feeling uncomfortable, phoning promoters and giving them the 'hard sell', but it *did* teach him the agency side of the music business and this experience would prove invaluable later on.

Given Jon's later involvement with studio production, one rather strange episode occurred while he was at LCA. One of the directors, Johnny Jones, had taken on a band called *The Tea Set*, who had made a demo recording which Jon thought had potential as a single. As a result of voicing this opinion, he was invited to produce it, as he recalls: "The session was set for a Sunday morning and I met up with the band outside the studio — which was all locked up. Although we waited for a couple of hours, nobody arrived to let us in, so in the end we gave up and went home. I don't remember any explanation being forthcoming and *The Tea Set* was never mentioned again." So Jon's debut as a producer would be delayed for a few years!

Still 'semi-pro', Jon was playing every gig he could, including many depping jobs, garnering as much experience as possible...weddings, bar mitzvahs, circus bands, jazz and blues; even one gig with naked female contortionists! Once, after giving Chico Arnez, a then famous bandleader a lift home late one Saturday night, he was invited up to meet the daughter: "...you're just the sort of boy she should meet!" With such a heavy workload, it was no surprise that he was getting noticed by other musicians, one of whom was Graham Bond. One Sunday, around lunchtime, drawn by the sound of a big band, he had wandered into the 100 Club in Oxford Street and seen Jon play at an *NJO* rehearsal. He mentioned to Dick Heckstall-Smith that, if ever the drum chair became vacant in his band, Jon would be ideal. Well, it seemed that the time had now arrived. Ginger Baker was leaving to form the 'supergroup' *Cream*, with Jack Bruce and Eric Clapton, but when Bond finally offered Jon the gig, it created a dilemma for him — he would finally have to confront the idea of becoming a professional musician. It was decision time!

Graham Bond was one of the main exponents of British modern jazz and R&B, blowing outrageous alto sax, playing great Hammond organ and singing a mean blues. Since he often did all three almost simultaneously, he dominated any stage he was on. He first came to national prominence in Alexis Korner's groundbreaking *Blues Incorporated*, which included Jack Bruce on double bass, Peter 'Ginger' Baker on drums and Dick Heckstall-Smith on tenor sax. Before long, Graham persuaded Alexis to incorporate an organ trio spot into the act, featuring Jack and Ginger, which went down a storm with the crowds. This gave Graham ideas and very soon the three of them left to form the *Graham Bond Trio*, which then changed its name to the *Graham Bond ORGANisation*. Eventually, in September 1963, Dick was added to the line-up, after he left *Blues Incorporated*.

Richard Malden Heckstall-Smith was born in Ludlow on 26th September, 1934, into a family with connections to the higher echelons of society. As Dick's son, Arthur, explains: "My father's paternal grandfather, Malden, was the head of a shipyard on the Clyde and the editor of *Yachting Monthly* from 1921–1926. He was one of three brothers, the others being Brooke and Smithey, all deeply involved in the yacht racing world with a number of respected books on the subject to the family name. Brooke's son, Anthony, authored the book *Sacred Cowes* in 1965, which contains fascinating tales of yachting with the elite and aristocracy of the time. It included a story I always remember, of sailing with the German Kaiser just before the outbreak of the First World War and the Kaiser expressing sadness at the prospect of not being able to go sailing with the King any more." Notwithstanding such connections, Dick's immediate family were not particularly wealthy...probably something akin to Orwell's 'lower upper middle class'.

Dick's father, Hugh, was a teacher at Stowe Public School and kept up the family's literary tradition by also becoming an author. While at Stowe he taught future cinema heartthrob, David Niven, who apparently never forgot him. Hugh was also Captain of an artillery company in the First World War. In his autobiography, *Doubtful Schoolmaster* (published in 1962) he amusingly relates how, during the battle for Ypres in Belgium, returning from lunch with a surfeit of wine in him, threw caution to the winds and strolled back to rejoin his company...reasoning that the Germans were not actually *aiming* at anybody in particular, with their so-called 'neutralising' fire. Suddenly, a shell exploded nearby and the shrapnel badly injured his leg, putting him, to his great relief, out of the war.

In addition to a number of physics reference books and a 1957 publication, *Atomic Radiation Dangers*, in which he tried to explain in lay terms what the consequences of atomic war would be, he also regularly lectured on science and religion. Despite these apparent convictions, his autobiography reveals an unceasing self-analysis — 'am I doing more harm than good?' His inquiring, probing, yet introspective mind was typical of the man who strongly influenced Dick throughout his life, though there was a downside, as Arthur confirms: "Unfortunately, my granddad could be a bit of an intellectual bully." So perhaps it was no surprise that Dick decided to do something completely different with *his* life.

The family eventually settled in Elgin, Scotland, where Dick attended the famous Gordonstoun School. It was around this time that he first heard soprano saxophonist Sidney Bechet...in particular his *Creole Blues*. He played his album *Bach Goes to Town* 'into the ground' (this album would also influence Barbara Thompson later). Ravel's orchestration of Mussorgsky's *Pictures At An Exhibition* was another seminal album for him. In due course, he succeeded in persuading his father to fork out £10 for a Maltese soprano saxophone. As he explained to *New Musical Express*: "I was undoubtedly the greatest copier of Bechet the world has ever seen — vibrato, timing, rhythm and approach, but Bechet on a very bad day!" By 1949, the family had moved to Devon and Dick left school to enter Cambridge University. However, having fallen out of love with formal education and after working on his father's farm, he decided to study agriculture, but quickly became more interested in joining the university jazz band. His saxophone playing was improving quickly, so much so that, in 1955 he won a silver cup for his solo at the Inter-University Jazz Contest. The panel of judges was headed by bandleader Sandy Brown, who made a mental note of Dick's talent.

At the end of the three years, it was time to leave university. Arthur believes some strings might have been pulled: "We wondered if Hugh used his influence to get Cambridge to award Dick his degree. It was obvious he wasn't actually studying anything and certainly had no plans to go into agriculture." Jon Hiseman remembers Dick being proud of being the only M.A. Cantab. in tractor driving! Shortly after leaving Cambridge, he bought himself a tenor sax. All of this musical activity left his father cold...convinced that his son was wasting his time. However, this was the '50s and Dick was about to get 'called up'! National Service was still in force in Britain — two years to serve your country in one of the Armed Forces. In his book, *The Safest Place in the World* (re-published as *Blowing the Blues* in 2004), Dick relates, with typical understatement: "The nearest thing I made to a political decision in those days was to register as a conscientious objector." In fact, it was a bold move to be an open dissenter in this era: "At the subsequent tribunal, I pleaded my case as a schoolboy pacifist and was rewarded with 18 months hospital work instead of 18 months gaol." In the event, he only served eight months; five months at St Bartholomew's Hospital, Smithfield, and three gruelling months in another hospital, suffering increasing bouts of back pain. He was finally discharged from his National Service commitments with a slipped disc; it was the first serious back trouble he'd had, but wouldn't be the last.

Just before Christmas 1957, Sandy Brown rang Dick and asked him to join his band. Before long, he was at the Humphrey Lyttelton Club (later the 100 Club, Oxford Street) playing a few weeks' stint with the band. He was aware he was serving an apprenticeship, but eventually felt the music wasn't challenging him enough. By now he knew that he wanted to become a professional musician and his chance came when, in the spring of 1958, he had a call from Ronnie Smith to join his band for season at Butlin's holiday camp, Filey. As the only horn player, he was promised solos, so he accepted the offer...but it didn't turn out to be the great musical adventure he had hoped. In fact, the mundane nature of the residency is brilliantly parodied by cartoonist *Biff* in Dick's book. The illustration shows a couple dancing right in front of Dick, who was playing but thinking "Only forty minutes to go before that Biriani!"

At the end of September 1958, the season over, Dick returned to the family home in Totnes, Devon to marry a beautiful young girl called Gary. She had arrived from Austria the previous year and had only been in the UK for a few weeks when she saw Dick at the Lyttelton club: "I loved jazz and I think we noticed each other that first night. I saw him again a few weeks later in the basement of another club in Soho. I was chatting to one of his friends when he came over. It wasn't long before we were dating." There would be no honeymoon, however, as he had a gig in Bristol the following day. They lived in an Islington bed-sit and Gary describes what it was like being married to a musician: "He was always practising, even when I was sleeping!" Though life was far from easy, they managed and six years later, Gary presented Dick with a baby son, Arthur.

Over the next few years, Dick played in various jazz bands and, after his infatuation with Bechet waned, he became strongly influenced by American saxophonist Wardell Gray, all the while developing his own bebop-influenced style. Times were hard however...by night he was blowing at thriving clubs like the Nucleus and Café de Artistes, but during the day, though barely able to stay awake, he worked at Dobell's, a jazz record shop in the Charing Cross Road. This lack of sleep would eventually lead to him using stimulants...as Dick wrote in his book: "They were amphetamines and they were magnificent. They kept me bright-eyed and bushy-tailed — able to go without sleep for quite long periods." Within a couple of years he was adding alcohol to the mix and, under its influence, began cutting out everything that didn't lead him directly to 'the safest place in the world'; the stage. During the years 1959–1961, he took any gig that paid, including playing in the *Johnny Burch Quartet* (with Ginger Baker) and the *Basil Kirchin Small Band*, even switching to baritone sax for a job with *Jerome Robbins' Ballet:USA* on a five month world tour.

By the early sixties, Dick was becoming disillusioned with the jazz scene. Fortuitously, rhythm and blues was beginning to gain a foothold in the London clubs. He had liked the blues since his schooldays, listening to artists like Muddy Waters and Leadbelly, but was even more interested in those blues bands playing with rock-based rhythm sections. However, the saxophone wasn't an instrument much welcomed by blues purists, so Dick's decision to switch to playing blues was quite a risky move. Gary recalls: "It was getting harder and harder for Dick to find a jazz gig and we were quite hard-up, so when Alexis Korner offered him the gig with *Blues Incorporated*, he jumped at the opportunity."

In his book, Dick explains that the kind of music he liked was 'full-blooded and free of self-imposed restrictions': "I began to feel that jazz audiences and jazz musicians alike had somehow got on the wrong road, browbeaten into believing that it wasn't quite right to enjoy themselves too openly..." He obviously felt there was something missing in the jazz scene, which he found in abundance with *Blues Incorporated*. The fact was that Dick was attracted to music that didn't have too many rules...he preferred to make up his own!

There weren't any record shops selling blues records in the early '60s. Even the famous Swing Shop in London was really just a jazz shop that also stocked a few blues albums. In spite of this, it became a magnet for fledgling fans and for rising blues musicians like Jeff Beck, Eric Clapton and *The Rolling Stones*. The R&B scene was relatively new and *Blues Incorporated* had to work hard to break in. But, as the number of paying customers began to dramatically increase, it wasn't long before some of the jazz venues began a metamorphosis into blues clubs. Thanks to the pioneering work of Alexis Korner and Cyril Davies building up the British blues scene, legendary blues artists such as Muddy Waters and John Lee Hooker were soon flying over from the States to play in the UK, often backed by groups such as *John Mayall's Bluesbreakers*; yet these blues giants were to remain almost anonymous in their own country for many more years to come.

Jon didn't immediately accept Graham Bond's offer to join the band. It was a big move, as the *GBO* were one of *the* bands to see — with its fantastic rhythm section of Jack Bruce and Ginger Baker, the ferocious attack of Graham Bond playing alto sax and Hammond organ simultaneously — and the wild blowing of Dick Heckstall-Smith. However, by mid 1966 the *GBO* was in a state of flux and had been for some time. Increasing friction between Jack and Ginger had forced Jack to leave the band some months previously but now, unbelievably, Ginger Baker was also leaving...to form *Cream* with Jack!

Graham Bond never got over what he saw as 'that betrayal' and having added trumpeter Mike Falana to the line up, decided he didn't need a bass player at all...he could play those lines with his left hand — though, charlatan that he was, he never did get into playing bass lines with his feet, like Jimmy Smith. Jon tells the story in Harry Shapiro's excellent book...*Graham Bond: The Mighty Shadow*: "Mike Taylor told me that Graham was looking for a new drummer as Ginger was leaving and advised me to go for it, but I said I didn't want to. Graham then rang me at the booking agency and asked me if I wanted to join and I said no, but he was very persuasive." He certainly wasn't giving up with one phone call. Part two of the match was played on away turf, as Jon told Shapiro: "I went with Mike Taylor to where Graham was living on the Sheen High Road. Graham took me up to his bedroom and rolled a huge joint, of which I had a puff or two. Graham's joints were magnificent, like miniature bonfires...I remember this very cultured man sitting, cross-legged on the end of the bed, telling me about his magnificent *ORGANisation* which I would be a fool not to join." Bond regaled the youngster with wondrous visions of a golden future — £35 a week (three times what he'd been earning at the day job), at least twenty five gigs a month and potential stardom...all backed by the august Robert Stigwood Agency.

There was no doubt Bond 'talked a good game', so what could possibly go wrong? Jon finally agreed to join...and at this point had to face up to telling his parents that he was turning professional. It was early July 1966.

As it turned out, Jon made his band debut before Baker officially left. It seems Ginger couldn't make a gig at the Ram Jam Club, Brixton early in his notice period and, following several frantic late afternoon phone calls, Jon filled in: "I didn't have a clue what I was doing and I had no rehearsal, but my ability to play ambiguously and feel my way through came to the fore. I had no real background in R&B either, having never heard any original American blues artists, although I *had* heard a lot of blues bands at the Marquee and the Flamingo and of course, played with the *Wes Minster Five*."

For some time, Jon had been aware of a rhythmical shift taking place, as the syncopation of swing and jazz was overtaken by the much 'squarer' rock feel. It fuelled quite a debate amongst the 'old school' of jazz musicians, many of whom perceived it as 'dumbing down'. Jon remembers stopping off late one night at a motorway service station soon after he had joined Graham and talking to a couple of older jazz musicians about this very subject: "You mustn't get involved, you mustn't play this eight-in-the-bar thing. You could be a great jazz drummer," Ian Carr and Don Rendell told him. Jon thought they were from a different planet, later explaining his reaction to this debate on *Rocklife* on WDR in 1994: "For me this shift into a squarer eight feel was a very natural thing that I felt more comfortable with....And even though I eventually learned to play the jazz rhythm, it always seemed second hand to me. I felt instinctively that a European drummer, whatever his style, was not going to contribute much to that special American language."

Chris Welch of *Melody Maker* reviewed one of Jon's early gigs at the Marquee on the 8th August, enthusiastically headlining his piece: 'Go Johnny, go!' The set included *Wade in the Water, Night Time is the Right Time* and *Oh, Baby!* Obviously a drummer of Ginger's reputation would be missed and his fans in the audience were doubly unnerved when they first saw Jon's two bass drum set-up. The roadies later told Jon that Graham had boasted long and loud to Ginger of his replacement's extra bass drum, which he had seen at the Ram Jam gig. Ginger immediately went into Drum City and purchased a second one. While the Baker fans might have been sceptical of the new man's abilities, Chris Welch (who was an amateur drummer himself) offered a neutral, but positive, verdict: "Jon proved to be not only a worthy successor to the departed Ginger Baker, but a fantastic technician and an individualist who is already altering the sound of the band. Jon himself is also making the transition from a pure modern jazz drummer, and judging from the audience reaction, he can make the fans happy." Chris thought the Baker fans were well and truly silenced, especially when they heard Jon's solo. As he related recently: "He had more technique than Ginger, and he could play so many more things, although he wasn't as brutal." The truth is that Jon wasn't troubled by being compared to Ginger, as he had only seen him for the first time a couple of days prior to taking over and only knew him by reputation. There is one thing, however, that Jon regrets about those early days of the band...the promo picture taken on Barnes Common, with him wearing sunglasses and a fez, which turned up in magazines and newspapers for years!

With Chris Welch's 'rave' review still ringing in his ears, Jon soon began to realise that Graham's promises were wishful thinking...The promised £35 a week was never forthcoming, the travel arrangements were chaotic and although the playing was an exhilarating experience, after several weeks Jon decided he'd seen enough. The organisation of the *ORGANisation* couldn't go on the way it was. He confronted Graham about the irregular finances of the band and told him he was going to leave unless they were put on an even keel. Bond pointed him in the direction of Dick, who showed him a tatty diary that passed for the band's accounts ledger. As Jon had only been receiving odd sums of money from time to time, not amounting to anything meaningful, he volunteered himself for the job of band accountant. A few years earlier, Bond had faced the same questions from Ginger Baker, but Jon's more practical approach was rather different.

By the time Jon joined the *GBO*, he had been living in Mike Taylor's old flat in Kew, having left home and taken over the lease when Mike could no longer afford it. Mike's lifestyle was degenerating, largely due to his increasing use of drugs and, by this time, he was virtually penniless and dossing around in various 'squats'. Barbara had also finally moved out of her parents' house, partly as a result of falling out with her stepfather, upon whom Jon had not made a good impression. She recalls: "We were going on a camping holiday to Italy to see my cousins. I had got a sleeping bag and we were messing around in it when my stepfather came in, and having a Victorian attitude, promptly banned Jon from the house. We weren't even doing anything interesting!" Barbara initially shared a flat with a girlfriend on the other side of the river in Chiswick, but was spending more and more time at Jon's place and soon, things came to a head. Jon: "I was with Bond and I'd get back early in the morning and Barbara would be asleep in the single bed. The group rarely stayed in hotels, driving out and back from London every night and I was getting no sleep, and not just for the obvious reason. In the end, after nodding off while driving on the motorway early one morning and being woken in the nick of time by the ever watchful Dick, I told Barbara she could only sleep over on my days off — but they were few and far between." Jon then left for a short tour of Scotland and on his return a few days later, at the crack of dawn; Barbara was fast asleep in a large *double* bed!

Following his ultimatum, she'd searched the adverts in the local newsagents and found just the thing. Using her initiative, she had gone out onto Chiswick High Road, flagged down a lorry and asked the driver if he wanted to earn a fiver delivering a bed. Jon succinctly commented later: "It kind of let me know where my real talents lay, in no uncertain terms!"

Graham Bond always blamed the band's dire financial circumstances on Robert Stigwood, maintaining they were being ripped off in some way. Not knowing who to believe and unable to get to the bottom of all the mumbo jumbo, Jon suggested a meeting with Stigwood; even taking a concealed tape recorder in with him[4], in case anything incriminating was let slip. Stigwood was charm itself and obviously didn't know anything about the day-to-day survival of a band on the road. However, his assistant, Robert Masters, suggested in a separate meeting that the band was not being well served by the office and would be better off elsewhere. Jon came to realise later that Masters had in fact, engineered their departure by playing on their fears, because the office didn't believe that the *ORGANisation* would ever have a hit record and just wanted rid of them. Whatever the case, the upshot was that they no longer had a manager or agent!

After Jon had played just a few gigs, Graham had announced that they would be recording a single to kick-start the new band. The climax to the live show was always *Wade in the Water*, which opened with a solo pastiche of Bach's *Toccata & Fugue in D Minor*, with Graham at the 'cathedral organ'. They recorded this, plus another track, in just a few hours, at the original Olympic Studio in North London, though as the session was presumably financed by Stigwood and that relationship foundered, this single was never released and Jon believes the tapes have now been lost.

In August of that year, they were approached by the Starlite Agency, run by the avuncular Peter Walsh. His bookers had told him that the *GBO* was one of the hottest groups on the club circuit, so from a business point of view, he was quite interested in taking them on. But his enthusiasm was tempered by Graham Bond's reputation as a volatile character and someone who was 'doing' drugs. However, he got on well with Jon and with his fears somewhat allayed, he offered the group a six month contract, conditional on Graham getting 'clean'.

The last week of August 1966, saw Jon completing the first proper band accounts, with his accounting experience gained at Unilever coming to the fore. A gig at Manchester's Jigsaw Club realised £75...a considerable sum in those days, but with the cost of keeping four musicians and two crew on the road, plus having to maintain the vehicles and gear, Jon soon came to realise that the band had probably been running at a loss for some time. However, he kept it going as best he could, living from hand to mouth...'robbing Peter to pay Paul', at the same time getting to know Dick Heckstall-Smith and enjoying the voyage of discovery that was Graham's musical vision.

Bond was a complex character who lived totally in his own world — a world skewed by constant pot-smoking and heroin use, which produced grandiose visions, often powerfully expressed. Jon quickly found that, faced with Graham's demands for money to support his habit, he had little control over expenditure. By turns charming and aggressive, Graham was at best inspirational and at worst thoughtless, devious and irrational...bringing to mind the famous line in *Citizen Kane*, where Leland exclaims: "Charlie Kane's not brutal, he just does brutal things!"

In order to comply with Peter Walsh's condition and to achieve it in time to be back on the road for the lucrative run-up to Christmas, roadie Pete Bailey realised that Graham would have go 'cold turkey', i.e. to stop 'using' and suffer the terrible withdrawal symptoms. He also knew that this would be impossible, unless he got him away from his 'connections'. So, it was decided that they would go to Ireland from mid-September to early October. The erstwhile leader, together with his roadies, hired a boat and set off down the river Shannon. On their return, the trip was hailed as a triumph of mind (Graham's) over matter, since both roadies proclaimed that, against all the odds, the maestro was finally 'clean'! Dick was sceptical, to say the least, maintaining that there was never any genuine attempt to turn the situation round, since Graham had taken his 'stash' with him!

Jon believes it more likely that he only took a couple of days supply of heroin and clearly remembers the situation when they resumed working: "I turned up at the first gig after their trip, to find Graham quite mad as a result of what seems to have been a nightmarish ordeal — one from which, in my opinion, he never fully recovered. He fixed me with his 'eye' and implored me to believe that he had to be the strongest man alive to have survived this trial by fire successfully and that as a result, the future would now be bright for him and his 'chosen ones'! He then showed me the upper part of his body, covered in bruises that he said had been caused by throwing himself around the confined spaces of the boat during the withdrawal period. Pete Bailey confirmed this apparent success by telling me that, towards the end of his suffering, Graham had pleaded for his life, so Pete had gone to Dublin, and found 'the only heroin in Ireland'. By the time he returned however, Graham was 'through to the other side', so they threw it overboard! In my naivety I was impressed, to say the least, but it was clear to me that Graham wasn't right. Although no-one mentioned anything to me, it's possible they had also taken LSD on board to alleviate his withdrawal symptoms, but too much of that stuff could easily have resulted in the man I saw before me!"

To add insult to injury, an advance against earnings had been procured from the Starlite Agency to pay the cost of the trip and the musicians' wages during this enforced break — so, in reality, the cost of the trip had been funded by the band!

FOOTNOTES

1. Mike Taylor did eventually find a degree of popular success, but, ironically, as a songwriter for *Cream*. Ginger Baker managed to pull him together long enough for the pianist to contribute three tracks for the *Wheels of Fire* album, in 1968. They were *Pressed Rat and Warthog*, *Passing the Time* and *Those Were the Days*, all co-written with Ginger.

2. Tony Reeves was also involved in some interesting projects at this time, including producing an album of *Beatles* covers with the *NJO's* Bob Leaper. Called *Big Band Beatle Songs*, it featured two drummers, Ronnie Verrell and Kenny Clare. He found playing between the two of them very confusing, as he didn't know who to follow. Another project was at the actor frequented Garrick Club in London, playing 'avant-garde' jazz with Laurie Morgan and Trevor Watts. Tony: "I decided to test the theory that avant-garde music was all about bouncing off each other and interacting. One night I just played anything I liked. I expected somebody to say something after the gig but they didn't!" Jon (who has admitted to enjoying *playing* this music) later affectionately dubbed it, 'bubble & squeak'.

3. Designed by architect and acoustician John Storyk, Electric Lady Studio was built specifically for Hendrix and was designed to generate a relaxed ambience so as to encourage Jimi's creativity, but at the same time, provide a professional recording atmosphere. Engineer Eddie Kramer enforced this by refusing to allow any drug use during session work. As things turned out, Hendrix would spend just four weeks recording there, mostly during the final phases of construction. A launch party was held on August 26, 1970 and the following day Hendrix laid down his last ever studio track: a cool and tranquil instrumental known only as *Slow Blues*. He then boarded an Air India flight for London to perform at the Isle of Wight Festival. He died less than three weeks later.

4. The tape recorder, in a soft bag, was not a cassette machine — portable versions of those did not arrive until the early '70s. This was a 3¼/7½ ips reel-to-reel recorder, battery powered, which used 3¼ inch spools and had a clear plastic lid. The sound quality was remarkable and Jon had been using it for some time to play taped LP tracks in the car, as the *GBO* travelled up and down the M1 Motorway. If only Jon could find that Stigwood tape now......

*"Jon's pulsing, wall-of-sound effect
was large and immediate;
from the first night he loosened
the band's feel."*
DICK HECKSTALL-SMITH

Chapter 4

THE OLDEST YOUNG MAN
IN THE BUSINESS

HAVING TO ENDURE THE MAYHEM AND MADNESS surrounding the *GBO* was Jon's 'baptism of fire' in his new life as a professional musician...it wasn't at all what he had expected. For the other band members, however, a relative outbreak of calm followed Jon's arrival, which had quite a sobering effect. Mike Falana called him 'the oldest young man in the world'...for Dick it was another reminder of how bad things had previously been, due to the volatile relationships that had existed between Graham, Jack and Ginger. However, some remnants of the old regime still had to be dealt with. The 'roadies' were a father and son team, the two Pete Baileys. Pete Senior was very supportive throughout but the son saw Jon as a soft touch and had been taking various liberties, like disappearing at crucial moments and 'forgetting' to pack the drums. Dick relates in his book: "Jon finally rounded on young Pete and physically hung him up on a band room coat hook by his collar and threatened him with an extra special beating up if he heard so much as another whisper out of him." Jon strongly refutes that this happened on his watch, maintaining that it was probably 'another drummer' sorting out the recalcitrant roadie. However, there were some problems that needed addressing with Pete Junior, so, relying on the status that being 'paymaster' gave him, Jon simply waited for the right moment and, pulling rank he didn't really have, threatened him with the sack, which seemed to do the trick. Fortunately, the incident never got back to Graham.

Not long after the Irish 'debacle', came a band meeting at Pete Bailey's flat, when Graham delivered a two-hour lecture on the hideous profundity of his sufferings, chief among them being his betrayal by Jack Bruce and Ginger Baker...'after all the risks he had taken with his personal life, to say nothing of the creative effort he put into the band on their behalf!' "I personally found it all completely credible..." is how Dick recalled it in *The Safest Place in the World*. "Typical Dick!" retorted Jon recently: "I found it all absolutely *incredible*! Graham was consumed by jealously — he couldn't bear to hear those successful hit singles released by *Cream*, which canny DJs were now playing in many of the clubs...*immediately before we went on stage!*" Now, as Dick noted, Bond's paranoid rant, shifting the blame for all his sufferings was, this time, devoid of any warmth or humour; he had changed...but not for the better! Dick began to think that it was the beginning of the end for the *GBO*, or at least, *his* role in it. As the nights got colder and the touring harder, the unpleasantness increased. Jon was convinced that Graham was surreptitiously 'back on the gear' and unlike Dick, he was less prepared to give him the benefit of the doubt. He saw him for what he really was and this inevitably led to confrontations. Dick remained equitable and calm throughout these conflicts, having long since developed very effective avoidance techniques. The start time of the gig was of crucial importance to Dick, as he needed to consume up to a whole bottle of Scotch in order to achieve that perfectly focused state of mind in which he liked to play...any delay and his calculations were thrown off, causing him to became grim-faced and silent. Alcohol was the way he 'cocooned' himself from all the strife going on around him.

In 1965 the band had recorded two albums with the Jack Bruce/Ginger Baker line-up. *The Sound of 65* and *There's a Bond between Us*. They were released on the Decca label, but had sunk without trace, which is a shame, as they contained some interesting and groundbreaking work. Earlier in 1963, the band had been definitely jazz-based when Graham was playing more alto sax and the extent to which the band had changed can clearly be heard on both these records, with their inviting blend of soul and jazz, combined with Graham's bluesy vocals. Dick always felt that the change of direction hadn't been consciously planned, but had just evolved. Significantly, the jazzier sections come over as more accessible and, even though they were recorded in a hurry, they stand up well today.

That original line-up would be a hard act to follow, but it wouldn't be long before the new band got the chance to make its own recorded statement. In the latter part of 1966, just after Mike Falana had left the band, Polydor Records showed interest in recording them. Jon and Dick attempted to conduct negotiations without Graham, but the company exec insisted on seeing the 'main man'. Dick describes the event in his book: "We wheeled Graham in and he did a 'blinder' on the guy. He was taken back by the sheer G-force of it all!" The upshot was an album deal with an advance of £500...half for studio time and the rest for the band. There was no time to prepare though and within a couple of days they went into Olympic Studio from midnight to 6am and blasted out nine songs, with Jon doing his best to produce whilst trying to control Graham's manic optimism. When it came to paying for the studio time and getting the tapes, the £500 had 'evaporated'! Graham had apparently picked it up earlier and Dick always maintained, with a chuckle, that he spent it on 'abracadabra' gowns, as by now, he'd become obsessed with the occult. So the tapes stayed locked in Olympic's vault, in true Orson Wellesian fashion! Well, that was Dick's view of what happened, but Jon's take is somewhat different! As he later told Harry Shapiro: "I went to see a guy from Polydor and told him about the band, although he *had* heard of us. I told him we needed a record deal and some money to buy equipment etc." The executive asked if there was anything he could hear and after some persuasion, agreed to pay up to £250 for them to record some demos. So, Jon phoned Eddie Kramer at Olympic and booked the session. They went in a couple of weeks later and played live right through the night, with no overdubs. Jon explains what happened next: "The tapes went into the vault, pending payment. I went back to Polydor, but the guy I had dealt with had been recalled to Germany. I played the mono monitor mixes to his successor, who laughed and threw me out." Jon is still convinced that, at some point, Graham had got the money out of the record company and spent it on heroin. Whatever the truth...the Polydor deal was 'dead in the water'!

The remarkable coda to this episode is that these tracks were eventually released, together with some other earlier 'live' tracks from the original band with Jack and Ginger, as *Solid Bond*, in June 1970. Out of the blue, Jon got a call from Graham, asking where the tapes were and the next thing he knew the album was out! Doubtless Graham Bond made some money from the album, but none of the other musicians saw a penny! On the whole, the reviews were favourable, but concentrated on the earlier material, with *Records & Recording* misguidedly commenting: "It does seem a pity that commercial considerations should have led Bond and his associates away from jazz — the Klook's Kleek (early material) sessions hint at a real musical future." The truth is that it would probably have meant oblivion if they *had* continued in that musical direction. A single, from the '66 session, *Walking in the Park* c/w *Springtime in the City*, was also released, but, again, sank without trace.

Meanwhile, as they entered 1967, life on the road wasn't getting any easier, as a glance at the March date sheet shows. In one six day period they played Guildford, Sheffield, Newcastle, Leicester, then back to Guildford and Woking! This frenetic touring was not without danger. They travelled in a 1959 Bedford van, with the gear in the back and no bulkhead between it and the passengers. Once, returning from a gig in Southampton, the van crashed and overturned, with the Hammond organ ending up on the seat where Jon usually sat! Fortunately, he had driven to the gig in his own car and was already back home, drinking coffee with Dick and Graham, when the call came about the accident. They immediately set off back down the route and discovered the vehicle on its side in a ditch. Miraculously, no one was injured!

With such extensive travelling, it was almost inevitable that accidents would sometimes occur. In 1969, Jack Bruce and Pete Brown wrote *Theme for an Imaginary Western*, as a tribute to all the bands who 'schlepped' up and down the motorways of Britain in search of fame and fortune. The song was almost certainly inspired by Jack's own experiences on the road with the *GBO*.[1]

The band eventually signed with Page One Records in January 1967 and went into the DJM studio to record a single. The session happened to be on same night that Jimi Hendrix played *Hey Joe* on *Top of the Pops*. Sometime around midnight, Mitch Mitchell (Jimi's drummer) dropped by for a chat and a drink. No one realised, at the time, the sensation that Jimi's TV appearance would cause. By contrast, the *ORGANisation*'s single *You Gotta Have Love, Babe*, hardly made any impact, selling just over a thousand copies. It seemed the band was going nowhere. They were still the 'band to see live' and a big club draw, but they needed a hit to take them to the next level and financial security. The signs weren't good though, and it seemed that the end of the *GBO* might be fast approaching. Around this time they played a charity gig in Woking and as Jon recounted to Harry Shapiro, the promoter had provided a bottle of Scotch for the band. It was asking for trouble: "We went into the dressing room and I chose this moment to tell Graham some truth that he found extremely distasteful and after the inevitable shout-up, Graham drank the whole bottle!" Things went downhill from that point. Graham played chaotically and non-stop for over an hour, driving most of the audience away until the hall was almost empty. Dick recalls that Graham wasn't even aware anything had gone wrong: "After the gig, we drove the mumbling hulk back to the address he'd given us as his latest resting place — and deposited him on the bed fully-clothed but unconscious." When they returned the next afternoon, he was still in the same position and the thought crossed their minds that he might even be dead! Such was the self-destructive nature of Graham Bond. Jon probably never saw the best of him; by the time he joined the band, Graham was already on a slippery slope of his own making. He does, however, recall one magical night, jamming with Graham, along with Mike Taylor and an Indian drummer. He remembers the playing as 'extraordinary' and thinks he might still have the tape somewhere. Who knows...perhaps one day it might see the light of day.

Graham Bond wasn't the only one having trouble with the booze, as Gary Heckstall-Smith recalls: "When Dick was playing a gig he would drink a bottle of whisky, but he never appeared drunk. I remember there was one time, however, when he did a gig and came on to a Christmas party afterwards. He looked rather odd and I asked what the matter was. 'I'm drunk', he replied, 'I've had two bottles of whisky.' Yet he wasn't an alcoholic in the true sense, because when there was no gig, he wouldn't drink at all. He drank because that's how he felt he could best play." It's clear, though, that Dick was doing serious, long-term damage to his body.

Even though the schedule with Bond was hectic, Jon was still able to fit in recording another album with Mike Taylor. Unexpectedly, both Jack Bruce and Ron Rubin turned up to play bass on the session...it seems that Jack had got his dates mixed up. On some tracks they actually play together, an experience that both Mike and Jon said they enjoyed greatly.

The album, another in the Lansdowne Series of jazz releases, was called *Trio* and Jon remembers Mike being particularly pleased with this title, referring, as it does, to the instrumentation, rather than the number of players. It was released early in 1967 and, with Jack Bruce's name on it, there was some scope for media promotion, which was just as well, as Taylor wasn't giving interviews, or even playing live at this point. Back when *Pendulum* was recorded, Mike was just smoking cannabis, but since then, he had discovered LSD and now seemed to be retreating more and more into his own fantasy world. Indeed, at one stage, producer Dennis Preston was seriously concerned that the album might never be completed. So fragile was Mike's mental state that, on one occasion, he threw his manuscripts into the dustbin outside the flat he and Jon shared at the time. Fortunately, Jon arrived home in the nick of time and managed to rescue most of it...including a suite for three drummers, apparently written for Jon, Ginger and Phil Seaman, titled *Horn, Gut and Skin*, which was inspired by the Great Pyramids at Giza.

In spite of Jon rescuing it, this work remained in manuscript form and was never performed.

With Mike Taylor apparently coming apart at the seams and Graham Bond also showing signs of going off the rails, it appeared that the two people who did most to kick-start Jon's professional career seemed to be hell-bent on destroying themselves!

Trio was re-released in 2004 and the *Guardian*'s John Fordham reviewing it, wrote: "Taylor is a highly rhythmic pianist whose dense chord clusters often travel in tandem with Hiseman's sensitive and flexible percussion. His handling of standards such as *All the Things You Are* is enigmatically fascinating, while his own rhapsodically wayward *Just a Blues* is a lot more than just a blues."

After the Mike Taylor sessions, it was back to the harsh reality of *GBO* business for Jon. Although there still seemed to be life in the band, it was all becoming extremely unpredictable. In July 1967, *Melody Maker*'s Chris Welch witnessed what was to be one of Jon's last gigs with the band. He described it thus: "Loud, hypnotic and neurotic is the music of Graham Bond. It wails, screams and tears at the senses for minutes on end, demanding either complete attention or complete rejection...Graham is seen as a constantly urging demonic power, inspiring his musicians to endless toil with harsh, violent vocals and organ." Chris recognised the hit-and-miss nature of the band, but still acknowledged Bond's incredible charisma, even if he was becoming more and more unreliable. Towards the end of Jon's tenure with the band, he and Dick drove to a gig at Northwich Civic Hall, arriving around mid-afternoon. The Borough Treasurer was waiting for them, cheque in hand, and insisted on paying Jon in advance, as he and his family were about to leave for a holiday. Graham, who was travelling to the gig by train, 'did a noddy' after shooting up in the toilet, slept through his stop, and finished up in Edinburgh. With the cheque in his wallet, Jon decided the gig had to go ahead, so with Pete Bailey Senior, who could just about manage a 12 bar blues, playing the Hammond organ, Jon and Dick endlessly swapped solos, keeping the beat danceable. The completely instrumental set went down surprisingly well and amazingly, the venue's agent phoned the following week to re-book them!

At another out-of-town gig, Graham found himself, after the show, without any heroin, having failed to 'score' earlier. Driving back, just after midnight, a raving Bond laying across the rear seat in the throes of withdrawal, Jon (with the stoic Dick at his side) drove, hell-for-leather, to the all-night chemist in Piccadilly, the only place Graham would be able to score or get methadone, the NHS substitute. His craving assuaged, Graham then turned on the charm, suggesting he buy them both an early breakfast. Nice gesture...except that, as usual, he had no money, so Jon paid...again!

By now, things were grinding to an inevitable halt. With all these shenanigans, it's hard to believe that the musicians stuck it for as long as they did. A lot was due to Jon, who was not only the band's accountant, but also its conscience. His steadfast refusal to treat Graham any differently to anybody else was courageous, but it frequently resulted in arguments and there is inevitably a price to pay for confronting a person who, to all intents and purposes, had lost touch with reality. Dick's view was: "Only Jon would come out with iron hard statements about what was wrong with Graham to his face, all of which could have contributed to his decline."

Jon and Dick had always been convinced that it was a big mistake not to replace Jack Bruce. Jon: "By not having a bassist, you removed a whole element from the band that not even Graham could compensate for. This essential element is missing from the *Solid Bond* tracks." Bond's reasoning will never be known, and while Jon thought it was down to his ego — a power trip, Dick believed he did it just to save money. Perhaps it was a combination of the two.

What fascinated Jon was the uncanny way Graham seemed to be able to foresee trends. Though his musical background was steeped in modern jazz, he always had his finger firmly on the wider musical pulse. He undoubtedly helped to create the '60s blues boom in Britain, but he was also one of the first to champion the use of 'sampled' sounds when he took a Mellotron on the road. During Jon's spell with the band Graham began dressing in occult-style cloaks and robes and talking up the new 'psychedelic' bands like *Pink Floyd*. In spite of this vision, commercial success always eluded him. Maybe with a lucky break or two, things might have turned out very differently, but this begs the question: 'Could he have coped with that success and the constant glare of publicity it brought?' He may well have gone to pieces even quicker that he did!

Undeniably, both Jon and Dick gained fantastic experience from their time with the band. As Jon admitted to Harry Shapiro in 1978: "In terms of the buzz and the high that I got from playing — *and* in artistic terms, my best days were with *GBO*." Dick would also look back, with incredible fondness, to his days with the musical maverick that was Graham Bond.

In the year Jon spent with the *GBO*, he really didn't have to make any adjustments to his style of playing. As he told *Melody Maker* in 1968: "Pop drumming is extremely difficult. When I was with Graham Bond I didn't take any notice of the conventions of pop drumming. I played what I had always played." An important part of Jon's early technique was not using the hi-hat for keeping time, claiming that it allowed him more freedom to develop his twin bass drum technique. Chris Welch even quotes Jon as saying in an interview that he had 'declared war' on the hi-hat. Initially, in the jazz context, Jon had tried playing with each bass drum tuned to a different pitch, but later decided to treat them as one drum, played with two feet. In another interview given in 1967, he was clear about his approach: "I just don't want to go 'tick-tock' all the time. Actually, I do keep time — in my head anyway — even in what sound like completely free bits. But the point is that, strict time is too limited in its emotional range — and I like to communicate emotion. I can do this by building tension and then relaxing it — by making some parts edgy and getting others to float along."

In the final weeks of the band, Graham asked Pete Brown to write some new material for them. At the time, Pete couldn't really play an instrument, so he sang the melody into a tape recorder: "Graham said the songs were great and asked me to join as singer." By now though, things were moving far too fast to take him on board! Finally accepting that he could no longer cope with, or control events, Jon left the band in July 1967. Unsure of his next move, it was Colin Richardson, now working for the Rik Gunnell Agency, who suggested putting him up for the job with Georgie Fame, who was looking for a drummer at the time. This would, however, mean Jon having to modify his approach somewhat, as the *Blue Flames* needed more of a 'funky' feel. It also meant a temporary parting of the ways with Dick...though he couldn't have known at the time that their musical partnership would resume sooner than he thought — and would last, on and off, for the rest of Dick's life!

During his year with Bond, Jon and Barbara's relationship had grown steadily stronger. Barbara had joined *She Trinity*, an all-girl group, originally from Canada who had enjoyed some success with their single *He Fought the Law*, as well as recording a version of *Yellow Submarine*. An appearance at ex-boxer Billy Walker's club, The Upper Cut, billed them as 'Britain's No.1 All Girl Group'. Keyboard player Eileen Woodman recalls: "I thought then and still do, that Barbara was an excellent player — her party piece was playing two saxophones at once, much to the amazement of all." Eileen recalls the band always went down well with their curious mix of blues and jazzy instrumentals, as well as the more usual pop and soul numbers. A particular favourite with audiences was *Wade in the Water* which, Eileen recalls, used to go on 'forever'...echoes of the *Graham Bond ORGANisation*!

Barbara had been with the group about a year when there was an incident that would eventually lead to her leaving. They were booked to do *The Kathy Kirby* show on BBC TV, but when she found that they were expected to wear skimpy costumes, black fishnet stockings and suspenders with Victorian lace-up boots, she flatly refused. She did get as far as trying them on, but 'went bright red with embarrassment'. The other two tried to insist, but Barbara was adamant..."You won't catch me wearing stockings and suspenders in public!" was her parting shot (a quip that would later come back to haunt her). To her amazement, the following morning, a hoard of reporters was on her doorstep: "When I opened the front door we were swamped by journalists with flashing cameras. They had heard about my so-called stand against female musicians being exploited." The next day, there was a large picture of her on the front page of the *Daily Express*, as well as coverage in some of the other papers.

Though the *She Trinity* gig had been fun to start with, this incident, combined with the musical limitations of the band caused Barbara to become frustrated. She recalls: "When I joined, they'd had a modicum of success with a top ten hit, but now they felt in need of something different, and they were hoping that I would help them to greater things." The problem was that they were technically quite limited, plus neither of them could write, so they were stuck with playing 'covers'. They did, however, play some incredible gigs, including three concerts supporting *The Who*. Even so, after a year, Barbara had had enough and left.

Still living in the Kew flat that Jon had taken over from Mike

Taylor, J&B were starting to get complaints about noise from the neighbours, so they agreed that the only solution was to buy their own house, preferably a detached one. After a brief search, they found the house of their dreams in Shepperton and beat off the opposition in a 'Dutch auction' with a bid of £8,350. They borrowed £3,350 from Barbara's mother and Jon went off to the Halifax Building Society in the Strand to secure a mortgage for the rest. The interview went pretty well with all the forms quickly completed, when Jon got a shock: "I was asked for the date of the wedding and for the first time in my life I was speechless. How had this not occurred to me? I hesitatingly replied that as far as I knew there wasn't one. With frowning disapproval, I was told that they didn't 'hand out mortgages to unmarried couples'. So much for the swinging '60s!" When Jon told Barbara that the mortgage was no problem, but they had to be married to get it, she didn't turn a hair — calmly checked her diary and announced that she was free on the last Saturday of the month! However, when she rang her family with the news, Barbara discovered her mother was playing in the Roehampton Tennis Club final on that date. In the end, a compromise was reached...marriage in the morning and tennis in the afternoon!

Jon Hiseman and Barbara Thompson were married on 29th July, 1967 at Sheen Registry Office, before a small gathering of guests that included Dave Gelly and Neil Ardley. Following the wedding reception, they all trouped out to watch Barbara's mother play in her tennis final, but when the 'well refreshed' group's good-natured heckling got a little too boisterous, putting her off her game, she sent them all packing and went on to win the match!

Their 'big day', however, hadn't exactly got off to a very auspicious start. Graham Bond (who was at this time 'of no fixed abode') arrived at daybreak from a gig to doss down in the adjacent flat to Jon and Barbara. Around 7am, without bothering to knock, he entered their room, sat on the end of the bed, fixed them with his 'eye' and proceeded to harangue them for an hour about the world's injustices. Both naked, they had little choice but to lie there and take it! Bond was still peeved with Jon for leaving, which he perceived as another heinous betrayal. Jon is still convinced that Bond was by now completely mad, due to the cocktail of drugs he was consuming daily. Jon has never taken drugs, though he did, on one occasion, have to wipe Graham's blood off the walls of the toilets at Watford Gap services, after he had 'shot up' there. In fact, Jon claims never to have actually witnessed Bond using drugs...like Dick he effectively managed to block such things out.

Jon and Barbara's marriage was never likely to be conventional. Married on the Saturday, the very next evening they were both gigging with the *Don Usher Band*. Then the following day, Barbara left for a six-week tour of American Air bases in Germany with the *She Trinity*. Jon spent all of the next month working on their new house, helped by fellow drummer, Keef Hartley and largely funded by his new wife's tour wages that she dutifully sent home from Germany. Barbara's own career was going quite well and as she didn't want to trade off Jon's name, she retained her maiden name when working. Jon had grown up with his mother following her own career, so for him, this was nothing unusual. Actually, Jon has never really come to terms with the concept of having a 'wife' and still calls her 'Thomps'. It would be many, many years before he got over the slight feeling of surprise when Barbara was addressed as Mrs. Hiseman. That's not to say there weren't any teething problems. Jon: "Right from the word go it was obvious that Barbara wasn't going to do all the cooking and cleaning while I just sat back and had my meals served to me. It wasn't up for discussion — it was simply a fact of life. There was a lot of coming and going and sometimes it seemed that we only saw each other when we passed on the stairs! I might have had a particularly hard three days gigging, only to get back and find that Barbara had been writing a half hour piece for radio and the place looked like a bomb had exploded. If I hit the roof for a minute or two, it didn't make the slightest difference; Barbara was always going to do what Barbara was going to do!" Such situations were inevitable given their respective careers and they both had to accept that this was probably going to be the way of things.

By the time Barbara returned from Germany, Jon had started with *Georgie Fame and the Blue Flames* and in October 1967, he left for his first foreign tour. Flying in a commercial airliner for the first time and being served hot towels and a meal, Jon remembers getting the feeling that somehow he'd finally 'arrived'. It was all a far cry from the treatment the *GBO* had routinely received. The band was booked to play the Jazz Jamboree in Warsaw then on to the Jazzoveho Festivalu in Prague, as part of an impressive bill that included the *Charles Lloyd Quartet*, the *Roland Kirk Quartet* and Jean-Luc Ponty. For these two dates Georgie took only a quartet comprising Jon, Lyn Dobson on tenor sax and flute, with Rik Brown on bass guitar. A high quality video of this performance surfaced recently in America and when Jon viewed it he was astonished to realise that they were virtually playing as a jazz quartet, with everyone taking long solos; a far cry from the usual *Blue Flames* soul sound that had impressed Jon all those years ago, at the Flamingo all-nighters. With Fame, Jon was certainly playing to much bigger audiences, but there was a downside...as he told *Melody Maker* in March 1968: "I found that Georgie Fame required a much more conventional drummer and I had to apply myself to simplicity for the first time, but I don't really think my style ever fitted. It was good discipline though and once again I learned a lot."

The quartet played a couple of other gigs in Poland on their own. One was, rather unusually, in a works canteen a few hours north of Warsaw. The equipment, which was travelling by road, hadn't arrived by the time the concert was due to start and the audience was getting restless, so Georgie went on and played the house piano, with Jon providing the rhythm by shaking a box of matches into the mike! Desperate measures...but the audience appreciated the effort and applauded warmly.

Back in England, coming up to Christmas, Georgie Fame was booked into a two-week cabaret at the Mayfair Hotel in London. This time, the band included ace guitarist John McLaughlin, soon to be tempted away to America by Miles Davis. Jon recalls fondly: "Georgie loved to hear us jamming and told the band to play heavy jazz for the first twenty minutes — then he would come on to: 'Ladies and Gentlemen, the star of our show — Georgie Fame!!'" Jon can still picture Georgie, 'bopping away' in the wings, grinning from ear to ear, as they played further and further 'out': "After a few nights, Georgie's manager, Rik Gunnell, turned up and was horrified. But he got his own back by screwing us on the fee for the residency. While I enjoyed the relative sanity of working with Georgie, I wasn't really a funk player and didn't have enough control then — I was more used to floating and shading. Not actually owning any funk records and after so many years of unfettered improvisation, poor acoustics and very little studio experience, my timing, by today's standards, was suspect."

Soon after this, they found themselves in the North of England, playing the club cabaret circuit, and one night, after the show, Georgie mysteriously took off and drove down to London for a recording session. Jon later found out that it was to record *Bonnie & Clyde*, probably his biggest hit, blatantly written to cash in on the movie of the same name. In retrospect, Jon can see that it made sense to record it using session musicians, but at the time he felt quite hurt — and to rub salt into the wound, as the single zoomed up to the top of the charts, he had to play it every night, complete with snare drum 'machine gun' effects!

In early February 1968, Georgie Fame had to fold the band. *Bonnie & Clyde* had become an international hit and he was in great demand for TV appearances, but all they needed was

Georgie — miming in a black pinstripe suit and fedora hat, with a pretend machine gun under his arm. In 1970, Fame confessed to *Melody Maker*: "Just before *Bonnie & Clyde* sidetracked me into cabaret, I had a great new band with Jon Hiseman, but that hit turned me into a solo artist." The bottom line was, the management weren't going pay the band for doing nothing, while Georgie was away doing TV shows. So Jon was out of a job again, but, with a few phone calls to some of his old contacts, it wasn't long before he had plenty of 'one-off' gigs in the diary.

During this period, Jon got a phone call, out of the blue, from Graham Bond. It was around 6pm and he was calling from Klook's Kleek, the North London club. He had a problem — his drummer hadn't shown up and would Jon fill in?[2] Though unwilling to admit it, Jon quite missed the excitement of playing in Graham's manic musical environment, so, despite his misgivings, he loaded his drums in the car and drove to the venue. Later, Jon described that evening as 'one of the greatest playing experiences of my life'. The set kicked off...then as each number segued into the next, they moved seamlessly back and forth through their old repertoire: "I realised that Graham's ego was driving him to show me just what I had been missing, to catch me out, to lose me, but he couldn't — I knew the numbers too well. This was absolutely my game, though we were both enjoying this spontaneous musical adventure in equal measure. We played non-stop for about fifty minutes or so,[3] finishing up with the inevitable drum solo. The audience was astounded at this bravura performance and for years after people came up to me and told me that they still remembered that night!"

As it happened, John Mayall chanced to be in the audience that evening — but it would need another bit of luck, and a nudge from an old friend, to pave the way for Jon's next career move.

FOOTNOTES

1. In view of the amount of time all the musicians mentioned in this book spent on the road, it's worth noting Pete Brown's lyrics to *Theme for an Imaginary Western*.

When the wagons leave the city	where the laughter sounds
for the forest, and further on	
Painted wagons of the morning	O the dancing and the singing
dusty roads where they have gone	O the music when they played
Sometimes travelling through the darkness	O the fires that they started
met the summer coming home	O the girls with no regret
Fallen faces by the wayside	Sometimes they found it
Looked as if they might have known	Sometimes they kept it
O the sun was in their eyes	Often lost it on the way
and the desert that dries	Fought each other to possess it
In the country towns	Sometimes died in sight of day

Music by Jack Bruce, Lyrics by Pete Brown
Bruce Music Ltd/Warner Chappell Music International

2. Jon wasn't the only drummer that received a last-minute panic call from Graham Bond. In a recent conversation with Jon, Keef Hartley related the following story: "Graham called me one night to ask if I could get to Klook's with my drums as soon as possible. So, with no rehearsal, I played a set — all the while cursing you and your bloody technique — Graham was playing all this tricky stuff that you must have worked out with him. When the gig finished, the promoter Dick Jordan asked me if I wanted the money. I thought this a bit strange, but realised that Dick must have known that, by this time, Graham's heroin habit was such that he often 'forgot' to pay the band — which, I guess, is why he was always being let down. Anyway, I grabbed the fee, deducted my share and gave the rest to Graham, who immediately shot off into the night to score!"

3. Jon first witnessed a jazz group play an entire set non–stop (segue) at the Antibes Jazz Festival in 1965. He and Barbara had driven to the festival on their way to Italy. It began with Elvin Jones, drummer with the *John Coltrane Quartet*, coming on stage and hammering nails into the floor in front of his bass drum to stop it 'creeping'. From there, he gravitated naturally to warming up on the kit which turned into an extended solo. Eventually the rest of the group, John Coltrane, McCoy Tyner and Jimmy Garrison walked on – and suddenly they were into the first tune. After each of *their* solos, the piece finished with another drum solo that segued into the next tune. This went on for the whole set, until Elvin was again alone on stage, soloing -- finally throwing down his sticks with a flourish and walking off. Jon remembers being astonished that the French audience really didn't get it. The next night, the quartet performed the incomparable *A Love Supreme* for the whole set, with Coltrane at one point *playing* to heaven on his knees. The French audience didn't get that either, but Jon and Barbara were held spellbound both nights. They had only known each other for six months at this point, but already they were sharing great moments together. Jon, in particular, never forgot the effect that Coltrane's first night had on him and remembers thinking, during that gig with Graham Bond at Klook's Kleek, that this was the fulfilment of some kind of dream.

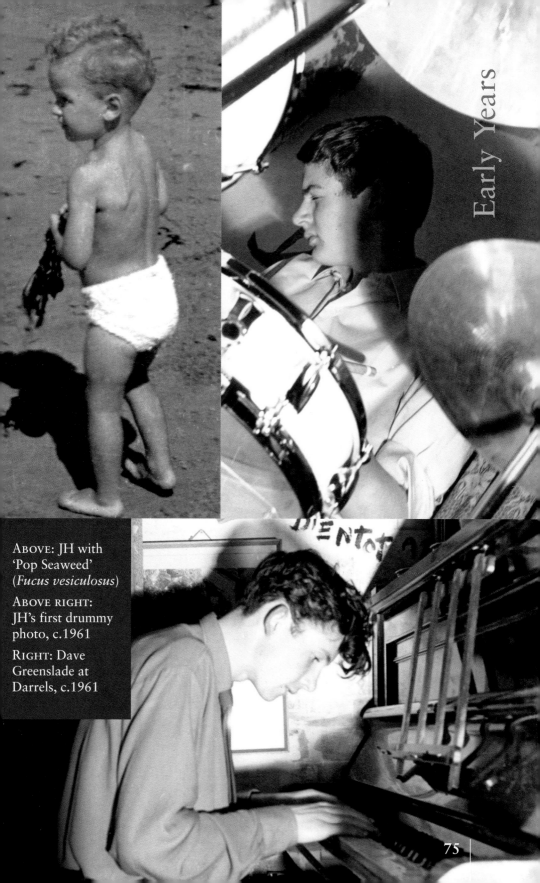

ABOVE: JH with 'Pop Seaweed' (*Fucus vesiculosus*)

ABOVE RIGHT: JH's first drummy photo, c.1961

RIGHT: Dave Greenslade at Darrels, c.1961

BELOW: JH's 21st Birthday in June '65 with Jill Hiseman and Barbara

RIGHT: Barbara and JH's Wedding Day, 29th July 1967

BELOW RIGHT: JH with Coltrane LP and Practise Drumkit, c.1964

Early Years

ABOVE: *The New Jazz Orchestra* at the Marquee Club, Wardour Street, mid '60s — Front row left-right: Dave Gelly, Trevor Watts, Barbara Thompson, Les Carter (silhouette); Middle: Dick Hart, Paul Rutherford (obscured), unknown, John Mumford; Back: Tony Reeves, Ian Carr, Bob Leaper, Mike Phillipson, Tony Dudley

BELOW: *NJO* c.1968 — Neil Ardley conducting left-right: Dick Hart, Derek Wadsworth, unknown, Mike Gibbs, Dick Heckstall-Smith, Dave Gelly, Jimmy Philip, BT

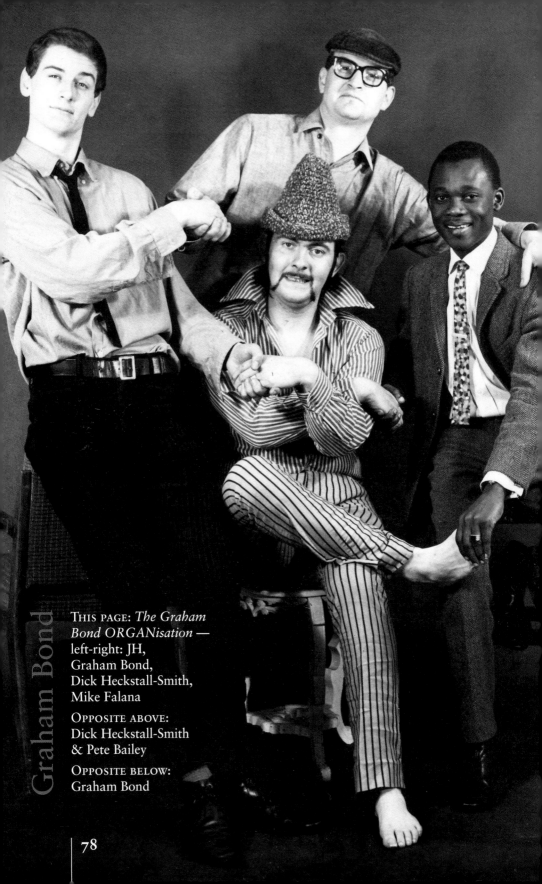

THIS PAGE: *The Graham Bond ORGANisation* — left-right: JH, Graham Bond, Dick Heckstall-Smith, Mike Falana

OPPOSITE ABOVE: Dick Heckstall-Smith & Pete Bailey

OPPOSITE BELOW: Graham Bond

Date	Venue		Fee	Cash pd to S.A. by Arts	Chques recd by S.A.
Aug 24	Bournemouth		75. 0. 0.		59. 2. 0.
26	Kingston	o/s	75. 0. 0.	10. 0. 0.	
27	Manchester		75. 0. 0.	75. 0. 0.	
28	Newbury		60. 0. 0.		60. 0. 0.
31	Norwich		66. 0. 0.	66. 0. 0.	
Sept 1	Portsmouth		75. 0. 0.	75. 0. 0.	
2	Derby		82.10. 0.	82.10. 0.	
3	Birmingham		85. 0. 0.		85. 0. 0.
5	Edmonton		65. 0. 0.	65. 0. 0.	
9	Leicester		82.10. 0.	82.10. 0.	
10	Cheltenham		78.17. 6.	78.17. 6.	
11	Bedford		60. 0. 0.	60. 0. 0.	
14	Eltham		65. 0. 0.	65. 0. 0.	
15				75. 0. 0.	75. 0. 0.
16				80. 0. 0.	80. 0. 0.
17					
18					559. 2. 0.

Payments				
Aug	23	Wages		245.
	27	Band expenses		31.
	30	Wages		245.
	31	Advance to Road Manager		30.
Sept	6	Wages		245.
	"	Band expenses	31. 6. 8.	
		less refunded	2.18. 8.	28.
	13	Cash for Cardeys - van hire		70.
	"	Wages		245.
	"	Band expenses	66. 0. 0.	
		less refunded	20.16. 4.	45.
	19	Band expenses		64.
		3 weeks holiday pay - Graham Bond		180

79

Barbara

Pop girl quits over TV 'bikini'

MUSICIAN Barbara Thompson, who quit a pop group after refusing to wear a "bikini" costume, relaxes at home last night.

Barbara, aged 22, took one look at the costume the BBC wanted her to wear in a Kathy Kirby show and said: "I will not wear that in public. It is too sexy."

Other members of the all-girl She Trinity group pleaded with her. But Barbara said: "I'll leave the group first."

She said at her Chiswick flat: "I am a musician not a stripper. The costume was just too much—a black mesh bikini top with tights."

OPPOSITE ABOVE: JH playing with *GBO* (Bond hated the 'bank manager' haircut)

OPPOSITE BELOW: Barbara wearing the *Ivy Benson Band* uniform in '64

OPPOSITE RIGHT: Barbara quits *She Trinity* in '67

ABOVE: *The Kit Kat Club Band* from the musical *Cabaret* in '68 — left-right: Jenny Russell, BT, Pat Sheridan, Jean Mercer

LEFT: Barbara in 1968

81

ABOVE: Barbara & *Art Themen Quintet* at the Marquee, December 22nd, 1969 — left-right: Tony Levin, BT, Dave Green, Art Themen, Howard Riley

RIGHT: Barbara in '69

Barbara

"If we're ever going to form this band of ours, it's got to be right *now."*
DICK HECKSTALL-SMITH
to Jon Hiseman

"I decided to make my own music because there just wasn't anyone else to work with."
JON HISEMAN on the reason for forming *Colosseum*

Chapter 5

THE GATHERING OF THE CLAN

DICK, DESPERATE AS ALWAYS FOR MONEY AND WITH A FAMILY TO SUPPORT, only stayed a few weeks after Jon left the *GBO*, mainly to ensure that he got wages owed to him. He asked Bailey Senior to sort it out and the roadie rummaged through assorted paperwork, found an exercise book and there, on one of the pages, was scrawled in Graham's handwriting...'Dick — £24'. Seems the boss wasn't completely disorganised after all! So, Dick got his money and left. Amazingly, at this point, he thought that his days as a pro-musician were over and seriously considered becoming a heavy goods driver. In the nick of time, he got a call from John Mayall asking him to join the *Bluesbreakers*. It was September 1967 and the new job brought sanity, efficient organisation, a solid musical environment and the bonus of his first American tour. However, after a few months Dick began to miss the white-hot intensity of the *GBO*...not that he wanted to return to it. Damn it...John Mayall was just too courteous and fair.

Meanwhile, after Georgie Fame disbanded the *Blueflames* in early February, 1968, Jon had returned to playing whatever gigs came along, just to keep some money coming in, conscious of the fact that there were mortgage payments to keep up. In March 1968, he gave a controversial interview to *Melody Maker*, in which he made some forthright statements about the current crop of drummers. It showed that he wasn't afraid to put his head above the parapet: "Several things really irritate me about young pop/rock drummers; they hit the drums so hard, they hit them so badly and they leave the stick on the drumhead for too long after each beat. There's a lot of clumsy 'sticking' and some of the kits are set up in such a way, it's a wonder *anyone* can play them!" He went on to accuse some drummers of blindly copying guys like Keith Moon. The interview ends with two pieces of advice to aspiring drummers: "Play with a piano trio, in order to learn control," and recognise that there was no substitute for hard work.

Jon continued playing the circuit into April and although it wasn't the best of times for him, a crust still had to be earned. About this time, he was called in by Arthur Brown to play on his new single, *Fire*. Of course, Jon had no idea that it would turn out to be not just a hit, but also a future classic. Recently, Internet gossip has placed a question mark over who exactly was the drummer on the record, because it's certain that Drachen Theaker and possible that Carl Palmer also recorded it. However in a recent conversation with Arthur, Jon mentioned that he was in the studio when Kit Lambert (manager of *The Who*) was producing and Arthur suddenly became certain that this version was the one released. On the session, Jon also played on the 'B' side — *Give Him a Flower* and the discerning listener can hear him singing in the chorus! Jon's take on all this is: "When *Fire* was released, my mum went out and bought it — as mums do — and when I next visited...proudly played it. So, I got to hear it pretty soon after the session — and it never occurred to me that it wasn't me!"

Shortly after the epic gig at Klook's Kleek with Graham Bond, Jon arrived home about 1am from a gig with the *Cole Richards Combo*, to find John Mayall sitting in his car, waiting for him. Apparently there had been yet another shake-up in the *Bluesbreakers*, resulting in drummer Keef Hartley's departure, and Mayall wanted Jon to replace him. He had decided to take the band in an overtly jazzier direction, which was fortuitous for Jon. Whether Mayall had discussed the situation with Dick before or after seeing Jon play at Klook's Kleek is not known, but Dick had certainly put in a good word for him: "I told Mayall that where jazz and powerhouse rock was concerned, it was all pluses. In the field of blues, I didn't know." Mayall's response was to indicate that 'it would all work out in the end' — which appeared to be his standard response to any tricky situation. Musically, the new band had plenty of potential, as Mayall had recently added a three-piece brass section. Apart from Dick, there was Henry Lowther on trumpet and violin (Henry had also been a member of the *New Jazz Orchestra* and *Group Sounds Four & Five*) and Chris Mercer on tenor sax.

85

These 'jazzers' were balanced by having 'boy wonder' blues musicians, Mick Taylor (guitar) and Andy Fraser (bass), though both would eventually leave for the *Rolling Stones* and *Free* respectively. It was an eclectic mix of personnel and had the potential to create something special.

Playing with the *Bluesbreakers* required Jon to rethink the kit he used. He told *Talking Drums* in 1997: "*The Bare Wires* album was made with a two bass drum set-up, but I recorded that within three days of joining. I soon realised it was ridiculous to use a kit like that when I didn't need it." He pared it down to one ride cymbal, one crash, hi-hats, bass and snare drum. No tom-toms — if he wanted that sound he just flicked off the snare wires: "This was absolutely right for the very 'street' blues that John was playing live — and I really enjoyed it."

Andy Fraser left the band just before Jon joined and still hadn't been replaced, so he recommended his old friend Tony Reeves. It was clearly another step toward jazz, but Mayall went for it. That left Mick Taylor and John Mayall as the only 'blues musicians' in the *Bluesbreakers*!

For the past few years Tony had been concentrating on his studio career at Pye Records. He'd always had ambitions to be a record producer and his chances improved considerably when he suggested to producer John Schroder that a cover version of the Vince Guaraldi instrumental track, *Cast your Fate to the Wind*, might have 'hit' potential with a new arrangement. It was recorded with Tony playing bass, Johnny Pearson on piano, Kenny Clare on drums and a string section. Released under the name *Sounds Orchestral*, it did indeed make the charts, peaking at No.5 in the UK and 10 in the US. They went on to make two albums, which also sold well. This success led to Tony working with Tony Hatch..."a fantastic experience!" and as a freelance producer in his own right, with the *Alan Bown Set* and *Episode Six*, a harmony group which featured Ian Gillan and Roger Glover, who would later find fame with *Deep Purple*.

The offer to join John Mayall also came at a good time for Tony as he was keen to return to playing, though it would mean 'going electric'. Hitherto, his attitude had been that it wasn't really a 'proper' instrument, but deep down, had realised that he would have to play one eventually if he was to have a future as a musician. He had, in fact, just bought his first bass guitar, an Epiphone *Rivoli* and had already tried it out on a gig with the *Don Usher Band*. Although he was a relative novice on the instrument, after joining the *Bluesbreakers* he practised diligently and learned fast. Suddenly Mayall, who always liked to keep his musicians on their toes, announced that they were to record an album straightaway, with no rehearsal. Tony explains how they were briefed: "We'd go round his flat and he would play records as an example of the feel he wanted." Henry Lowther was somewhat bewildered by the 'ad hoc' nature of it all, though his offer to join the *Bluesbreakers* had been just as laid-back: "I went to a gig with Dick, and John Mayall was there. He just said to me 'want a job?' And that's how I got in the band."

It was a remarkably jazzy line-up for a band that was called the *Bluesbreakers*, but it underlined Mayall's willingness to experiment. Actually, Jon considers Mayall to be similar to Miles Davis, in that they were both 'catalysts' in their field. Neither of them changed their own way of playing over the years, but by using musicians who reflected the changing musical styles, they maintained their own relevance. So, in April 1968, the new line-up went into Decca's studio in West Hampstead, London, to record the *Bare Wires* album. It was a John Mayall/Mike Vernon production and the result proved pretty controversial to many Mayall fans, who were hoping for another blues classic like the earlier *Beano* album, but it would, nevertheless, turn out to be one of Mayall's most enduring works.

Soon after recording finished, the new band appeared at the Marquee. Henry Lowther recalls: "We'd do spontaneous things at gigs, though *I* always liked things to be more worked out. After the gig, John would say 'let's keep that bit in'. So if we could remember it the next night, we'd play it again." It wasn't long before Tony Reeves was put on the spot by the bandleader: "At one of my first gigs with him, he pointed at me and said 'solo'. I had no idea it was coming. There was about a two-second pause and I was away. It was good leadership to throw people in at the deep end." Though unexpected, it wasn't so surprising, as he'd already impressed Mayall in the studio with a good bass solo. Most of their gigs were played to packed houses, which had its drawbacks...at one particular venue (the Fisherman's Arms) the musicians couldn't even get a drink, as the interval just wasn't long enough for them to fight their way to the bar.

Life on the road with the *Bluesbreakers* was very different to that of the *Graham Bond ORGANisation*. They tended to play one-off, random dates, whereas Mayall's tours were more carefully routed, especially when playing abroad. Notoriously 'careful' with money, John once famously announced to a Swedish audience that the band had no hotel booked, so if any young ladies would be prepared to provide accommodation for his musicians, this would be greatly appreciated. Apparently, there was no shortage of offers!

Gary Heckstall-Smith remembers: "When the *GBO* played the UK they would come home every night and as there were no foreign tours, I still saw a lot of Dick. With Mayall though, he was away a lot." Being married to a musician was never easy and Gary also had young Arthur to take care of, so it just wasn't possible to get to many gigs. As it was, things weren't going too well between them and it looked like Dick might soon have to find somewhere else to live.

Bare Wires was scheduled for release on 21st June, 1968 — Jon Hiseman's 24th birthday. With its mixture of jazz and blues, it would prove to be too radical a departure for some reviewers. *Rolling Stone* magazine considered it a "disastrous episode for Mayall...sloppy orchestration and poor material." On the other hand, Chris Welch of *Melody Maker* waxed lyrical: "...absorbing music, richer in content than any previous British group album apart from *Sgt. Pepper* and *The Thoughts of Emerlist Davjack* (*The Nice*)...it features his most talent-packed band to date." *Record Mirror* was just as enthusiastic: "...a remarkable showcase of one of the most inventive and authentic blues outfits on the scene." It would eventually turn out to be Mayall's biggest UK chart success, reaching No.3.

Following the release of the album, Jon, ever watchful, had noted that the crowds had become much bigger than they had ever been for Graham Bond. Late one night, on the way back from a gig, he asked Mayall if he knew how many people there had been in the audience and how much they had paid. Though John never let on what the band was earning, Jon had calculated roughly what the door take was. He soon convinced Mayall that the band's fee should be increased to reflect their pulling power. Mayall's initial reaction was jovially non-committal, but a few days later he triumphantly reported having shocked the bookers by instructing that in future his fee should be doubled. Apparently, there had been little protest. As Jon had suspected, the agency bookers had rarely bothered going to their gigs and, of course, the promoters always downplayed the crowds, and thus the fee.

Meanwhile, the band continued to tour, but time was already running out for this line-up. On the 31st May, playing a gig in Zurich on the same bill as Jimi Hendrix, Tony Reeves had a premonition that something wasn't quite right when Mayall didn't call on him to solo that night — or the next. It seems that he already had another change in mind. What Tony refers to as 'the night of the long knives' was imminent and Henry Lowther, for one, didn't see it coming: "After a gig at Kew, Mayall asked everybody back to his flat and told us he was changing the band." The whole brass section of Chris, Dick and Henry was sacked, along with Tony Reeves. But, then Mayall appeared to reconsider Dick's position, mulling whether to keep a saxophone in the line-up. After a few days, John finally told Dick, with a rueful grin: "Sorry, it's bad news." Mayall explained the changes to Chris Welch: "On the *Bare Wires* album, we used the brass section properly, but in clubs it didn't work out. There are two ways to use a brass section; either with arrangements, which you can get anybody to play — or to feature them all as soloists." Mayall admitted there had been a lot of pressure with so many good musicians queuing up to solo, with the result that some were underused. Mayall decided to keep Jon and Mick Taylor and brought in Steve Thompson on bass guitar. The quartet then embarked on a series of gigs with no rehearsals and with no 'pad'. John would just kick off the set by vamping on organ, guitar or harp and the rest of the band would come in after four bars. Maybe it was a return to basics that Mayall was after. In fact, Jon found the spontaneity very enjoyable.

So Dick found himself unemployed again and with no idea of his next move. He'd just split up with his wife, Gary and his gut feeling was that his next gig should be more radical. At the height of all the *GBO* madness, Jon and Dick had often discussed their dream of a band with no passengers, lunatics or drug addicts. It seemed to Dick that anybody who was any good was either completely mad, or heading for an early demise from drug use. On one of his last gigs with Mayall, Dick said to Jon: "I don't know what I'm going to do now, but sure as hell I'm going to have to do something quick or I'll be dead. If we're ever going to form this band of ours, it's got to be right now." Jon wasn't sure, but over the next few weeks, as he gigged with the quartet, he started to think that he might be letting the window of opportunity pass by. As it turned out, Mayall had planned a holiday in America in order to suss out the scene and the Hisemans were going to spend this time at a family-owned villa in Frascati, just outside Rome, where they had holidayed every year since 1965. In this peaceful environment, Jon could ponder the weighty matter — whether or not the time was right to form his own band.

Away from the pressure of touring and recording, Jon began to realise that he might have had the best out of the blues scene and that Dick was right...now *was* the time. Jon had been tossing ideas around in quiet moments and slowly the way forward became clear. The final decision came to him suddenly and with absolute clarity.

Towards the end of their holiday, he and Barbara spent the day sightseeing in Rome. Jon was a serious student of Roman history and had spent much of his spare time on the road reading up on the subject: "We were on the high point of the Forum overlooking the Senate House on the left and the Colosseum on the right. I had my head in my hands, Barbara leaning on the rail next to me, shaded by the cypress trees behind us. It was a very hot day. I turned to Barbara and said: "I'm leaving John Mayall. I'm going back to London and I'm going to form a band and call it *Jon Hiseman's Colosseum*." Her reply was typical: "Go for it!" The name had come to him almost as he spoke and he also had very definite ideas of who he wanted with him in the band, so on his return he immediately set about gathering the clan. Mayall soon got wind of Jon's plans on the grapevine and phoned him: "I hear you're leaving us," he laughed. Jon never forgot that royal 'us', but at least there was no acrimony from the ever-gracious Mayall.

Early in August '68, before Jon had everything finalised, Jack Bruce got in touch with him. *Cream* was just winding down and Robert Stigwood had given Jack some money to make an album of his own and as it was going to be jazz-based, he wanted Jon and Dick Heckstall-Smith on it. The seeds were planted when they played a 'one-off' gig at the 100 Club in Oxford Street a few weeks earlier. He called the album *Things We Like* and it included stuff written by Jack when he was 11 years old! Respected jazz guitarist John McLaughlin also makes a guest appearance but, in spite of the stellar line-up, the record company thought it uncommercial and didn't release it until after Jack's solo album, *Songs for a Tailor*, two years later.

When recording with Jack had finished, with Dick already on board, Jon next contacted Tony Reeves. He had made great strides while playing electric bass with Mayall and Jon liked his front-line approach. It was all coming together nicely — the next to join would be another old friend. Tony: "I seem to recall Jon saying to me, 'Now we need a keyboard player,' and me replying, 'Well, what about Greenie? — he's the obvious choice'." As it happened lady luck was on their side — Dave Greenslade had now been with *Geno Washington's Ram Jam Band* for about 18 months and, in his own words, was "ready for a change."

Of all the members in Jon's fledgling band, Dave was probably the one with the strangest musical career to date. After taking the job with French singer, Teddy Raye, he found himself heading for Morocco — via a long overland trek by way of Paris, Southern Spain and a ferry crossing. They were often broke and therefore hungry, as Dave remembers: "We had just enough money for a single lunch, so one of us ordered and started eating, then we each took turns to have a piece of the meal. The waiters didn't know what was going on!"

On their arrival, Teddy Raye hired a clapped out Dormobile, piled all the gear precariously on the roof and set off. Before long, they found themselves stranded in the middle of a flooded plain. The police came and rescued Teddy and his wife, who drove off, promising to return later to pick them and the gear up. Dave takes up the story: "When night fell, people appeared from out of the long grass. Carl Daykin, our drummer, who had been to this part of the world before, said we should go with them as things could turn nasty. After a short trek, we arrived in front of a reed stockade. The chief was obviously hoping we had money. I explained that we were English and told him about the Queen, none of which seemed to make much impression. We were finally allowed to rest on the floor of the chief's hut, where we were bitten by hundreds of bugs." They were so exhausted they fell asleep immediately, but were woken by shouts, searchlights and armed police who, alerted by Teddy, had brought trucks to carry them and their gear into Casablanca, where they eventually arrived, huddled under a large plastic sheet. This then, was Dave Greenslade's initiation into life as a professional musician!

The band spent three months playing Marrakesh, Rabat and Casablanca, with such success that they appeared on a local TV show every week. Eventually, Teddy Raye decided they should return to Paris to try their luck, but instead he split from the band, who continued to gig as *The Big Four*, playing a mixture of R&B, covers and rock 'n' roll.

Dave, having now seen some of the world, decided to return to London. While he was looking for work, John Gunnell, his old 'boss' at the Flamingo, put him in touch with Chris Farlowe who was looking for an organist and happened to have an upcoming date at Klook's Kleek. When he got there, Dave was surprised to discover that the gig was also the audition and there were several other musicians waiting and each played a couple of numbers, with Albert Lee, the band's lead guitarist, calling out the chords. Dave must have impressed, because Farlowe immediately asked him to stay on. He was still playing the Bird organ, but soon traded it in for a Hammond L100. He recorded two albums with the band, but unfortunately didn't get to play on Farlowe's major hit, *Out of Time*, as it was arranged with a string section backing. The Jagger/Richards song made No.1 at the same time as England won the World Cup in July, 1966.

After playing with Chris for three years, enjoying the marvellous guitar playing of Albert Lee, he was headhunted by Geno Washington, after his old friend Clive Burrows had recommended him. It was good to work with Clive again; Geno was a great 'live' performer and even though he found it musically naive, he enjoyed the fantastic audience reactions. After a year and a half though, Dave had had about enough, so when Jon Hiseman called to ask if he wanted join his band, he promptly agreed. "The timing was right, as I was at a point in my career when I was looking for a change."

Initially, *Jon Hiseman's Colosseum* was very much an instrumental group. Jon, Dick, Tony and Dave had all served their apprenticeships in a variety of ways, but were now ready to be in their own band and play their own music. Jon firmly believed that the days of covering other people's material were well and truly over. He was also convinced that the band should have no 'stars'...everyone would play an equal role. Dave recalls: "When Jon first called me, he couldn't tell me much because he wasn't sure how it was all going to work." What Jon *did* say, however, was that they would write their own material, ignoring the fact that none of them had much writing experience. Dave, however, was ready for the challenge: "All my various influences, since the age of seven, would enable me to write in an original way. *Colosseum* was a melting pot and its music came about because of the chemistry of the different people in the band." Dave was prepared to take a big pay cut to play in this new band -- with Geno Washington he had been earning a colossal £90 a week, but now the financial future looked uncertain again. Only time would tell if he had made the right decision.

Jon approached his old friend Colin Richardson to ask him if he was interested in managing his new band. Colin, who was working for Bron Artistes Management by that time, suggested that Jon come in to discuss representation with his boss, Gerry Bron. Gerry was the son of the legendary music publisher, Sydney Bron and his musical background lay more in the classical music of Bartók, Ravel and Stravinsky. He had built up a very successful operation managing and producing established artistes such as Gene Pitney, *Manfred Mann* and the *Bonzo Dog Doo Dah Band* — however he had never produced anything like the kind of music *Colosseum* would be playing. Colin recalls how it happened: "I didn't want to leave Bron's to take a flyer on an unknown band, so I suggested that I talk to Gerry about the possibility of the office representing them." Things had kind of come full circle, as Colin's career had been intertwined for several years with the four *Colosseum* founder members. When he had worked at the Gunnell Agency, he was the booker for Georgie

Fame, Chris Farlowe, John Mayall and Geno Washington, in whose ranks were to be found at one time or another...Jon, Dick, Tony and Dave.

Rehearsals started straight away at St Matthew's Church Hall, Elephant & Castle, London. The plan was to write some material, lick it into shape, then invite Gerry Bron down to hear it and, hopefully, be impressed. The first day's efforts produced results beyond expectations, as Dave remembers: "I started a riff and Dick developed the middle section." Jon then created the bridge passages by playing the rhythmical shapes on the drums and the rest of the band adding their ideas. The Roman connection was made when Jon decided to call it *Those About To Die — Morituri te Salutant*. It was destined to be their unofficial signature tune well into the next millennium, as well as the title track of their first album. The gladiatorial theme seemed to sum up their situation...they didn't waste time or creative energy worrying that they might not make it — as Jon remembers: "We felt comfortable with each other and there was an atmosphere of self confidence, born I think, from all the varied experiences each of us had had in the music business. In some ways, I think we all felt as if we'd just come home." Since they had all foregone other opportunities to join the band, there was also the imperative that they had to deliver the goods...or else! Another piece was started that first day, as Tony Reeves recalls: "I remembered a riff that Mick Taylor used to play in the Mayall band. I changed it into a bass line, the others chipped in with their bits and *Debut* was born." Dave recalls that: "It gave us a good start but at that stage we didn't know quite where we were heading." For the fledgling writers, these were exciting times and their confidence was growing, but Jon was determined to add vocals to the music. In order to keep the band to a five-piece and placate Dick, who did not want to lose touch with the blues, it was decided to look for a guitarist who could also sing.

An advert was placed in *Melody Maker* by Colin's secretary, Jan (the future Mrs Dave Greenslade). The response was swift and overwhelming; there were over 240 applications, of which approximately 60 made it to the auditions, which started on Monday 23rd August and ran for three days. They tried out four applicants an hour, from 12 noon until 5pm. It was an especially punishing schedule for Dave Greenslade, who, first off, had to make sure each one was in tune. This looked easy enough on paper, but it didn't turn out that way, as Dave recalls: "There was a bloke from Newcastle who came in with a dubious looking guitar. I said 'give me an E'. The note he gave me was somewhere between E and F sharp. He said 'I know it's in there...I *built* the guitar!'" One guy made a particularly memorable impression, unfortunately for the wrong reasons. Dick recalls him: "Then there was 'Flashing Fingers', he had a green velvet suit, glamorous, shoulder-length blonde hair and looked magnificent. We saw him waiting in the line at the far end of the hall...nobody who isn't really great would have the bottle to dress like that, I thought." Dave agreed: "He was polishing his guitar and we thought — this guy's the one!" Tony referred to him as 'the guy with the amazing disappearing fingers'! He started to play, but was quickly halted by Jon, who complained that he couldn't hear a note. Adjustments were made to the amp, but they never did get any sound out of him. In the end, Jon thanked him politely and told him he wasn't quite what they were looking for!

One of the other unsuccessful applicants went on to much bigger things. Jon recalls: "Ted Turner, later to become well-known in *Wishbone Ash*, had great potential and we told him so, but he was very young and very inexperienced. I was looking for a front man and at that time, he could only play a simple blues — I needed someone with a broader approach."

Another young hopeful was James Litherland, who had travelled down from Manchester. Having just left his job, after nearly coming to blows with his boss, he'd bought his regular copy of *Melody Maker* and seen the advert 'Guitarist wanted for *Jon Hiseman's Colosseum*, featuring Dick Heckstall-Smith'. With nothing going on, he decided to apply. He didn't know who Jon was, but he had heard of Dick, having seen him with Graham Bond. Little did he know, at that moment, that the phone call he was about to make would change his life.

He arrived on the first day of the auditions, guitar in hand and awaited his turn: "I was nervous, but I had nothing to lose." He recalls: "The band was formed in a circle and you had to play in the middle of them. At the right time, Dick would point at you and say 'now' and that was the signal to play the solo. I had a stroke of luck, as they played *Backwater Blues* by Leadbelly and I knew how to play *and* sing it." He was one of the few who *did* sing and for this reason he stood out.

At the end of the third day, as soon as the last guitarist had left, a short- list was compiled and the following Friday set for the final audition. The constant workload had taken its toll on Dave Greenslade who had caught flu and needed the break to get over it! James was on the short list, but almost didn't make it. Not having his own phone, he'd left his neighbour's number with Colin Richardson: "A couple of days later, whilst talking to my mother, I found out that the neighbour had gone away for a week or two. I immediately phoned the office to tell them that I had given them a useless number and Colin came on the line to say that he had been trying to contact me and could I come down to London for an expenses-paid second audition?"

In the event, James got the job and didn't hang around: "I came back home, finished with my girlfriend and told my mother to pick up my cards from work. Come Monday morning, with my guitar, my amp and a suitcase, I was back on the London train, without a second thought." What James didn't know at the time, was that they hadn't, in fact, considered him to be the best guitarist, but he *was* thought the best singer. The band had also been impressed by Jim Roche, a local lad (he lived only half a mile from the rehearsal room), who was clearly a good jazz guitarist, but couldn't sing. Initially, this had ruled him out, but, unsure of James's soloing strength and against

Jon's better instincts, it was decided to add the second guitarist to play lead.

Jon found the auditions a painful experience — so many hopefuls, so few with any real ability. So, why did the band choose to audition at all? Surely they knew a good guitarist that would fit the bill? Jon later explained to *Beat Instrumental*: "We had name guitarists enquiring about the band, but I thought it would be more stimulating to introduce fresh musicians — to dig them up, show them to the audiences and let them create their own following." However, Dave Greenslade's personal view was: "We didn't actually know another guitarist who was prepared to work for £20 a week!"

James Litherland was born in Salford, near Manchester, on 6th September, 1949. He got his first instrument, a blown-out harmonica, from his uncle Les Holland, a fan of the famous harmonica groups like the *Morton Fraser Gang* and the *Three Monarchs*. Later, James switched to guitar, one of his first influences being Lonnie Donegan. He'd been learning for some time before he actually saw one being played (echoes of Jon Hiseman). It was during a BBC play and he was transfixed, so much so that the next day he went out and bought a chord book, learnt a few 'shapes' and wrote his first song. He listened to records, slowing down the speed so he could work out what was going on more easily. At 11, he joined his first band, the name of which is long forgotten.

Whilst still at school, he started listening to the blues. It was fortunate that, at that time, there were several American blues musicians touring the UK and James got the chance to see legendary stars like T-Bone Walker, Sonny Boy Williamson, Sleepy John Estes, Sunnyland Slim, Howlin' Wolf and Willie Dixon. Then James met up with a fellow enthusiast, Roger Gibson and formed a blues band, but it wasn't long before the blues boom petered out and he started listening to soul music...*Dancing in the Street* by *Martha & the Vandellas* was a big influence, but he was also impressed with *The Who*. He recalls those days: "My first serious band, called *The Puzzle*, was with a guy at school called Steve Bolton, who later played with Paul Young and also, funnily enough, *The Who* (he played on their 1989 tour). When *The Puzzle* got in the local paper, the deputy head threatened to expel us. He said 'You'll never make a living playing music' and he was probably right, but I'm glad I didn't listen to him. The next group I was in, *The Go Go*, played Motown and we also copied a London 'mod' band called *The Action* — they were our heroes." After leaving school, he took a succession of boring jobs in local factories and warehouses, none of which gave him any sense of reward, other than on getting his weekly pay cheque. Then the day came when he bought that all-important edition of *Melody Maker*!

It wasn't long before Gerry Bron, clearly excited by Colin's initial briefing about the pedigree of the new band, was keen to see how things were progressing, but they kept fending him off until they felt they were completely ready. The momentous day eventually arrived, as Gerry recalls: "They played a couple of numbers — the first one was *Those About to Die* — and Jon said to me 'What do you think?' I said 'Absolutely fantastic!' 'No, no, what do you *really* think?' said Jon." It took a while for Gerry to convince him that he meant what he said. He then told Jon to come in to the office and bring a list of what he needed to get started. The following day, Jon read through and signed management and agency agreements, together with a contract that enabled Gerry to record the band and then license the resulting albums to major record companies in different territories around the world. Jon then went to Lloyds Bank in Tottenham Court Road, where Gerry had opened an account for the band, with Jon as signatory. Jon: "We had a £4,000 overdraft and I was writing cheques for the van, PA and wages. You try to do that today within 24 hours of an audition." It was all down to one man putting his money where his mouth was, trusting his instincts and having the courage to back them up; that man was Gerry Bron.

With rehearsals progressing well, Colin Richardson got busy setting up the first gigs for October. Jon explained in an interview with *Beat Instrumental*: "Once you've got a manager, an agency and with gigs bearing down on you, it's amazing how much work you can get through." Dick also described the buzz to *Beat Instrumental*: "It's exciting music and we want to excite people with this band, because I feel that jazz musicians can often be too tepid." Jon recently said: "Once you create a band you also create a personality with a life of its own and it has to be fed. As long as the writers and musicians feed it, the band stays alive." Easily said with hindsight, but the difficulty of feeding the beast would later come home to haunt *Colosseum*.

Rehearsals continued apace and everyone seemed to be coming up with ideas and it fell to Jon to keep a grip on things. He was very good at getting the best out of people, but would never force anybody beyond their capabilities. Dave recalls: "Jon was a good arranger and he had a flair for musical shapes. Riffs were kicked around by us all, but Jon was good at knowing how to link them. He knew what was needed once the framework of music was there." Tony Reeves clarified this: "He couldn't arbitrate about a chord sequence or melody line but he was good at recognising what fitted and sounded right." Jon recollects: "The band was rehearsing and writing in the round — in those days nobody was presenting finished material in demo form, because at our level the technology did not exist." The *Colosseum* creative process can be summed up as anyone and everyone throwing ideas into the mix, with Jon restructuring and uniting them so they could be presented to an audience. Later, he would also contribute some of the most enduring lyrics for their music.

While the band was honing its act, Gerry Bron was trying to secure a record deal, but finding it hard going. Gerry recalls those frustrating early days: "The worst problem we had was that the record companies didn't understand what the band was doing. I remember taking Martin Davis (of United Artists) to a gig. He said it was too complicated and uncommercial, so he wasn't interested." As always, the record companies were several steps behind the fans and it would be a while before they woke up to this new music that fused rock and jazz. However, Gerry had worked a lot with Philips Records in the past and, using his track record there, persuaded them to sign *Colosseum*. Looking back, he's certain Philips didn't have a clue as to what they were getting, but they obviously trusted his instincts. Eventually, it was agreed that *Colosseum*'s first album would be released on Philips' sister label, Fontana. Jon felt quite elated — it was the same label that the *Dave Brubeck Quartet* was on.

Gerry Bron saw his role thus: "The manager should only think up the ultimate long-term schemes that help the band progress and become successful. Colin Richardson was my right-hand man and I left the everyday running to him." Around this time, Jon and Gerry lunched together at the Star Steak House, off Soho Square. It was here that Jon gave Gerry a shock, as Jon remembers: "We discussed *Colosseum*'s recording policy. I told him that we were an album band and we didn't release singles. With a wry smile, he said, 'Well, I'd like to think that we could sell as many albums as I have singles.' I then told him, 'if we do something that, in your professional opinion, could be a hit single, then go ahead and release it — but I haven't put this band together to make singles.'" However, most of Gerry's success had, hitherto, been with producing and selling 'pop' singles and he never quite gave up hope that he could produce a hit for *Colosseum*.

Meanwhile, booking the band out was going like a dream, since, according to Colin Richardson, their pedigree meant that all the regular venues took them without hesitation. The Bron Agency had expanded with the addition of Don Kingswell (later to become tour manager for the 'doo-wop' revival band *Sha Na Na*) and Jim Godbolt. These two 'old hands' sat in a smoke-filled office overlooking Oxford Street, making a mixture of hot and cold phone calls to promoters. Don was a larger than life character, who chain-smoked and always had cigarette ash down his lapels. Jim was a dour, cynically funny man who would later edit the Ronnie Scott house magazine *JARS* for many years. Both were good at their job, though in different ways. They were later joined by a hot-shot young booker, Steve Barnett, who went on to manage Gary Moore for a while before moving to America to join the famous Hard to Handle management company, eventually climbing the corporate ladder to become President of Epic Records and CEO of Columbia Records.

Though *Colosseum* was busy preparing to make their live debut, this didn't preclude some of the guys taking on other projects from time to time. *The New Jazz Orchestra* was about to record their second album, *Le Dejeuner sur L'Herbe*, the cover of which was a recreation of the famous painting by Edouard Manet. Photographed by Tony Reeves, it displayed Jon and Neil Ardley in period dress, with two semi-naked female friends of Barbara's. It was three years since the release of *Western Reunion* but for this new album, three members of *Colosseum* would be involved. Jon Hiseman and Tony Reeves had played with the orchestra since its formation, but now Dick was also on board for the first time. In the event, Tony decided *not* to play bass as he was producing the album, so Jack Bruce was drafted in to make his debut with the *NJO*, taking time out from preparations for *Cream*'s farewell concert. Dave Gelly noted in his diary that rehearsals were scheduled for the 15th and 16th of September, with just two days' studio time to record the album. On paper it was a daunting situation for any producer but Tony wasn't concerned: "It wasn't daunting, it was a pleasure. It didn't need much producing anyway. But you had to know all the relative balances of the brass. I did the job because I was the only one who was a producer." Barbara Thompson, Dave Gelly, Henry Lowther and the usual members were there, together with some new faces — percussionist Frank Ricotti (man of a thousand sessions) and trombonist/composer/arranger Michael Gibbs, who wrote the original big band version of *Tanglewood '63*.

While Jon, Dick and Tony were making the *NJO* album, James

Litherland was a worried man. He had been experiencing severe stomach pains for quite a while and they were getting worse, eventually peaking during a studio session he was doing for Mike Hugg of *Manfred Mann*. He ended up rolling on the floor in agony and was rushed to hospital in Fulham, where appendicitis was diagnosed and an immediate operation was ordered. Back then this was a much more serious affair than the keyhole surgery practised today. The incision was larger and took longer to heal, so recovery was slower. To make matters worse, *Colosseum*'s debut was imminent. By the time James was released from hospital, he had little more than a week to get fit.

Colosseum's first gig was actually two nights, at the Scene Two club in Scarborough on 11th & 12th October 1968 and their fee was £150 (for both nights). They preferred starting off 'out of town', hoping to be able to fix any problems out of the limelight, but such was the excitement in the music press that Chris Welch, who had been a fan of Jon's since his Graham Bond days, was detailed by *Melody Maker* to cover the event. Unfortunately, the venue was not without its problems, as Dave's Hammond organ had to be got to the stage by somewhat unconventional means, as Jim Roche recalls: "The staircase was too narrow to be used, so it had to go up the outside wall on a kind of window cleaner's cradle; it was probably used to get the beer in. In the high wind and rain, the roadie was hanging on to the organ and the chains at the same time, as it swung from side to side. That's when I realised roadies were not just drivers and deserved every respect."

The gig went well enough, though Tony Reeves didn't think it was the right venue, but accepted that they had to start *somewhere*. James hadn't completely recovered from his operation and struggled his way through the show with a big piece of cotton wool stuffed down his trousers to protect his wound. Chris Welch's review was positive, comparing the band with heavyweights *Jethro Tull* and *The Nice* and singling out the two young unknowns for special mention: "James, from

Manchester, sings blues with strength and feeling, while Jim blows uncommonly fine guitar. Their twin guitar sound is a groove." In spite of Chris's praise, Jim felt uneasy: "I was more concerned with the gaping holes which were becoming apparent in my knowledge of musical theory. I hadn't paid my dues, so you could say I was intimidated by the situation, though never by the members of the band. You simply can't learn what takes years, in a couple of months."

The show comprised mainly original material plus a few covers, one of which was included to highlight James' bluesy voice — Dave and Jon had been knocked out by the Rod Steiger/Sydney Poitier film, *In the Heat of the Night*, the soundtrack of which featured Ray Charles singing the Quincy Jones-penned title track, and the eerie flutes of Roland Kirk.

Colin Richardson recalls being at Klook's Kleek in North London for one of the early gigs and remarked on the great atmosphere. The band was definitely creating a buzz. Jon, however, didn't have it easy that night, as the stage was made up of four sections that weren't level and his drums straddled the divides, which meant that he felt as if he was balanced precariously across a chasm. In spite of this, they went down very well; though Jon, with his music business background, was under no illusions...as yet the audiences weren't exactly breaking the doors down to see them! They planned to spend at least a month on the road before going into the studio, as Tony recalls: "I am a strong advocate of playing material first before recording, because you can reshape things according to the audience reaction." For Jim Roche, it was the first time he had ever been in a studio, but expert help was at hand: "The fondest memory I have of Dick — a hero of mine from the Graham Bond days — is of him taking me to some other recording sessions to educate me. He was a lovely man."

"Jack Bruce was important to me, because he confirmed what I was beginning to suspect — most listeners don't know what is intended and only hear what you have done... and often there's a big difference."
JON HISEMAN

Chapter 6

Morituri Te Salutant — THOSE WHO ARE ABOUT TO DIE SALUTE YOU

"We mainly played the club circuit back then. I knew the breakthrough had come when we played Brunel University. We were shown into this hall and there were rows of seats. I thought we must be in the wrong place but they said 'no, you're playing here.'"
DAVE GREENSLADE

JIM ROCHE'S FEARS ABOUT HIS PLAYING PROVED TO BE JUSTIFIED — he was clearly not fulfilling the promise of his audition performance. Jon felt that they were *all* on a steep learning curve and wanted to encourage a spirit of adventure, with plenty of risk taking. Unfortunately, it became clear that Jim's standard of playing in the first few days was as good as it was going to get in the short term and they simply couldn't afford to keep him on as a passenger. In the end, as bandleader, Jon had to bite the bullet and tell him he was out. Jim recalls the moment very well, as he was never sacked in a more gentlemanly manner: "I was disappointed, but not surprised. It did however, bring long-term benefits in making me realise there was much more to the music than playing the notes...and that the music is much more important than the individual."

Meanwhile, James' playing had been improving, so Jon decided to revert to his original plan of combining guitar and lead vocals. It was a big step up for James, who also began to write material for the band, but he was well aware that he lacked the experience of the other guys. Colin Richardson recognised that James was a little awestruck at first, "but fitted in quickly." It had all happened so fast...James recalls: "One minute I was in Manchester and the next I was in London. It was like a dream." Apparently, he had also acquired a nickname when he'd commented to one of the band, "you're as thick as a workhouse butty!" Having explained to the incredulous Southerners, that this northern 'delicacy' consisted of fried chips between two slices of bread, i.e. a 'chip butty', Dave Greenslade promptly accorded him the nickname 'Butty', which immediately caught on...hence *Butty's Blues*.

A somewhat disconsolate Jim Roche knew he'd let a great opportunity slip by, admitting to *Melody Maker* in 1970, that he had played like an idiot while he was with *Colosseum*: "After that, my range of musical interests expanded and my stage terror began to decrease. I worked with many fine musicians and learnt something new every time. Music is like that. The more you learn the more there is to know."

On the 1st November, 1968, *Colosseum* played the first of many gigs at the famous Marquee Club, London in a schedule that was already becoming quite hectic. Three days later, they were in Pye Studios laying down tracks for their debut album. The sessions began at the civilised time of 2pm and went through to midnight, with Gerry Bron producing and Tony Reeves as co-producer. Four days were booked, but according to James Litherland, Jon wasn't happy with the drum sound he was getting on some of the cuts, so the decision was taken to change studios. Gerry Bron recalls: "We only went to Pye in the first place because Tony Reeves said he knew the desk there, but the sessions were pretty disastrous so we moved to where I wanted to go in the first place, Lansdowne Studios." Jon later remarked that the drum booth at Lansdowne was too oppressive...maybe one reason why his own studio, Temple Music, doesn't have one.

As if life wasn't already hectic enough, midway through recording, Jon had to fit in a concert with the *New Jazz Orchestra* at London's Conway Hall. Not only was he in the *NJO* rhythm section, but he was also playing with the opening act, which was supposed to be the *Mike Taylor Trio*. On the night, however, it was Howard Riley who sat down at the piano...Mike Taylor having performed his disappearing act once again!

By all accounts, the *NJO* set didn't start off too cohesively, but in the second half they settled down and got into their stride. Christopher Bird of *Melody Maker* was there and described the climax of the concert: "The final number, a fifteen minute version of *Dusk Fire*, with the brass section led by the impressive Derek Watkins, and featuring great solos by Dave Gelly, Jim Philip, Jon Hiseman and Tony Reeves, was tremendous."

Being in the *NJO* was always a juggling act, with its musicians having to fit the one-off concerts around their regular gigs.

For Barbara Thompson though, it was a fruitful time, as she was fast becoming a successful musician in her own right, having mastered an impressive array of instruments...soprano, alto, tenor and baritone saxes, as well as flute and clarinet! Even though it was the swinging '60s, it was still a male-dominated world and the music biz was no exception — unless you were a singer. She got used to seeing disapproval on the faces of musicians who didn't know her and always felt she had to prove herself.

At the time of the *NJO*'s Conway Hall gig, Barbara was performing nightly in the West End musical *Cabaret*, with Judy Dench in the lead role. Set in a nightclub in pre-war Germany, she played sax in the onstage, all-girl *Kit Kat Klub* band, who were clad in stockings and suspenders...which were every bit as racy as the ones that Barbara had refused to wear with *She Trinity*. On this occasion, however, she felt that it was justified as it was a stage role — plus it paid the bills while Jon was forming his band.

During the show's run, Barbara got to know the actor Barry Dennen and they became great friends. He played the 'Master of Ceremonies' (the male lead in the show), winning high praise for his performance and would subsequently play Pontius Pilate on both the original album and Broadway production of *Jesus Christ Superstar*. The production wasn't without its problems though and Barbara remembers there were occasional backstage tensions: "The Palace Theatre dressing room was a great refuge for me, as sometimes that part of showbiz, with its artificiality and false bonhomie, really depressed me. I had an old Ford Anglia car at the time and often dropped Barry off at his Chelsea Mews flat after the show. I was full of admiration for him as he was an incredible performer, but also great fun to be with." Barbara and Jon remained in touch with him long after the show ended and he even co-wrote a song for *Colosseum* later.

Even though it wasn't the happiest of experiences for Barbara, the regular income continued to support them both while

Colosseum was trying to break through. However, working six nights a week in the theatre, it was very difficult to do any other work, but when the *NJO* were offered the Conway Hall gig, she arranged for the very capable Kathy Stobart to 'dep' for her in the *Kit Kat* band, pleading sickness. Unfortunately, she was rumbled when her name appeared in the subsequent press reviews and the management decided to make an example of her. She was put on two weeks' notice, which got a lot of sympathy from the cast, but a week later it was announced that the show was to close anyway...ironically, on the last day of her notice!

Meanwhile, back with *Colosseum*, James Litherland had grown in confidence since those first gigs in Manchester, when his nerves were so bad he felt as if he was going to have a heart attack. It was a great opportunity 'fronting' a major band but it bought with it considerable responsibility for someone so young and inexperienced. As James recalls: "The pressure I was under to be a front man, which I didn't audition for, drove me to drink vodka before the gig — first, a quarter of a bottle, then half. I soon realised that I couldn't carry on like that and I stopped pretty quick." Jon, however, doesn't recall being aware of any problems and always thought James was most professional.

Jim Roche's departure gave the band a chance to take a break from gigs and work on honing the act. They dropped numbers that weren't working, polished up the more successful numbers and brought in new material. Then it was back to business! On the 17th December they recorded *Top Gear*, John Peel's ground-breaking radio programme on the BBC, performing *The Road She Walked Before*, *Those About to Die*, *Backwater Blues* and *Debut* amongst others. Programmes such as this played a very important part in a band's career as they enjoyed high listening figures. Jon recalls: "It's amazing to remember the power of radio back then...especially John Peel's show. *Colosseum* actually played several of their famous numbers on these shows for the first time, because it gave us a recorded version to analyse and when I announced them at a subsequent gig, the audience would applaud *en masse* — incredible!"

On the 3rd January 1969, the band returned to Lansdowne Studios to finish recording their all-important first album. With two producers in the studio, there could easily have been friction, but as Tony Reeves explains, there was a clear division of labour between them: "Gerry Bron understood the recording technicalities, but the music less so. He seemed happy to leave the performance decisions to me. I got on with him very well, respectful of his business knowledge but confident of my musical knowledge." Adrian Kerridge, who engineered the sessions, found this arrangement less conducive: "Working with two producers, each with his own idea of what it should sound like was very hard at times! Had I been left to get on with it without so many producers (including the two cents' worth from the band) I think the results would have been better." For Adrian, the fact that *Colosseum* had such a unique sound made it more important to keep the production as uncomplicated as possible. Up to that point Gerry had mainly produced pop records and this was quite a different kettle of fish, as he recalled recently: "With *Colosseum* I wasn't going to tell some of the best musicians in the country what to play, but I might have made the odd suggestion." Despite these minor tensions the album was finished in three days and would prove to be an important steppingstone in the band's career.

James Litherland's recollection of the Lansdowne sessions is of Jon seeming much happier with his drum sound. Interestingly, Jon disputes this, which just shows how perceptions of what was actually going on, differed. Gerry Bron enjoyed recording the band, but admitted that working with Jon wasn't always easy: "Jon was very opinionated and very sure of what he wanted, but in fact he wasn't always as correct as he thought." At one point, Adrian Kerridge asked Jon to take the front head off the bass drum, because he couldn't record it properly. Jon refused, but according to Gerry, he subsequently realised that Adrian had been right. Jon recently reflected on all this: "There is no doubt that when I was a young man I did not suffer fools gladly and tended to jump right in with both feet, so I certainly alienated people. Adrian was quite right about how to 'mic' the bass drum for this band — I should have taken the front head off, because he wasn't going on about whether the drums sounded authentic, but how the sound of the drums *worked in the mix*. I learnt a lot about all that later on, but my main problem was always the monitoring — the speaker systems the studios had in those days bore no relation to the kind of domestic speakers we had in our homes and we were, and still are, recording music that people listen to in everyday situations. The layout of the control room at Lansdowne Studios was particularly bad at that time since the only person who could really hear the mix was the engineer. We were a band trying to make creative decisions based on what we were hearing and we didn't have the experience to hear *through* the studio, so it was really difficult for us. Studio monitoring was only sorted out when new technology arrived in the early '80s. Actually, in my view, those early album recordings don't do justice to the sound of the band — I knew that at the time, but didn't understand what was going on. I'm not blaming anyone though — as a band we *were* very sure of ourselves, even though we were relatively inexperienced."

Recording the album actually brought the band closer together and provided Jon Hiseman with some useful insights into the bargain: "It's important to remember that bands and their managers become like families. They spend so much time with each other that they can forget the social niceties — everybody pitches in. In the end it's all about getting it right...or as right as you can, whatever it takes. I soon learnt how to listen closely and ask awkward questions. Everybody was very generous in passing on their skills and the most important thing I learned was not do anything unless the way forward is clear — and it becomes clear at the oddest of moments."

With the album in the can, the band and Jon were pleased and satisfied with the end result, in spite of the problems they'd had with the sound. As a first album, it certainly had some strong tracks and confident performances, notably *Those About to Die*, *Walkin' in the Park*, *Mandarin* and *Debut*. For a band that aspired to play jazz-rock, it is surprisingly eclectic, as it included blues, a classically inspired piece and a track with Eastern influences. This diversity is, in fact, the album's main strength, as it sustains the interest and whets the appetite for a follow-up, which, as they gained more experience and honed their song-writing abilities, stood every chance of being even better.

Jon's work on the album is richly satisfying. For a drummer with no formal tuition, his technical ability is impressive. Jon had always preferred to work things out for himself, however long it took, and this personal approach to problem-solving certainly paid dividends. He learnt to think things through quickly, which contributed to his very individual style. As Dick noted when Jon joined Graham Bond: "His pulsing, wall-of-sound had an immediate and positive impact, but even though he can create a great wash of sounds, he always seems to have it under control." Jon maintains his playing has always been about 'making the incomprehensible, comprehensible', and there is no doubt that, both on and off the drum kit, he was always a good communicator.

One thing that Jon was keen to communicate was emotion and he began to understand that, at the drumkit, he was a kind of conductor with a lot of control over the way the music was perceived. "I can produce tone colours that either sharpen the music or blunt it," he told *Melody Maker*. Jon's playing posture was very unusual too...his upper body upright and his head still, giving the impression of being in complete control, which Jon is quite happy about, but as he admitted recently, it would be the late '80s before he could play something and be sure of how it would sound to the listener.

Jon Hiseman has been called the complete drummer but, in reality, there is no such animal as, at some point, everyone's limitations are exposed. In 1970, Jon was brought in at the last minute to record a session for Eric Clapton, which turned out to be a most uncomfortable experience. Jon explains: "They couldn't have picked a worse drummer for their music — I didn't understand what they wanted or why they kept telling me to 'be lazy and lay back on the beat'. I came from a jazz background and my whole concept of playing at that time was to play right up on the beat. Later, when I became more experienced — playing in bands other than my own and after I had built my own studio and began listening back to myself regularly, I learned to play the beat in slightly different positions, to suit the music." The bottom line was that, at this time, he was great at playing *his* way, but not much good at playing like anybody else.

Colosseum's musical mix was what gave them their unique sound, but there was still the occasional 'bone of contention'. As Dick Heckstall-Smith noted in his autobiography: "Jon's authority leaked from administration to fill the vacuum in musical policy." Four of the band wrote the music and Jon was contributing lyrics...but who decided what was used? Many a band encountered problems when stronger personalities tried to promote their own, often inferior, material over better stuff from the less pushy ones. With Jon at the helm, that was never going to happen, because he knew that his most useful role was to stay neutral and select the things that worked best. That way he was able to set and maintain the direction, as well as the standard, of the material. As time went on, the writers, Dave Greenslade especially, were able to present virtually finished songs that fitted the *Colosseum* ethos. The success of this system is borne out by the fact that, in 2010, the band was still playing much of this original material. Even Dick admitted that, without such strong leadership, they might have ground to a halt and everyone agreed that Jon was most effective in this role. Ultimately, it was his band and he called the shots! However, that's not to say he didn't want the others to contribute to the overall running of the band. Dick acknowledges in his book that Jon broached this subject quite early on: "Jon told me quietly and seriously that he needed me to take a more positive role on the organisational side. He felt disappointed that I had not done so spontaneously. I felt awkward; I didn't want to hear it. The real issue was how the band came into existence; the way the band had been born made it his, not ours." Dick's partner, Christine Roche, confirmed his dilemma: "He would come back home and moan, saying 'Sure it's Jon's band, but it is also *our* band'. Dick always felt guilty about not doing more, but he just wasn't able to. He wasn't good at dealing with non-musical things and would only deal with what interested him." Faced with Dick's recalcitrance, Jon became resigned to continue doing everything himself, but this would eventually catch up with him.

Dick did, in fact, question the band's musical philosophy quite early on, as he mentions in his book: "Each member should be able to express himself musically without deliberately focusing on originality. In this way, the band as a whole would not suffer from the stultifying burden of self-consciously trying to do something new." Jon still doesn't really understand what he was going on about. He knew that Dick aspired to be the world's greatest blues saxophonist, bending and shaping notes the way a guitarist could, and that he saw *Colosseum* as a platform for this. Right from the start, Dick had made it clear that he thought they should be primarily a blues band, but Jon was aware that if they were, when the blues boom came to an end, so might they. "My idea was a fusion of jazz and rock, but I knew that instrumental music had a small audience, so I also wanted to do what Graham Bond, Georgie Fame and John Mayall were doing with vocals." Even Dick acknowledged that *Those About to Die* had only a tenuous link to the blues, though it does contain a blues sequence, but like most of *Colosseum*'s music, it is actually a fascinating hybrid of styles. In the event, people came in droves to hear their unique blend of music and Jon's policy was

114

vindicated. As time went on, blues featured less and less and Dick enthusiastically embraced the new, more ambitious, material — especially when persevering against the odds with his ill-fated showcase piece, *The Pirate's Dream*.

Colosseum was now almost constantly on the road, both in the UK and Europe, going down a storm everywhere. As new material emerged, it was added to the show and then further developed in performance. Live recordings of the band from this period indicate that in between the vocals there was a great deal of improvising. The *Shields Gazette* quotes Jon as saying at the time: "I will never go back to playing purely improvised jazz...all the themes and songs *we* play are precisely worked out and it's only within that framework that members of the group are free to improvise." The 'free' jazz that Jon and Tony had played with Mike Taylor was essentially unstructured music. Mainstream jazz and blues solos are usually very structured; and Jon's idea was to marry these to rock rhythms, add a vocalist and thus appeal to a much wider audience. For Tony, improvisation was what made the music exciting and challenging, explaining: "It only took a quarter of a second of eye contact and you knew something was going to happen — you heard the change and went with it. It wasn't planned, but the idea may have been hinted at the previous night." It was a risky strategy and it didn't always work, but it was all part of the process of developing the new material on stage. One of Jon's most enduring concepts was that audiences shouldn't know where the written music stopped and improvisation began. Jon: "Later on, Barbara's way of integrating her writing with the improvisation was so clever that, after a few gigs, not even the band knew where the joins were!"

Inevitably, there were frequent post-gig 'inquests' and often, when Colin Richardson went backstage to congratulate the guys on a great show, he would find a heated discussion going on about the things that had not happened the way they should have. These exchanges, though exhausting, were, in fact, a healthy way of evaluating their performance and ironing out any flaws, as well as throwing up ideas that could be incorporated into the next performance. Colin recalls: "They were all level-headed people, so these disagreements never got out of hand and things quickly returned to normal." This was the fundamental reason why Jon and Dick had wanted 'no passengers and no lunatics' in the band, having seen at first hand the damage they can do from their time with the *Graham Bond ORGANisation*.

Their debut album, *Morituri te Salutant (Those Who Are About To Die Salute You)* was about to be released. The sleeve reflected the Roman theme of the title and depicted the band 'cowering in terror' against the backdrop of an original Roman mosaic. The cover design, as was usual at that time, came from the record company's in-house art department and the band had little or no say in its design. At the photo session, they even tried on some Roman regalia, but that idea was quickly dumped! When Jon eventually saw the finished artwork, he hated the photo...but by then it was too late to change anything.

On 19th March, 1969, two days before the album came out, the band took part in the filming of *Supershow*, an ambitious project which brought together an impressive roster of some of the top names in jazz, blues and rock, playing in various permutations and culminating in a giant, all-star 'jam session'! Filmed over two days in a disused linoleum factory in West London, the list of star musicians included Roland Kirk, Eric Clapton, Stephen Stills, Jack Bruce and Buddy Guy. The event was produced by Tom Parkinson and filmed by Colourtel TV Productions in front of a small invited audience. *Colosseum* played two tracks from their about-to-be released album and in the finished film, their powerful performance of *Those About to Die*, was chosen as the opening sequence, though it was slightly marred by the list of credits scrolling over it. Their other contribution, *Debut*, has everyone in fine form, with Tony Reeves resplendent in a 'mandarin-style' jacket and sunglasses: "How pretentious was that! I remember thinking it could be a cool thing to do. The joke was they were a really cheap pair." James Litherland was in seventh heaven, just to be there! Whereas most of the guys in the band had seen a lot of these artists before, he hadn't and was thrilled to be amongst such a stellar cast.

Colin Richardson recalls that there was a lot of hanging around, but not much time for rehearsal or sound checks. Nevertheless, *Colosseum* turns in a great performance, as do the individual members when 'sitting-in' with other line-ups. Among the highlights of the film is the scintillating performance from Buddy Guy and Roland Kirk on *Stormy Monday* and *Slate 27*, which featured Dick and Roland Kirk both playing twin saxes. This was somewhat ironic, as Dick had avoided playing two horns in the early days *because* it was Kirk's speciality. Dick recalls being challenged to do it by Ginger Baker when they were with Graham Bond. He dismissed the idea at first, but when he tried it, he loved the sound, though he never found it easy to do well.

Jon had met Roland Kirk a couple of times before, once on tour with Georgie Fame and again when he and Barbara saw him at Ronnie Scott's Jazz Club, sitting in front row seats with Ronnie and comedian Marty Feldman. Barbara was very excited to see Kirk, as she had learned some of his solos off by heart from his albums, as part of her early attempts to understand jazz. Roland often played two or more instruments at once and this had inspired both Dick and Barbara to try it. She recalls the night at Ronnie Scott's for a special reason: "On his famous *Here Comes the Whistle Man*, he gave out penny whistles to the audience and asked us all to play along and of course I joined in with gusto. I've always been blessed with a good ear, so I played all the right notes and Roland, who, like many blind people, could hear incredibly well, picked up on what I was playing and to my embarrassment, stopped the band and asked who was playing over there, pointing to where I was sitting." Chatting with the star after the show, Jon was surprised to learn that Kirk had, on a previous UK tour, asked for him to be in his rhythm section, as he'd been impressed by his work on the Mike Taylor sessions. Unfortunately, Jon had been out of town and therefore never got the message.

During the filming of *Supershow*, Jon introduced Dick to Roland and mentioned that he (Dick) also played dual saxophones, to which Kirk, ever competitive, replied that he doubted that he played them in tune. Dick's laugh had a hollow ring about it. Later, when they were on stage together warming up, Dick played a few notes on the two saxes — Roland swivelled round to Jon on the drums and said with a grin, "Told you so!" To dwell on this though, is to miss the point. Here you had two forceful musical personalities together on stage, metaphorically 'locking horns'. Jon also recalls Eric Clapton, playing on *Slate 27* with Kirk et al, muttering that he wasn't good at jazz and obviously feeling uncomfortable in that milieu.

Two days later, Jon received a letter from producer Tom Parkinson congratulating the band on their contribution and saying: "I hope we can work together again in the future." The letter was dated 21st March, 1969, the day that *Those Who Are About To Die Salute You* was released. Colin Richardson had organised a press reception at Ronnie Scott's, where the band previewed some tracks from the album, which were well received by the assembled media. The subsequent reviews carried headlines like: 'Great! This grabs you by the hair'; 'A Salute from the *Colosseum*' and 'One of the finest drummers in Britain'. The Danish publication *Politiken* raved: "If you miss this record, you might as well throw yourself to the lions. If one is to believe the reviews in the UK trade papers, it is the whole truth and nothing but the truth, as *Colosseum* is the spring sensation in London."

Philips released a single, *Walkin' in the Park* c/w *Those About to Die* which, whilst never a hit, picked up valuable radio play throughout Europe. Very soon, the band was invited to appear on *Beat Club*, Germany's most important and relevant music TV show, the first of several such appearances over the next two and a half years as their stature grew.

With the album's release, the band's reputation spread like wildfire and their schedule became ever more hectic. Urged on by Jon, the writing flowed, as they came up with new ideas. However, the material was now being written less as a group and more by partnerships and individuals. On 25th March, they were back in Lansdowne Studios to start recording the next album and three days after that they appeared on the prestigious BBC TV programme *How Late It Is*. Then, in early April, their first European tour was due to start, but prior to this Jon and Dick were booked to record some sessions with Jack Bruce for his first solo album, *Songs for a Tailor*.

Though Jack had known Jon for quite a while, he'd known Dick much longer, even before the days of the *Graham Bond ORGANisation*. As a 16 year old, Jack had seen Dick on the cover of *Melody Maker* and thought he looked cool and wrote to him. Dick replied, (Jack still has the letter!) suggesting that he should look him up if he was ever in town. It was the beginning of a lifelong friendship, during which Dick turned him on to the great novelists, introduced him to Ginger Baker and told him to watch out for a guy called Eric Clapton!

For this project, Jack had surrounded himself with some great players. They included Chris Spedding and George Harrison playing guitars and Henry Lowther on trumpet. The sessions went well, Jack's music being enhanced by Pete Brown's visionary lyrics. Two tracks in particular made a big impression on Jon Hiseman: the intriguingly titled *Rope Ladder to the Moon* and *Theme for an Imaginary Western*, both of which would later be recorded by *Colosseum*. As it turned out, the recording of *Rope Ladder* on *Songs for a Tailor* is the only track that Jon does not play on, although he did record a much freer, jazzier version. Jon supposes that it didn't sit so well with the rest of the tracks and after he went off on tour, Jack, anxious to finish the album, got John Marshall in to play drums on the song. Jon was very impressed with John M's cool 'take' on the track and made it the basis for his playing on all *Colosseum*'s subsequent versions.

Most people perceived Jon as a forceful personality, not slow to voice his opinions but, surprisingly, he was quite insecure about his own ability as a drummer. Jon recalls that while recording Jack's album *Things We Like*, Jack praised his playing on one of the slower tracks, saying no one else could have achieved the same effect. Jon was quite taken aback, since privately, he was always his own fiercest critic: "That changed the way I thought about myself and what I did. When I listened back to recordings, all I had ever heard was what I thought of as the mistakes, so Jack was important to me, because he confirmed what I was beginning to suspect — most listeners don't know what is intended and only hear what you have done...and often there's a big difference."

The Bruce sessions over, *Colosseum* flew out to Copenhagen to record a radio show, followed by six live dates. It was their first foreign tour and the first time they were billed as a 'supergroup'. The opening concert was in the biggest hall they had played to date, with a surprisingly large crowd waiting to see them. The audience reaction was terrific, as were the reviews. The newly released album sold 3,000 copies in the first week in Denmark alone, which was a quite an achievement for a jazz-influenced band in a new territory. Things were looking very promising!

One of the Copenhagen gigs was held in a disco type club situated in an upstairs restaurant where the equipment had to go up by lift...not an ideal situation. After the gig was over, a problem arose. The roadies came and told Colin Richardson that the power to the lift had been switched off at midnight (which had long passed). This astonishing revelation, which the club owner had failed mention before, led to heated arguments with him and the tour promoter, but to no avail. There was no alternative but for everybody to help manhandle the gear downstairs. Colin was furious that such key information hadn't been mentioned when the gig was booked. When he finally got back to the hotel, it was very late and, though he was extremely tired, he found he couldn't get to sleep. After a while, feeling quite ill, he wondered if was something serious was happening. Colin recalls: "I was sweating but at the same time feeling cold. Eventually, after a few hours I got up, went next door to Dick's room and whispered to him 'Dick, I'm not feeling too great'. Without hesitation, he got up, asked a couple of questions, then called a taxi and took me to a doctor, who diagnosed an anxiety attack brought on by stress and exhaustion. He then thrust several Valium tablets into my hand and told me to get some rest." Dick's unhesitating action prevented what might have been a serious situation, but it just goes to show the kind of trials and tribulations of life on the road.

Even though Jon had always maintained that *Colosseum* was an album band, Gerry Bron still wanted them to record a single, but he realised that it wasn't going to happen voluntarily. Hoping to persuade Jon, Gerry called on Tony Hazzard, a successful in-house songwriter. Tony had already written hits for *Manfred Mann*, *The Hollies*, Cliff Richard and *Herman's Hermits*, but the $64,000 question was, 'could he write something that would suit *Colosseum*?' With some reluctance, and after listening to several demos, they eventually went with a song called *Tell Me Now*. The final result was uninspiring and even Gerry Bron was deflated. Tony Hazzard[1] recalled recently: "I was quite pleased with the demo and remember going over the song with them in Lansdowne Studios when they were recording it, but I assume it didn't work out so they scrapped it." Some time later, it was recorded by a group called *High Society* and duly bombed! Many years later, in August 2009, a *Colosseum* 4 CD box set was released (*Morituri te Salutant*) which includes this rare track.

However, when the band listened to *Tell Me Now* while preparing this compilation, nobody could remember who had written it! After some email exchanges, it was agreed to attribute the lyrics to James and the music to the band. Having registered it as such, Jon then discovered by pure chance that he was mistaken and quickly revised the credit. Interestingly, even Tony Hazzard's recall was hazy: "When Sanctuary Records put out a double album anthology of my stuff called *Go North — the Bronze Anthology*, I couldn't recall recording the song either."

On 25th April, 1969, *Colosseum* played the first of four nights at the prestigious Montreux *Golden Rose* TV Festival. The fee per show was a derisory £75, plus expenses, but was justified by the promotional value of appearing before an 'invitation-only' audience comprising TV producers, press and other industry and media heavyweights. The deal also included performing three songs for Swiss TV, which would subsequently be offered to Eurovision for screening in other countries. It was all setup by Colin Richardson, who saw it as a means of breaking into the European markets. It seems to have worked, as only a week after the *Golden Rose* they found themselves in Hilversum, Holland, for another TV show.

The times were indeed 'a-changin". In addition to the club circuit, the universities and colleges around the country were opening up their larger venues to the general public, with their 'social secretaries' often taking a year out to become, in effect, professional promoters, but with the advantage of having considerable funds to work with and little pressure to make a profit. Several of these fortunates used this experience to go on to become important figures in the music biz. These student-promoted gigs invariably paid better fees than the clubs and the audiences were ideal for groups like *Colosseum*, who always received rapturous ovations.

The band had now been working together for just over six

months and confidence was growing. When they started out they had little idea of how they would go down with the public. Yes, the management had faith in the band, but it was only now beginning to dawn on them that they were actually becoming successful. Everyone has a different take on when the turning point was. For Colin Richardson it was reading the review of their first appearance in Belgium: "We got the press cutting of the gig and it read 'Kolosseum Kolossal'. I knew then that we had a winner. Though it was clear that Europe still wanted our 'pop' artists, there was a definite sense that things were changing." With Tony Reeves, it was more of a general feeling: "I can't remember the exact gig, but there was a large audience that erupted into loud, unqualified approval as we went on stage, which gave the impression that we had become reasonably successful." Dave Greenslade felt that there was a palpable difference in the way that their audiences were beginning to appreciate the music: "We mainly played the club circuit back then and I knew the breakthrough came when we played Brunel University...we were shown into this hall with rows of seats and I thought we must be in the wrong place but they said, 'no, no, you're playing here'. The audience actually sat down and listened to the music...it was a new departure and I never saw it coming. They were starting to take our music more seriously."

For Jon, the realisation dawned that things were happening for them when they returned from that first tour of Denmark. Driving off the ferry and straight to a gig at the Leas Cliff Hall in Folkestone, they arrived to find a huge crowd milling about outside the venue. There were exhausted mutterings from the back of the van along the lines: "the bloody office has booked us as the support act; let's go on home!" However, it turned out that the office had omitted to call them during the tour with the all-important news that the album had charted...the crowd was, in fact, there to see *them*!

FOOTNOTES

1. Most of *Colosseum*'s members worked with Tony Hazzard at one time or another, as he recalls: "Dave Greenslade once played in my band for a while, which was very noble of him since he was really a jazzer and I was more pop/folk/rock. Another lovely chap was Clem Clempson who played on my album *Loudwater House* and once I even got Jon to play on a demo of mine at Chipping Norton studios. His wife, Barbara Thompson, also played flute on a TV jingle I wrote for the Furniture Exhibition at Olympia, which subsequently won an award at the Cannes Film Festival."

"You lived on your nerves."
JON HISEMAN'S TAKE on life
on the road

*"I was putting on a South East London
accent, sitting around the pool
with Dick, saying: 'Let's have a go
at* Lost Angeles.'"
DAVE GREENSLADE on the genesis
of a classic track

Chapter 7

EARTHQUAKES & SMOG

WITH THEIR DEBUT ALBUM OUT AND SELLING WELL, there was no time to sit back and enjoy the moment. *Colosseum* needed a busy schedule to keep financially afloat, but the punishing regime was beginning to take its toll. Jon knew that the only way for a band to hone its 'chops' was constant gigging, but he also knew the danger of creative 'burn out'. The truth is that life on the road was hard...and it could also be dangerous. In the early days, *Colosseum* travelled in a Ford Transit double wheelbase van with standard seating, but later they had the idea of fitting decommissioned aircraft seats, which were more comfortable but did little to improve safety, because no one ever bothered to use the attached seat belts.

The mileage that a gigging band clocked up certainly increased the odds of an accident, especially when tiredness kicked in. Jon admitted in one interview: "I sometimes wonder when I kiss Barbara goodbye, whether I will, in fact, see her again or whether some maniac driver is going to sandwich us between a van and an articulated lorry! You can't travel on a motorway without seeing accidents and blood on the road." He recalls one occasion, travelling on a German autobahn in a blizzard...the roadside littered with wrecked cars. It looked as if an enemy aircraft had strafed the motorway! Such was the reality of life on the road.

In an interview with Sidney Nelson of the *Nottingham Evening Post*, Jon confessed: "All of us are a little bit worn out from playing practically every night of the week and we're fed up with what we've been playing lately." Actually, what they *were* getting tired of was performing the same material every night. Jon makes the point that, if you're the kind of band that concentrates on showmanship, with little or no improvisation, it's relatively easy to do long tours, as you can 'switch off' and just go through the motions. "The audience can't tell the difference because it's note perfect and it looks like everybody's having a great time. The problem for an improvising band is that it doesn't work that way. You have to be on the case every moment of every gig and if, for one reason or another, it's not happening, the audience knows it too. That's a continual pressure and stress of a kind the 'entertainers' never feel."

Everything pointed to a pressing need for new material. *Colosseum* had put down a couple of new tracks prior to Jon and Dick recording *Songs for a Tailor* with Jack Bruce, which was a start, but Jon was aware that more effort was needed: "We want to come up with something different and we want something that will make our audiences sit up. It could be that some of our new sounds will not appeal at first, but I hope the fans will bear with us."

In early June 1969, Jon was invited to be the guest reviewer for *Melody Maker*'s 'Blind Date' column. Examples of several different musical styles were played to Jon in quick succession and he showed, once again, that he wasn't afraid to speak his mind. Of a track by the *Woody Herman Big Band* he wrote: "that's always been our hang up with big bands here — we never get to play together enough to be that good." About *The Who*'s *Tommy*: "I don't think whoever is singing here has enough of a mystical quality...but Keith Moon is a gas. He's had lots of acclaim from the punters, but nobody seems to take him seriously — they should." On Archie Shepp (free jazz): "I don't know any drummer...who can imply rhythm and still be free." *Don Ellis* (modern jazz big band with attitude): "It doesn't matter whether the time signature is 4/4, or as here, 7/4 — the main thing is the beat that's going on." Elvis Presley: "Great — takes me back to my schooldays." *The Beatles*: *Ballad of John & Yoko*: "this sounds like somebody doing an Elvis impersonation — Peter Sellers did it the same way — it's got exactly the same echo as those early Elvis records." *The Miles Davis Quintet*: *Frelon Brun*: "That's Anthony Williams goofing on eight — the feel he gets gives me the horrors, but it was great — I must buy it." His final review was of the *Bee Gees' Tomorrow*: "I'm not familiar with their work and nobody whose judgement I trust has said to me that I must listen to them. I don't understand the purpose of this record. In fact, I don't understand the purpose of any of these singles." Jon's attitude to the singles market isn't so surprising, given his preference for albums and his certainty that *Colosseum*'s audience shared that preference. Nevertheless, his views made for an entertaining article!

The band returned to IBC Studios on 17th June to finish off the all-important second album. The result would exceed everyone's expectations though, at the time, neither band nor management could have predicted the impact this album would have. It was decided to call it *Valentyne Suite*, after the concept piece that takes up the whole of side two. The contrast with their first album is striking — on *Those About to Die*, they are virtually an instrumental band with a singer, but on the new album, James's voice is used to great effect on some very good songs that fit well with the instrumental concept piece. It's clear that the band is comfortable with both genres and this time round they weren't afraid to leave space on some of the cuts to give the music a chance to breathe. Clearly, six months of successful concerts, healthy album sales and good reviews had given the musicians much greater confidence in their abilities as writers, as well as players.

Gerry Bron's opinion is that, even though others may have contributed to the writing, there is no doubt whose trademark is was stamped upon it: "I always thought Dave Greenslade *was* the *Valentyne Suite*. It's a magical recording, it's got a feel about it and it's their best track." Jon wrote the sleeve notes whilst watching Neil Armstrong's historic walk on the moon on a small black and white TV, perhaps sensing that in its own modest way, this album might make history for them. Even before its release, both band and management had the feeling that it was something special, but nobody realised that it would also help set the benchmark for later concept pieces in progressive music. It has certainly stood the test of time and still sounds incredibly fresh after 40 years.

With *Valentyne Suite* in the can, the band returned to Montreux, this time to appear at the renowned *Jazz Festival*, on a bill that included Ella Fitzgerald, *Clarke Terry's Big Band*, John Surman and, rather more unusually, *Ten Years After*. How *Colosseum* played at the festival is lost in the mists of time, but what is remembered is the 'impromptu' performance by the casino pool as a publicity stunt, delighting the many punters that witnessed it. As it was a warm, sunny afternoon, Dick decided to play 'topless', so to speak, and at the end of their final number, immediately jumped into the pool to cool off. *Almost* the stuff of which legends are made!

Jon generally hated those early festivals, as the organisation was often incompetent and the dressing room/toilet facilities were usually awful, though Montreux *was* an exception. He didn't like the swimming pool gig though, considering it to be a cheap stunt. However, he soon realised that *Colosseum* was being booked on jazz festivals as a way of boosting crowds, in what was an ailing genre. On several notable occasions the posters proclaimed *Colosseum* as top of the bill (which they never were at rock festivals), but the organisers, whose main interest was still in the 'purer' forms of jazz, often continued treating them as second-class citizens. By now the band was carrying much more equipment than the average jazz group and was seldom given enough time to set-up or soundcheck, often only getting the regular 15 minutes usually allocated to jazz groups. If they took longer, which they often did, it ate into their performance time. But the writing was on the wall...*The Beatles*/Hendrix/*Stones* revolution had already sounded the final trumpet for the Golden Age of Jazz.

Back in England, Jon was now writing a regular column for *Beat Instrumental* magazine and in it he comments that he had been impressed by Ella Fitzgerald and the *Tommy Flanagan Trio* at

Montreux, but the musical offerings from the other American bands he described as 'unproductive audience fodder'. Pulling no punches, he made it clear that he felt the European musicians on the bill should have been taken much more seriously than they were. In the same article Jon wrote frankly about the perils of crossing borders as a musician: "As any seasoned traveller will tell you, entering foreign countries is becoming ever more difficult in this modern age; and should you also commit the cardinal sin of having long hair and carry a guitar case, or even be seen *talking* to somebody who does, then life is made doubly difficult. We are always singled out for currency checks and the customs officials are usually at their most sarcastic. Why is it that European statesmen and politicians impose so many restrictions and conditions on the free interchange of people from one country to another? When will they realise that travellers clutching their bottles of duty-free Scotch and perfume are nothing to be frightened of? When we arrived hot and tired in Switzerland we were all searched — not for drugs or currency, but for the extra bottle or two of Scotch — as apparently had all the musicians bound for the Montreux Jazz Festival!"

On the 28th June 1969, *Colosseum* played the first *Bath Festival of Blues* and though the stage was tiny, the bill[1] was huge. The day hadn't got off to the best of starts though, as Dick had managed to leave his saxophones behind at the hotel, but in spite of having to play on borrowed instruments, he still managed to make his usual fine contribution to what turned out to be one of their best gigs to date. The band went on third of 16 acts, around mid-afternoon getting a great reception. Ordinarily, the band would have hung around to check out the 'competition', but their agency had other ideas. Back at the office, it had been spotted that *Colosseum*'s early performance had apparently given the band an evening off — which would never do. A 'double' was therefore arranged, with the Van Dyke club in Plymouth, so, immediately after coming offstage, they had to set off for their second gig of the day!

Another notable appearance for them was at Selby Abbey in Yorkshire, with *Pink Floyd* headlining. The *Yorkshire Evening Post* dispatched an 18-year-old cub reporter to review it and, with an audience of around 2,000 people crammed into a marquee, he watched as *Colosseum* kicked off with *Walkin' in the Park*. The rookie scribe was hooked! "It was *Jon Hiseman's Colosseum* who took the place over. Let's not call them a pop group, jazz band or anything, but let's call them fantastic and they didn't indulge in any sky-high solo improvisations. Each man knew his limits and despite the wide ranging mood of the band, the tight and changing arrangements demanded that each member respect others." This journalist didn't stay with the *Post* for much longer...his destiny lay elsewhere. He would reappear some eight years later as the lead guitarist in his own group...*Dire Straits*! Yes, the 'cub reporter' was none other than Mark Knopfler.

Knopfler had perceptively observed something which had concerned the band since its inception. What kind of music *did* they play? Some called it jazz-rock, but this specific term was mainly used in the early to mid '70s to describe bands like *Mahavishnu Orchestra*, *Weather Report* and Chick Corea's *Return to Forever*. There were many different descriptions of progressive music of the late '60s. Some labelling caused a few smiles...one journalist wrote that he went to see *Colosseum* expecting to hear 'progressive pop', but came away convinced that, if you took away the amplification, they would have sounded like a good mainstream jazz band! The truth is that when a trailblazing band appears on the scene, it's not always easy to categorise them. Film-maker Tony Palmer described their music in 1970 thus: "Pop excitement combined with jazz discipline and classical structure." Even stranger was Radio Luxembourg's description of *Those About to Die* as 'Hard Rock Heavyweight Album of the Week'! It does seem clear, however, that combining jazz with rock rhythms opened the eyes and ears of many other musicians, as would be borne out later, when they played the Fillmore West, in San Francisco.

Prior to their first American trip, they returned to Denmark for a short tour that included a TV show and an appearance at the Copenhagen Jazz Beat Festival with *The Byrds*. One member of *Colosseum* who loved playing foreign tours was Tony Reeves. He was known to eat his way through countries: "I liked to partake of the cuisine and I was blown away by the Danish food on board the ferry. There were huge tables with open sandwiches of smoked eel." On the 28th July, the day after the festival, the band took part in a jazz workshop with Alexis Korner, where Jon outlined some of the frustrations of writing original material: "It takes something like three months for a number to be perfected. And even then there is a chance it might never be played in front of an audience." This comment illustrated the one problem that would always hang over the band — a continual shortage of usable new material. This would become critical in 1971, but right now, it was off to the USA for their first tour.

James Litherland was about to get a reality check regarding the band's wage structure. The American tour was to last four weeks, so the guys went to the office to collect an advance on their wages which was to cover personal expenditure while away. James recalls: "Tony and Dave were taking more than me to the States *and* leaving more here to pay the bills. When I pointed this out to the accountant, he was surprised I didn't know that they were being paid more than me. I was very upset. I would have expected Jon to get more, as he was working hard running things. Dick also a little more as he was a featured name, but certainly not everybody. I felt betrayed and insulted. I was very near tears from both anger and hurt. I thought I was pulling my weight as I was singing, playing lead *and* writing." Gerry Bron wasn't surprised to hear of the two-tier wage structure: "James was the new boy and he was never treated on a par with the others in the band. It does seem possible that he was getting less than the others, though somebody ought to have told him." At first, Jon was quite surprised when he was reminded about this, but the more he thought about it, the more likely it seemed that James *was* paid less, given his lack of experience and the need to keep overheads down. The other members all received equal pay throughout — and still do. Though the band had, by now, achieved a measure of success, their expenses still exceeded their income and, with frequent reminders from Gerry Bron as to who was funding the operation, any wage increases were unlikely.

At the time they left for America, each member of the band was earning £20 per week — except, it seemed, James. Of course, they all received *individual* publishing royalties for the songs, or parts of songs each wrote for the band when they were released on the albums and whenever they were performed or broadcast. The advances they received from the record companies, as the artists performing on the albums, were used for the day-to-day expenses of running the band and to pay the studio costs. It would be the late '70s before these advances would be recouped from record sales enabling them to receive further royalties.

To say that *Colosseum*'s first USA tour was a leap into the unknown is an understatement. As they would quickly discover, only the language was the same. Dick had toured there the previous year with John Mayall and was looking forward to being reunited with his new partner Christine Roche, who he'd met at the famous Café Au Go-Go, New York, where she worked as a waitress.[2] Gerry Bron and Colin Richardson had gone over a few months earlier, to set the tour up with booking agents Action Talent Inc. in New York and Associated Booking Corporation in Los Angeles. On the band's arrival at Kennedy airport, they took taxis into a hot and humid New York City, where they hired a U-Haul van for the equipment. With Gerry at the wheel, they set off to find the instrument hire shop. James, Tony and Dick took their instruments with them, but organ, drums and amps had to be hired for each region they played. Jon hated playing on any kit that wasn't his own and still does to this day, so *his* tour was not going to be much fun. All the gear came supplied with flight cases; something they had never seen before. Unsure of where they were, they pulled over to ask a pedestrian for directions and as they did, the man cowered back, as if about to be gunned down. When he realised that they were just asking the way, he recovered his usual New York aggression and snarled: "What the hell do you think I am, some sort of talking map?" and walked off, leaving everyone in the car dumbfounded. Welcome to the USA!

Some weeks before *Colosseum*'s American tour started, Barbara flew to Los Angeles with her mother to try to trace her estranged half-sister, Jane. Prior to leaving, Barbara had been for a chest X-ray and the results had come back showing that she had tuberculosis! Jon's father phoned him with the bad news and by the time the band arrived in New York, she had already been admitted to a Los Angeles hospital and was receiving treatment that would keep her there for most of *Colosseum*'s tour. She was in fact released just in time to join up with them and even to appear in some of the home movies that Jon shot in and around a hotel pool. Though Barbara had to stay on heavy medication for the next three and a half years, surprisingly, it didn't affect her playing.

The band found that New York was full of surprises...not all of them pleasant. For Tony Reeves, it was the gun toting cops and for Jon it was the casual violence, which he wrote about in his *Beat Instrumental* column: "In the first few hours we were there, we saw a taxi driver being hauled from his cab and savagely kicked, until the police arrived with sirens wailing. In fact, the police sirens never stopped." On the lighter side, they all enjoyed the big breakfasts, with their sausages, waffles and maple syrup, though it hardly made up for the frequent mayhem going on around them.

The tour unfortunately didn't get off to the best of starts. They were due to open in Bridgeport, Connecticut, but when they arrived, they found that they were a day late! Somebody had blundered badly! So the first gig they actually played was the three-night stint at the famous Boston Tea Party, where they were reunited with *The Byrds*. Quite a few British groups had played there before, including *The Who*, *Ten Years After* and *Family*, so the audiences were well used to seeing UK bands and they usually got a warm reception. *Colosseum*'s show was taped by a member of the audience and when Dave Greenslade heard it recently, for the first time, he was astonished at the length of the *Valentyne Suite*: "We knew no fear!" he said of the 25 minute plus version...almost ten minutes longer than the original recording.

One minor point of interest at the Boston gig was the Carnaby Street 'fashion statement' from Tony Reeves, who sported an outfit that Dave Greenslade drily referred to as 'the Pakistani policeman's uniform'. It featured a 'Nehru' collar and was made from orange brocade, a kind of heavy curtain material which Tony admitted, was 'totally impractical'. Dave usually wore what can best be described as a tablecloth, whereas Dick, who was never into stage clothes, wore any colour as long as it was black, accessorised with a 'bum bag' which, according to Dave, contained a selection of foodstuffs and the 'makings' for his very strong roll-ups (known as 'Dick's nasties'). Indeed, the band had always enjoyed a reputation for wearing somewhat exotic stage garb, prompting the girls in the office to jokingly christen them *Jon Hiseman's Clothes Museum* (according to Dick). Colin Richardson, however, believes this name actually originated as a 'mickey-take' from Mick Abrahams of *Blodwyn Pig*.

Jon liked Boston and, after their successful debut there, much of the tension that had built up while hanging around the 'Big Apple', evaporated. Not only did they appreciate British bands there, but also the countryside was very similar to rural England...quite literally a breath of fresh air after the garbage filled streets of New York. Jon gave *Melody Maker* a report on the tour and the newly released album: "We've done extremely well in Boston and the album suddenly leapt into the charts, and it's only been out for three or four weeks." Jon had been given this momentous news by the local representative of the US record company but, as he soon learned, it was typical American music-biz bullshit!

After the Bridgeport fiasco, the Tea Party gig restored the band's morale somewhat. What they hadn't fully anticipated, however, was the vastness of America and the diversity of audience taste, which would present new challenges as the tour progressed. Right now, though, it was off to San Francisco for three nights at Bill Graham's famous Fillmore West.

For James, this gig was particularly exciting, as he had a Mike Bloomfield album that had been recorded at Fillmore West and now, here he was, about to play there on the same bill as *Chicago Transit Authority*. While Jon was watching them from the wings, one of *CTA*'s brass section sidled up to him and complimented him on *Colosseum*'s performance, remarking 'how neat it was to hear jazz solos played over rock rhythms!' A few years later, their bass player and singer, Pete Cetera, was interviewed in *Rock Star* magazine about the band's roots and was asked about the jazz influence. He mentioned how *Chicago* was formed before *Blood, Sweat and Tears*: "There was another band that got that jazz/rock label. I remember *Colosseum* and the guy who played two horns at once." During the tour, *Colosseum* found there was a great deal of interest from local musicians, who quizzed them about their music and how it worked. Jon, in turn, was impressed with the diversity of bands that played at the Fillmore.

The weekend of 15th of August is legendary in the history of rock music, but *not* because *Colosseum* played the Fillmore West. It was the weekend of the Woodstock Festival and it is rumoured that *Colosseum* could have appeared there, "but that wasn't possible, as we were already committed to play the Fillmore," is how James Litherland remembers it. Jon had a differing view: "We played the Fillmore West and of course had no idea that Woodstock would turn out to be such an important festival. Bill Graham ran the Fillmore, but was also involved with booking some of the bands at Woodstock and I always assumed we got screwed in some subtle way. That's probably nonsense, of course, but I always regretted missing that opportunity." *Had* they played Woodstock it would have upped their profile in the States considerably, but it has to be filed under 'might have been'. They were getting *some* exposure though, as on that weekend the band had one of their first airings on a new American radio show called *Best of British*.

For Tony Reeves, it was the easy pace of the tour that he remembers: "It was fairly leisurely — usually three days on and three days off. It was a nice paid holiday around America and I felt in some way that we were getting the rewards of our success." Jon always had his movie camera with him and filmed plenty of footage of the tour, including the guys relaxing by a hotel pool.

After the Fillmore, they headed down to Los Angeles, where they were booked for six nights at the Whisky a Go Go. The 'City of the Angels' initially proved to be something of a disappointment, as it was shrouded in acrid smog on their arrival and there were frequent 'foul air alerts'. Dave was filled with apprehension even before landing: "We saw this dark orange cloud as we flew in and I realised we were going to have to breathe it." The air was so bad that police cars were patrolling the streets, warning people to avoid over-exertion. Then James got a scare when he inadvertently wandered into a rundown area and was chased out by the local gang. It was certainly the culture shock of the tour and Jon was astonished at the state of what was supposed to be the 'flower of modern civilisation'. From the humblest car valet to the snootiest Maître d', from the width of the smiles to the insincerity of the praise, from the promise of the food to the attentions of those 'California girls' — nothing was as it seemed. Everyone was trying to break into the Hollywood big time, writing scripts, attending auditions and bragging about whom they had met — all buoyed up by the fantasy that someone famous had said that they had 'real talent'. Jon summed it up to *Beat Instrumental*: "We found ourselves in a kind of half world, where everything was sex, deodorant commercials and 'will he ever kiss me again?'"

The headlining band at the Whisky was the *Bar-Kays*. Most of the original group had been killed in a plane crash in 1967, but the surviving members had now re-formed the band. Jon caught their act and thought they were amazing, especially the two drummers. He was less impressed by the venue though — considering it to be more a 'drinking den' than a music venue. Neither did he like the fact that, apparently, it was customary to allow fans into the band rooms, which meant that, in Jon's words, they encountered "all sorts of madmen...and mad women!" Dave was pretty realistic about their time there: "When you are playing a club for six nights, you can't expect a fantastic ovation every night. It was just so exciting to be there and in those days, it was a big deal to play the States." Jon, however, was actually quite disappointed with the reaction on the West Coast and couldn't understand why they just didn't 'get it'. All Gerry Bron remembers is that most of the girls were wearing see-through tops, which left little to the imagination.

Their experiences in the city aptly referred to as 'La-La Land', inspired Dave and Dick to write a song. It was Dave who came up with the title: "I was putting on a South East London accent around the pool with Dick and I said, 'Let's have a go at *Lost Angeles*'..." and the name stuck. Christine Roche recalls: "Dick had a wonderful relationship with Greeners; they would just be doodling around and he would come up with a phrase which Greeners would then add to. It was organic...they were very creative together. Later on, Dick developed a similar rapport with Clem Clempson."

Lost Angeles ultimately evolved as a group effort, with various combinations of the guys going to the Whisky in the afternoons to work on it. On the whole, they just felt happy to be playing in America, but privately Jon recognised that, despite their promising start in Boston, they hadn't really managed to make much of a breakthrough. He was only too aware that there would be a hard slog ahead if they were to have any chance of making it in the States.

After the LA experience, the band flew back east to New York for two nights at Ungano's, where Dick was finally reunited with Christine, the love of his life. She would later move to England and they would stay friends until Dick's death in 2004. Christine has a slightly bizarre memory of the Ungano gig. One night, during Jon's drum solo, a girl got up and started stripping right in front of him, but Jon, ever the consummate professional, didn't even notice! "He was so focused — it was amazing." Quizzed about this recently, he laughed: "I don't recall many specific incidents because weird things happened all the time!"

After New York, they headed up to Detroit, where they were booked to appear with the *Keef Hartley Band*, who *had* just played Woodstock. The dowdy looking venue was somewhat inappropriately called the Grande Ballroom, which was located in the middle of a black ghetto and pretty run down. Also, as it was only a year or so since the '68 race riots, a degree of caution still had to be exercised.

Colosseum was scheduled to open the show, which Gerry Bron straight away objected to, telling the promoter that, in the UK, Keef's band supported *Colosseum*. The promoter backed down and reversed the running order, so the *Keef Hartley Band* played first and went down a storm to a packed hall. Jon and the guys were looking forward to a similar or better reception, but what Gerry didn't know (or Keef Hartley for that matter) was that there was an 11pm curfew for everyone under 21. One minute there was an enthusiastic packed audience and the next it was 'one man and his dog'! So the two nights there ended up being pretty much a fiasco!

As the tour had progressed, James had become more and more self-confident and more prepared to voice his opinion. Following the disastrous first night at the Grande Ballroom, he happened to be in the hotel lobby when Jon and Gerry Bron came out of the lift. "That was a dumb thing to do," James volunteered, which didn't go down too well. Driving around Detroit, the band was reminded only too clearly that some parts of the USA could be quite dangerous. Dave recalls that the security staff at the venue wouldn't let the band leave until everyone was ready, as there had been a murder in the car park the previous week. Relieved to be putting Detroit behind them, it was back to the 'Big Apple' for the final leg of the tour

The return visit to New York brought about two quite memorable occurrences. The first was when Jon and Dick were in the hotel lift and two Texans got in. Jon recalls: "They were wearing Stetsons, bootlace ties and cowboy boots. Dick was tall, bald and bespectacled -- I had long hair down to my shoulders. The two 'good ole boys' stood opposite us and after a moment one said to the other, out of the corner of his mouth: 'The things yer see when you ain't got yer gun!'" The second occurrence was while the band was doing a photo shoot in the subway. A passerby buttonholed Jon and asked him if they were a group. Jon said they were, whereupon the man said that he was also in show business. Jon takes up the story: "In a strong Bowery accent, he told me, 'I write garbage for television...you know like, after an episode of one of those cop shows, they always finish with a happy, laughing end to make people more receptive to the adverts — well, I write those bits, the end bits — I write the garbage!'"

The final dates of the tour were at New York's Electric Circus, where Dick had another slightly odd experience, this time onstage. He was in mid-solo, when he heard the sound of his sax change perceptibly. He looked down to see some guy dragging his microphone stand away. Quick as a flash, he stepped on his fingers to stop him. This was quite something for Dick, as he wasn't an aggressive person, but later he confessed that he was quite proud of his reaction, though a couple of fans warned him to watch out, as things could turn nasty if the culprit returned. Fortunately he didn't. Christine recalls that Dick was always a bit apprehensive when in New York, but never felt threatened onstage. Some of the others were also a bit concerned about the city's reputation for violence, but never really felt personally threatened.

So, with their first US tour behind them, it was pretty clear that they'd hardly scratched the surface of this huge and perplexing country. Dave realised how relatively naïve they were when he went to a gig in a bar at the Ramada Inn Hotel: "I was walking down the stairs and I heard this great jazz band playing. I expected to see a bunch of seasoned veteran musicians, but they were just kids. I thought 'Why are *we* here in New York when they have bands like this?'"

It was never that likely that *Colosseum* would crack the American market at their first attempt. Jon was aware that nearly all the bands that *had* succeeded had done so by touring as support to a big name artist. This hadn't been an option for them, so they found themselves playing to audiences who didn't know them or their music. Even when they went down well in one area, they had to start again from scratch in the next. Thus, their success on the East Coast where jazz was alive and well, hadn't counted for much on the West Coast, where AOR ruled and their pioneering form of jazz-rock was unlikely to make a big impression. Nevertheless, given that the tour had been organised on a shoestring budget, it was a reasonable first step, though it wouldn't mean much unless other tours followed...and quickly. But, for one reason or another, this didn't happen.

Jon's comments on the tour now make strange but interesting reading. He really didn't like America much and rather gives the impression of someone trying to make sure that he never had to tour there again. He felt a constant undercurrent of insecurity that wasn't even alleviated when he was playing. This was probably due to the mostly lukewarm reaction they'd received from audiences compounded by having to play hired drum kits that, as he recently admitted, he didn't really have the skill to cope with in those days. What really bugged him, though, was the fact that the drum solo always went down a storm, but he was well aware that the long-term success of the band couldn't be based on a drum solo.

They flew back to the UK on the 8th of September and just five days later they were off to Holland and Germany for a short tour, during which Jon gave James Litherland the unexpected news that he was fired. This came as a shock to many people, including Colin Richardson: "I was surprised when Jon let Butty go. I wanted it to be a happy band because that makes for good music and as far as I was aware, everything was fine." Jon put out a statement that was partly a public relations exercise, which ended: "It has therefore been amicably agreed that he (James) should leave *Colosseum* to form his own band," and continued by acknowledging that James's song writing talent had blossomed and he was now a force in his own right. Dave remembers James as a good guitarist, but always felt they needed someone stronger: "The *Colosseum* rhythm section — keyboards, bass and drums — is a mighty fearsome animal, so it's difficult for anybody to play in front of that." James, however, then showed that he was made of the right stuff. After being told he was out of the band, (the night before going on stage at the famous Star Club in Hamburg), Colin Richardson remembers that he played the gutsiest performance of his career, with the crowd going berserk at times. Jon Hiseman remains reticent about James' departure, except to say that it was a collective decision.

Looking back now, James has no regrets about the parting of the ways as he remembers being somewhat uncomfortable with things anyway: "I think they wanted a flashy guitar player and I was under pressure to jump around on stage. I was not happy with the musical direction because I wanted funk and drive. I wasn't into technique, I was into songs. When I first joined the band I was star-struck but, over time, that changed." Maybe it had to do with his background as a Northerner being very different to the other members of the band. James sums it up: "I don't think the band could see it. There was nothing malicious about it but they didn't take my age into account, my background or my take on life." But as one door closes, another one opens — it wasn't long before James moved on to the next phase of his career and formed his own band, *Mogul Thrash*. He had spent less than a year with *Colosseum*.

FOOTNOTES

1. The Bath Festival of Blues (June 28th, 1969) — list of artists in order of appearance:

1. *Just Before Dawn*
2. *Deep Blues Band*
3. *Colosseum*
4. *Taste*
5. Roy Harper
6. *Keef Hartley Band*
7. *Edgar Broughton Band*
8. *Liverpool Scene*
9. Champion Jack Dupree
10. *Chicken Shack*
11. *Blodwyn Pig*
12. *The Nice*
13. *Led Zeppelin*
14. *Principal Edwards Magic Theatre*
15. *John Mayall's Bluesbreakers*
16. *Fleetwood Mac*
17. *Ten Years After*

MC: John Peel

2. The Café Au Go-Go had been closed down a few years before, but had later reopened. The reason for the temporary closure was yet another 'bust' for the iconic anti-establishment comedian Lenny Bruce, who performed there many times. In fact, one of his last performances was at the club, just before his untimely death in April 1964, from a heroin overdose.

*"This remains one of the best gigs
I was ever involved in. I was
so proud that all my old mates from
Tamworth were there to see it."*
CLEM CLEMPSON on the Lanchester
Arts Festival

Chapter 8

A GIANT LEAP FOR COLOSSEUM

JON HISEMAN DIDN'T NEED TO SEARCH for a lead guitarist to replace James Litherland — he'd already spotted a likely candidate when *Colosseum* had played Oxford University back in June. The support group had been a blues trio called *Bakerloo* and the band's young guitarist, Dave 'Clem' Clempson, had made a big impression on him. Soon afterwards, *Bakerloo* had hit problems and the trio had parted company, leaving Clem with the name and a contracted gig to fulfil. He managed to get drummer Cozy Powell and bassist Dave Pegg to fill in, and the gig went so well that plans were mooted to continue. Before anything could be formalised, Clem got a phone call from Jon Hiseman asking him if he would like to try out for *Colosseum*: "It was too good an offer to refuse. I spent a couple of days learning the tracks from the wonderful *Those Who are About to Die* album and travelled to the band's rehearsal room in Elephant & Castle. Within an hour or so I'd become the new guitarist in one of England's most exciting bands." This was the big break he had been looking for.

David Clempson was born to Dennis and Betty on 5th September, 1949, in Tamworth, in what is now part of the West Midlands, but grew up in a council house in the nearby village of Wilnecote. There was, in fact, some musical history in the family...his grandfather had played violin[1] and led the *Elite Dance Band*, which included three of his great-uncles on sax, piano and bass. David's interest in music began at the tender age of four, when his parents bought him a toy piano. In no time at all, he was picking out well-known tunes of the day on the school piano and was noticed by one of his teachers, who suggested to his parents that he would benefit from some formal tuition.

So, encouraged by his parents, he went to a piano teacher for lessons, but soon discovered that he didn't like the discipline: "Whatever fun I'd been having figuring out the tunes I'd heard on the radio was replaced by tedious hours of practising the scales, arpeggios and other exercises, to prepare for the next lesson." Around this time David discovered football, when he saw West Bromwich Albion play. He was immediately hooked and from then on, when he wasn't studying or practising music, he was playing football with his mates. David also loved going on the Sunday evening family walks, which always ended with a visit to the local Working Men's Club. It was here that he saw a local band, *The Wanderers*, and was greatly impressed by the guitarist who played a fantastic looking guitar. It was a Fender Stratocaster and the young lad suddenly felt a burning desire to play it. For the time being though this was out of the question, as it would disrupt his piano studies.

Academically bright, he attended Atherstone Grammar School, where his schoolmates soon nicknamed him 'Clem'. His infatuation with the guitar continued unabated and it wasn't long before he bought a cheap acoustic model, persuaded two of his friends to do likewise and formed a band, which they called *The Adders*, playing mostly *Shadows* numbers and the like. By 1964, they had changed their name to *The Vipers* and were playing Working Men's Clubs and garden fêtes. A flyer of the time invited people to *Come & Shake to the Vipers* — all for 2/6d! Their 'highpoint' came when they supported the legendary Screaming Lord Sutch at the Coalville Village Hall.

A couple of years later, Clem, now 17, went to his local record shop to buy a *Yardbirds* album, but it was out of stock, so he bought a *John Mayall's Bluesbreakers* album instead: "It was the legendary *Beano* album, so-called because Eric Clapton is reading the *Beano* in the cover photo. One track in particular changed my life; the slow blues called *Have You Heard*." At that moment, Clem realised what he wanted to do with his life and even though 1966 was a vintage year for English football, the game simply ceased to exist for him: "I became totally immersed in learning how to make my guitar do what I'd heard on that *Bluesbreakers* album, and subsequently on blues records by Muddy Waters, Howlin Wolf, Buddy Guy,

BB King...and then along came Jimi Hendrix and *Cream.*" No question...he was hooked!

After another name change, this time to *Harwell Reaction*, they graduated to playing colleges and parties, but Clem was becoming disheartened as he felt that the other guys in the band weren't taking things seriously enough. So, when Tamworth's top band, *The Pinch*, asked him to join them, he jumped at the chance. They were soon spotted by local entrepreneur Jim Simpson, who already managed another local band, *Earth* (later to become *Black Sabbath*). Jim took them under his wing, brought in a new bass player, Terry Poole, and changed their name to *Bakerloo Blues Line*, which was later abbreviated to *Bakerloo*. Keith Baker[2] then replaced the original drummer, John Hinch and the line-up was set. They played venues like Birmingham's Elbow Room and Jim Simpson's own club, the legendary Henry's Blueshouse, in the city centre. Clem recalls those magical days: "We backed people like Champion Jack Dupree and Duster Bennett, and regularly hosted jam sessions with local heroes like Robert Plant, John Bonham, Tony Iommi, Ozzy Osbourne, Spencer Davis and Cozy Powell."

However, it was at another Birmingham venue where *Bakerloo* got their national breakthrough. Clem remembers it clearly: "It was whilst playing the well-known local club, Mother's, that legendary DJ and broadcaster, John Peel heard us and invited us to London to record for his Sunday afternoon show, *Top Gear*. That was when things really began to take off and we began to travel further afield for bookings around the country's blossoming club scene." At this point, Clem decided to quit his job as technical author and illustrator at the Reliant Motor Company and become a professional musician.

Bakerloo were soon signed by Harvest, EMI's new progressive label and Clem got his first taste of studio work. Their debut album was recorded at Trident Studios, with Gus Dudgeon, who was in the early days of what would be an illustrious career as a producer. Clem helped to broaden the band's sound by summoning his earlier keyboard skills and playing piano and harpsichord. By the time they played the Oxford University gig, he had, in fact, seen *Colosseum* a couple of times and liked their music, so when he got the call from Jon Hiseman, following the break-up of his own band — he didn't take much persuading!

After only a few rehearsals, Clem made his debut at the Top Rank Suite, Cardiff on October 8th, followed a few days later by an appearance at the Newcastle Arts Festival. The *Evening Chronicle*'s reviewer was there, but was confused by the change of personnel, as he mentions James Litherland in his report. The main thing is that it was a great review, with the headline 'The Colossal sound of *Colosseum*.' Most of the reviews around this time were so good that they could have been written by their own press office. One exception, however, was *Melody Maker*'s Richard Williams, who caught their Marquee gig and commented, rather pompously: "I've a feeling that they may be getting a bit carried away with technical expertise for its own sake," singling out *Those About to Die* with this withering remark: "It was played at such a ridiculously fast tempo, even Hiseman, wonder drummer that he is, couldn't handle the pace." Ouch! Maybe it was a sign that the band was getting a bit blasé playing the older material. In an interview with *Record Buyer* in 1970, Jon does mention *Those About to Die* saying: "It's not popular with us as we have played it so many times." More recently Jon elaborated this point: "It's well known, with instrumental music in particular that, after playing the same numbers over and over, you try to find the same excitement that you felt when you first played them. The easy way to keep up the pressure is to play them faster and faster. Many famous bands have fallen prey to this…I had the same problem with all my '60s and '70s bands, but now we are older, and hopefully wiser, the tempos are slower and more consistent."

Clem had clearly made a good start with the band and was brimful of confidence. He describes those early days: "I'm sure I was quite nervous about the audition, but having been given the gig, I certainly wasn't overawed. Although they were all obviously very accomplished, I felt I had plenty to offer too, bringing something extra to the band — it was all very exciting." Dick also noted in his book how seamless it all was: "Clem fitted in quickly, his innate musicality showing in everything he did." Things were going so well that Jon issued this upbeat press statement: "In recent rehearsals it has become startlingly apparent that Clem is not only the most logical replacement for James, but will also be a major contributory force to *Colosseum*'s future."

As well as learning his musical parts, Clem also had to get on top of the vocals — not an easy task. About this time, the band celebrated its first anniversary that Bob Dawbarn wrote about in *Melody Maker*. In the article, Jon talks of being pleased with their progress, but was proudest of the fact that the band's individual identities had been successfully established: "*Ten Years After* is really just Alvin Lee and a rhythm section and there are other bands like that. It's a difficult thing to get across to the public, as generally, they will only accept one person to the detriment of the others in the band." It was at this juncture that Jon decided to drop his name from the masthead. Henceforth the group would be known simply as *Colosseum*.

Meanwhile, their record company had been reviewing the marketing strategy for all their progressive bands. *Colosseum*'s debut album had been released on the Fontana label, but with stablemates like *Wayne Fontana & the Mindbenders* and Julie Felix, it wasn't surprising that the promotion department was unsure how to handle them. In fact, very few record companies had recognised the burgeoning progressive/underground movement, but now things were about to change. *Valentyne Suite* was to be released on Philips' new specialist label Vertigo[3], which was the brainchild of an innovative young executive, Olav Wyper, who had just joined the company. He had pitched the idea of a label based on the CBS marketing model in the States. His plan was to find bands that were progressive musically and wrote intelligent lyrics, a profile that *Colosseum* fitted perfectly. Colin Richardson recalls the meeting he attended with Gerry Bron: "Olav didn't have a desk in his office; you sat round a coffee table in easy chairs. I thought his ideas were exciting, as well as making good business sense." The clincher was that a sizeable marketing budget would be made available to back the new venture. They also commissioned hip young designers who were into the music and who came up with the unusual Vertigo 'swirl' label design, which later took on iconic status. They also came up with a series of memorable album sleeves that were totally 'off the wall' — the *Juicy Lucy* cover, for instance, had a buxom, naked woman covered with fruit. The *Valentyne Suite* sleeve, though, was more intriguing, depicting a woman dressed in white — possibly symbolising virginity — on a hillside, with a giant candlestick. Jon has lost count of the number of fans who surmised that this apparition was Barbara Thompson but, in fact, she was an agency model.

Valentyne Suite was released in the final week of October '69, carrying the catalogue number 'V01' as Vertigo's debut album. Press reaction was mainly very good, with the *Lincolnshire Chronicle* calling it: "the most interesting album I have heard for a long time." *Disc*'s review singled out: "a raucous bluesy thing called *The Kettle* and a cacophonic *The Machine Demands a Sacrifice*. It's jazz, but pop-ular"! However, the *New Musical Express* seemed somewhat underwhelmed: "While full of praise for the music and the energetic performances, it seems lacking in direction and climax." *Melody Maker* concentrated on Jon's drumming with the headline 'Suite success for Hiseman'. Chris Welch's eulogy continued: "He is never obtrusive and Jon's great strength is his self-discipline which enables him to harness his great technique for the good of the band. The result is that the band swings far more than many a name jazz group." Possibly the funniest comments came from fellow-drummer Buddy Rich, when he was the guest reviewer on *Melody Maker*'s *'Blind Date'* column and Chris Welch played him *The Machine Demands a Sacrifice*. Buddy seems confused: "I don't like this kind of thing, because it offers me no challenge, though I haven't heard a lot of other drummers do better. He sounds as if he fell down a flight of stairs carrying tympani!" What probably misled Buddy's rather conventional ears, was that unusually, the drums on this track had been overdubbed in eight layers. It was never an attempt to compete with his very traditional style and Jon, a great admirer of Buddy's technique, is still proud of that comment. In spite of the mixed reviews, *Valentyne Suite* sold well, going straight into the UK album charts, peaking at 15.

Clem's early gigs were interspersed with intense rehearsals, as the band worked hard to refine the act. Before he could draw breath, he was off to face his first foreign audience when *Colosseum* flew to Prague for the Jazz Festival, taking them behind what Winston Churchill referred to as the 'Iron Curtain'[4]. It would prove to be something of a culture shock for the band, as the atmosphere was very different from the optimism two years earlier when Jon had played there with Georgie Fame. Since then the Soviet invasion had brought with it deprivation and repression...there was a distinct tension in the air.[5] Dave remembers: "When we walked the streets, people either wanted to buy my leather jacket or dollars — although everybody was very hospitable." Clem was probably the most affected: "The Russians were occupying Prague and wherever you saw a Soviet soldier, he would always have a Czech officer with him to prevent anyone lobbing a grenade at them. I had never been to a country that was so different." He later described meeting the Czech people as a 'humbling experience'.

Prior to the concert, Jon decided to go out to the foyer of the theatre and give away some albums, which, in those days, were virtually unobtainable in Czechoslovakia. This almost caused a riot and he had to be rescued by a worried Colin Richardson, who couldn't believe Jon's foolhardiness. As well as that, Dick was later 'kidnapped' and taken to a Saturday afternoon jazz club, where he was politely instructed to play by his 'gentle and studious captors'.

There was also a tense moment during the concert when Jon wanted to dedicate the *Valentyne Suite* to Alexander Dubcek[6]. On hearing of this plan, the promoter told Colin Richardson in no uncertain terms that this was not permitted! The venue was a wonderfully ornate old theatre and the atmosphere was tremendous. The band put on a thrilling show, but Jon, still smarting from being denied the chance to pay his tribute, was determined to make *some* kind of political statement. So, part way through his drum solo, during a passage of hi-hat work, he started whispering into the hi-hat mike: 'Dubcek–a–Dubcek–a–Dubcek' to the rhythm. The audience picked up on what Jon was doing and then, exchanging disbelieving glances with each other, surreptitiously joined in. Colin Richardson recalls being quite concerned, but secretly thrilled by the moment. Jon was just elated at having made his point. *Melody Maker*'s Jack Hutton was there and reported: "Their set was intensely moving and every musician was involved in what he was doing. Clem Clempson had a sense of immediacy about his playing and was totally compelling." It seems that *Colosseum* had managed to draw back that 'iron curtain', if only briefly.

The Prague trip was certainly a memorable one and Dick devoted several pages of his book to update his own political views in the light of it. It's hard to understand why Jon felt impelled to get involved in volatile Czech politics, when he hadn't made any similar gesture on the racial situation during their American tour. Jon's view is that, in order to take a stand you need to have a measure of power or leverage. In the USA they were unknown —

nobodies, while in Prague they were rock celebrities — and this made all the difference.

Hardly were they back in the UK, than they were off again for an eight-day tour of Denmark and a week after that, they were booked to record another *Top Gear* session for John Peel, with Barbara Thompson augmenting the band. After several months in development *Lost Angeles* was finally ready to be unveiled and the version performed here was eight minutes long and featured solos by Clem and Dick. It was an ideal opportunity to 'test drive' it, as the band would soon be recording the next album. The programme would also showcase a new piece by Tony Reeves called *Arthur's Moustache*,[7] notable for a 'special effects' bass solo and a delightful understated sax riff from Dick.

Early December saw the band back in IBC Studios to record tracks for the second American album, *The Grass Is Greener*. The first US release, on Dunhill, had been timed to coincide with their American tour and it had been decided to include the best of the tracks recorded up to the end of May 1969. It was effectively a compilation of *Those About to Die* and the first two movements of the *Valentyne Suite*. To complete it, *Beware the Ides of March* was tagged on to the end and throughout the American tour this was played as the last movement. Back in the UK, *The Grass is Greener* was recorded as the actual last movement to the suite and this is still the version performed today. For the next US release, they now needed to record four new tracks. It was also important for Clem be given a chance to get some recording 'under his belt'. One of the new tracks was *Rope Ladder to the Moon*, the Jack Bruce/Pete Brown song. They also recorded Mike Taylor's *Jumping off the Sun* and a version of Ravel's *Bolero*. Listening to these tracks today, it's apparent that Clem's playing added greatly to the band's overall sound, but there was now something lacking vocally. Clem enjoyed the sessions until the time came for him to sing: "I'd never been very confident about my vocal ability, and during my time with

Bakerloo I'd always wanted to find a great singer for the band. It was probably soon after these first *Colosseum* sessions that I began to suggest to Jon that we should look for someone whose vocal ability would match the instrumental prowess for which the band was renowned. I still cringe to this day when I hear my vocals on those tracks!" Jon, though, still wanted to keep the personnel at five and hoped that Clem's voice would strengthen over time, but gradually, the realisation grew that this problem would eventually have to be addressed

The latter half of 1969 saw the media's interest in so-called 'progressive' music growing. Geoffrey Cannon of *The Guardian* singled out three bands that he thought worthy of particular note: *The Nice*, *King Crimson* and *Colosseum*. Having seen each of them several times, Cannon explains what he thought set them apart: "They don't give the same concert six months later or on successive nights. It's what *progressive* music means; the music of these bands progresses from session to session." He then proceeds to qualify this by saying that, though he was exhilarated by the live performances, he found all their studio albums disappointing and conjectured as to why this was the case: "The virtues of these bands in concert have become obstacles to their recorded work. It's difficult to transfer an inspiration derived from improvisation on to record." The studio version of *Lost Angeles* is a good case in point. It's a decent enough effort, but it lacks the punch of the live version recorded later in 1971. In fact, it could be argued that the fully developed live performance epitomises what *Colosseum* was all about.

In early December 1969, a memorial concert was held at the London School of Economics to celebrate the life and music of Mike Taylor. His body had been found that summer, washed up on the beach at Leigh-on-Sea at the mouth of the River Thames. It was rumoured that he might have committed suicide by jumping off Beachy Head, but this was never verified. Jon remembers the last time they played together. He had visited him at his 'squat', where he had seen a strange looking 'music machine' which Mike had constructed. It consisted of two circular upright columns attached to a long board, with a roll of 'music' wound around them — the 'notes' on the score consisted of intermittent coloured lines. Vertical bamboo canes of matching colours were placed at intervals round the roll and each musician was assigned a colour. The score was then moved round by turning a handle on one of the columns and when your coloured line on the score appeared behind your cane, you started playing and when that line ended, you stopped. What you played, or what instrument you used, was left entirely open. It was a clever way to direct free improvisation and Jon always thought this system could have been used to great advantage with young children. He also recalls, however, that Mike was as 'high as a kite' at the time and laughing a little too much!

The story of Mike Taylor's brief life is the all too familiar tragedy of drugs clouding an original and creative mind…altering his perception of the world around him and causing him to lose touch with reality. Who knows how much more he might have achieved had he not gone down that road.

Christopher Bird of *Melody Maker* was at the memorial concert and reported that: "The ensemble was led by Dave Gelly, who, in addition to playing well, conceived the whole idea and mapped out the general strategy of the evening. Humanity without sentimentality, musical intelligence without intellectual aridity; these were the hallmarks of Taylor's music. I hadn't realised before just what a loss to the scene his death has been."

As 1969 ended, Jon Hiseman could reflect on a year of solid progress for *Colosseum*. They had the valuable experience of their first US tour under their belt with another planned for the following spring. They had steadily increased their fan base through powerful live performances and their two albums, though Jon still had some reservations about these. He told

Record Buyer that he felt the albums were already out of date by the time they were released. Jon was honest, almost brutal, about *Those Who are About to Die Salute You*: "Many of the performances weren't good enough, because we were a young band. We were still feeling each other out. At the same time I'm proud of it, in that we successfully fused two separate musical genres, rock and jazz." The general consensus at the time held that *Valentyne Suite* was a superior album and it was certainly better received by both the music press and the fans, but Jon was still unhappy that the actual making of the album had stretched over a six month period. "We were fighting all the time with tracks we'd put down when we were a different band." It's true to say that many artists find it difficult to revisit their earlier work, because they will always see ways of improving it. However, Jon understood that any album was only a snapshot in time, and learned to live with it.

One thing was not in doubt though — Jon Hiseman was now recognised as one of the best drummers around. He once described playing the drums as 'walking a tightrope', adding that it often drove him to the brink of mental and physical exhaustion. 'Playing the band and not the drums', meant integrating his style with the music, while at the same time providing an ever-shifting backdrop that put the drums on more of an equal footing with other instruments. Though an 'instinctive' drummer, he had also paid his dues with many hours of practise and study. His brush work on *Elegy* from their album *Valentyne Suite*, is a good example of this instinctive feel which was perceived in Germany as quite revolutionary and a 15 minute segment in a radio programme was devoted to analysing it. One critic noted: "When *Colosseum* really get into their stride, one gets an absolute barrage of sound, as well as a ceaseless variety of superbly constructed rhythmic patterns...yet it's a drive that still retains its subtlety."

All of this added to Jon's growing reputation as a

groundbreaking drummer, but it was his dynamic drum solos that really made his name. Described as 'a thunderously powerful spectacle'…it wasn't just the fans that were blown away! Eric Bell and Brian Downey of *Thin Lizzy* recall seeing *Colosseum* at the Marquee, as Eric relates: "Jon Hiseman was in the middle of his drum solo — I looked at Brian and he had his mouth open in awe. It was just tremendous to watch." Since Ginger Baker had recorded his legendary *Toad* drum solo, many drummers vied to outdo him with ever longer and louder efforts. For quite a few journalists though, the drum solo was the signal to repair to the bar. So, why were Jon's solos so different and compelling? Jon explained his approach to Chris Welch: "When I play a solo it's an entirely musical thing, just like a flower opening. If it wasn't, it would be boring technical nonsense. I don't think in technical terms when I play. I like to create a bubbling thickness of sound and layers of rhythmical patterns." In spite of this apparent success, Jon always felt he had a lot to learn and, as the band got busier, lamented the fact that he was unable to practise enough to extend himself further.

It was pretty obvious that *Colosseum*'s music was different to most other bands. In an interview with Rob Partridge of *Record Mirror*, Jon explained his strategy for keeping it that way, saying: "I don't listen to anybody but us!" In truth, the group was so busy that there wasn't much time to listen to whatever else was going on. Jon always maintained that the band was never 'just a gig' for them…*every* musician played every performance from the heart. All of their careers, so far, had lead up to this…they were finally playing *their* music, on *their* terms and, seemingly, at the right time! However, Jon would be the first to acknowledge the source of their inspiration: "We owe much of the groundwork to Graham Bond. He brought jazz musicians like Jack Bruce, Ginger Baker, Dick and me together in a rock context."

In early 1970, *The Grass is Greener* was released in America with almost the same artwork as *Valentyne Suite*. The first US album, it was rumoured, had sold over 100,000 copies, but Jon was never able to verify this. *Cashbox* welcomed the new release enthusiastically: "This talented and extremely creative group comes through with a blockbuster album, which is bound to stir up listener interest through the sheer force of its presentation and the imaginative approach." Ravel's *Bolero* is singled out as an example of this. Before long, some of the UK fans heard that the US album contained new material, as yet unreleased in Europe and were buying it on import. Gerry Bron, however, was unimpressed with the American record company: "Dunhill didn't know a thing about the market for bands like *Colosseum*. They promoted the band in a pop-orientated way. It just didn't work." To make matters worse, plans for *Colosseum* to support Jack Bruce in the States fell through. In a cryptic press statement, Gerry Bron announced: "Within the past few days, we have been advised of substantial changes in the originally negotiated arrangements." So, it was 'back to the drawing board' as far as their transatlantic aspirations were concerned.

The first few days of 1970 found *Colosseum* back on the road doing TV and live dates in Europe, including their first gigs in France — two shows at the famous Paris Olympia, where they received a standing ovation from a euphoric audience. The feeling of satisfaction at having acquitted themselves so well in such a prestigious venue was slightly tempered by having to be up and away early the following morning in order to make it to the next gig, which was at the Winter Gardens, Weston-super-Mare. Back to earth with a bump!

In the latter part of January, Colin Richardson was heavily involved with the Lanchester Arts Festival, a student led, mixed media project in Coventry. He had been appointed booking consultant in the latter part of 1969, a role which, the following year, would give him the opportunity to bring off something of a major 'showbiz coup'…the first 'live-on-stage' appearance of

Monty Python's Flying Circus. For the current year though, he had already booked the UK premiere of *Jack Bruce & Friends*, featuring American stars Larry Coryell and Mike Mandell, together with ex-Hendrix drummer Mitch Mitchell. Sharing the bill was *Colosseum* and the *New Jazz Orchestra*, playing live together for the first time…an idea that partly stemmed from the *NJO* brass and reed sections playing on the studio version of *Butty's Blues*. Given the close musical relationship that had always existed between Neil Ardley and Jon Hiseman, it was a naturally symbiotic combination, which would prove to be both musically satisfying and exciting. For Jon it was all part of the plan, as he told *Melody Maker*: "When I formed *Colosseum* I was consciously trying to create an environment in which we could involve a band of this size." His real ambition went even further: "The ultimate goal is to produce a 20-piece band whose members are individually as well-known as *Colosseum*. It's impossible, of course."

On the night, the *New Jazz Orchestra* opened proceedings with Dick, Tony and Jon in their 'big band' roles. The Lanchester College newspaper in reviewing the concert, wrote: "The Mike Gibbs composition *Rebirth*, showed what a ridiculously accomplished set of musicians they were, while *Dusk Fire*, by Michael Garrick, had Tony Reeves playing the best bass solo I've ever heard." The *Guardian* and *Melody Maker* echoed this praise in their reviews, *MM* going on to report: "Jon Hiseman swung beautifully through every number giving one of the most tasteful displays in drumming and stamping his style memorably on everything." Ronald Atkins of the *Guardian* was equally impressed: "Few drummers in this country can touch Hiseman for sheer technique, and he obviously takes every chance to vary his patterns."

This *NJO* gig was also something of a milestone for Barbara Thompson, as she got her first chance to play a major solo in public, in a stunning duet with Henry Lowther. Jon recalls: "She played on Mike Taylor's *Study*, a very hypnotic slow ballad and it brought the house down. I learned the big lesson that night that you didn't have to go in with a sharp stick to get an audience reaction. I was seldom able to apply it with *Colosseum*, but I applied it later to Barbara's career. She was fantastic that night, I was so proud of her."

After the *NJO* left the stage, Dave Greenslade and Clem Clempson came on and *Colosseum* played their set. They kicked off with *Lost Angeles*, by now considerably longer than the studio version, followed by the old Graham Bond staple *Walkin' in the Park*. Next came *The Machine Demands a Sacrifice*, which featured Jon's drum solo, inspiring the college paper to write: "For those of you who saw the first solo, the second was even better and for those who saw the second, Jon had been on stage for over six hours when he started." It's quite likely that most of the crowd were there to see Jack Bruce, but already they were experiencing some seriously powerful and memorable music...but the best was yet to come! The *NJO* musicians returned to join *Colosseum* for the final two numbers, the first of which was *Butty's Blues*, featuring some forceful playing from Dick, but the highpoint of the performance was always going to be the closing piece, *Valentyne Suite*, scored for the whole ensemble by Neil Ardley. At one point during the performance, Dave Greenslade was suddenly aware of the significance of the moment: "This was amazing for me, Jon and Tony, as we had seen all those great big bands when we were kids...and now I found myself playing Hammond in the middle of this marvellous brass section — it gave me a great buzz." The Suite's climactic ending prompted lead trumpet Bob Leaper to hurl his horn high in the air, deftly catching it on its return flight. It was a fitting climax to a memorable collaboration. Jon congratulated Clem after the show, saying it was the best he'd heard him play and the college paper also singled him out for his outstanding performance. There was good reason for Clem to be so fired up and playing so well that night: "This remains one of the best gigs

I was ever involved with. I was so proud that all my old mates from Tamworth were there to see it." Colin Richardson concurred: "It was an amazing concert…without doubt, one of the highlights of my music biz career." The *Guardian*'s Ronald Atkins was amazed by the crowd's good humour, as they sat shoulder to shoulder in stifling heat: "No one grumbled and no one collapsed; they sat quietly while the music played and clapped and cheered when it stopped."

Dick saw it as a milestone for *Colosseum*: "Of all the outrageous things to attempt — the *NJO* incorporated into the set, playing Neil Ardley's arrangements to some of our recorded numbers. The hall was packed to the rafters and the reception we got started off as enormous — and ended up gargantuan." The Lanchester college paper went into overdrive: "Then, back came the *NJO* for the final 40 minutes of the best music I have ever heard here…words cannot do justice to the reality. Quite simply, it stopped the show." The final word is from Jon: "Lanchester was just amazing! We played to a total of 5,000 people over the two shows. Dave Gelly told me afterwards that it was more people than he'd performed to all year!" Jon goes on to say: "While most gigs are lost to memory, this concert stays fresh in my mind…it has left an indelible impression of just what can be achieved when everything comes together on one magical evening." It was also clear that the success of this collaboration ensured that there would be further such concerts in the future.

Jack Bruce's set, of course, was also well received, with Jon joining the audience to dig it, enthralled by the drumming of Mitch Mitchell: "He was just wonderful that night — his was a talent I much admired, but I think he got lost somewhere along the way."

Barbara had, in fact, played in Coventry before. In the early part of 1969 she had formed the *Barbara Thompson/Art Themen Quintet*. Art Themen was a very talented tenor saxophonist who had known Jon and Dick for many years (he's also Arthur Heckstall-Smith's godfather). They had played the Belgrade Theatre, Coventry and a *Melody Maker* review read: "Opening with John Coltrane's *Promise* they played some interesting modern jazz with Barbara and Art both blowing fluent tenor, soprano and flute." The audiences tended to be on the small side, but Barbara enjoyed the artistic freedom. She told *Melody Maker*: "Musicians have got to get the idea they can make a living from jazz out of their minds…it's a pipe dream." In spite of this remark, since her *Cabaret* experience she had made the decision never turn down the opportunity to play jazz *just* because it didn't pay. Barbara always kept several projects on the go, including composing music and writing arrangements. She also seems to have had a thing about drummers, as she also played on Keef Hartley's album *Battle of North West Six*, which Hartley then performed for a John Peel 'live special' with a 14-piece big band, featuring Barbara in the sax section.

Two days after the memorable Lanchester Festival gig, Barbara made her first public appearance with *Colosseum* on *Beat Club*, a German TV show filmed in Bremen. Colin Richardson was a good friend of the producer/director, Mike Leckebusch having previously booked *Manfred Mann* and the *Bonzos* on the show. Barbara remembers she wore a strange outfit: "It was the time when the Indian squaw look was really in, and the make-up department at the German TV station went to town on me." Barbara reprised her flute playing on *The Machine Demands a Sacrifice* which she had performed on the *Valentyne Suite* album. Clem, who had by now settled in and had gained confidence, gave an inspired vocal performance.

1970 had certainly got off to a good start, but unfortunately, there was another crisis looming on the horizon!

FOOTNOTES

1. *Colosseum*'s publicity was handled by Frances van Staden, a press officer at Tony Barrow International. In an early biog of Clem, it was stated that he'd inherited a 200-year-old Stradivarius from his great grandfather, but unfortunately this was complete fiction.

2. All three of *Bakerloo* went on to greater things. Drummer Keith Baker joined *Uriah Heep* and played on their second album *Salisbury*, while bassist Terry Poole joined the *Graham Bond ORGANisation* for a short 'spell'! (sic)

3. The Vertigo label later took on legendary status, with a stable of artists that included *Black Sabbath*, *Ian Carr's Nucleus*, Rod Stewart and *Manfred Mann Chapter III*.

4. There is some dispute as to whether it was Churchill who first coined the phrase, 'Iron Curtain'. Hitler's Minister of Propaganda, Joseph Goebbels, mentioned it in February 1945 when it was clear that Germany had lost the war and it's quite likely that Churchill would have heard the term then. He is certainly on record as having used the term in his speech at Fulton, Missouri in 1946, at which point it seems to have stuck in the public consciousness.

5. Jan Palac set himself alight in Wenceslas Square, Prague, on 16th January, 1969 as a protest against the Soviet intervention. He died three days later.

6. Alexander Dubcek was deposed as the reforming Czech Communist Party Secretary on 17th April, 1969. He was appointed Ambassador to Turkey, but was eventually expelled from the Communist Party and spent the next 18 years working as a clerk for a Slovakian lumberyard. In 1989, following the 'Velvet Revolution', he was reinstated and elected Chairman of the Federal Assembly. He died in a car crash, under somewhat suspicious circumstances, in 1992, *just* before he was to give evidence against several KGB officers.

7. *Arthur's Moustache* was only ever recorded for broadcast and never released during the lifetime of the original band. It was, however, included in the 2009 boxed set, *Moriture Te Salutant*.

*"My mum and dad were there and they
were so proud. We had gone to Promenade
concerts there when I was sixteen."*
DAVE GREENSLADE reminiscing about
Colosseum's first gig at the Royal
Albert Hall

'*Farlowe joins* Colosseum'
BANNER HEADLINE in *Melody Maker*

Chapter 9

'FARLOWE THAT...!'

WHEN THE SECOND AMERICAN TOUR FELL THROUGH, all the stops were pulled out to find replacement gigs in the UK, one of which was in Stroud, a small town in Gloucestershire and a little off the beaten track for *Colosseum*. Jon was upfront about it when interviewed by the *Stroud News & Journal*, saying that he felt it was important to reach as many parts of the UK as possible: "This was one of the places that came in to the office, so I jumped at it, even though the fee was lower than we would normally charge." The gig went down well to a packed audience who were especially impressed by Tony's bass solo during *Arthur's Moustache*. Jon also revealed to the newspaper that they had been offered dates in South Africa, the promoter having assured them that they could play to mixed audiences, which Jon and the band insisted on. Reluctantly, they had to pass on the offer, as the British Musicians Union banned all performances in the Apartheid State and no compromise was possible. Since South Africa eventually did move bloodlessly to become a democracy, it must be said that history supports the MU stance.

Nowadays, when certain 'name' artists make all kinds of outrageous demands for their dressing room requirements, it's interesting to note that, in the late '60s, things were very different. When *Colosseum* played The Place in Stoke on Trent, it was the promoter making the demands of the artist, by way of a notice on the dressing room wall: "Excessively loud playing, swearing and obscene language are not appreciated. Under no circumstances will girls be allowed in the changing room. Playing short sets does nothing to enhance either an Artiste's reputation or the professional presentation of The Place." Any band playing there that ignored these rules did so at their peril!

Colosseum's original road manager had been Colin Smith, but many others had come and gone as the rigours of the road took its toll. Among the later roadies was Kenny Smith, an unflappable Liverpudlian, who went on to manage the *Eurythmics*. By the summer of 1970, it was Scott Thompson and his sidekick Clive Davies, a somewhat unlikely double-act, who took care of all the stage 'backline', as well as the PA & lighting, with Scott mixing the live sound from a control desk sited in the centre of the audience. Harry Isles, who had taught at Southport Art School, but had given it up for a life in the music business, was hired as the band's 'personal' driver after being secretly auditioned — by driving them to a gig! Harry also happened to be a talented photographer, with an artistic flair that he later put to good use, taking many excellent photos of the band on the road. When he started with *Colosseum*, he only had about six months' experience, but soon learned that Jon Hiseman had a tremendous respect for the road crew, knowing that the band's safety on the 'killing fields of Europe', (Jon's expression) was in their hands. He was also aware of the role they played in how the band's performance was perceived. Harry recalls: "I remember coming back from a gig and a few of the band were whingeing about their monitor sound and things like that. Jon turned round and really gave them a dressing down and told them if they couldn't tell Scott exactly what they wanted, he wouldn't be able to help them." Harry also remembers Dick fondly, recalling that one of his wackier ideas was to run his car on the gas produced by chicken shit! Harry remembers *Colosseum* as a happy band, but that Jon was definitely the boss.

Even though the band was gigging almost non-stop, any gap in the date sheet had them back in rehearsals, which usually consisted of working out new ideas and running through any pieces that were in development. However, there was a downside to their rarely taking breaks, as Jon revealed to Brian Jones of the *Western Daily Press* after playing the Bath Pavilion: "It's vastly different when you start back gigging again after several days of rehearsing. It takes a concentrated effort and our performance felt very shaky to us." Jon even admitted that he hadn't really woken up until after his solo, continuing: "We weren't working too well until the end of the gig." Dick had his own ideas as to why the gig hadn't gone well: "Three hours' practice in the morning never does a gig in the evening any good — but what also worries me is that we were playing for us and not the audience." This was another problem that would later come back to haunt them.

By now there was an undeniable feeling that *Valentyne Suite* was becoming something of an albatross around their necks and at the back of everyone's mind was the pressing need for new material, but their hectic schedule meant that they had to do a lot of their collective writing at the sound checks. At one Marquee gig around this time, *Walkin' in the Park* was the only previously recorded piece they played, as they were trying out so much new material on the audience. Jon now feels this policy was a mistake. "We never had much in the way of studio time anyway and all our tracks were being thrown at the wall very quickly, often in whatever time we had before leaving for a gig. Up to this point, we had never actually rehearsed in a studio environment and recorded mainly what had proved successful on stage. But of course we judged the success of the studio performance on how close it was to the stage version and I later came to realise that you can't really equate the two."

Everyone's thoughts were now on the imminent recording of their next album. On March 31st, the band recorded a BBC radio session, *Sounds of the Seventies*, which featured three new pieces written by Jon, Dave and Clem — *Bring Out Your Dead*, *Time Lament* and *Daughter of Time* plus, at a later session, another song called *Downhill and Shadows*. This new material was very different to *Valentyne Suite*, as Jon explained to *Record Buyer*: "I don't think many of our fans want to sit through a fifteen minute song...quite a few have told us our albums are too demanding, which is interesting."

In early April 1970, the band played the Cologne Rock Festival, as well as being named 'Group of the Year' by a German TV programme, which resulted in even more offers to tour there.

Soon after their return to the UK, a press release was issued announcing that Tony Reeves was leaving the group to concentrate on record producing. Tony, it seems, had been unhappy at the direction the new material was taking the band (even though he had co-written *Downhill and Shadows*) and felt that it was time for a change. However, he also confessed that he had been less than pleased with his own performances for a while, admitting: "My playing was terrible on *Valentyne Suite*. It was egocentric and far too intrusive. I was not doing my job properly." He agreed to stay on while a replacement was found, but this would turn out to be quite a long and tortuous process.

Around this time, Jon received a call from Keith Emerson, who had just 'dissolved' his three-piece group *The Nice* to form a new trio with ex-*King Crimson* bass guitarist Greg Lake and was looking for a drummer to complete the line-up. The phone call was quite short and to the point. Jon recalls: "He asked me how serious was the *Colosseum* thing and was I available. I told him I was not." Jon would, however, get to work with Keith a couple of years later.

Following the success of *Colosseum*'s Lanchester Arts Festival concert with the *New Jazz Orchestra*, plans had been made for further dates together and the first of these was at the famous Fairfield Hall, Croydon on May 10th. The *NJO* opened the first half of the concert with a confident and powerful performance. After the interval, *Colosseum* played their usual set and then, as at Lanchester, the *NJO* brass and woodwind sections returned for the climax of the show. A new arrangement of *Rope Ladder to the Moon* was unveiled and a version of Neil Ardley's *Shades of Blue* which featured Clem playing a beautiful acoustic guitar intro he had written. Clem had recently met classical guitarist John Williams at Ronnie Scott's Club and it was rumored that he'd asked about the possibility of taking tuition from him. Clem recalls: "I really was quite keen to learn some classical guitar and had taught myself several pieces already. But I had an insurmountable barrier to any chance of becoming a really good player, because I could never grow the nail of my right-hand index finger. It was always destroyed by being mashed against the strings during all those long *Colosseum* solos."

Barry Shinfield of the *Croydon Advertiser* reviewed the concert, focusing his piece on Dick, with the headline: 'Can you be 35 and still play pop?' Shinfield was transfixed by Dick's charismatic stage presence, but makes some strange observations about *Downhill and Shadows*: "Dick was well away; chin stuck out, eyes closed, leg in frenetic action, communicating through his two saxes on a free-flowing, assured solo in which he seemed to bend notes in full flight. Clempson tried to follow on guitar but was temporarily lost. Then, as the others grinned, he retaliated by upping the tempo which made Heckstall-Smith sweat to keep up." Jon never ceases to be amazed at how some journalists misinterpret their performances: "The idea that Clem was temporarily 'lost' is ludicrous and 'upping the tempo' presumably means he played more notes in his phrases, but the 'tempo' definitely stayed the same!"

A few days later, before the next joint concert with the *NJO*, *Colosseum* were scheduled to make the first in a series of films featuring rock bands, which would be shown on the cinema circuit as support to the main feature. Stablemates *Juicy Lucy* were also taking part and both bands would be filmed playing to an invited audience at the Questors Theatre, Ealing. The project was a joint enterprise between Lion Television Services and Oakhurst Enterprises Ltd, the production company set up by the film star Stanley Baker. He was something of a rock fan and had already been involved with promoting music festivals. In the director's chair was Tony Palmer, who had directed the film of *Cream's Farewell Concert* in 1968.

Chris Welch was sent by *Melody Maker* to cover the event and according to his report, setting up the cameras and lighting the set took up most of the morning, with Tony Palmer pacing around, looking harassed. Around midday they ran the sound checks and by early afternoon, Palmer was ready to begin filming. *Colosseum* kicked things off with *Lost Angeles*, exchanging grins at odd moments — then *Juicy Lucy* followed with a short set that included their recent single *Who Do You Want*. The concert ended with both bands jamming on the blues classic *Going to Chicago*, with Paul Williams on vocals. Afterwards, everyone repaired to the local pub, only to be refused service because of their long hair! This was probably just as well, since *Colosseum* had a 300-mile trip to Newcastle the next morning.

The film eventually went out on release with *Hoffman*, starring Peter Sellers. Unfortunately, this film turned out to be a rare Peter Sellers 'turkey' (though, ironically, many Sellers fans now consider it a classic), so the exposure wasn't as great as had been hoped.

The third in the series of *Colosseum/NJO* concerts followed, just over a week later, at Birmingham Town Hall. The *Birmingham Evening Mail* gave it the thumbs up, but the next one at the Queen Elizabeth Hall, London received mixed reviews. Derek Jewell, from *The Sunday Times*, loved the individual performances of both *Colosseum* and the *NJO* and was generally approving of the augmented numbers, but he did have some reservations about the finale: "The level of decibels at which *Colosseum* performed totally defeated the *NJO*, whose massed force of eleven horns was submerged by Clempson's amplified sound alone. All the orchestra could do was to blast hopefully away in support of the general electronic commotion, which was a waste of all its strengths." *Billboard*'s Peter Halstead, though, didn't see it the same way: "The *NJO* lost some of its subtlety when playing with *Colosseum*, but gained in the feeling of something racing through the blood. Their dynamic range and scope of primary colours fused with *Colosseum* to stunning effect!" Two further dates, one in Portsmouth and the final one at the Brighton Dome, completed this brief tour.

Two similar collaborations took place that summer, and though they were officially *NJO* gigs, Neil Ardley invited Jon, Dick, Clem, Tony and Dave to participate. Only *NJO* repertoire was performed, with one exception — Neil's arrangement of the Jack Bruce/Pete Brown composition *Rope Ladder to the Moon* (which would soon feature in *Colosseum*'s show). It had become part of the *NJO*'s repertoire after Jack Bruce had played bass on their second album, *Le Dejeuner Sur L'Herbe*, and on occasional live gigs since. Neil apparently recorded this concert for his personal archive (unbeknownst to *Colosseum* and their management!), and a CD was released in 2008, a few years after his death.[1]

The second concert took place at the Playhouse Studio, London on the 28th of June and was recorded by the BBC for inclusion in their series *Sounds of the Seventies*. Five pieces were performed, including the Neil Ardley composition *Shades of Blue*, with Clem reprising his acoustic 12-string guitar intro. By mid June, Tony Reeves had officially left *Colosseum* to become creative director of Les Reed's Greenwich Gramophone Company, so this broadcast brought about a swift reunion with his old band-mates. However, the undoubted highlight of the session was the Mike Gibbs composition *Tanglewood '63*. Mike had played trombone with the *NJO* for sometime and this track made such a big impact on Jon that it later became part of *Colosseum*'s repertoire.

There's no doubt that the *Colosseum/NJO* concerts were a great success. Dave Gelly remembers them with great fondness, but recalls there was something of a downside: "That whole tour was a high spot in the *NJO*'s life, but it may also have marked the beginning of the end. It was so successful that we got asked to do all kinds of unsuitable things with rock acts. The only one that we agreed to do was a short tour with Eric Burdon (without the

Colosseum rhythm section), which was fine for what it was, but not really us. Don Rendell was in the band at the time, and he said to me, 'I don't want to do to this kind of project and it isn't the reason why I joined this band.'" So, even though the *NJO* had achieved considerable stature by this time, it was beginning to look like its days might be numbered. As it turned out, this remarkable big band continued to gig sporadically over the next few years, but eventually Neil Ardley decided that he preferred to work with smaller line-ups and to record under his own name.

After a lengthy search, they found a replacement for Tony Reeves. He was Louis Cennamo, who had previously played with Peter Frampton and *The Herd*. Now he was leaving *Renaissance*, because they had just lost two key members and were in the process of dissolving. Louis recalls: "I'd had quite a lot of session work coming in and one or two offers from bands, the biggest of which was *Colosseum*. Earlier Clem Clempson had come into the dressing room after a *Renaissance* gig in Birmingham and asked if I'd be interested in playing with the band." So Louis joined and was thrown into the 'deep end' somewhat, as there was only time for a couple of days' rehearsal before *Colosseum* started recording their third album.

It was the summer of 1970 and the festival season was in full swing. On the 27th of June, *Colosseum*, now with Louis Cennamo on bass, returned to Bath for their second appearance at this popular event, alongside an impressive list of over 20 acts[2] including *Pink Floyd*, *Led Zeppelin*, Frank Zappa. The typically British summer delivered a mixture of sun, wind and rain, prompting one musician wag to christen the occasion — 'cold Bath with showers'. In fact, some of the showers were quite violent, with lots of electricity in the air...causing Grace Slick of *Jefferson Airplane* to comment anxiously to Chris Charlesworth of *Melody Maker*: "It's too wet and we'll get electrocuted. They don't have summers like this in New York!" It turned out that the promoters had seriously underestimated the size of the crowd, which resulted in the approach roads being very congested. This delayed several of the groups that were appearing, including *Colosseum*, who were eventually rescued by a farm vehicle trundling across the fields to escort them to the backstage area! These delays had the knock-on effect of rendering the onstage timetable virtually obsolete, but in any case Jon had developed a savvy strategy for festivals, as Colin Richardson explains: "Jon asked me to try and ensure that they went on around 4.30pm and as the promoter Fred Bannister liked Jon, he was happy to agree." Most bands jockeyed for the later spots, but Jon maintained that it was better to go on earlier, before the crowds got too drunk, fell asleep or became restless from hours of sitting on the ground. With one of the highlights of the show being Jon's drum solo, nothing would be worse than subjecting a drunk or tired audience to 15 minutes of 'hitting the skins'! As it turned out, it was nearer 7pm when they finally made it onstage, but Jon's plan still worked a treat — and, at the climax of what Chris Welch described as 'an uncharacteristically brutal' drum solo, the crowd rose to its feet and gave him a standing ovation. To Jon, it looked like a hundred and fifty thousand people were heading down the hill towards him — it was an extraordinary moment! Such was the incredible audience reaction to *Colosseum*'s performance, that *Melody Maker* made it their lead story in their centre-page spread on the Festival. *The Bedford Record* wasn't quite so impressed though, commenting that the band was 'technically good, but soul-less'. Now that they had been playing the circuit for a while, it appeared that the honeymoon with the press was over and they were beginning to get the occasional negative review.

Apparently some of the festival was filmed (photographs show what appear to be TV or movie cameras on stage with *Colosseum*), but no one seems to know whether any of this footage survived. The photos also show a chaotic scene on stage, with dozens of people milling around! The aforementioned access problems meant that no band appeared when they were scheduled to and with many bands over-running, the music continued throughout the night, with *Canned Heat* finally playing their set about 6am on Sunday morning! The second day wasn't much better...so it was around breakfast time on the Monday morning when Dr. John eventually brought the Second Bath Festival to a close!

Just a few days later, on Friday 2nd July, *Colosseum* played one of their most important gigs...the Royal Albert Hall, supporting the American group *Steppenwolf*. This arose out a reciprocal arrangement, set up by Gerry Bron with Reb Foster Associates, who managed them and *Three Dog Night*, both of whom were huge Stateside at the time. This deal was supposed to have *Colosseum* support one of them on an American tour, thus giving them exposure to their stadium audiences, which would hopefully achieve the breakthrough they needed.

In those days, the Royal Albert Hall was a dream gig for a rock act, though, as Dick commented, it was not without its problems. "It was the first time I'd attended that ornate home of dreadful acoustics." Dave remembers that: "My mum and dad were there and they were so proud, because we had all gone to Promenade concerts when I was 16." It was a big occasion for the band, especially for the newly-arrived Louis Cennamo: "Louis was a nice man, but when we played at the Albert Hall he found it all a bit daunting," was Dave's impression. The concert, however, was a triumph — but that didn't stop Jon's mother asking him, after the gig, when he was going to get a *proper* job!

For this concert, the band made a radical decision. Having climaxed every show for the past year with the *Valentyne Suite*, they decided to drop it! There had been a growing feeling within the band that it encouraged lengthy improvisation, which meant that it had become far too long. As Dave Greenslade explained to Chris Welch of *Melody Maker*, it was taking up a third of the show, which curtailed the introduction of new material. *Disc* commented that it was a brave decision to drop one of their most popular and well-received pieces.

The *Financial Times* review of the concert reported that the band was just too loud: "The group were hell bent on deafening its audience, while possessing in Dick Heckstall-Smith, the most talented 'odd-man-out' in British pop; he blows a superb saxophone. In contrast, as soon as *Steppenwolf* were onstage, we were able to relax. Their drummer (Jerry Edmonton) coaxed rather than drove them on and their guitarists accompanied rather than bullied." It seemed that a pattern was emerging in their relationship with the press. It's difficult to ascertain whether these adverse reviews were merited. So many bands start off getting good notices, then, as journalists get bored with those they had been championing, they switch to supporting new favourites...often referred to as 'build 'em up, then knock 'em down'. Controversy is always good for selling newspapers and Chris Welch of *Melody Maker* was well aware that, occasionally, a fellow journalist would attack a band that a colleague liked, even though they both worked on the same paper! Commenting on the *FT* review, Dave Greenslade admitted to Chris Welch that: "I suppose sometimes we do go on for too long and *are* too loud." Dave also agreed with what Dick had said after the Bath Pavilion gig...that occasionally they were just playing for themselves. Jon, horrified at the reviews, thought that the infamous Albert Hall acoustics and the fact that they were too far apart onstage, made them uncomfortable from the start, as their interactive way of playing relied on them being able to see and hear what each other was doing.

A day after the Albert Hall concert they played the Top Rank Ballroom, Cardiff — then took a timely break, which allowed Jon to review the four tracks that they had recently recorded. It had become clear that Louis Cennamo wasn't working out, so would be asked to leave the band. Louis admitted recently how hard it had been for him: "I remember there wasn't time to adapt my style to fit in. I came into a busy schedule and had to learn too much, too quickly and I was too young to cope, so never got to show what I could do. It was difficult joining a band that was so tight together, having played so many gigs — they all knew their parts so well. The more I tried to change my style to anchor the band the less it seemed to work. In *Renaissance* I was there from the beginning and had a hand in the creation of the music. I had time to develop my contribution over several months of leisurely rehearsals, but with *Colosseum*, everything was already arranged and just seemed to require the bassist to slot in. In the end I remember feeling just sort of exhausted, trying too hard to get it right and then I switched off."

A poster that still hangs in Jon's office today proclaims *Colosseum* the 'hottest live outfit around', but the main criticism levelled at them was that their records lacked the drive and spontaneity of their live performances. Hitherto, the band had always 'run-in' new material onstage and then tried to reproduce that live energy in the studio, seemingly without success. Jon now felt, rightly or wrongly, that this approach must change, outlining his solution to *Music Now*: "We have separated ourselves into a stage *Colosseum* and a studio *Colosseum*. All the numbers (on the new album) were arranged with the studio[3] in mind." However, progress was hampered for two reasons; they still needed to find a new bass player and, on top of that, Clem was becoming increasingly unhappy singing lead vocal and was pushing the band to find a more powerful singer to take over.

So, between gigging several days a week, they also had to fit in recording for their all-important third album, but several tracks had to be left unfinished until they found a new bass player and, hopefully a new lead singer...all of which explains how they would end up spending more time on the third album than the first two combined!

For a while now, Clem and Jon had been 'eyeing up' *Juicy Lucy*'s vocalist, Paul Williams. Gerry Bron agreed to get him into the studio to sing on the Jack Bruce/Pete Brown anthem *Theme for an Imaginary Western*. Everyone was delighted with his performance, so much so that he was immediately invited to join the band. Dick was especially pleased, as he'd always rated Paul highly. However, things became a little tense when *Juicy Lucy* found out and the offer was suddenly declined. Gerry Bron: "The manager of *Juicy Lucy*, Nigel Thomas, had obviously put a lot of pressure on Paul...I was convinced he really wanted to join *Colosseum*."

After this disappointment, they concentrated on finding a new bass-player. Clem recalls several contenders being auditioned, but none were right for the band. Finally, just before their scheduled, and badly needed, three week holiday break...fate took a hand and their prayers were answered — in the shape of Mark Clarke.

As a good friend of Liverpudlians Bob Adcock (Jack Bruce's personal roadie) and Kenny Jones, who had been *Colosseum*'s driver, Mark had been hanging out with the crew for a number of weeks and had therefore also got to know the guys in the band. They were aware that he played bass as he and his group had supported *Colosseum* at the Liverpool Philharmonic Hall just a few days before the Albert Hall concert. Mark even recalls that Dave Greenslade asked him if he thought he could handle the *Colosseum* bass slot. He and Clem were also jamming and singing together on odd occasions and eventually Clem was impressed enough to take the plunge and invite him along to a recording session. Thinking it was for a backing vocal, he was somewhat surprised when he saw his own bass guitar there in the studio. Jon then asked him if he knew *Rope Ladder to the Moon*, which he did. Mark recalls: "I played my arse off, but I never looked at it as an audition because I didn't think I had a chance as I seem to remember Jack Bruce's name being mentioned as a candidate at one point." After playing for about 30 minutes, Jon came out with the killer line, 'Do you wanna job?' Four words that changed his life there and then and, for Mark, it was a dream come true.

Mark Clarke was born in Liverpool on 25th July, 1949. His mother had been a violinist with the *Liverpool Philharmonic Orchestra* and with such a musical pedigree it was no surprise that he started piano lessons at the age of just four. By the time he was 14 he had progressed well enough that his teacher thought he should try for a music college in London, but the family just couldn't afford it. Around this time he took up bass guitar and, after leaving school, joined a local band called the *Downbeats* whilst working for his father's upholstery company in the daytime. Like Dave Greenslade, he also took the risky step of accepting a foreign gig — in Portugal, but it only lasted six weeks, after which he came back to Liverpool and joined another local band, *St James Infirmary*.

Jon really clicked with Mark's playing right from the off: "For me, the bass player has to be transparent, and that means his natural way of playing has to be my natural way. I have never really liked playing 'tight' with the bass for very long, by that I mean playing the same rhythm on the bass drum as the bass line. I prefer the two parts to be different, but complementary — I guess that's due to my early immersion in jazz. But it also means that we *do* have to be inside each other's heads, even if subconsciously. So, I can instantly tell when somebody feels the way I do. I get a wonderful ride with Mark and I'm a great fan of his voice." Mark returns the compliment and remembers how playing with Jon made a lasting impression on him: "There's just no way to describe how hard it can be to play with Jon as he can play some tricky stuff, but when we click we are one of the best sections on earth, and nobody I ever played, or play with to this day, has *that* magic, *nobody*...I really am proud of what happens on stage between us sometimes..."

Mark's debut with the band was something of a 'baptism of fire', as his first gig was at a festival in Aix-en-Provence, France, in front of many thousands of people. Dave recalls him hurriedly learning his parts, en route: "We had no rehearsal, so we jotted down the chord charts on the back of a Piccadilly fag packet and told him, 'This is it, mate, so good luck!'" As if that wasn't fraught enough, two days after their return they were back in the studio to continue recording the third album. Then, just a few days after that, they were appearing at the prestigious National Jazz & Blues Festival at Plumpton, in Sussex. Mark Clarke recently recalled his initiation: "Being asked to play with what was then one of the biggest bands in Europe was one thing but to do my first gig in front of masses of people without any rehearsal, surrounded by television cameras — that was just plain 'brown trouser' time."

Plumpton was the 10th in the series of Jazz and Blues festivals organised by Harold Pendleton, owner of the Marquee club. In its earlier years it had been the major British festival, but had lately been somewhat overshadowed by Bath and the giant Isle of Wight Festival. In spite of this, Pendleton managed to get artists of the calibre of *Deep Purple*, *Taste*, *The Groundhogs* and *Family* to appear. Harry Isles remembers this festival very well: "I recall driving to the gates and there stood this hippy. I heard Dick say 'I bet he's going to call us *man*'. He came over and said to me, 'Who are you, man?' and we all fell about." The hippy, looking rather bemused at the hilarity his question had triggered, returned to his position at the gate. The *Melody Maker* review carried a picture of the band showing new boy Mark, on bass. *The Morning Star* was ecstatic: "*Colosseum* finally broke through the cricket match-level of applause and really brought the audience to its feet. They provided the most inspiring set of the festival." It is ironic that, although Jon hated festivals, they invariably received such plaudits.

Collectively and individually, the band's performance was a triumph, with *Melody Maker* stating that *Colosseum* had provided the two best solos of the weekend. It was the kind of accolade that Jon received on a regular basis, but Dick's unrestrained performance also got a rave notice on this occasion: "It was the sort of brass blowing that cuts partings into your hair and sets your toes rubbing their way through socks. He screamed, searched and found rasping patterns of blue notes that were free, but handled with a subtle mature feeling!" Purple prose indeed, but it summed up Dick's playing to a 'T'.

Arthur recalls that watching his father perform often caused him a great deal of stress: "It used to make me sweat like hell — *he* was fine, but I felt all the fragility of what he was doing. He would push himself into musical corners that were hard to get out of. He often discarded his roots and he took incredible risks." Jon confirms that this really was the musical essence of Dick, but also points out that he was occasionally almost *too* individualistic. As he recently explained on an Italian website: "He was a rough, tough tenor sax player, driven by demons...he never played the way you expected and often he went down a tunnel of his own making, often at the expense of the show. But at his best, he was a unique and recognisable voice and that's the best kind of musician you can be."

After Plumpton, the band resumed recording, though by now they had switched to IBC Studios. Towards the end of August, the sessions were interrupted by a short tour of Scandinavia, which included major festivals in Stockholm and Turku, Finland. Then, in early September, they were booked to appear at the Fehmarn Festival, in Germany. The impressive line-up included Jimi Hendrix, *Canned Heat* and *Ginger Baker's Airforce*. *Colosseum* had played many festivals over the long hot summer and they tended to become a blur, but this one stood out, though for the wrong reasons. Even the way they came to be there is slightly bizarre. The office somehow found out that *Colosseum's* name was on the bill, even though nobody had contacted them, let alone *booked* them! They immediately phoned the organisers threatening legal action and were promptly offered a substantial fee to appear.

The offer was eventually accepted, on condition that the entire fee was paid upfront and *Colosseum* flew to Hamburg, where they met up with Hendrix and *Canned Heat*. Jon relates what ensued: "We got to the site about 8.30pm and the rain was coming down in sheets. The police had rigged up searchlights, I assume to control the crowd. The storm was unrelenting, with a force nine gale driving the rain horizontally across the stage. There was no food or drink; the whole thing was a nightmare. Finally, *Sly and the Family Stone* decided to brave the elements and set up on stage to a forest of crouching umbrellas. Then, with the amps on and the band ready to go, the canopy over the stage tore and most of the band's backline was drenched in rainwater!" A very nervous stage manager agreed to sign an affidavit stating that it would be too dangerous to perform. Adding to the general mayhem, a number of German Hell's Angels were roaming around, looking very menacing. So, it was straight back to the airport, without appearing, and home to the warmth of the recording studio. During this epic saga, Jon bumped into a very sick Jimi Hendrix several times and was horrified at the state he was in. As far as Jon could see, no one in his entourage seemed at all concerned and it brought back Jon's worst memories of the Graham Bond era. Tragically Jimi was dead within a few days of returning to London.

Since Paul Williams had turned down the offer to join the band, Clem continued singing lead vocals. As Jon, Dick and Dave had all cut their teeth on jazz, vocals had always played a secondary role for them. Though Jon's original concept was for a band with a lead vocalist, his preference had been to combine the role with that of lead guitarist. Now, back in the studio, it had become clear that the new material required a much more powerful singer. Jon told *Beat Instrumental*: "I started writing lyrics in the middle of last year and quickly became interested in voices and vocal quality." By now, they had auditioned several singers without success, but as a result, the way forward had become clearer. A new *Colosseum* was evolving, one that could make the most of the two good singers they already had in Clem and Mark, together with a more powerful lead voice out in front. This might also improve their chances of cracking the American market.

Meanwhile, pressure was mounting to finish the album and it was at this point that Dave Greenslade suggested bringing in his old boss, Chris Farlowe. At first glance, this would appear to be a strange choice, since he was best known as a powerful blues singer, who'd also had some 'pop' success. Oddly enough, Jon had never heard him sing live, nor was he aware of his number one single, *Out of Time*, so he got a copy of his *Mama Rosa* album, listened to it and was mightily impressed. Dave told Jon that Chris could usually be found at his militaria shop in Camden, London. In fact, he was at that time recovering from a bad car crash and had been out of action for a while. He'd read in *Melody Maker* that *Colosseum* were looking for a singer, but hadn't thought anything of it. Chris related to *Disc* how this strange visitor came to his shop one day: "Jon asked if he could have a word with me and for a moment I thought maybe I owed him some money. He then explained that *Colosseum* was looking for a singer and would I like to have a go? I learned the numbers in a few days and recorded them right off. Jon was knocked out!" So was Gerry Bron, who was delighted with Chris's performance.

With Chris now fronting the band, a great new bass player and two fine back-up singers, Jon and the rest of the guys felt ready to face the world anew. This line-up would become the definitive *Colosseum* which, 'with the odd break', would still be playing together in the new millennium.

Chris Farlowe was born John Henry Deighton on 13th October 1940 in Essex. When he was still very young his family moved to

Islington, in North London. He'd always wanted to be a singer and by the age of seven was singing along to his mother's piano accompaniment. At thirteen he was listening to skiffle and learning the guitar. He soon formed his own band, calling it the *John Henry Skiffle Group*, which won several talent competitions and played a few local gigs. John's voice stood out even then: "I was only small as a kid but I had a voice which should have belonged to a six-foot fairground barker. It helped to build up a large local following." Their greatest success was winning the All England Skiffle Contest against hundreds of other bands. The prize...a princely £25!

After he left school, John decided he wanted to be an apprentice joiner and as the skiffle boom was dying out, he formed an R&B group, *The Thunderbirds*, but at the same time also signed solo deals with various labels, recording under different names. One such record was the classic *Stormy Monday Blues* performed as *Little Joe Cook*. The producer, Guy Stevens[4], thought it sounded American, so the artist's name should too. The record got a positive reaction, many reviewers thinking that the singer was black, but John wasn't even aware of its release. Around this time he decided to change his name anyway, choosing the surname of an American jazz guitarist, Tal Farlowe, and eventually settling on 'Chris' for a first name, purely because he thought the two names went well together. *Chris Farlowe & The Thunderbirds* were launched in 1961 and were soon having success on the club circuit. They recorded their first single *Air Travel* for the Decca label, but switched to Columbia for the follow up, *I Remember*, in '63. Neither charted, but Chris was gaining in experience and confidence. He got to know manager and club owner Rik Gunnell while appearing at his all-night venue the Flamingo, eventually signing a management deal with him. In 1965, after recording five singles for Columbia, he switched to Andrew Loog Oldham's Immediate label and pretty soon had his first hit with a Jagger/Richards song called *Think*, which went to No.37 in the charts. Then in the summer of 1966, came his first and only

No.1, with another Jagger/Richards collaboration, *Out of Time*.

Meanwhile, *The Thunderbirds* were going down a storm at gigs, which was no surprise, as the band included musicians of the calibre of Albert Lee on guitar and later a *very* young Carl Palmer on drums. In '67 Chris had another hit with a Mike D'Abo song, *Handbags & Gladrags*, which later became a much-covered classic. Then, in 1968, at the suggestion of the Gunnell Brothers, Chris disbanded *The Thunderbirds* and spent the next six months in America, trying to make some kind of impact there. He didn't — and returned home disappointed. Having by now parted company with Immediate, he recorded an album for Polydor, called *From Here to Mama Rosa*, as *Chris Farlowe and The Hill*. It was a much more progressive sound than his previous bands and Penny Valentine of *Sounds* was one of the few journalists to pick up on this, commenting: "One of the saddest things about his career, as far as I am concerned, was the lack of enthusiasm shown by the public to a brilliant album he made with *The Hill*. If people had listened closely enough they would have detected a strong change in the Farlowe as they'd known him."

So...on the front page[5] of *Melody Maker*, dated 26th September, 1970 — a banner headline announced to the rock world the news: 'Farlowe joins *Colosseum*!'

FOOTNOTES

1. Review of the Camden Arts Festival CD release (reprinted with permission):

The New Jazz Orchestra (a.k.a. *NJO*) led by composer/arranger Neil Ardley was Britain's most prestigious and adventurous big band in the 1960s. Under Ardley's visionary leadership the band developed the foundations for the modern European Jazz big band sound. Although incorporating the classic American big band tradition of Duke Ellington and the more modern approach of Gil Evans, Ardley managed to steer his band into uncharted territory, using his unique approach to instrumentation and bold arrangements. At the time this album was recorded live at London's Camden Jazz Festival in May of 1970, Ardley was already moving rapidly towards the exploding Jazz-Rock

Fusion genre, creating one of the first, and magnificent at that, examples of Jazz-Rock Fusion big band. Compared to American bands at the time, like *Blood, Sweat & Tears* or *Chicago*, Ardley's approach is definitely much more refined and orchestral and uses a wider arsenal of the Jazz vocabulary, being therefore much more sophisticated. Having at his disposal some of the best British Jazz musicians (and then also Jazz-Rock Fusion musicians) he was able to turn the *NJO* into a 'mean' and powerful Jazz-Rock Fusion ensemble, which truly fuses Jazz and Rock to the max. This of course brings us to the players and more specifically to the fact that this version of *NJO* incorporates in its midst the entire line-up of one of the greatest British Jazz-Rock groups, *Colosseum*. Dick Heckstall-Smith (saxophone), Clem Clempson (guitar), Dave Greenslade (keyboards), Tony Reeves (bass) and Jon Hiseman (drums) all play here, and even a couple of tracks the band recorded on their albums are present, in a big band arrangement of course. With the members of *Colosseum* as a core of the band and with other notable players like Henry Lowther and Harry Beckett (trumpet), Dave Gelly and Barbara Thompson (saxophone) and even an ultra-rare appearance of Michael Gibbs on trombone, this is truly a superb group, able to face any challenge Ardley's arrangements may present them with. BTW the presence of the *Colosseum* members is not incidental, as both Reeves and Hiseman were *NJO*'s founding members and Heckstall-Smith appeared on the *NJO*'s second album entitled *Le Dejeuner Sur L'Herbe*. Seven of the tracks present on that album are also included here, which turns this recording into an updated live version of that timeless classic. The original recording tape of this concert had quite a few technical problems, but was painstakingly and beautifully restored to life with an exceptional sound quality considering the circumstances under which it was recorded.
Adam Baruch www.adambaruch.com

2. List of Bath Festival performers:

The Byrds, It's A Beautiful Day, Johnny Winter, *Colosseum, Jefferson Airplane*, Frank Zappa, *Country Joe*, Joe Jammer, *Hawkwind, The Pink Fairies, Canned Heat, Led Zeppelin*, Donovan, John Mayall, *Moody Blues*, Dr John, *Pink Floyd, Fairport Convention, Flock, Santana*, Keef Hartley, *Hot Tuna, Steppenwolf*, Maynard Ferguson, Compere: John Peel.

3. This wasn't strictly true, as *Downhill and Shadows* and *Bring Out Your Dead* had already been incorporated into the act and would be on the third album.

4. Guy Stevens, who died in 1981, produced albums for *Free, Spooky Tooth* and *Mott the Hoople* whose name he had, in fact, come up with. He is probably best known for producing *London Calling* by *The Clash*, who were so impressed they wrote a song dedicated to him called *Midnight to Stevens*.

5. In fact, it's always amazed Jon that *Colosseum* got that front cover banner headline at all — considering that Jimi Hendrix had died the week before. This edition of the *Melody Maker* was the earliest one that could report his death as it had occurred just after the previous week's deadline and the national press had been covering the story in full for almost a week. Actually, most of the page is a photo of Jimi in full flight with the sub-heading 'Hendrix Blues.' Jon recently purchased a fine copy of this edition of the *MM* from an American collector and the front cover is reproduced in the second section of photos in this book.

"The bastards had gone!"
CHRIS WELCH'S REACTION when
stranded in Germany

*"Never give a drummer an
even break!"*
JON HISEMAN

Chapter 10

"O, THE SUN WAS IN THEIR EYES"

The final session for *Colosseum*'s third album was on 23rd September 1970, at Lansdowne Studios. Jon was never very happy there — it was too dead and the monitoring was tricky — but he rated the facilities and liked the young in-house engineer, Peter Gallen, finding him very 'simpatico' to work with. The album was to be called *Daughter of Time* and, as Jon had hinted, would be a departure for the group. They had also changed their approach to the production, spreading it over four months. Jon told *Melody Maker*: "I got so involved on working on this album I forgot about being a drummer for a month or so."

Over the time it was recorded, the band had two different singers and two bass players, so it was amazing that the album had the cohesion and consistency that it did. Barbara plays on the whole of side one, this time being duly credited, which she hadn't been before. In June 1970, she was featured in *The Sun* newspaper with the headline: 'Plugging in to the new sound' and a photo of Barbara perched on a high stool, playing soprano sax, while Jon pushed a vacuum cleaner, looking rather resigned. The article mentions Jon as being in *Colosseum*, but still paints a rather misleading picture: "Barbara is in great demand, working with three orchestras, which leaves Jon house-bound in London much of the time, doing the washing and tidying up." To their eternal chagrin, these pictures were then syndicated throughout Europe! They got it right about Barbara though — she was playing in several orchestras at that time, including John Dankworth's, the *NJO* (of course) and Mike Gibbs'. As well as this, she made odd appearances with Keef Hartley's *Little Big Band*, Alan Cohen and Gordon Rose.

Meanwhile, Chris Farlowe was wondering how he would be received by the *Colosseum* faithful. His first gig was at Newcastle Polytechnic on the 25th of September, 1970. As usual, Jon introduced the proceedings, talking about the recently completed album and explaining that Chris had only had three days to learn 11 complicated songs. Just in case though, Chris had a music stand with his lyrics on — an unusual sight indeed for a rock singer! At one gig, a gust of wind blew them all over the floor, inducing mild panic. Phil Penfold of *Melody Maker* was there to witness Chris make a slightly shaky start with *Rope Ladder to the Moon*, but things quickly improved: "He came more into his own on *Downhill and Shadows* when the slow beginning gave his soulful voice a chance to warm up."

Chris weathered the next couple of gigs successfully, but admitted to *Music Now*: "I was worried stiff that people would throw bottles and shout, 'Get out of *Colosseum* you old pop singer.' At our first gig a lot of people were shouting for some of my old numbers." In the same interview, Jon explained the band's new 'modus operandi'. There would be more rehearsal time, even though this would reduce the number of gigs they played which, in turn, would deplete their income. Jon felt it was important to get off the live treadmill that just bred fatigue and staleness. This was quite a brave decision as, at that time, they were still paying off a £9,000 overdraft for their equipment.

Harry Isles remembers that, in those days, bands carried their own PA (Public Address) systems. He recalls the laughable situation at festivals, where all the bands laid out their gear onstage in the order they were playing, including their PAs! Sound engineer Scott Thompson admitted that the ever-increasing amount of equipment[1] created quite a few problems. The varying size of venues required a lot of expertise to get the sound right every time. In an interview for *Sounds*, he explained: "On stage, every one of the band is so loud that they can't hear anything but themselves...but we've been doing a lot of experimenting with monitors and I think we've solved the problem." Indeed, over time *Colosseum* saw many improvements to equipment technology. For the first two years, the volume of the guitar, bass and organ amps was set by the musicians and what came through their speaker cabinets was what the audience heard — and this decreed the overall loudness of the band. The PA system at the sides of the stage was only used for Dick's saxes and the vocals, with the drums usually heard acoustically. No one had a monitor — each musician hearing the other's sound bouncing off the venue walls! Just before the band's demise, when they were playing much bigger venues, they took delivery of a massive Dynacord PA, under an advertising deal, which had a great sound but wasn't very hardwearing. When, shortly after, the band broke up, the manufacturer demanded its return, though they were not best pleased at the terrible state it was in.

Generally it was the smaller gigs that had the better sound, as the band could balance itself more easily. It also helped that these venues were usually packed to the rafters, thus soaking up the sound so the audiences didn't have to contend with any echo. In the bigger venues, or those with poor acoustics, it was more difficult. Amplification technology was forging ahead and as a result, guitars were often too loud, so when Scott mixed the sound, he could only increase the volume of the PA to compensate. The complicated arrangements that *Colosseum* played would still challenge most state-of-the-art equipment today, but in the autumn of 1970, the press was certainly commenting on their increased volume levels — *Melody Maker* published a letter from one irate fan which read: "I've never heard such an uninspiring dirge as *Colosseum* at Barking Technical College; volume doesn't drive a band."

Jon was true to his word and, from October 1970, the band rehearsed for more days than they played gigs and this would pay dividends when they came to record their fourth album. In mid-November, they set off for yet another German tour, this time supporting *Free*, who were riding on the back of their No.1 hit, *All Right Now*. The tour was put together by major German promoters, Lippman & Rau, who had started out promoting internationally established jazz and blues acts, but were now embracing the new rock music *and* they were already *Colosseum* fans.

At the first concert, it was clear that the audience were predominantly there for our heroes, but as *Free* had a hit record the promoters had decided they should close the show. *Colosseum* finished their set to tremendous applause, but when *Free* went onstage, they found that a good half of the crowd had disappeared! Jon and a couple of the others were anxious to hear *Free* and snuck into the rear of the auditorium, but were immediately spotted by several of the audience, so they had to beat a hasty retreat when more and more fans stood up, turned round and began to applaud. Colin Richardson recalls: "In a way, it was an unfortunate pairing and Island Artists agent Alec Leslie, who was looking after *Free*, buttonholed me on the train the next day and suggested that it might be better for all concerned if the playing order was reversed. I thought that this showed a canny perception on Alec's part as well as a degree of humility." Jon, though, was less pleased — he was happier with the original arrangement, always preferring to play early, "while I'm still young!" The band still fondly remembers this tour, as it made a pleasant change to be travelling by train and staying in hotels close to the stations. All very civilised!

It had been decided to invite Chris Welch to join the tour for a couple of days on a 'facility trip,' all expenses paid by the band. He joined them in Nuremburg, toward the end of the tour and the plan was that he should see at least a couple of gigs. He was, however, so exhausted when he got to the concert that evening that he actually managed to nap for part of *Colosseum*'s set, even during Jon's drum solo! Unfortunately, the part he *did* manage to catch was fraught with major technical problems, as Chris later noted: "*Colosseum* suffered from a PA fault and voltage drops, which hit Dave Greenslade's organ (putting it out of tune)." It was all rather unfortunate and resulted in what was probably one of their worst sets ever! Later, in a somewhat acrimonious 'post-mortem', the group complained that they couldn't hear each other — apparently, Scott *hadn't* completely solved the monitor problems. It was at this gig that Colin Richardson was offered a *Colosseum* 'bootleg' album from a fan, but declined to buy it. Jon did though, and this simple act would later prove to be significant. The evening was capped with the discovery that the tyres of the group's equipment van had been slashed and 'Capitalist Pigs' scrawled in the dirt covering the rear windows. At that time, there was a student-led movement in Germany, probably the remnants of the 1968 unrest, claiming that 'music should be free', a somewhat naive point of view, given the cost of setting up and running a band. As an interesting postscript, Jon recently had a guy come up to him at a German gig who told him that, as a boy, he had run away from home and hitched halfway across Germany to see their show. Unfortunately, the local police had caught him afterwards, just as he was leaving the hall and he was driven back to his home, albeit in some style in a police Mercedes.

Chris Welch was staying in the same hotel as the band and after partaking of a few 'nightcaps' with some of the guys, fell asleep, fully clothed on his hotel bed. Upon waking, somewhat later than planned, he went down to the lobby to find that *Colosseum* had left without him. Everybody had checked out except Chris Farlowe, who always travelled in his own vehicle when touring Germany. He couldn't be much help though, as his Range Rover was packed with Nazi militaria, bought to sell in his London shop. So, our intrepid reporter was left with little option but to fly back to London. Over the years, this anecdote has taken on quite a humorous aspect, but at the time it wasn't thought funny at all. In his subsequent *Melody Maker* column, Chris was spitting venom: "The bastards had gone...never has a group ditched their scribe, with scarcely a Deutschmark to buy a crust in a strange city. I felt like a character from a Kafka play and expected men in leather overcoats to begin interrogation." Having got this off his chest, his sense of humour reasserted itself with the 'tongue-in-cheek' suggestion that some reparation could be made by buying him 'a set of wine glasses and a pop-up toaster'! With *his* tongue firmly in his cheek, Colin Richardson dutifully delivered said items to the *Melody Maker* office in a large box marked 'Payola'![2]

Apparently, it was crew member Harry Isles who had been detailed to keep tabs on Chris Welch and he was duly 'carpeted' by Jon. Harry remembers how the incident demonstrated his boss's positive leadership style: "Jon was always keen to sort out any problems before they were allowed to fester. After I lost Chris on the tour, I had an argument with him. I was pissed off, as I had enough to do looking after the band. But on the plane home, Jon said 'This isn't going to affect your relationship with the band, is it?'" In fact, the unfortunate incident was soon forgotten and things quickly returned to normal.

Though Chris Farlowe had flown out to Germany, his friend and ex-*Thunderbird* guitarist, Bugsy Waddell, had driven out and joined him. Chris explained to *Disc*: "They told me I can please myself what I do over there as long as I make all the gigs on time." *Colosseum*'s Press officer, Frances van Staden remembers driving around with Chris, while he picked up bits and pieces of Third Reich memorabilia. However, Harry Isles recalled that Chris wasn't always very discreet: "I remember him walking into a hotel in Germany and going up to reception with two SS uniforms on coat hangers and the receptionist being quite shocked." Jon also recalls another occasion when they were fogbound in a Munich hotel and napping in the foyer while waiting for their transport. He woke up to find a Nazi toy soldier perched on his chest, aiming a rifle right between his eyes! It was part of a Nazi war game that Chris had set up around him. Prior to joining *Colosseum*, Chris had, in fact, been door-stepped by a *News of the World* reporter running a story on people who dealt in Nazi memorabilia. Chris told *Music Now*: "He asked me if I liked Hitler, so I said 'Yes, sure'...then I took him outside the shop, pointed at the brand new Buick Riviera parked there and said 'Hitler bought that for me, didn't he? He took so much from the people he conquered...I'm just taking a little bit back.'" Chris's interest in militaria first surfaced when he toured Germany with the *Beatles* in the early '60s and he subsequently became very knowledgeable about Nazi Germany and the history of World War II. However, as the supply of these artefacts dwindled, Chris turned his attentions to the iconic designs of the '50s American diner and the classic jukeboxes of the period.

The German tour ended with the TV show *Beat Club*, on 25th November. They performed spirited versions of *Take Me Back to Doomsday* and *Tanglewood '63*. By now Chris Farlowe had over 25 gigs under his belt and had obviously settled in well. Dick was very impressed with him, writing in his book: "He was a veritable master for whom nothing, no vocal melody line of anybody's invention, was ever difficult to perform. Once he'd got it in his head, he invariably did it with Olympian skill and with a voice that was second to none." Dick also noted that Chris was very adept at vocal improvisation and ad-libbing, as well as having the ability to push his performances ever higher.

With rehearsals now going well, plenty of new material in the pipeline and a band with no weak areas, it was becoming clear to Jon that the best way forward would be to make a live album...but right now, it was time for everyone to meet the *Daughter of Time*!

Colosseum's third album was released in mid-November, while they had been away on the German tour. The press reaction was mainly favourable, with some reviews noting the impact Chris Farlowe's arrival had made. *Record Mirror*'s headline was: 'Farlowe adds vocal power', followed by: "It's amazing what a combination of *Colosseum* and Chris Farlowe can do." They were, however, also of the opinion that Jon's drum showcase, *The Time Machine* (the only live track on the album) didn't fit well with the rest of the material. *Music Now* commented that:

"*Colosseum* has come of age in the recording studios. This really is an excellent album, it seems to create a mood and a consistency that their previous efforts had failed to do." *RTR* thought it was easily their best album to date and *Sounds* observed that: "it was a logical extension to the *Valentyne Suite*, but even more atmospheric." Chris Welch's review was probably the warmest, raving that: "It adds up to their most satisfying production to date and *The Time Machine* is one of the most staggering drum solos yet recorded in Britain." Chris also noted that: "Occasionally, there is a tendency to 'busy-ness' stemming from the enthusiasm of the players in passages where many instruments are making their statements." This criticism was one that cropped up occasionally, but nobody could deny that they were successfully developing a new sound.

Jon's reaction to Chris Welch's rave review of the drum solo track on the album was typically modest: "People tell me *The Time Machine* is the best I have ever played, which I refuse to believe. But I just kept going and somewhere I am playing four different rhythms. It's a pity that drum solos are nothing more than crowd-pleasers...and for keeping my weight down!" Nevertheless, it still makes for exciting listening (one of the few drum solos that achieves this distinction). It was around this time the band played a wonderful trick on Jon. When he finished his drum solo and the band returned to play the 'out' theme, Jon looked up to discover they were all playing each other's instruments and nearly fell off his stool, laughing. "Never give a drummer an even break!"

The Daughter of Time is considered by many to be *Colosseum*'s best studio album (although the *Valentyne Suite* surely remains their best composition). They had learned how to be a studio band and not just make a 'live' record in the studio. There is a certain inner strength to the material, with strong melodic lines and thought provoking lyrics. The string quartet on two tracks, *Time Lament* and *Daughter of Time*, adds another interesting dimension, all of which consistently engages the listener. It's true that some *Colosseum* fans were somewhat confused by the album, as very little of it was ever played live, though Jon had signalled this in interviews preceding the album's release. It's generally thought that this was their worst selling album, but when Philips converted their accounting to early computer technology some years later, the royalties got lost in the system and as a result were never properly accounted for. At the time, though, Jon exuded confidence, telling Jerry Gilbert of *Sounds*: "There's no question that this is the best album we've made." He is also on record as saying that it was the best of their sleeve designs, though there are many who might disagree with him; in fact, Gerry Bron apparently didn't like any of *Colosseum*'s covers, while Jon confirmed recently that the *Daughter of Time* sleeve was the *only* one he could live with.

Jon's new approach to the way they worked in the studio would cause controversy amongst their followers. One fan fired off a letter to *Melody Maker* after the album's release: "As a fanatic of *Colosseum*, I dispute the lavish praise given by Chris Welch to *Daughter of Time*. In the case of *Time Machine* it is justified, but the rest was a disappointment and not a true representation of *Colosseum*'s progression during the last year or so." However, another fan disagreed: "This was definitely the best *Colosseum* album for me. I'd bought *Valentyne Suite* after seeing them live, but it was the sound and feel of *Daughter of Time* that really 'pushed my buttons'. I still listen to this album today, and it's as fresh now as it was then." The sales figures certainly reflected these mixed views, as the album only made it to No.23 in the UK charts.

Mike Love of the *Beach Boys*, reviewed the title track, *Daughter of Time* in *Melody Maker*'s 'Blind Date' column and it's clear that he had no knowledge of *Colosseum*: "Is it that big, huge band that was recorded at the Albert Hall? What *haven't* they got in this band — it's quite good really." It seems they were winning over the most unlikely fans, though Love's reference to

196

the live Albert Hall recording suggests, maybe someone was talking to him about *The Time Machine*.

The decision that the next album would be 'live' was taken in early November, as Jon revealed to Jerry Gilbert of *Sounds*: "We plan to do a live album next, as I think we've made our name as a stage band and I don't think we've really communicated well on record, although we're obviously coming to terms with the studio now!" In *Music Now* he explained: "There are many numbers that we do on stage, such as *Lost Angeles* that we just can't do in a studio. A live album will give us the chance to record all those numbers."

In the run-up to Christmas, they had two important gigs in the date-sheet. The first was the Lyceum Christmas Party on the 10th of December, supported by stablemates *Gentle Giant*. Jeff Starrs of *Melody Maker* was there and took special note of Jon's drum solo. He described how Jon gradually developed it, withholding the climax expertly and gripping the audience: "He then proceeded to build it up again, this time laying patterns on the cymbals and finally back onto the drums for the climax. With his arms flailing round like a windmill, he even had the audacity to juggle with the sticks whilst playing a roll on the snare drum."

Two days later they travelled to Amsterdam to play the famous Concertgebouw.[3] Dutch group *Golden Earring* were supposed to be the support band, but as they had just had a massive hit with *Radar Love*, all the advertising had their name above *Colosseum*'s. The local newspaper must have given their music critic the night off and sent their sportswriter instead, as the review read as if it was a football match. Colin Richardson was quoted as saying: "Our lads are never at their best at an away game," which Colin totally refutes: "I made no such comment. It's complete fiction!" *Golden Earring* certainly had a lot of fans there, as they weren't far from their hometown, The Hague. The reviewer, doggedly persisting with the football metaphor, judged *Colosseum* to have come off second best: "*Golden Earring* won the match and The Hague celebrated their victory till the late hours."

Apart from one more pre-Christmas gig, the band resumed rehearsals, fitting in six solid days before the end of the year, concentrating on writing the new material they needed for the live album they planned to record over a series of concerts early in 1971.

FOOTNOTES

1. Scott Thompson, head roadie and sound engineer, listed the Dynacord equipment to *Beat Instrumental* as: "4 x 12 inch speaker cabs for the bass guitar and organ, and 2 x 15 inch speaker cabs for guitar. The PA comprises four large reflex cabinets about 3 ft x 5 ft tall with eight smaller cabinets to spread the sound around. Then you've got the monitoring system, comprising eight cabinets and a big mixer 'about the size of a large TV set' (and they were large in those days!). We also carry four spare speaker cabs and spare speakers. On top of all that, there's the Gretsch double drum kit and the A100 Hammond organ." Scott continued: "One time we were in Belgium trying like hell to make a festival in Germany. There was ice on the road so I was taking it easy. Anyway, we got caught in one of those gutters they have on the sides of their roads and went into a slide, spinning round and round for what seemed like hours. The van finally came to a halt and we thought we'd made it, but she just slowly rolled over onto her side. It was about six bloody freezing hours before anybody could get to us. Once righted, we drove as fast as we could for the German frontier...but they wouldn't let us through, because they claimed we had 'a dangerous van'. They're bastards those German customs! So we hired another van on my credit card, re-loaded the gear and drove through, leaving the old one in the customs car park. We made the gig and the band went down a storm!"

2. 'Payola' was quite prevalent on both sides of the Atlantic around that time. It involved record companies giving 'backhanders' to radio DJs (amongst others) to ensure their records got plenty of 'plays', thus boosting sales and hopefully getting them into the charts.

3. The Concertgebouw is one of the world's foremost classical/opera venues and was first used as a rock venue on 29th September 1969 for the European premiere of *The Who*'s rock opera, *Tommy*.

*"Don't keep chasing happiness;
let it take you by surprise."*
FROM *Skellington*, lyrics by Jon Hiseman

*"The day I'm satisfied with a performance,
I might as well give up"*
JON HISEMAN

Chapter 11

THUMBS UP!

EARLY IN THE NEW YEAR, THE *New Jazz Orchestra* WAS ASKED to record a live show for BBC Radio as part of a series called *Jazz Scene*. Billed as *A Study in Contrast*, Neil Ardley, once again, invited four of *Colosseum* to join them (neither Chris Farlowe nor Mark Clarke took part). It would turn out to be the last of such collaborations. Dave Gelly remembers it as the largest ever *NJO* line-up with 19 musicians in all.[1] The set included two Mike Taylor pieces, a Jack Bruce song called *The Immortal Ninth*, *Tanglewood '63* and a new work from Barbara Thompson called *Terre de Miel*. Humphrey Lyttelton compered the programme, which was broadcast on Sunday 14th February. It was a fitting, if low-key end to what had been an exciting partnership.

Meanwhile Jon, impressed with how Chris, Clem and Mark's three-part harmonies gave the band another dimension, thought that *Tanglewood '63* would be an ideal vehicle for their distinctive sound and convinced the others that it should be incorporated into the act. It required much painstaking rehearsal, because their version took Mike Gibbs' original brass and saxophone lines and scored them for sax and organ with the three voices 'scat-singing' the main melody parts. The piece quickly became very popular with their audiences, which pleased Jon no end, as it epitomised everything he had set out to achieve with *Colosseum*. As Jon recalls: "My original idea of cutting-edge jazz and blues solos, together with interesting and challenging songs, seemed to have come to fruition, though it had taken more than two years to get right. Mark and Clem's voices blended perfectly and Chris bought a vocal power to match the band in full flight — all of which made the difference." Mark Clarke explained in an interview with *The Wembley News*: "Our collective musical policy binds the musicians together, but it is more of a general understanding of what each individual member wants to play, rather than a set formula." Mark's rock background helped him give a more solid rhythmic foundation for the band: "At first I was just tagging along with what was going on, but now I feel I am contributing something positive to the band and the music." In the run-up to the live album, the new material was proving to be quite complex, so the basic structures were being well rehearsed, leaving plenty of space for solos, which Mark described as 'planned improvisation'. In addition, they now had a virtuoso lead vocalist who also contributed his own improvisations, becoming, in a way, a sixth instrument.

Chris Farlowe was much more relaxed now than when he was a solo artist as he felt a lot less under pressure. He explained to Keith Altham of *Record Mirror*: "I don't have to do my wrestling act with the microphone because the audience has come to listen. I don't have to play at being Chris Farlowe anymore. When we go back to the States, we'll kill 'em!" The next American tour, though, always seemed to be 'just around the corner'. However, not everybody was convinced that Chris was the right choice. Harry Isles recalled recently: "I never felt Chris was the ideal lead vocalist. He's got incredible technical ability, but he didn't seem part of the band to me — he didn't feel right. I always thought that Paul Williams of *Juicy Lucy* would have been better." Dave Greenslade had no such doubts: "We needed someone with the kind of vocal strength that can compete with the powerful *Colosseum* sound...and that someone is Chris Farlowe." There were certainly still some who preferred the original band, but the vast majority considered this line-up the definitive *Colosseum*.

Chris had also been in talks with Gerry Bron, who was keen to record him in his own right. He told *Sounds* that he was no longer concerned about hit singles, as being in *Colosseum* changed his attitude to music. He hinted that the rehearsal sessions in December had been fruitful: "We're working on a live album, and one track, *The Pirate's Dream*, has an arrangement by Dick that's the most incredible I've ever heard," — though he would later come to modify that opinion. They were still using their radio sessions as a way of making demos and on January 20th the band recorded the *Robin Black* show when they premiered *The Pirate's Dream* and *Skellington*. The lyrics for the latter were written by Jon for Clem's blues-based music and he considered them to be his most successful so far. Indeed, the song proved so popular that it's still in the show at the time of writing. On the other hand, Jon and Dick's vision for *The Pirate's Dream* was so ambitious it would almost sink the ship.

Around this time, Barbara told Roy Hollingsworth of *Melody Maker* that she didn't think she would continue to be involved with *Colosseum*: "To me now, *Colosseum* is such a complete group, they don't need anyone else." Towards the end of the interview, he asked what *her* future plans were and she replied that she was very busy playing commercial dates with various bands, studio session work and writing material for several jazz projects. Paying tribute to her husband's support, she said: "Jon gives me a lot of help, especially rhythmic help. He's got a marvellous ear for shaping music and often helps me with my new material." Barbara was already making a name for herself on the jazz club circuit and gaining recognition for her original compositions.

On the last day of January, Jon was driving round the Heathrow perimeter road in a blinding rainstorm, *en route* to the airport for a flight to Glasgow where *Colosseum* was to play the University. Glancing in the rear-view mirror, he thought some 'nutter' was tailgating him. Jon tried to accelerate away and put some distance between himself and the car behind, but it kept on his tail. After a few minutes of this, a ghostly blue light suddenly started flashing behind him, so Jon pulled over. A very wet and irate airport police officer then got into the car, angrily accusing him of speeding. Jon's response was to get out a pen and paper and demand the officer's details, saying he would counter prosecute for dangerous driving. After they had both calmed down, the police officer proceeded with the painfully slow process of booking him. Jon told him that he had a plane to catch, which brought forth the reply: "Afraid you've 'ad that, sir." Eventually Jon was allowed to drive on to the terminal where he discovered all flights were cancelled due to industrial action — something the policeman *must* have known. Jon's solution was to charter a small private plane. Later, explaining to *Melody Maker* the reason for this seemingly reckless largesse, Jon just said that they didn't want to let the students down. Phil Parker, an avid fan of the band, was at the gig: "They didn't turn up till around midnight, but I would say that the ensuing performance was the best I ever saw from the band. They were on top form that night, winning many new fans amongst the thousand or so who were there and getting a long, rapturous, standing ovation at the end." Ironically, Jon never heard another word about the alleged speeding offence!

With the recording dates for the live album imminent, the band was busy honing the new material at the pre-gig sound checks. This made for long days, with a lot of hanging around at the venues. Everyone was well aware of how much was at stake, which also increased the pressure on them. They all had their different ways of coping — Dick's method was described previously, but Mark Clarke handled it differently: "I did suffer from nerves and still do. I just get very quiet and before any gig I try only to speak to the guys I'm working with — the band and the crew, though I also tried booze for a while." Clem admitted: "I often suffered from stage fright and I still do, but I think it's more because of shyness than nerves! I always seem to feel under scrutiny when I'm onstage, which may be a result of the fact that my entire musical life as a child seems to have consisted solely of preparing for the next exam." Dave Greenslade's attitude was more sanguine. He considered that it was quite healthy to be nervous — the trick was learning how to control it. Chris Farlowe seemed never to suffer from pre-gig nerves and could often be found fast asleep before a performance! Jon Hiseman admitted that he sometimes had problems with nerves and recalls often being sick in the toilets before some of the bigger gigs: "I'd get nervous standing at the side of the stage, watching the other bands. They would go down so well, singing their pretty songs and strutting around like peacocks and I would think we were so far 'off the wall' that the crowd wouldn't like us." He also found that listening to other drummers was often difficult — especially when their approach was *so* different to his that he wondered whether *he'd* be able to play at all! Maybe two years on the road was beginning to take its toll, or was it just that he never really *did* have complete confidence in his own ability? Whatever the case, it always seemed that his nerves disappeared once he got on stage and started playing. These were undoubtedly difficult and worrying times for Jon and he recently admitted that he often felt he was walking a tightrope in the weeks leading up to the live album recording.

After another short tour of Scandinavia in early February, detailed planning for the live album got underway. Jon remembers that both Gerry Bron and Phonogram (as Philips Records were now known) had been against the idea of a live album from the start, the perceived industry wisdom being that they just didn't sell. However, copies of the 'bootleg' album recorded at the Circus Krone in Munich (*Colossal Live*), had been turning up everywhere for autographing — indeed Jon had *bought* one at the Nuremburg gig. Using this as a lever, Jon persuaded Gerry that it was worth a try. Originally, they were going to record just one gig and hope it would be a good one, but this was deemed to be too risky, so several concerts were recorded, though no one can remember exactly how many. The first 8-track recording was at the University of Kent in Canterbury on the 12th of February 1971. The band arrived with quite an entourage. Hedley Leyton (of Bron Music, the publishing arm) was in charge of logistics and Gerry Bron, who rarely went to gigs, was there as Executive Producer. Two engineers manned the Granada mobile recording unit, then there were *Colosseum*'s five 'roadies' and Lansdowne's studio engineer,

Peter Gallen. The mobile wasn't due to arrive until 1.30pm, which was cutting things fine, but the group still managed to fit in two and a half hours of rehearsal, fine-tuning the material. The support act was the acoustic duo *Tir-Na-Nog*, so once set-up and balanced, *Colosseum*'s gear could remain undisturbed on stage until show time.

There was no set schedule for the number of gigs to be recorded — the gear would be taken to every suitable gig until it was agreed they had enough material for an album. The third of these was at Manchester University on the 13th of March 1971. Nobody remembers much about the gig except that there was an almighty row in the dressing room afterwards as tensions boiled over. Nobody thought things had gone well and presumably everyone was trying to deal with the fact that they weren't getting anywhere — though it *was* generally agreed that the acoustics that night had been the best so far.

Desperate to get *something* in the can, they returned five days later to play a second show, for free. Steve Peacock of *Sounds* was there: "For the Manchester students it was something of an end of term party and the hall was packed, with people being turned away at the door. *Colosseum* seemed rather subdued and a bit apprehensive about the whole thing — perhaps the 'now or never' atmosphere of the gig was weighing on their minds." Peacock noted how the band got off to a slow start, but got into their stride after the third number. He was particularly impressed with the way Jon 'gelled' the band, writing: "I've always considered him to be a technically good drummer, rather like a well-oiled, versatile metronome, so it was a joy to find that he could play with so much feeling and sensitivity, while the other members of the band proved to have the same balance of technical skill and spirit." With the audience screaming, stomping and clamouring for more, Jon picked up the microphone to announce a surprise encore: "We're going to do a number that we did earlier which we weren't too pleased with...then, as a special treat we'll do something we haven't played for a long time." There were massive cheers as the crowd realised he meant *The Valentyne Suite*. So, at least it was being considered for the live album.

The day after the gig, they listened to the tapes and soon realised that their performance hadn't been anywhere near good enough. At this point, Gerry Bron put his foot down and said they would record just one more gig and if they still weren't happy, the project would be abandoned. Even though the idea of making a live album was a good one, Gerry was probably right to call time on it, as they could have gone on forever trying for the perfect performance. The final recording took place at the Big Apple, Brighton on the 27th March, but it didn't seem to be any better than the other performances and Jon in particular, was very despondent — the live album was very close to his heart.

In spite of being unenthusiastic about the whole idea, Gerry suggested going back to Lansdowne to listen to some of the early efforts in a studio setting. After spinning through several shows, they ran the tapes of the first Manchester gig and it began to dawn on them that some of it *did* have that special 'spark' — plus the recording quality was good and the few goofs made could easily be 'fixed'. Jon had announced an encore, even though he didn't have a clue what it would be. Jon: "When we went off stage — with the audience yelling for more — the recriminations started immediately. I remember being mentally and physically exhausted after a very long day and Clem, in particular, was angry about something and didn't want go back on to play another of our complicated arrangements, so he decided to play a blues, which started in the traditional way — an instrumental chorus, then Chris coming in and singing one of his favourites, T-Bone Walker's *Stormy Monday Blues*. It was a genuine first take with no rehearsal. Later, in the studio, we overdubbed some parts to tidy it up, but the magic of Chris's entry is still being relived every night on tour, some 39 years later!"

Colosseum Live is unjustly neglected in the pantheon of live albums. Everybody acknowledges great examples like *The Who's Live at Leeds* and *Deep Purple's Made in Japan*, etc, but *Colosseum Live* compares well to either of them. Admittedly, the sound isn't totally crystal clear and does have a harsh edge to it, but that just adds to the excitement of the performance. Peter Gallen, at the recording desk, finally succeeded in capturing the essence of a *Colosseum* live gig...and then some! The album didn't please everyone though — one disappointed fan wrote to *Melody Maker* asking why there was no solo from Dick on *Lost Angeles*. The fact is, the band continually switched solos around and Dick seldom took one on it anyway, so the disgruntled fan must have been at one of the few gigs when he did. *The Valentyne Suite*, which was only recorded at the second Manchester concert, was never seriously considered — there was just too much good new material. Gerry Bron always teased the band by telling them they would never better the studio version anyway!

In early April, the group left for a tour of West Germany with *Gentle Giant*, the highpoint of which was a concert during the *London in Berlin Week*, a prestigious cultural exchange exhibition. Their following in Germany had been building up steadily since their first tour and was now reaching new heights. As they went on stage at the Deutschland-Halle, there were scores of armed riot police in evidence. *The Wembley News* interviewed Mark Clarke afterwards: "We had been warned that Berlin audiences were the coolest around and that even top groups received at most, a ripple of applause, but at the end of our set the crowd loudly demanded an encore. The riot police were instantly on their feet, visors down, shields up, ready for trouble." Mark remembered their roadie appearing and telling them they *had* to go back onstage, as the crowd was going mad. They played two encores, the first group to earn this accolade at the venue, which was probably the beginning of their eventual legendary status in Germany. Clem commented that, while

Colosseum, *ELP* and *Soft Machine* went down well in Germany, groups like *Black Sabbath* were less well received at that time — possibly because the German audiences generally preferred more complex music. Jon's drum solo was still 'doing the business' with the crowds as Clem told *Melody Maker*: "They're always different. Some nights Dick and I fall about when he does something that Elvin Jones would have done, but then it doesn't go down so well, while another time he'll play something really simple with a few tricks and the audience storms the stage." Some of these tricks were illusory — one fan wrote to *Melody Maker*, asking how Jon managed to bounce his sticks off the snare drum during his solo. Jon would never have been admitted into the *Magic Circle*, as he sportingly revealed the secret: "What you do is to throw the sticks up in the air, let them revolve once and catch them. Once you have mastered it, you can play things on the drums and throw the sticks up whenever you have a free hand."

Jon always gave the impression of being someone who never lost his cool, but one fan, Roger Farbey, recalls a surprising incident at the Marquee: "During the obligatory, but far from routine drum solo, Jon suddenly stopped and shouted, "turn that fucking light off," to some idiot who was aiming a strobe light at the drums while he was playing." Jon always told the crew to dim the lighting during his stick juggling routine, because if there were lights directly in front of him, it created a strobe effect with the airborne stick which meant he couldn't see it well enough to catch. On one occasion, in Italy, the lights came back on halfway through, with hilarious consequences! He missed one stick, but, keeping the rhythm going, he grabbed another from the bag hanging on the deep tom-tom and up it went. Still blinded, he missed it again and this time it landed behind him — another stick, another miss...then another and so on till the bag was empty and the stage behind him was littered with sticks. Jon takes up the story: "When I finished, the whole audience was on their feet, applauding wildly and I suddenly realised that, from their perspective, I appeared to have thrown up and caught an impossible number of sticks, whilst continuing the solo. I guess I should have kept it in the act, but could never bring myself to con audiences on a regular basis."

Colosseum's busy schedule continued unabated. The live album was mixed and ready to be pressed in time for a June release, though first they had to complete the process of changing record labels. Like so many of Gerry Bron's acts, *Colosseum* was signed to his Hit Record Productions which leased its albums to the major record companies for marketing and distribution. For some time now, Gerry Bron had been less than happy with the Vertigo label, as he recalls: "They did nothing for *Colosseum*. They'd said they were going to be highly selective but they were signing three acts a month, so they weren't being very selective at all — although Olav Wyper always claimed that they did great things for us." In the light of this, Gerry decided to form his own label, Bronze[2], so as to be better able to control the way his artists were marketed. He immediately signed *Colosseum*, *Uriah Heep*, *Juicy Lucy* and *Paladin* (*Colosseum*'s support act on a few of their recent gigs). The launch party for the Bronze label was held at Ronnie Scott's Club in May, attended by David Betteridge of Island Records, the new label's distributors. The Bronze name seems an obvious choice now, but it didn't occur to anyone immediately. In fact, Gerry had offered a cash reward to whoever came up with the best name. He recalls: "Bronze was suggested by Iain Clarke, who at the time was *Uriah Heep*'s drummer. It was so obvious, we just couldn't believe it. Why hadn't we thought of it?" Iain got the princely sum of £5 for this flash of inspiration.

The publicity machine kicked into gear, building up to the release of the live album with Jon giving a series of revealing interviews, the first of which was with Steve Peacock of *Sounds*. Jon had had plenty of time to reflect on the *Daughter of Time* album and was aware some fans were disappointed that none of the tracks had ever been played live, admitting: "We really fell down over that last album; groups need identity — it's essential and I think we lost ours. Now we're trying to retrieve the situation...we respond to the audiences and if they react positively we can give all the more back. We're very conscious of the people who buy our records and who come to our gigs." Peacock asked whether all the changes of personnel had altered the original plan, but Jon was quick to defend the earlier line-ups: "I think that on good nights, even in the early years, we did transcend the material, though perhaps we do it better now. In the beginning, over half the show was material from our albums, or things that people wanted to hear and we were slaves to that, but now I think we just go on and be ourselves."

Another interview was with *Melody Maker*...a group discussion with Robert Fripp and Maggie Bell. The confrontation with Fripp could only be described as prickly, but it got to the heart of the vibrancy of the current music scene. Jon advanced the idea that it was the musicians who were influencing the direction of progressive music. Fripp totally disagreed, arguing: "Musicians have very little to do with the music and the music business has *nothing* to do with the music!" He felt that it was the music *press* that created trends. Jon countered by citing his own example of making *Colosseum* economically viable — after all, he had formed a band that played relatively non-commercial music, but which *had* become successful. "Nobody really believed that we would become accepted and play major tours in foreign countries...the idea was in *my* head, not the audience's, nor in the newspapers." The discussion then went to the question of what audiences wanted to hear. The consensus seemed to be that it was music they already knew and were familiar with. Fripp felt that most of *their* audiences sat waiting patiently for the two or three numbers at the end that they recognised! Jon thought it was important to introduce the newer music during the set and save the 'hits' for the encores. Fripp retorted that they didn't do encores! Touché!

Pondering this exchange, Jon now believes that artists may drive their work forward on several different fronts, but it's the public that decides what is commercially successful, by voting with their wallets. He also thinks that the record companies allowed their grip on the music biz to slip in the '60s and the artists took more control of their own destiny, viz: *The Beatles/Stones/Cream*/Hendrix/*King Crimson/Yes/Colosseum et al.* It was, of course, too good to last!

By the beginning of the '70s, record companies finally realised that there was a progressive music boom and a whole slew of 'specialist' labels appeared almost overnight. How successful these labels *really* were, is a matter for conjecture, but by the late '70s, the major record companies were firmly back in control and remained so for the next 25 years.

In early June, the band embarked on yet another German tour, to coincide with the release of *Colosseum Live*. The 'working title' of the album had been *Thumbs Up* — another nod to Jon's fascination with all things Romanesque. An artist friend of Chris Farlowe even produced a cartoon showing the band being torn apart by lions in a Roman arena, but it was crudely drawn and, though a good idea, there wasn't the time to develop it. They also had an amusing idea for a Monopoly-style board game ('gear truck turns over on motorway — miss gig, lose £1000'; 'groupie diversion — 3 in a bed, miss 2 turns'!) but, in the end, the design that was chosen for the gatefold sleeve was by the well-known album sleeve artist Marcus Keef, and turned out to be seriously contentious. The back of the gatefold sleeve depicted a 'graffiti artist' daubing the title of the album in red paint onto a white wall, with the front cover showing him after (ostensibly) being shot in the chest! The intention, one assumes, was to shock, but because the picture is so blurred, it didn't really succeed in this. The inside of the sleeve has a montage of photos of the band, plus a few other associated personnel, taken by Harry Isles during recording. The band was nonplussed by the cover art and

Jon hated it: "What the hell has it got to do with my band?" What made things worse was that no one at Island Records had any explanation as to what the thinking was behind the idea.

Just as controversial as the artwork was another unusual feature of the packaging; the records came in red plastic inner sleeves with foam strips attached, which were supposed to clean the record as it was taken out. Clem admitted to *Melody Maker*: "We have a bit of trouble with the unusual sleeve design. Not everybody in the band is knocked out by it — it would have been better just to have a normal sleeve." Jon remembers Gerry phoning to say that the first copies had arrived and immediately going to the office to check them out. Seizing an album from the top of the pile, he opened the gatefold — the inner sleeves flopped down and both records fell out onto the floor! Jon was enraged: "I said I wanted it changed, but was told that it was too late. David Betteridge, boss of Island Records, whose art department had commissioned the cover, tried to calm me down. I told him, 'the outer sleeve design is awful, but we haven't even talked about that because of the *inner* sleeves. It's the worst idea I've ever seen!'"

The Press reaction to *Colosseum Live* was mostly excellent. As usual, Chris Welch reviewed the album for *Melody Maker* saying how impressed he was by Clem's 'remarkable' performance on *Skellington* and highlighting the way the individual talents blend on the album. He also singled out Dick's 'incomparable playing' on *Tanglewood '63*. Many critics considered the track that most summed up the album was *Lost Angeles* and Chris agreed: "Here the drama is piled on, as ideas come tumbling from all the musicians, playing at the peak of involvement and excitement."

New Musical Express wrote that the band had finally captured on record the full essence of their live performance, with the rhythm section coming in for special praise: "Hiseman and his bassist, Mark Clarke, play so well together that it becomes frightening at times. Such is their energy they constantly spur Chris, Dick and Clem to the point where they frequently bubble over with joyous exuberance." *Disc* also gave it a good review ending with: "If you can't get to a *Colosseum* gig, this is the next best thing." *Sounds* was less enthusiastic: "I agree that in the past *Colosseum*'s records have been rather cold, compared with what they could do live...it still doesn't do them justice because, in places, the sound balance is very odd and the performances, however fiery and full of life, in some way lack the considered quality that has previously been their strength." Despite this lukewarm review, *Live* went on to become *Colosseum*'s best selling album.

It's clear from the interviews Jon gave around this time, that he felt the current line-up of the band was just about right, but they also reveal the strain he was under. His responsibility for the overall organisation of *Colosseum* was total, which meant he invariably had too much on his plate. One *Melody Maker* journalist asked him what he would do if any member of the band were to leave. Jon replied: "It would be very difficult to find replacements and I don't know how willing I'd be to go on with it. So much of what I do is administration and production — sometimes I forget I'm a drummer! Occasionally, I think I'd just like to go back to gigging and play with some of the good musicians who are around." Nevertheless, Jon was sure that this was for him *the* band — a delicate and symbiotic balance of unlikely personalities, who together were capable of producing music greater than the sum of its parts. This had always been his vision, but he was also aware of its inherent fragility — just one little tremor could cause it to collapse like a house of cards.

Footnotes

1. The line-up was: Nigel Carter, Bud Parks, Harry Beckett, Ian Carr, Henry Lowther (trumpets); Derek Wadsworth, Robin Gardner, Mike Gibbs (trombones); Dick Hart (tuba); Barbara Thompson, Don Rendell, Brian Smith, Dave Gelly, Dick Heckstall-Smith (saxes & woodwind); Frank Ricotti (vibes & percussion); Dave Greenslade (piano & organ); Clem Clempson (guitar); Jeff Clyne (bass & bass guitar); Jon Hiseman (drums); Neil Ardley (conductor).

2. After being set up in 1971, the Bronze label enjoyed early success with *Uriah Heep* and throughout the '70s built an impressive roster of bands that included *Motorhead*, *Osibisa*, and *Manfred Mann's Earth Band*. Bronze released 96 albums in all, 40 of which went into the UK or international charts. The Bronze catalogue was sold to Castle Communications in 1986, when the Bron Organisation went into liquidation.

*"Dave recently reminded me that, at one
of the many arduous rehearsals
devoted to the piece, Chris said he had
to go to the toilet and we never saw
him again that day!"*
Clem Clempson on *The Pirate's Dream*

Chapter 12

Colosseum in Ruins!

*"The shit hit the fan for me following
the Albert Hall concert. After that,
I was just waiting for an excuse that
no one would argue too much with —
and Clem provided it."*
Jon Hiseman

THE SUMMER OF 1971 FOUND *Colosseum* WITH THEIR USUAL
FULL DATE-SHEET, which included an appearance at the Reading
Festival on 27th June, sharing the bill with, among others, Rory
Gallagher. The weather on the day was awful, even by British
standards. Just how bad, was summed up by the *New Musical
Express*: "*Colosseum* went on with the wind and rain blowing
straight into their faces. They turned in a professional
performance and got a tremendous reception, with Chris Farlowe
giving impromptu renditions of *April Showers* and *Singing in
the Rain*, capturing the spirit of the moment." *Melody Maker*
reported that fluctuations in the power supply caused some
problems: "The balance was awry, with the bass inaudible for
most of the time. Clem Clempson's fine lead solo in *Skellington*
lacked the force needed to carry it off. Jon Hiseman executed the
obligatory drum solo in an excerpt from the *Valentyne Suite* —
the amazing crispness of his playing was demonstrated
throughout the performance." Jon's solos were still getting
glowing accolades, but they were also a bit of a poisoned chalice:
"I thought it had become an albatross around my neck and
always felt bad if it took the solo to get the crowd going — it
meant we had failed as a band. I offered to drop it, but the band
wouldn't have it, maybe because it gave them a chance to get
to the bar!"

Around this time, Jon flew out to Rome to appear with Frank
Zappa on a televised debate about 'the impending demise of
western civilisation and, with it, the collapse of capitalism'!
Arriving at the studio, they found there were four nationalities
taking part, each receiving simultaneous translation, so they
could follow proceedings — it was just like the UN! Jon: "This
was prime time television and a team of eminent European social
scientists, social workers and politicians were discussing the
break-up of society, as evidenced by the 400,000 young people
who attended the Bath and Isle of Wight festivals. One by one
they took the floor, having a wonderful time fear-mongering to
their own public and publicly castigating us as the leaders of the

revolution! Despite our ridiculing the whole premise, they would not be deterred. When Zappa was asked to play the programme out on solo guitar he 'hoisted the flag of revolution' by playing 'gobbledegook' phrases interspersed with deafening bursts of feedback. The pundits, of course, congratulated themselves on their perspicacity!"

This mind-set had been brought about by the student unrest of 1968, when many European states had overreacted to what they perceived as a threat to society. Jon had personally experienced something of this backlash outside a venue in Germany. Mistaken for a fan, he was manhandled by the police for no other reason than being there, resulting in a lot of bruising to his upper arms. Tony McPhee of the *Groundhogs* was involved in a similar incident, also in Germany and about the same time. Jon considered that the 'revolution' was merely a loss of respect for authority, primarily due to the previous order being so heavy-handed. When he and Barbara had first visited Frascati, Italy in 1965, Barbara was about to go into town wearing a mini skirt. "You'll be arrested by the police and bought home in a police car, dressed like that," laughed her cousin, Susanna and loaned her something more modest.

In July, Jon and Chris gave a revealing interview to Roy Carr of *NME*. The headline trumpeted '*Colosseum* want an American challenge.' Their non-stop touring of the UK and Europe was paying dividends and they were in constant demand, but this was a double-edged sword. They were now headlining at most venues in Europe and going down a storm, but they needed new challenges. Chris told Carr: "That's why we need to go to the States — it'll do us the world of good and make us work a lot harder." The 'on/off' American tour situation was becoming farcical. Tour plans had been made a couple of times, but for one reason or another hadn't materialised. This interview confirmed that they were still hungry to go, but Jon was aware of the pitfalls. They were practically unknown there and if the audience reaction wasn't positive enough, it could have a serious effect on band morale. Meanwhile, they just had to wait and see whether an American tour ever became a reality.

In August they were back at Lansdowne Studios, where they demoed *The Pirate's Dream, Same Old Thing, Sleepwalker* and *Thank God for Things that Grow*, none of which turned out very well at all. Jon had become increasingly interested in the mysteries of recording and had taken the multi-tracks recorded at Lansdowne and mixed them in several different London studios, trying to pinpoint why they always sounded so odd to his ears. He decided that the best sound was at Advision, where many progressive bands recorded and where the in-house engineer was the talented Eddie Offord. Following the abortive session at Lansdowne, Jon persuaded Gerry Bron to let them try out the new studio. The recording quality was everything Jon hoped for, but the music, unfortunately, wasn't. Both *Colosseum* and management agreed the experiment hadn't worked.

The band had never thought of themselves primarily as writers; first and foremost they were musicians, but writing had now become all-important. They realised what was needed to top the live album, but the last two studio sessions had sown seeds of doubt about their composing abilities. It wasn't all bad news though — there was still plenty of evidence of their success. Proof of that came on the 15th of August, when they broke the attendance record at London's Lyceum Theatre. Jon was in the dressing room waiting to go on when the manager poked his head round the door and announced: "Full house and police are outside, controlling the crowd. I could let in another two hundred or so and we can split the proceeds 50/50." Jon agreed. It's possible it was at this gig that the first public airing of the ill-fated *Pirate's Dream* occurred. The next day they were in the TV studio for an appearance on *The Marty Feldman Comedy Machine* for ITV. They were in august company, as Spike Milligan and the legendary film-maker Orson Welles were also taking part. The show enjoyed high viewing figures, as Marty was one of Britain's top comedians at the time, so it was terrific exposure for the band. Marty was obviously aware of Jon and *Colosseum* as he been at Ronnie Scott's Club with Jon and Barbara when Roland Kirk was playing. Jon wanted a drum kit with visual impact for the TV show, so Ivor Arbiter of Drum City, loaned him a Ludwig Vista-Lite kit, with see-through acrylic shells. When it was set up, Spike Milligan[1] wandered over. "He told me we should fill the deep tom-tom with water and put goldfish in it!" Jon recalled with a grin. It was quite unusual for a band like *Colosseum* to appear on this kind of show as this kind of family entertainment TV tended to be the province of the more pop-orientated acts.

On the last weekend of August, *Colosseum* had a UK festival double-header. The first, on the Saturday, was at the Weeley Festival, Clacton-on-Sea, 'organised' by the Clacton Round Table as a fund-raiser. The festival itself was a shambles, partly due to a serious error of judgement by the promoters in employing Hell's Angels as security. Predictably enough, they proceeded to run amok, assaulting members of the public and turning over some stands, although it has to be said that, backstage, most of the groups were unaware of the chaos. The Festival's MC then hilariously introduced the band as '*Colosseum* and Chris Farlowe'. Nevertheless, the *New Musical Express* reviewer was very impressed with their performance: "*Colosseum* is an exciting band to watch. Their closing number brought forth an excellent reaction and if we'd been out front to see, maybe we could have reported a standing ovation." The press, who were all cowering backstage and couldn't hear the announcements, had to rely on their knowledge of the music to identify who was playing, which probably explains why no songs were named in the reviews. Chris Charlesworth of *Melody Maker* managed to recognise their opener, *Lost Angeles* and explained why he thought they always went down so well at the big open-air events: "What a perfect festival set it was, every ingredient for a large rock crowd was there; the heaviness, the blaring riffs and, above all, the musicianship — both stunning and funky at the same time."

Next day, the band set off on the long drive to the Kendal Festival in the North of England. It was a much smaller event, with a crowd of around 6,000 and it rained almost continuously. Penny Bosworth of *Melody Maker* gave *Uriah Heep* a pummelling, but was much kinder to Hiseman's men: "*Colosseum* must, by now, be a veteran festival attraction, though Chris Farlowe's voice was cracking under the strain." Chris signed off with: "Thanks, you were a better crowd than that Weeley lot." By any standard, it was a successful weekend, but the *MM* reviewer had picked up on a worrying sign; Chris Farlowe was having difficulty keeping his voice in shape with the massive workload.

On 2nd September, the band recorded another BBC session, taping four tracks: *Jumping off the Sun, Sleepwalker, The Pirate's Dream* and *Upon Tomorrow*. Three days later they were appearing at the Palermo Festival in Sicily, but in-between, had a couple of UK gigs to wrap up. The first was in Cheltenham and the review in the *Gloucestershire Echo*, though quite positive, criticised the structure of the show and hinted that they were perhaps losing their way and becoming a bit self-indulgent: "Several numbers have been written around a solo, in order to display the talents of each member. After sitting through six of these ten minute breaks, I was beginning to feel that the set was turning into a mere showpiece of individual playing, instead of the brilliantly arranged melodic pieces, for which they are famous." Jon recently commented on this criticism: "This particular review was right on the money and it was my fault in a way, because Graham Bond had demanded a drum solo from me every night, as Ginger had always done. The drum solo led to the long sax 'solo, solo' (as we called it — a solo without accompaniment), first on the *Valentyne Suite*, then on *Tanglewood '63*. We then featured a long guitar 'solo, solo' on *Skellington*. Clem eventually, and quite rightly, became very anti the whole 'solo, solo' thing. With all those 'solo solo's' in one show, we realised that we had a problem — all except for Dick, who 30 years later, was still defending his right to a long 'solo, solo' on *Tanglewood*."

One of the band's most important onstage assets was the individual virtuosity of its members, but ironically, this was beginning to sow the seeds of their downfall! The situation was exacerbated by the constant gigging, which left them no time to work on correcting the problem. In such circumstances, it isn't long before serious disagreements start to crop up.

Palermo turned out to be quite challenging, as the *New Musical Express* reported: "They came on to lukewarm applause, but that all changed very quickly. With their dramatics and stage expertise they began to get through to the kids." When they came off stage, though, the recriminations started, as Clem recalls: "We played a very rough set on a typically chaotic festival stage and as soon as we came off, Jon had a terrible go at me for being too loud...I was already very pissed off, because I'd walked out on stage expecting to use my own amplifier, but found I had to use an amp I'd never seen before and it sounded absolutely horrible. So the last thing I needed was to feel like I was being made the scapegoat for the crap set we'd played." In some respects, *Colosseum* was becoming more and more of a pressure-cooker — and over the coming weeks, things were going to get worse.

Mid-September, they left for a tour of Italy, where they were building a strong fan base — the *Live* album had charted and, of course, their name aroused a lot of interest. Clem recalls that, when they played Rome, Chris suddenly ad-libbed a chunk of the *Beatles* hit, *With a Little Help From My Friends*: "Chris always likes to spring little surprises when he's singing *a cappella*, as he does at certain points in the set and on this occasion, he started singing the famous *Beatles* tune, so it was nothing unusual really, but then Mark and I joined in and maybe made a bit of a meal of it. Jon is rumoured not to have liked it much, but the audience loved it! The next night, it was as if Jon and Dave were out for revenge, as they suddenly and unexpectedly broke into the jazz standard *Night in Tunisia*."

In spite of the fantastic audience reactions and being in one of his favourite countries, Jon wasn't happy. They were being 'stalked' by Dee Anthony, the American manager of *Humble Pie*, whose lead guitarist, Peter Frampton, was about to launch a solo career. Jon suspected that he was checking out Clem as a possible replacement, but he also seems to have been impressed by the band, as he actually tried to persuade Jon and *Colosseum* to sign with him. Jon knew that Anthony had a reputation for shady dealing — in any case they were under contract to Gerry Bron and he had no intention of being drawn into Anthony's seedy subterfuge. As it turned out, Anthony, seeing Clem's impact upon the excitable Italian audiences, decided it was *him* he wanted.

During all this, Jon remembers having a distinct feeling that the wheels were coming off the wagon. It seemed the band was gradually dividing into two camps, the rockers and the jazzers, which was *not* a healthy state of affairs. The situation wasn't helped when, a week after their return from Italy, they flew to Scandinavia for a short tour. Chris Farlowe didn't go with them as he'd apparently lost his voice (though it was rumoured that he'd been away too long and had problems at his shop). Either way, it meant Clem had to take over the lead singer's role again, which, in turn, affected what they played in the set, as certain numbers had to be dropped. All this left Jon feeling, for the first time in a year, that they 'didn't have the goods on them' and this adversely affected his normally upbeat and positive attitude. On the surface, he seemed fine, but he was having difficulty hanging on to the drumsticks — they kept slipping out of his hands — he felt he'd somehow lost his sense of touch. He still managed to get through the tour though...and there were, as always, a few laughs. Colin Richardson remembers one incident, when a 'wannabe rock-star' suddenly appeared: "It was at Uppsala University in Sweden. A somewhat inebriated student decided to accompany Jon's drum solo on a grand piano, sited on the floor of the auditorium. It was obviously bothering Jon, who couldn't figure out where the noise was coming from, so I bundled the guy off as quickly and quietly as possible, much to his bewilderment!"

Their hectic schedule continued, as they criss-crossed Europe with alarming frequency. After Scandinavia, it was back to the UK for three gigs, then out to Germany for concerts in Berlin and Munster. Chris Farlowe, back singing lead after regaining his voice, took advantage of the trip to buy some American Civil War rifles. Germany was now firmly established as *Colosseum*'s number one market and their popularity was simply phenomenal, though one souvenir programme amusingly described Chris Farlowe as a 'progressive Tom Jones'! A new number had been added to the set: *Sleepwalker*, which featured Mark on vocals and Clem, reviving his childhood skills, on piano. Interestingly, the 'ad-lib' from *With a Little Help From My Friends* featured again, so perhaps Jon wasn't so 'anti' after all. Steve Turner of *Beat Instrumental* was there and once again the Hiseman drum solo was singled out for praise: "He flashed around the kit at an incredible speed as well as juggling the sticks. Cracked cymbals, cut down to various sizes, were used along with Paiste cymbals and gongs, virtually a cymbal solo." The climax of the solo, however, was Jon simultaneously playing both bass drums, gradually building to a ferocious crescendo. At the end of the solo, he threw a handful of sticks into the audience and the crowd went mad...the noise was deafening. What they couldn't have known was — this was the last time a European audience would see *Colosseum* for 23 years!

Back home, a very special gig was imminent...a return to the Royal Albert Hall. The first time had been as 'support' to

Steppenwolf, but now they were headlining in their own right. It would prove to be a memorable affair, but not for the best of reasons. Christine Roche recalls feeling nervous backstage: "When I heard Dick's solo I was dying with fear — he always played so dangerously. It was amazing — he got a standing ovation and the packed crowd loved it. We went back there a few days later to a Bach concert and there was hardly anybody there!"

Colosseum's PA was really too small and of insufficient quality to overcome the unpredictable acoustics of the RAH. The sound onstage was atrocious and wasn't much better for the audience, on top of which, there was a rather unfortunate 'glitch', as road-manager Harry Isles recalls: "In those days the gear was set up and we just plugged into one 13 amp socket. I was walking down some steps, just offstage, when I felt my foot catch against something and everything went quiet. One moment *Colosseum*'s wall of sound was steamrollering them, the next — silence! I'd kicked the plug out! I rapidly replaced it and the band carried on playing!" The crowd was momentarily stunned, as was the band; it must have seemed as if time had stopped. Afterwards, Harry kept 'schtumm' and busied himself in the dressing room, pretending not to hear the investigation going on around him.

Melody Maker's Chris Welch was there of course and wrote a stinging review that reverberated throughout *Colosseum* and their management. The headline pulled no punches: "*Colosseum* — time for a rethink?" According to the *MM* scribe, the show got off to a good start, but: "...during Chris Farlowe's blood curdling yell, we were listening to a noise machine that had seized up. Until *The Pirate's Dream* the band were playing well, but from then a slow rot set in." Even Jon's drum solo didn't escape criticism: "...it went on too long and he seemed to be treading water, reducing the impact." Coming from one of their biggest fans, it was just about as bad a review as it could be.

Interestingly, Gus Brain of the *Morning Star* saw things quite differently: "*Uriah Heep* had the unfortunate job of opening the concert and was consequently overshadowed by probably the most complete band — *Colosseum*." It wouldn't have mattered if *NME*, *Disc* and *Record Mirror* had all come out with rave reviews, because what Chris Welch had written would have eclipsed them all. He had been there for their very first gig and had championed them ever since, which is why this review came like a thunderbolt from the blue — and it hurt! Chris later tried to justify his diatribe in a letter to co-manager Colin Richardson. It read:

Dear Colin,
I hope Jon has had time to cool off a bit after my review of the concert. Perhaps, demanding an entire 'rethink' was a bit strong, but I still felt there was something more than just bad acoustics wrong with the music. And some of our readers think likewise. I have taken the liberty of enclosing a genuine, unsolicited testimonial, as they say in the trade, which perhaps shows I was not alone in feeling a certain disquiet with the proceedings. How do you feel about it Colin?

But seriously folks, I hope we can thrash it all out with Jon when he is feeling a bit more communicative.
Yours Sincerely
Chris Welch

Secretly, some of *Colosseum*, Jon included, agreed with the review — Chris Welch had always supported the band and hitherto his reviews had been positive. He appreciated their risk-taking approach and their ability to produce music that sounded fresh and inspired. Perhaps three years of experimentation, personnel changes and continual touring had taken its toll. Had *Colosseum* possibly reached 'burn-out'?

In the midst of this turmoil, came some good news and some bad news. The good news was that a second USA tour had finally been set up. They were to support *Deep Purple*, opening in Buffalo on the 8th of December. This was the chance they'd been waiting for — *Deep Purple* was well established in the States and attracted good crowds, plus the bill included *Fleetwood Mac*, who were quite well-known already as they had a couple of American tours under their belt. The not-so-good news was, as Dick Heckstall-Smith wrote in his book, there were conditions: "Our set should be no more than 30- or at the outside 40-minutes long and there should be no Hiseman drum solo — our office told us that Ian Paice didn't fancy the competition." For a band that didn't play three minute tunes, but relied on a slow-burn build-up for effect, having their show 'censored' in this manner would result in them being practically emasculated.

In fact, a 30-minute set for supporting acts was about par for the course in the States and with three bands on the bill, they daren't overrun. Jon dreaded the whole idea, knowing there was no way that a set that short could give anything like a true impression of what *Colosseum* was about. He wasn't worried about dropping the drum solo, as he had always known that they don't help to sell records. America was all about high volume sales, which, for *Colosseum* as with all bands, was the 'crock of gold at the end of the rainbow'. Bear in mind...they were all still on wages of just £50 a week!

A couple of months earlier, Jon and Gerry Bron had flown to Los Angeles to meet with the head of Warner Bros, Joe Smith, who was very enthusiastic about the live album and a new deal had been struck. Now came the announcement that *Colosseum Live* would be released in the USA and Canada to coincide with the November tour. Pressure? What pressure?

Just as Chris Welch's letter landed on Colin Richardson's desk, the final straw landed on Jon Hiseman's back. Some weeks earlier, guitarist Peter Frampton had confirmed that he was leaving *Humble Pie* and Clem had now received a formal offer to replace him. He was obviously tempted and met with Jon to talk it over. Jon clearly remembers how it went down: "When Clem came to me and told me of the offer, I said, without hesitation -- you should take it...I'll fold *Colosseum*. The shit hit the fan for me following the Albert Hall concert. After that, I was just waiting for the excuse that no one would argue with too much — and Clem provided it. I remember feeling relieved, partly because I could now be sure of being present at the birth of our first child, our son Marcus. Clem saw it this way: "I was thoroughly disillusioned with what seemed a very contrived approach to writing and I just wanted to return to the simplicity of the blues." The sad, but unavoidable truth was — the *Colosseum* juggernaut had begun grinding to a halt well before this.

Various rumours circulated as to why Clem left the band — he recently put the record straight: "There was something in Dick's book where I'm supposed to have said I'd been offered some ridiculous amount of money plus 'the use of a Bentley'. *Humble Pie* weren't making anything like that kind of money when I joined, their only source of income at the time was the advances being received under the deal with A&M Records and Steve Marriott would never have been so stupid as to try to tempt me with such nonsensical promises. Dee saw me playing in Italy, then Steve went out and bought *Colosseum Live*, liked what he heard and invited me to his house for a chat. My decision was made easy by the miserable situation *Colosseum* had gotten into."

According to Paolo Hewitt and John Hellier in their book *All Too Beautiful*, the *Humble Pie* offer wasn't quite as clear-cut as Clem believed. The first two choices were apparently Rick Derringer and Joe Walsh, but both declined. Hewitt and Hellier also claim that it was Clem who made the first move, by phoning Steve Marriott and hustling for the gig. Jon definitely remembers warning Clem about Dee Anthony's dubious reputation, but this was shrugged off. He also heard Clem had allegedly been offered £200 a week and a Bentley. Of course, the music biz thrives on such rumours and like most newspapers, never lets the facts get in the way of a good story!

Jon's reaction was swift and decisive — he called a meeting with the other guys at a pub in Gerrard Street, told them about Clem and said that 'he was knocking the band on the head'. Oddly enough, he is somewhat hazy about the details of this momentous occasion: "I may well have intimated over the phone what the meeting was about, or I might have dropped the bombshell at the meeting. If Clem wasn't there it was because he was now well out of it. I don't remember any serious objection from anyone. There was nobody in there fighting for the band." Dave Greenslade, for one, *was* shocked as he hadn't seen it coming, but Mark maintains he had an inkling. What *is* on record is that Jon went to see Gerry Bron the next day and told him that *Colosseum* was 'history'. It hadn't been long since Gerry had launched Bronze Records and at that time *Colosseum* was the main band on the label. Gerry recalls: "Jon knocked on my door and said that he had something very important to talk to me about but I had someone with me. I told him I was busy, but he was insistent, so I said I'd speak to him outside the office." Suffice to say, Jon's news put Gerry Bron in shock.

The band's final gig was at Sheffield University on 23rd October 1971, which, in the past, had always been one of their best and most enjoyable gigs. On this occasion, however, there was a sense of anticlimax, which seemed to mirror their current circumstances. The audience was sparse, compared to their previous appearances, because the University authorities, in their wisdom, had banned outsiders, due to some 'aggro' between 'town and gown' in previous weeks. So *Colosseum* finally went out with a whimper, rather than a bang. There were those who thought that the logical step might have been to try and find a replacement for Clem, but it was soon clear that nothing was further from Jon's mind. The opening lines of of *Skellington*, as sung by Chris Farlowe, come to mind: "I lit a flame to happiness...smoke got in my eyes,"...which aptly sum up the band's situation in those final weeks

It's obvious that the main cause of the band's problems was a general malaise coupled with fatigue, and Jon Hiseman wasn't the only one who felt it. Even Gerry Bron admitted to being affected: "My reaction to Clem leaving was my biggest mistake as a manager, because I didn't try to dissuade Jon. I think I could have persuaded him, but for some reason I didn't. Maybe I was getting a bit fed up with it as well." The truth is that Gerry had a rising star in *Uriah Heep* and they got his creative juices flowing. Mark Clarke recently recalled *his* reaction: "I felt we had been on the road for years and it was as if there was just no will left and everyone wanted out. The tragedy was, we were still evolving — just a few weeks before in Bologna, after one of our best gigs, Jon told me for the first time 'you played brilliantly tonight' or something like that. On that night in Italy something changed and Jon felt it." Dick also made a valid point about Clem's leaving in his book: "His departure delivered a death blow to a debilitated creature. If it hadn't happened, the band might well have gone on, but it wasn't the real reason. A healthy band could have handled something as disastrous as the loss of a lead guitarist, but then again, perhaps, the lead guitarist of a healthy band would not have wished to have left."

Adding to Jon's concerns during the previous six months had been his sense of a 'sea change' in the music business. Harry Isles always said that if something wasn't right, Jon would pick up on it. Being the only one of the band who saw the books (kept by Bron's accountant) he noticed that receipts were dropping of and began to sense that the audience's enthusiasm for instrumental-based music was on the wane.

On the 6th of November 1971, *Melody Maker* trumpeted

'*Colosseum* Split' — with Jon citing 'musical problems' and asserting that the members of the group were all 'moving in different directions'.

During the summer of 1971, the band had been working hard on songs for the next studio album but they hadn't gone well. Dick put a brave face on it to Ray Telford of *Sounds*: "At present, *Colosseum* is rehearsing new material and a completely new show," — in other words, "shelving the old *Colosseum*." Dick also mentioned that there were some shorter numbers, but there is no doubt the flagship of this new direction was the lengthy *Pirate's Dream*. Dick wrote candidly in his book: "It started life as a twinkle in Jon's eye and gradually grew until it became a 12-minute epic albatross that hung around *Colosseum*'s neck." Jon admitted: "It was entirely my fault; I created the monster by writing an innocent set of lyrics — a series of disjointed jokes on the madness of dreams, but Dick thought they were fantastic and wanted to do something with them. I suggested it should contain a long, entirely written solo for the band to interweave round and the climax would be improvised solo trades. So the eventual structure was there from the beginning. Dick undertook to write the outline of the written section for sax and guitar and Clem worked closely with him at rehearsals, modifying the lines and adding harmonies etc." Chris's extraordinary vocal range was also showcased and initially he enthusiastically talked up the piece in the press. Dave sat stoically throughout, waiting to see what would develop — it was all a long way from what he wanted to write or play, but he didn't complain.

In the early days, Jon had always said that the band could try out a piece for a few months and if it didn't work, it would be dropped. Yet *Dream* had been in the pipeline for 10 months! It ought to have been apparent by then that, even with the constant tinkering, it wasn't working. Was this another indication that they were losing their way?

Oddly enough, Clem has a writing credit on it, though, as he admitted recently, he'd never really liked it: "I only got involved in the writing of *The Pirate's 'Nightmare'* (so christened by Dave) because Dick badgered me into helping him realise his fantasy of a long 'written' solo, which would be orchestrated for guitar and sax. The song, and the arrangement of it, summed up for me the direction I personally didn't think the band should be going in and I know that Dave and Chris also agreed with that. In fact, Dave recently reminded me that, at one of the many arduous rehearsals devoted to the piece, Chris said he had to go to the toilet — and we never saw him again that day!" Time certainly hasn't changed Clem's opinion. Jon recently sent him a CD of a *Colosseum* live performance, with a view to including it on a European tour. Clem: "I think it's quite atrocious, it's totally devoid of any emotion or taste and it's the perfect ammunition for anyone wanting to deride the whole prog-rock scene!"

Over the years, Dave Greenslade had written a lot of the music for the band, but this was a barren time for him: "The beginning of the end for me was *The Pirate's Dream*. It was a clever piece of writing, but I didn't feel comfortable and my heart wasn't in it. I didn't think it was right for us, but Jon and Dick really wanted to play that piece. I had done a lot of writing over the preceding months but it got kicked into touch. I was getting a bit confused and didn't know what to do next. We had lost our way..." Dave also feels that he was partly to blame: "...because if I had come up with some strong new material perhaps *The Pirate's Dream* wouldn't have been so important."

Jon remembers feeling increasingly desperate that no new material was forthcoming and was very conscious that any new album would be judged against the success of *Colosseum Live*. They had tried out material in both Lansdowne and Advision Studios and the general consensus was that they were getting nowhere. Dick told *Sounds*: "There is no one in *Colosseum* who is a natural songwriter, which means we write very slowly." They had played the *Valentyne Suite* to death and, bearing in mind that all the *Colosseum Live* material had been honed in live performance long before recording it, they were now desperate to play something new. With no other material on the horizon, they were stuck with *The Pirate's Dream*, which apparently was neither popular nor playable!

The odd thing is, Jon doesn't remember any really serious objections being raised. During all that time in rehearsal, he didn't pick up any tangible feeling of animosity or indifference to the piece. Yes, the rehearsals had been hard, but they invariably were — people were tired, bored and sometimes tempers got frayed — all the usual stuff — but never any serious discussion about not going ahead with the piece. The band always jointly agreed the programming of the show and it *was* included in all their final gigs. Jon, doggedly, still thinks it could have been saved: "We'd actually written too much — if about a third of the writing had been cut and the solo trades lengthened, it might have worked a lot better...but that's with the gift of hindsight. At the time I couldn't see the wood for the trees."

Some even thought that *The Pirate's Dream* would be the title of the next studio album, but even if it *had* become a reality, could it have saved the band? Mark Clarke thought it would have had disastrous consequences: "What I remember of that piece was that it didn't help us move forward as a band. In fact, it sent us off in all directions and split us right up the middle." The media response to *The Pirate's Dream* was mixed, often drawing the obvious comparison with *Valentyne Suite*, but two reviews do stand out — neither particularly favourable. The first, Chris Charlesworth's piece for *Melody Maker* on the Weeley Festival: "They played their new suite, with its moods and extended solos. It was an early public airing and it sounded too tight and over-rehearsed, but once they have been playing it for a while and the solos are more fluid, it will become a firm favourite in their repertoire." The second comes from Chris

Welch's review of the Albert Hall gig: "It is not intended as a put-down to say the *The Pirate's Dream* was a mess. There wasn't enough time for individual solos to develop and the rhythm section was generally so busy that the overall sound became blurred." Ultimately, he thought the new work had diminished the impact of the whole set.

Reading the reviews now, Jon feels that the piece was largely misunderstood: "Both audience and critics were probably expecting more of the same old *Colosseum* and their constant reference to unsatisfactory solos indicated they just didn't get the idea of a completely composed piece of music — they just thought it was poor improvisation. Having said that, regardless of what they did or did not understand about the premise for the piece, if it didn't touch them, it failed."

Dick also mentions in his book that, by mid-1971, Jon felt tired and isolated, possibly a contributory factor in the break-up. Jon admitted to Steve Peacock of *Sounds* in 1973 that the band lost sight of its *raison d'etre*: "The individual musicians, myself included, never fully understood what we had — what *Colosseum* was really about. We pulled for each other and for ourselves, but we never really pulled for the band. Nobody really sat down and thought 'what can I do for *Colosseum*?' Then the thing begins to fragment; it becomes more and more difficult to find new material and nobody was prepared to sublimate their own vision of the direction they wished to take, for the collective good." Of course, most bands hit problems sooner or later, but with six highly individual personalities such as these, the potential for a catastrophic loss of direction was always there.

Another consideration was Chris Farlowe's recurring bouts of sickness. Dick makes reference in his book to Chris pulling out of the Scandinavian tour: "Discussions were under way with a view to replacing him, as it was felt in some quarters that we might have to." Jon was also vexed by this problem and the added pressure it brought: "It was a very difficult time — I hated that tour without Chris. I knew we couldn't present ourselves properly. Also, his militaria business was taking more and more of his time and we wondered how committed to the band he was, which all became academic when these issues were resolved by the break-up." Chris explained in an interview with Steve Turner, why he was devoting so much time to his shop, saying that it made four times as much as he earned with *Colosseum*.

Colosseum's demise also prompted Colin Richardson to move on, as he explains: "I told Gerry Bron I was resigning straight away. I knew that with *Colosseum* out of the picture, my role with Bron Artiste Management was reduced, so I decided on a pre-emptive strike. Though Clem's departure was the catalyst for the break-up, I had a feeling that it came as a relief to Jon. He was aware that Dave and Dick were finding it ever more difficult to sustain the flow of new material and he knew that without that, the band would lose its momentum. Jon also knew that this would lead to the live performances stagnating, as well as delaying the all-important next album. All this put him under a lot of pressure and I sensed he was ready for a change."

One positive by-product of the break-up was that Scott Thompson and Clive Davies, the sound engineers, did a deal with Jon whereby they took over the van and some of the sound equipment to set up a PA hire company, Colac (*Colosseum* Acoustics) which became very successful, although Jon personally never saw any income from it!

Jon Hiseman is the first to acknowledge that *Colosseum* was a difficult band to market commercially, but added recently: "In the end, we didn't get the help we needed in order to make it internationally. When we were at our lowest ebb, struggling to find new material in those final months, we still got no help. Having said that, we *were* very headstrong young men and I ran a very self-sufficient operation. Gerry Bron and his dad were from a different era and they didn't fully understand us; they were hoping *we* had the answers. Later on, I made the same mistakes with my daughter's first album — so history repeats itself."

The simple and basic truth is that some bands last longer than others — in *Colosseum*'s case, three years seemed to be its allotted span. Perhaps, to take another line from *Skellington*, they pushed too hard: "don't keep chasing happiness...let it take you by surprise."

The last word is with Jon, who sums it up with typical candour: "The whole point was, we never faced up to our problems. We had worked so hard for three years, we were exhausted and we split because the way forward was not clear. Faced with the task of following up the live album without Clem, who had clearly lost confidence in the band, we had no alternative but to take a 23-year holiday! Seriously though, Chris Welch just stated what I already knew but couldn't face. In fact, a journalist can often say the things you can't put into words yourself and unlike so many 'hack' journalists, who know nothing and spin out publicity sheets, Chris knew the business intimately and had a great nose for the era. His was, in many ways, the voice of our musical generation."

A month later, Bronze Records rush-released *The Collectors Colosseum*, which included all the tracks on the US album, *The Grass is Greener*, that hadn't been released in the UK — together with James Litherland's under-rated *I Can't Live Without You*, from the very first studio sessions. Rumours that the album was an attempt by Bron to cash in on the split are completely without foundation. The fact is, it was already out in Europe and was scheduled for release in the UK early in 1972. It had been Jon's idea to provide a stopgap until the next studio album was ready. Also, for the European fans, it fulfilled a useful function, as over half of the album was new to most of them, but at the same time it heralded the end of the original band's recorded legacy.

Harry Isles once commented that Jon never harboured grudges and always moved on, but would that still hold true? The answer is that Jon, Dick, Tony, James, Dave, Clem, Chris and Mark stayed in touch and more importantly, have remained friends until the present day. On the 4th of December, 1971, just weeks after the ill-fated Albert Hall concert, Chris Welch got married — and a certain Mr. Hiseman joined in the impromptu jam session at the reception, together with the multitude of other notable musicians assembled for the event.

FOOTNOTES

1. When Jon was in his early teens, his father had taken him on several occasions to watch the recording of the legendary *Goon Show* at the BBC Theatre, Camden. Radio and TV shows always have someone to 'warm up' the audience, usually a comedian, but rarely a member of the show's cast. Unusually, the *Goon Show* 'warm-up' was by its stars, Peter Sellers playing drums (he had, in fact, started his career as a professional drummer), Spike Milligan playing a jazzy trumpet and Harry Secombe singing. These 'jam sessions' had almost as big an impact on Jon as their off-the-wall humour. Looking back, Jon now thinks that the *Goons*' surreal comedy had an incredibly liberating effect on him and his immediate circle. This gloriously anarchic commentary on British life blew away the relatively strictured thinking of early post-war society – the very thinking that prevailed with the 'toffs' running the BBC, who disapproved of the show, which they frequently and erroneously referred to as '*The Go On Show*'!

Colosseum

TOP: Bass drum
heads painted
by John Mayall

ABOVE:
Colosseum early
rehearsal

RIGHT:
Colosseum play
The Marquee

237

SHE'S THE COLOSSEUM'S SECRET WEAPON

YOU could describe tenor saxophonist Barbara Thompson as the Colosseum's secret weapon. For though Barbara, married to Colosseum's leader Jon Hiseman, never appears with her husband's group in public—instead, she leads her own jazz quintet—she does play on several of their records including their latest album, *Valentyre Suite*, tipped in this column a few weeks ago and now in the best-selling charts.

eite 40 · Bremer Nachrichten

Bremen

Rock + Bl

Top: Left-right: Dave Greenslade, Dick Heckstall-Smith, Tony Reeves, James Litherland

ABOVE AND RIGHT: BT in *Titbits*; BT and JH at *Beat Club*, Bremen

OPPOSITE: Bath Festival, 1970

MEMORANDUM TO THE COLOSSEUM

Friday 11th –
Saturday 12th October : Scene 2, Aberdeen Walk, Scarborough.

Equipment to arrive by 6.30p.m.
Artistes to arrive by 8.00p.m.
On stage between 9.00 – 1.00a.m. (1x75 mins. sp

(Collect £150 cheque on night)
Road Manager and Band to telephone SCAR:2506 by
: 5.00p.m. on Friday to reassure promoter you are
on your way.

: Redcar Jazz Club, Coatham Hotel, Redcar.

Equipment to arrive by 6.30p.m.
Artistes to arrive by 7.00p.m.
On stage between 7.30 and 10.30p.m. (2x45 mins.

(Collect £70 cheque on night)

: Eel Pie Island, Twickenham.

Equipment to arrive by 6.30p.m.
Artistes to arrive by 9.00p.m.
On stage 10.00p.m. (1x75 mins. spo

(Collect £55 in cash on night)

Thursday 17th October : Railway Hotel, Wealdstone.

Equipment to arrive by 7.00p.m.
Artistes to arrive by 7.30p.m.
On stage between 8.00 and 12.00 midnight.
(2x45 mins. spo
(Collect cash on night – £45 against 60% taking

Saturday 19th October : Possible Bradford Club.

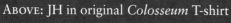

ABOVE: JH in original *Colosseum* T-shirt

RIGHT: Clem Clempson

BELOW AND BELOW RIGHT: Colin Richardson — *Colosseum* manager and editor of this book, with the boys and in the Bron office

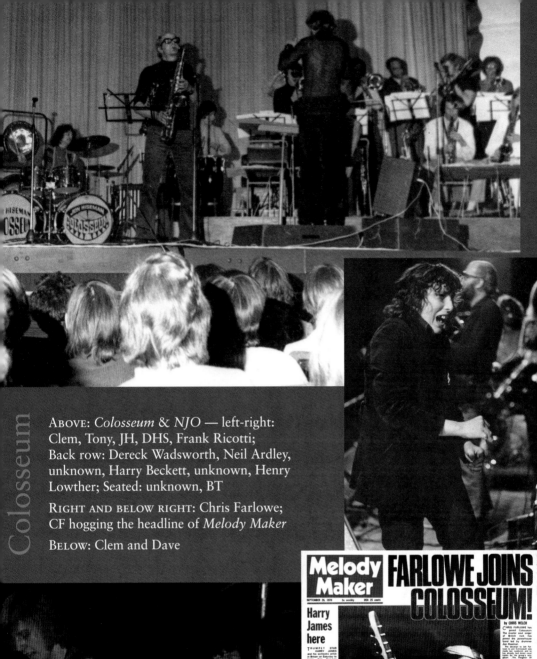

Colosseum

ABOVE: *Colosseum* & *NJO* — left-right:
Clem, Tony, JH, DHS, Frank Ricotti;
Back row: Dereck Wadsworth, Neil Ardley,
unknown, Harry Beckett, unknown, Henry
Lowther; Seated: unknown, BT

RIGHT AND BELOW RIGHT: Chris Farlowe;
CF hogging the headline of *Melody Maker*

BELOW: Clem and Dave

Melody Maker

FARLOWE JOINS COLOSSEUM!

SEPTEMBER 26, 1970   3s weekly   USA 25 cents

Harry James here

Why I smash guitars, by Deep Purple man Ritchie

SEE PAGE 26

Hendrix blues

241

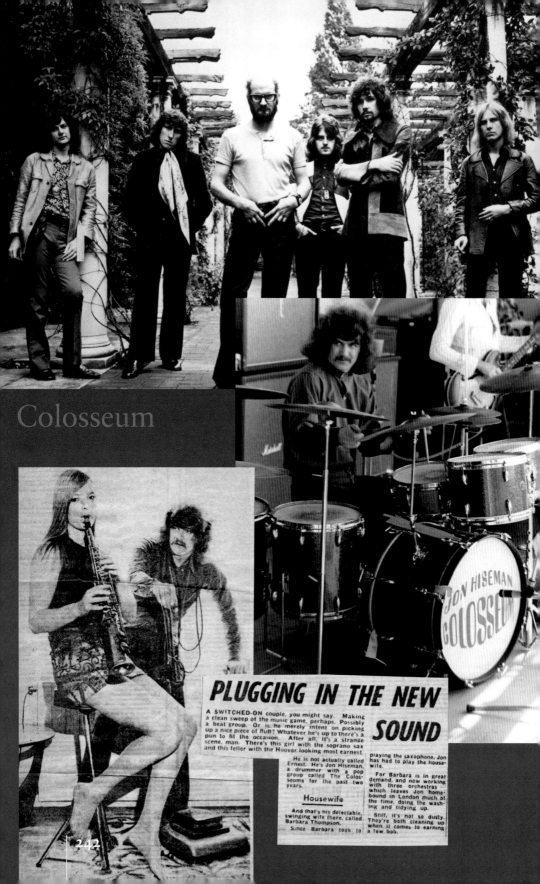

Colosseum

PLUGGING IN THE NEW SOUND

A SWITCHED-ON couple, you might say. Making a clean sweep of the music game, perhaps. Possibly a beat group. Or is he merely intent on picking up a nice piece of fluff? Whatever he's up to there's a pun to fit the occasion. After all, it's a strange scene, man. There's this girl with the soprano sax and this feller with the Hoover looking most earnest.

He is not actually called Ernest. He's Jon Hiseman, a drummer with a pop group called The Colosseums for the past two years.

Housewife

And that's his delectable, swinging wife there, called Barbara Thompson.

Since Barbara took to playing the saxophone, Jon has had to play the housewife.

For Barbara is in great demand, and now working with three orchestras which leaves Jon home-bound in London much of the time, doing the washing and tidying up.

Still, it's not so dusty. They're both cleaning up when it comes to earning a few bob.

LEFT: *Colosseum* publicity pic, 1971

BELOW LEFT: JH with his great Gretsch kit

THIS PAGE: The Classic *Colosseum* — left-right: Dave, JH, Chris Farlowe, Clem, DHS, Mark Clarke

LEFT: BT & JH, pregnant at the Manor, 1972

RIGHT: The original *Tempest* — left-right: JH, Mark Clarke, Paul Williams, Allan Holdsworth

RIGHT CENTRE: *Tempest* Logo; Allan Holdsworth

BELOW RIGHT: JH with *Tempest* Full Kit

BELOW: Recording DHS's *A Story Ended* — Chris Farlowe, Paul Williams, Graham Bond

A Story Ended

Tempest

TEMPEST

JON HISEMAN

245

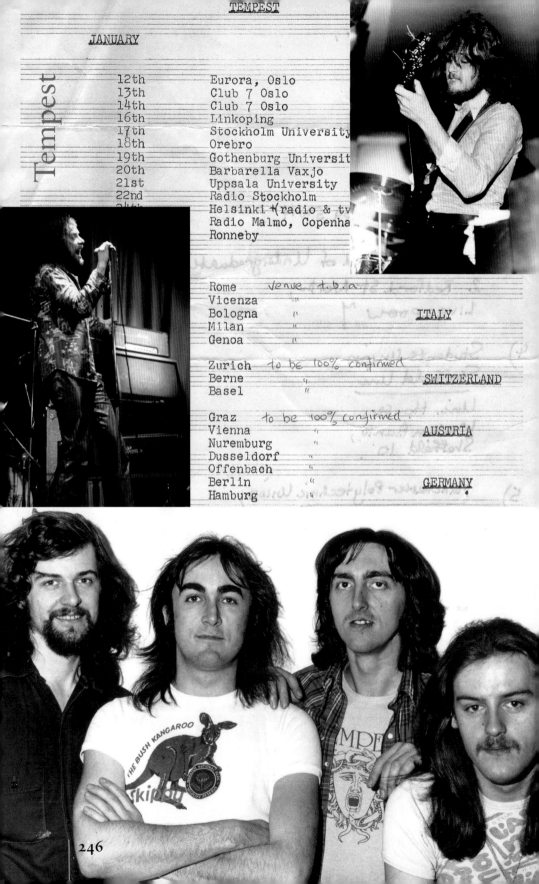

Tempest

JANUARY

12th	Eurora, Oslo	
13th	Club 7 Oslo	
14th	Club 7 Oslo	
16th	Linkoping	
17th	Stockholm University	
18th	Orebro	
19th	Gothenburg Universit	
20th	Barbarella Vaxjo	
21st	Uppsala University	
22nd	Radio Stockholm	
	Helsinki + (radio & tv	
	Radio Malmo, Copenha	
	Ronneby	

Rome	venue t.b.a	
Vicenza	"	
Bologna	"	ITALY
Milan	"	
Genoa	"	
Zurich	to be 100% confirmed	
Berne	"	SWITZERLAND
Basel	"	
Graz	to be 100% confirmed	
Vienna	"	AUSTRIA
Nuremburg	"	
Dusseldorf	"	
Offenbach	"	
Berlin	"	GERMANY
Hamburg		

246

OPPOSITE ABOVE: Paul, Mark

OPPOSITE BELOW: *Tempest* with Ollie Halsall and Allan together

ABOVE: The last *Tempest*, by now a trio — Ollie, JH, Mark

RIGHT: Ollie and JH

BELOW: *Colosseum II* signing contract — JH, Lillian Bron, Gary Moore, Gerry Bron

Colosseum II

Colosseum II

RIGHT: The boy protege, with THE Les Paul

BELOW: *Colosseum II* — left-right: Neil Murray, JH, GM, Mike Starrs, Don Airey

BOTTOM: DA in reflective mood; *Colosseum II* — John Mole, JH, GM

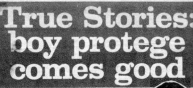

True Stories: boy protege comes good

Gary quits Skid Row and Thin Lizzy but finds happiness is a warm Hiseman

REMEMBER SUPER speedo guitarist Gary Moore? Well it seems a lot of you do gathering from enquiries that have filtered into the office. The last heard from Gary he was in Thin Lizzy — a short-lived stay. Then apparently Gary went to Germany to sort things out.

In fact, Moore's been in Britain since August when he met that ace skin beater Jon Hiseman. "We met out of musical frustration. We were both sitting at home thinking of packing it in. I didn't want to do anything unless it was with the best people."

Before we get into Moore's present plans let's take a look into his illustrious past. At only 22, Moore has matured into one of Britain's major guitar talents.

Moore's professional career began when he was sixteen with a band called Skid Row formed by bass player Brush Shields. Wasn't it in fact Brush who taught Moore

248

"It was so clean and simple — the antithesis of the complicated music I had played since 1966."
JON HISEMAN on *Tempest*

"There's no place I've not left in great haste, for the journey back home to you."
Foyers of Fun — lyrics by Jon Hiseman

Chapter 13

FOYERS OF FUN

AFTER THE BREAK-UP, JON HISEMAN PAUSED and took stock of things. A month or so earlier *Colosseum* had played the Zurich Jazz Festival and while he was there Barbara phoned Jon with the news that she was pregnant. Both of their careers so far had left them precious little time for a private life and Jon determined not to make any long-term plans, as he wanted to be present at the birth. He was, however, open to any short-term project that took his fancy and almost immediately one came up. *Emerson, Lake & Palmer* had just finished recording their latest album, *Trilogy* and Keith Emerson was now looking to lay down some solo tracks before their next American tour. He decided he wanted to use Jon Hiseman and the *New Jazz Orchestra*, including all the usual suspects — Ian Carr, Henry Lowther, Mike Gibbs *et al...and* a heavily pregnant Barbara Thompson.

After some discussion with Jon, Keith booked Olympic No.1 studio for the 24th and 25th of February. The first track they put down was Charlie Parker's *Au Privave*.[1] NJO stalwart Dave Gelly, who was on the session, remembers it being a difficult piece to master and several takes were required. Chris Welch of *Melody Maker* was there, observing their efforts: "Jon Hiseman was leaping around the control room, his face contorted as he detected mistakes in his playing that were not apparent to anybody else." According to Chris, there was a moment of magic when the combination of Keith's dexterity, the power of the *NJO* and Jon's superb drumming brought forth spontaneous cheering in the control room: "Keith grinned as the big band steamed into the medley of eight Parker themes, brilliantly arranged by Neil Ardley." The second track was Meade Lux Lewis's *Honky Tonk Train Blues*, with an Alan Cohen arrangement featuring a Dave Gelly clarinet solo, which unexpectedly became a minor hit for Keith in 1976. As there was still some time remaining, they recorded one more track, which, at Jon's suggestion, was a blues by Gary Burton, *Walter L.* The sessions were deemed by one and all to have been a resounding success and there was a definite feeling of anti-climax when they were over. Later, it was suggested that Jon and Keith should perform together somewhere, but as both of them were so heavily committed, this proved to be logistically impossible.

Neil Ardley had developed quite an interest in electronic music at the time and was fascinated by Keith's original modular Moog synthesiser, one of the early versions, which looked like an old telephone switchboard. It was an incredible piece of gear, with cables leading off in all directions and wasn't exactly easy to use, since each and every sound had to be created 'on the hoof', there being no system for storing pre-sets.

The *NJO* story is the stuff of legend, in a way. Dave Gelly recently summed it up: "It was never formally wound up. It sort of melted away as Neil's ideas developed and the rest of us pursued our various musical careers. Looking back, I'd say that we made a decisive break with the standard jazz big-band approach and created a band with its own distinct style and sound. Listening to the recordings again, after all these years, I honestly don't think anyone picked up where we left off. Jazz orchestras nowadays are more technically accomplished than we were, mainly because they've all been to Music College, but jazz is tricky stuff and too much polish leads to anonymity." The *NJO*'s legacy is enshrined in the two albums they recorded, *Western Reunion* and *Le Dejeuner Sur l'Herbe*, which are still in demand today.

Jon Hiseman hardly had time to draw breath before the start of his next project. Gerry Bron, who still had *Colosseum* technically under contract, was quietly optimistic that Jon and Dick would each do something of their own. Dick quickly expressed an interest in making a solo album, with Jon as producer and using the aborted Advision session tapes as demos. As Dick had also been working on-and-off with lyricist Pete Brown since the late '60s, he had plenty of other material in hand. He decided to split the album in half — one side would feature his work with Pete Brown and the other, the *Colosseum* material that had been scheduled for their fourth album. Having Jon produce was all-important, as Dick was determined to record *The Pirate's Dream* for posterity.

Dick assembled an impressive array of musicians at Richard Branson's new Manor Studio[2]. Richard had rung up Jon a couple of times hustling business for this new enterprise and he had booked two five-day sessions at the end of March and beginning of April 1972...not exactly a lot of time to record a whole album! Arthur Heckstall-Smith vividly remembers being taken to the studio in Chris Farlowe's new Range Rover, with his dad's partner Christine, and recalls that there was quite a positive atmosphere. *The Pirate's Dream* would form the crux of the album, using the same arrangement that *Colosseum* had played[3]. Although Paul Williams was the main vocalist on the album, it was decided that Chris Farlowe should sing on this track, as he had rehearsed it with *Colosseum* for so long. He was quite happy to do this, but Dave Greenslade decided to bow out[4]. Dick writes in his book that it was recorded quite quickly but Mark Clarke disagrees: "It took forever to record that whole work. I remember poor Graham Bond sitting in the Manor studio laying down the organ part a few phrases at a time." Jon remembers a very genial Bond, with young girlfriend by his side, exuding a ghastly kind of 'love for all mankind', but he could sense the ominous cracks beneath this façade.

With recording over, Jon felt he had finally woken up from *The Pirate's Dream*. They started mixing, but after a couple of tracks had been completed, the engineer Tom Newman was so exhausted that he couldn't continue. Though Jon and Dick were paying for his services from 10am to 10pm every day, he had also been working nights on a speculative Mike Oldfield project during studio 'downtime'. This situation, though frustrating at the time, presented Jon with an interesting challenge. It turned out that this 'other project' was the iconic album *Tubular Bells*, the phenomenal (and unexpected) sales of which laid the foundation for the Virgin label and, ultimately, the Branson Empire.

To digress for a moment, it's worth mentioning here how recording techniques had evolved in the few years since Jon first visited a studio. When he recorded with Mike Taylor at

Lansdowne and the *NJO* at Decca in '65, it was to a single-track tape recorder, i.e. in mono and the performance that the listener heard on the record was just as it was played in the studio. A couple of years later, the *Beatles* had famously used three- and four-track tape recorders to great effect, but by the time of the *Colosseum Live* album, eight-track recording was the norm. Any more than two tracks always had to be remixed to mono or stereo to make the master tape, from which the record was produced. Crucially for the rock and pop business, multi-track recording allowed overdubbing — recording on one track, while listening through headphones to what had already been recorded on the others — for example, when adding vocals or an instrumental solo to a 'backing-track'.

By the early '70s, the *modus operandi* for rock bands was for them to play together when recording the backing tracks, but with the drums isolated, usually in a separation booth. The drum track had to be absolutely right, as it was the rhythmic guide for the other musicians when they overdubbed their individual contributions, replacing or adding to, the original tracks. This meant, of course, that the drummer had to get it right first time, while everybody else could experiment with their parts. In theory, the drummer's role was over once the original tracks were laid, so he could either disappear into the night, or sit with the engineer while all the overdubbing went on. Jon, being Jon, always opted for the latter — watching, asking awkward questions and learning. Back at the Manor Studio, all this was about to pay off.

After giving him a 30-minute crash course on the idiosyncrasies of the desk, its signal-paths and the tape-machine's target audio levels, engineer Tom Newman staggered off to bed and Jon added the role of mix-engineer to that of producer. Feeling his way into it, the mixing of the shorter pieces went well enough, but after spending a frustrating and fruitless couple of days on *The Pirate's Dream*, Jon realised he needed several extra, and experienced, pairs of hands. The problem centred on the fact that the mixing desk, like all desks back then, had manually operated faders with which to adjust each track's level (volume). *Dream* was so complex that most of the eight tracks were full, with a variety of different instruments, vocals and effects. To create the stereo master tape, all the levels had to be manually balanced using the faders, while the piece was being played through. Make a mistake — and it was back to 'square one'!

So, Jon contacted the most experienced record producer he knew — Gerry Bron, who needed no persuading to lend his studio 'nous'. He immediately booked Lansdowne Studio, with engineer Peter Gallen. Jon recalls the painful process: "Gerry wrote a chart of what had to be done, where and by whom — he was the master of ceremonies. We had eight hands on the knobs and faders and everyone had to know their part. After many false starts and the inevitable killer mistakes near the end of the take, we finally recorded a complete stereo master."

As a result of seizing the chance opportunity to mix this album, Jon fell head-over-heels in love with the recording and mixing process, but most of all with the control it gave over the finished product. It would be 10 years before he would build his own 'state-of-the-art' studio and fully realise his dream, but as Jon admitted: "The lesson that stayed with me out of all this came from a chance remark made by Adrian Kerridge, then head of Lansdowne Studios. We were playing the tapes I had mixed at the Manor and Adrian popped his head round the door. 'What do you think?' I asked. He put his hand up in front of his mouth...'sounds boxy'[5], he replied thickly. I turned to listen — and he was right. I still had a lot to learn!"

Dick decided to call the album *A Story Ended*, inspired by his favourite poet, T.S. Eliot. It was released in August '72 on the Bronze label, to some goodish reviews, the one in *Sounds* concluding: "It's a fine accomplishment and far from being *A Story Ended*, it's just the beginning." Dick immediately began putting a band together, but soon realised that it wasn't as easy as he thought. He discovered that, to be a bandleader, you needed the ability to make quick, sometimes spontaneous, decisions, responding to situations over which you often had little or no control. This was not in Dick's nature — he preferred the time to think things through and then to discuss and plan everything. Consequently, he was under a great deal of stress — admitting in his book: "I was unhappy. The reason was, that *I* was now in control and I didn't want to be, but it wasn't that I didn't like being a bandleader or that I couldn't handle the responsibility." Or maybe it was the realisation that, as a bandleader, he would no longer find the stage 'the safest place in the world'.

Jon was still in the process of planning his future, when, on 19th June 1972, Barbara gave birth to their son Marcus...and the proud father was there to record his first cries. Keith Emerson and his wife, whose children had passed the baby stage, kindly donated their carrycot and changing table.

Earlier in the year, Jon had been out to Germany to guest on an album with Wolfgang Dauner's band, *Knasch* and to play the Frankfurt Jazz Festival with them. Jon remembers this gig as the first time he felt drunk going on stage — not that it took *much* for him to feel drunk! He was ashamed of how badly he had played, feeling he'd let the side down, so he was quite astonished when, coming off stage, he was given a big hug by promoter Horst Lippmann. Nevertheless, he made a mental note to stay away from booze till after the show in future!

About this time, Jon was considering an offer to work with Robert Fripp of *King Crimson*. On the face of it, this was a little strange, given their clash at *Melody Maker*'s 'round table discussion' in 1970, but musically it could have been very interesting. Jon told *Sounds*: "We met on several occasions and talked things over, but it became obvious that we disagreed about so many things, almost without saying them." By the time Fripp got back from America, it was clear that it wasn't going to happen. Jon did, however, get to play on Dave Cousins' (of the *Strawbs*) first solo album: *Two Weeks Last Summer*, while Keith Emerson was still chasing him to find out when they were going to finish *his* solo album.

While all this was going on, Jon was offered the chance to produce an album for an old friend; renowned jazz trumpeter (and future music biographer) Ian Carr. Jon had first met Ian when he 'guested' with *The Ian Bird Quintet* at the Jazzhouse, Blackheath and he had been a great source of encouragement to the young drummer during the time they both played with the *NJO*. Jon had also 'depped' occasionally with Ian's group *Nucleus*, and now Ian had turned to Jon for help and advice with his management and recording contracts. It appeared that his relationship with the band's manager, Pete King, had broken down and Ian wanted to deal directly with his record label, Vertigo. They, of course, were very receptive to the idea of the 'famed' Jon Hiseman of *Colosseum* producing the next *Nucleus* album and the result was that, in July 1972, Jon and the band met at Phonogram's studio to record *Belladonna*.[6]

Jon was quite clear that with a musical band like *Nucleus*, it was not his job to choose material or alter arrangements, but to act as a conduit between the sounds and visions in the musician's heads and the somewhat intimidating technology of the recording studio. For the mixing and mastering, Jon wanted the skills of Lansdowne's studio engineer Peter Gallen, who had worked on *Colosseum Live* and had recently remixed the *Pirate's Dream*. For the first time, Jon was in complete control. He was trusted by Ian and the band, but 'outside' the music, with no performing role. It proved both an enjoyable *and* instructive experience. Unfortunately, it wasn't the definitive *Nucleus* line-up and the album was not as well received as the band's previous two releases, but in Jon's opinion, one track — *Suspension* — remains one of Ian's most satisfying recordings.

Prompted by Gerry Bron, who was still reminding him that he was under contract, Jon began to think about forming another band. As before, he searched for another single-word, powerful-sounding name like *Colosseum* and after much thought settled on *Tempest*, which met with universal approval. Given the task of coming up with a logo for the band, brilliant young designer Fabio Nicoli asked what kind of music would be played and Jon presented him with a set of lyrics that he had just completed inspired by the Greek myth of Medusa (a Gorgon with writhing serpents for hair and piercing eyes — anyone who beheld her was instantly turned to stone!). Fabio created a stylised Medusa-head as the band logo and now all Jon had to do was recruit the personnel!

First in was Mark Clarke, who had joined *Uriah Heep* when *Colosseum* folded, but had left soon after due to their ridiculous workload, though not before co-writing the album track that would become a *Heep* anthem, *The Wizard*...which was quite surprising, as he'd never written anything for *Colosseum*. However, his newly discovered song-writing talent would be put to good use in *Tempest*. Mark recalls his reaction when he got Jon's call: "When we had the meeting that broke *Colosseum* up, I think it was me who may have felt the worst pain as I was just beginning to open up as a bass player, which Jon had noticed — that's why he asked me to start *Tempest* with him." In fact, also at the back of Jon's mind was that Mark might quickly develop into a lead vocalist.

Now Jon needed a guitarist and by one of those strokes of good fortune, happened upon a virtual unknown, Allan Holdsworth. He'd originally been spotted as a semi-pro playing at the Mecca Ballroom, Sunderland and had been persuaded to try his luck in London, and in no time at all he was playing in the house band at Ronnie Scott's Jazz Club. His name swept around the jazz circuit like a brush fire, but it was Jon Hiseman who got in first, as he told *Sounds*: "I got word that he was in London and he came round to my place. After he'd played for ten minutes I knew he was right." Jon actually already knew Holdsworth as he had played on the *Nucleus* album *Belladonna*, which Jon had produced a few months earlier. Allan Holdsworth was a quiet, almost morose character, who would often disappear for days at a time and then turn up just before rehearsals began. Holdsworth had started out playing piano and clarinet and didn't actually start playing the guitar until he was 17!

257

Gerry Bron got quite a shock when Jon informed him how the new band would operate. Jon was well aware that a band could lose money playing badly routed gigs, which happens when the agency's prime concern is filling the date-sheet. A substantial chunk of the band's earnings went on commission — 10% to the agency, 15% to management (as well as 50% of record royalties going to Bron's Hit Record Productions). Jon wasn't complaining, but it was always deducted from the *gross* fees; if the date-sheet had you travelling from Bristol to Glasgow, then down to Southampton and back up to Leicester — the cost of transporting band and equipment was quite considerable and was borne, of course, by the group. So Gerry was told, in no uncertain terms, that *Tempest* would only do well-routed tours — not one-off gigs.

Jon did have some clout in this situation as he co-owned the PA company, Colac (*Colosseum* Acoustics), run by Scott Thompson and Clive Davies, the ex-*Colosseum* sound crew. Apart from *Tempest*, their clients included *Steppenwolf*, *CCS*, *Steeleye Span* and *Black Sabbath*, so hiring equipment for one-off gigs would've been impractical. He was determined to avoid all the problems that had so badly affected *Colosseum*, but in order to achieve some continuity he decided that press and publicity would again be handled by Frances van Staden

Right from the off, Jon planned for *Tempest* to be quite different from *Colosseum*; solid rock rhythms underpinning intelligent songs and short solos. Jon was keen to put his ideas on the record, telling Tony Stewart of *New Musical Express*: "I want to break with everything except the improvisational element in my music — same punch, but much more song-orientated." Also, he wanted to alter his drumming technique by changing his grip from orthodox to 'matched grip', which he had tried to do before, but had found impossible while playing with *Colosseum*. He felt that the matched grip would make playing a bigger kit easier, as he told *Melody Maker*: "You don't get your arms crossing up — but it took me four months to get my matched grip as good as my orthodox." Jon now believes that, for intricate work, the orthodox grip is preferable, but making the change to the matched grip definitely changed the way he thought about what he was doing. It enabled him to approach *Tempest* with a new mental *and* physical approach.

The early rehearsals went well, but Jon soon realised that Mark wasn't a forceful enough lead singer to front the band and when recording began, Jon knew the vocals would have to be re-done later. Jon recalls: "Mark's voice was much lighter then and wasn't really suited to our kind of music. With hindsight, it might have been better to forget the big instrumental thing and concentrate on writing songs for him, but I doubt our audience would have accepted it." As luck would have it, Paul Williams had just left *Juicy Lucy*, so Jon promptly grabbed him, delighted that someone of his ability had become available at the crucial moment. *Tempest*'s first album was different to anything Jon had done before — mainstream rock, but with a touch of class. Jon explains what defined the music: "It was so clean and simple, the antithesis of the complicated music I had played since 1966." Jon was in the producer's chair, while the engineers were John Punter and Denny Bridges. Apart from the lyrics, much of the writing was done 'in the round' and though this was all new to Allan Holdsworth, he still contributed to five of the eight songs recorded.

On the domestic front, Jon soon realised that he and Barbara would need a bigger house now they had a baby, eventually finding what they wanted in Hinchley Wood, just off the A3 in Surrey. Jon was still in touch with his old 'sparring-partner' Keef Hartley[7], who Jon had replaced in the Mayall band back in 1968. Due to some devious misinformation from one of the other *Bluesbreakers*, Keef had for several years believed that Jon had conspired with Mayall to oust him from the band, but in fact, the offer had been a complete surprise to Jon. The misunderstanding was eventually cleared up and they resumed their friendship, which remains strong to this day. On the face of it, you couldn't find two more dissimilar characters, but Jon always had a sneaking admiration for Keef's simplistic but

259

groovy drumming, as well as his ready wit and banter. Keef started his working life as a plumber's apprentice, but carpentry was his real passion and as *Tempest* started rehearsals, he and Jon worked on the new house, just as he had at Jon and Barbara's first property five years before. In 1977, when they moved to the huge Edwardian house in Sutton where they still live, Keef was there, creating and fitting the hand-crafted kitchen and five years later, he would carry out all the specialist acoustic carpentry for the studio which Jon would build in 1982.

Meanwhile, Dick Heckstall-Smith's career moved ahead as he began touring with his own band, *Manchild*, to promote the recently released *A Story Ended*. He brought in James Litherland on guitar, but *not* as lead vocalist. James explains: "I was going through a 'guitar period' where all I wanted to do was improve my playing. I never really thought about my voice as that was something which had always been there." The other band members were Billy Smith on bass, Theodore Thunder on drums and David Rose on keyboards. After just a few UK gigs, Gerry Bron had managed to secure them a six-week American tour, opening for *Deep Purple* and *Fleetwood Mac* (strangely coincidental, as these were the two bands that *Colosseum* was supposed join on the aborted 1971 tour). Things ostensibly went well, but apparently not well enough as, on their return to the UK, Dick parted company with the Bron Organisation, by mutual agreement.

Dick had plenty of new material in hand, so it made sense to record another album. In April 1973, the band booked time at Escape Studios in Kent, but Dick began suffering with back pain, related to a slipped disc he'd had 20 years earlier. En route to the studio one morning, his back simply seized up and he spent the next few months laying flat on the floor of his Hampstead apartment. During this time he did a lot of thinking, with the net result that the album never *did* get finished. Having immersed himself in music since his schooldays, he now came to realise how little understanding he had of the 'real world' and how it worked. So, as soon as he was partially mobile again, he enrolled at South Bank Polytechnic to study for a B.Sc. in Social Science. It would be three years before he picked up the saxophone again!

Tempest's album, however, was by now 'in the can' and the band started preparing for their live debut. Harry Isles returned as tour manager, with Scott Thompson and Clive Davies (as Colac) doing sound and lights. Initially the plan had been to start the UK tour in November, but the time it took finding a lead singer scuppered that idea. Then Paul Williams' arrival was delayed by contractual problems, so their UK debut was re-scheduled for March '73. Such was the interest in Jon's new band, that it was decided to embark on a six-week swing through Europe, kicking off in Oslo on the 12th of January, followed by dates in Italy, Switzerland, Austria and Germany. During this tour, Jon was interviewed on Radio Free Europe (a US-run station broadcasting propaganda to the Eastern Bloc countries) and offered to send a *Tempest* album to anyone who wrote in. He had made a similar offer before, with *Colosseum* and then as now, the result was a flood of letters...this time, it was the Bronze label that received over 700 requests...Gerry Bron was not amused!

FOOTNOTES

1. *Au Privave* and *Walter L* were eventually released as part of Keith Emerson's *Off the Shelf* album in 2006. Jon and Barbara recently heard it for the first time since the recording and both were astonished at how good it was. Barbara was especially impressed with Keith's solo on *Au Privave*.

2. The line-up for *A Story Ended* comprised: Paul Williams, Caleb Quaye, Mark Clarke, Rob Tait, Dave Greenslade, Gordon Beck, Graham Bond, Jon Hiseman, Chris Spedding and Chris Farlowe.

3. In 2006 Jon Hiseman began to help compile a *Colosseum* box set — in the process listening to several different versions of *The Pirate's Dream*, and noted that the early versions were quite different to the one recorded on Dick's album *A Story Ended*.

4. The line-up for *The Pirate's Dream* might have been even more interesting, if, as Dick's private notes indicate, his preferred musicians, Keith Emerson, John-Paul Jones and John Bonham had played on it. Jon, however, is sceptical: "Dick had a lot of fantasies, but he would never have got those guys to learn that piece. John Bonham wasn't that kind of drummer. One of the biggest mistakes a musician or producer can make is to enjoy a great performance played in one context and expect to get the same magic in a different context."

5. Adrian Kerridge's remark, 'sounds boxy,' referred to Jon's mix sounding slightly 'forward' in the lower-mid frequencies, whilst the highs and lows were slightly muted. Recording in the early '70s was beset by problems of frequency response, i.e. the range of sound, from the lowest bass to the highest treble, reproduced on a recording. To start with, the studio could have a sound characteristic that would distort this response, as could the choice of microphones or the cables. The tape recorders were quite good at capturing what came down the lines initially, but as the tapes were played back over and over again (during the overdubbing and mixing process), the magnetic oxide rubbed off the tape, thus diminishing some of the higher frequencies. However, all this could be compensated for during the final mix-down to stereo, by using the mixing desk's equalisation (sophisticated bass, middle and treble controls, known as EQ), but only providing the studio loudspeakers were reproducing the music accurately — which they often didn't! Any such improvement, however, could be scuppered during the tortuous process of transferring the music from the tapes to the finished LP, especially while 'cutting' the acetate master. This was a dark art that, in Jon's experience, never reproduced music that sounded anything like it did on the original master tape. Jon breathed a huge sigh of relief with the advent of the CD.

6. After *Belladonna* in 1972, Jon went on to produce other albums for Ian Carr: *Snakehips Etcetera* in 1975, working alongside famed engineer Steve Lillywhite, then later that same year, *Alleycat*. Then in May 1988, Jon engineered *The Old Heartland* suite of pieces that were recorded in the TM studio. A few years later, Ian conceived the idea of writing several compositions based on Shakespeare's plays, which he wanted to record in Southwark Cathedral as a duo with pianist John Taylor on the cathedral organ. He chose Southwark Cathedral because of its proximity to the rebuilt Globe Theatre as well as it being Shakespeare's boyhood parish church. The recording took place between the hours of midnight and dawn on May 30th and 31st, 1992. There was, however, one problem...the noise of the trains crossing Southwark Bridge. So Jon had to track down the British Rail engineering works manager, who was most accommodating and agreed to bring forward some maintenance work, so that the trains could be halted for two nights. In Ian Carr's own words: "All the pieces were inspired by words from Shakespeare and this — plus several hours spent at the dead of night in that magnificent environment — made the whole experience a very powerful one." The album, *Sounds and Sweet Airs*, was later released on the Celestial Harmonies label. Sadly, Ian died after a long debilitating illness on 25th February, 2009, and the whole of the British jazz world mourned his passing. His artistic contribution on so many levels cannot be overestimated.

7. Hartley's career began when he replaced Ringo Starr as the drummer with *Rory Storm and the Hurricanes*, a popular Liverpool-based band. Subsequently, he played and recorded with *The Artwoods* (an R&B band that included a young Jon Lord on organ) then achieved some notability as John Mayall's drummer before forming *The Keef Hartley Band*, which mixed elements of jazz, blues and rock 'n' roll into a jazz-rock sound comparable to *Blood, Sweat and Tears* and *Chicago*. They played at the Woodstock Festival in 1969 and released four popular albums, including *Halfbreed* and *The Battle of North West Six*. In November 1974, the UK music magazine, *NME*, reported that Hartley, who had been largely inactive since his band broke up in early 1972, had formed a new outfit called *Dog Soldier* who recorded just one album, the eponymously entitled *Dog Soldier* in 1975. In 2007, Hartley released a ghostwritten autobiography, *Halfbreed (A Rock And Roll Journey That Happened Against All The Odds)* that recounted his life growing up in Preston and his career as a drummer and bandleader.

*"Unbelievable! — it was like being
a pop star!"*
JON HISEMAN'S REACTION after *Tempest*
was mobbed at the Venice Festival

Chapter 14

IN THE EYE OF THE TEMPEST

*"He was one of those people they
call a catalyst and I, for one,
feel I owe him a very great deal."*
JON HISEMAN on the death of
Graham Bond

WHEN *Tempest* SET OFF ON THAT FIRST TOUR, they were in uncharted waters. Although Jon and Mark had experience of headline touring, Allan Holdsworth and Paul Williams had not. It was the first ever tour for Allan and Paul had rarely, if ever, headlined with *Juicy Lucy*, so there was quite a lot of pressure. Jon was also worried that the audiences would be expecting a reincarnation of *Colosseum*, but putting on a brave face, he told Tony Stewart of *NME*: "*Tempest* will become as well-known or even better known than any of the other bands I've had and that's because it's the best thing I've ever done." It was a bold statement to make and he would find out if the UK fans agreed when their eponymous debut album was released. A Swiss fan wrote recently to Jon: "I have never ceased to remember one of my first concerts where I heard you live with *Tempest*, together with Allan Holdsworth on guitar. I liked the album (with the song *Gorgon*) so much that I bought it twice!! That gig must have been in 1972 or '73, in St. Gallen, Switzerland. I was 18. It was an unforgettable happening to me. I could not sleep that night, in fact, after the concert I waited on the train station for the first train in the morning to leave to Zurich."

The album was released in February, soon after their return from Europe. Of the many reviews, Chris Welch's was perhaps the strangest: "The result is thoroughly professional musically, but oddly the exercise has caused me several sleepless nights." The pain of his comments on *Colosseum*'s valedictory Albert Hall gig had faded, but maybe Chris was now sensing a conflict of interest between his loyalty to Jon and his professionalism. He remained close to Jon though, as was shown by his getting a 'sneak preview' of the early mixes of the album. His downbeat review continued: "Strictures are placed upon the freedom of the band to express itself, by the over-elaborate lyrics that Paul Williams has the task of translating into song. No matter how well performed, many take on the aspect of a poetry reading set to music." He concluded by saying that it was all rather 'neurotic', but with 'a promise of greatness.' While Chris wasn't convinced about the lyrics, Tony Palmer, the well-known film director, was — inviting Jon onto his radio arts programme expressly to discuss them. *Record Mirror* declared the album a triumph for Allan Holdsworth, but considered the music a bit dated and the *New Musical Express* weighed in with: "An enterprising debut from Hiseman's new outfit," and vindicated Jon by adding: "To me, this set owes very little, if anything, to the now defunct *Colosseum*. It's just four highly individual talents, who have achieved the near miraculous feat of blending smoothly at the first attempt." The reviews all seemed to agree on one point though — the band was more 'rock' than *Colosseum* had ever been. Jon told Steve Peacock of *Sounds*: "One of the things I wanted to do, was to develop a more economical style, driving the band along as much by what I didn't play, as what I did. I want to be less of a dominating force on stage, but I'm fighting a rearguard action, as promoters persist with selling us as *Jon Hiseman's Tempest*, because it's easier."

Now they found that their first UK dates had been postponed *again*, this time though, it was in favour of an American tour supporting *Fleetwood Mac*. It was only 13 concerts, but it was a chance to test the waters. The venues were quite small by US standards, as *Fleetwood Mac* hadn't yet had the major hits that turned them into the stadium-fillers they later became. So, they left for the States early in March and, on the whole, the tour went well, though Harry Isles recalls there were *some* problems. Confusion with flights resulted in the band and crew taking different routes and the roadies arriving late[1]. When they did eventually meet the fans, Jon was surprised to discover that they were extremely well informed about all his records, later confiding to Chris Welch that maybe one more US tour mfor *Colosseum* might have done the trick. About *this* tour, though, he was more measured, admitting that: "Though we went down a storm in San Francisco and a couple of other cities, we weren't really earth-shattering and the album didn't do much; we've a lot to learn and I'd rather build slowly." If Jon was relatively laid-back, that wasn't the case with Paul Williams. He had a *serious* fear of flying and here he was, taking up to three flights a day! Jon was well aware that, at times, Paul drank copiously to overcome his phobia, which, of course, had an adverse affect on his voice.

The album came out on the Warner Bros label and one of the first reviews was by *Rock* magazine's Gordon Fletcher, which centred on the conundrum of comparing *Black Sabbath*'s music to *Tempest*'s 'spellbinding instrumental virtuosity'! He was especially taken with the guitar work: "Holdsworth really begins to shine through the more you hear him. His playing draws from many idioms (especially jazz) and he shows amazing knowledge of his instrument's capabilities." High praise indeed! He wasn't so taken with Jon's playing though, finding it at times to be 'ridiculously cluttered'. Mainly, he was impressed by the fact that they had made the album after being together for only a few weeks and ended by saying he was looking forward to their next one.

Arriving in New Orleans, Jon and Paul had a strange and somewhat disturbing experience. After checking into the hotel, they arranged to meet in the bar for a drink. Jon arrived first, making his way to the far end of the very long, dimly lit room. When Paul got there, not noticing Jon he perched on a barstool halfway down. Suddenly, the guy on Jon's right got up and moved behind him, then, looking along the length of the bar, drawled: "You English — he a friend of yours?" indicating Paul. Jon replied: "Yes, we're in a band — he's the singer, I'm the drummer." The man then introduced himself as Sergeant Surpass of the New Orleans Police and said: "I'm sure glad you guys didn't make any false moves with yer hands, as I'd a shot yer for sure!" Shocked, Jon asked why: "You 'set the bar up' with your friend, by covering the till from two different angles," the officer explained. He then became quite affable and, as they chatted away, the drinks flowed. Jon actually got to handle a *real* revolver for the first time (taking him back to his 'cowboy' days in the playground) and couldn't believe how heavy it was. An hour and a half later, Jon and Paul poured the sergeant into his police car and, with some trepidation, watched him drive off into the night.

Jon felt at the time, that this was his most difficult tour yet. They were flying almost daily and he became steadily more and more exhausted. He remembers looking at his reflection in a hotel mirror and noticing his right eye twitching uncontrollably. Stress was not a word in Jon's vocabulary but he had the distinct feeling that something, somewhere was no longer under his control. Then there was the musical tussle going on between Allan, with his unshakable vision of a new guitar style, played at a volume which might easily overpower the songs that were the heart of the act — and Paul, struggling to cope with all the flying which was affecting his stage performance. Mark, meanwhile, remained stoically optimistic throughout, playing and singing beautifully.

The tour lasted five weeks and they were back in England by mid-April. After a week's holiday, they resumed rehearsals for their first UK tour, now set for June, whilst managing to fit in time to write material for their second album. This was exactly how Jon had planned it, after the pressure caused by *Colosseum*'s lack of writing time, rehearsals or breaks. Jon assured Chris Welch that the new band was beginning to establish itself: "I think the gamble of touring Europe first was staggeringly successful. We didn't take America by storm the way some groups are reported to do, but we had a great time and were well-received." Things seemed to be going well...maybe a bit *too* well!

Suddenly Allan dropped the bombshell that he wanted to leave the band and return to a jazz environment — this just a few weeks before their UK debut concert! He tried to soften the blow by recommending a young guitarist called Peter 'Ollie' Halsall to take his place, but Jon managed to persuade him to stay for the gigs already contracted, at least. Thus *Tempest* temporarily became a quintet, with Ollie fitting in smoothly right from the off. Jon described to Dmitry Epstein of the *Let It Rock* website, the difference in character between the two guitarists: "Allan was very meticulous, very clear. He had a vision about what he was trying to do. Ollie was a lunatic, a chameleon, but in any circumstance, he'd find a way to make it work and when we played we really hit it off — I thought he was great." Mark Clarke affectionately recalled: "Ollie was a very wonderful, quite complex man. If you think of Patrick Moore, the astronomer,

who was a bit of a wacko, well I thought Ollie was a bit too."
Ollie, like Allan, also played keyboards, an added bonus. Though
the band had gained musically, the balance had now changed and
Paul Williams began to feel there was less for him to do.
Tempest's music was becoming more instrumental and Jon
admitted to Steve Peacock of *Sounds* that this meant
performances had to be more organised. As Jon recalls: "Having
two guitarists with very contrasting styles and characters in the
band, it was never going to be an easy ride, as they were both
keen to play solos, though I don't remember any real rivalry
because they *were* so different. But Allan wanted to do his own
thing and I got the impression he didn't like standing around
while someone else played — it was soon clear to me he couldn't
wait to get away...and of course, Paul was right, the vocals *were*
being sidelined."

On the 15th of May, 1973, the band played their first BBC Radio
session — hosted by DJ Pete Drummond. They performed *Up
and On*, *Grey and Black*, *Strangeher* and *Foyers of Fun*. This
was the first time the British fans had heard their music and it
wouldn't be long before they saw them in the flesh. *Tempest*
finally made its debut on 27th May, 1973, at the Queen Elizabeth
Hall in London to positive press reaction, but for once it wasn't
Jon's drum solo that was singled out as the highpoint of the show,
it was the two 'axe-men' that stole the headlines. Tony Stewart
of *NME* wrote: "With ex-*Patto* man Halsall added and crossing
licks with Holdsworth, *Tempest* benefit from two guitarists who
rarely ease up..." Charles Le Vay of *Music Week* argued along the
same lines: "...but while the songs were all composed of
elementary rock figures, the natural emphasis lay on the excellent
guitar work of Holdsworth and Halsall; speed guitarists
extraordinaire." However, he signed off with the portentous line:
"Hopefully, Halsall will remain with the band. If he does,
together with Holdsworth, he's going to blow a storm with
Tempest." Sadly though, the die was already cast.

Just before the UK tour started, the band played a live BBC Radio
session at the Golders Green Hippodrome, hosted by Alan Black.

They performed seven numbers, mostly from the debut album, sounding tight and being well received by the audience. It seems this performance was bootlegged, though with the erroneous title: *Live in London 1974*! The ensuing tour went well, playing to almost full houses in most places, but in spite of this, Paul Williams, surprisingly, left the band when it was over. He recently went on record as saying that the songs were 'OK' but, for him, it just wasn't working. Jon decided not to seek a replacement, instead letting Mark and Ollie share the lead vocal role. Right after the UK tour, with Allan still hanging on in there, they headlined the Venice Festival, where they, quite literally, went down a storm! At the end of their set, screaming fans, rushing the stage, mobbed them. The security guards had no choice but to lock the band in their caravan for their own safety. When the mayhem had died down, they were hustled into cars and driven off, only to find themselves being tailed by fans on motorcycles and scooters. "I couldn't believe it. It was like being a pop star!" is how Jon later described the scene to *Melody Maker*.

It was soon after this that Allan Holdsworth finally quit and *Tempest* became a trio, which in fact, was really what Jon had in mind all along. Unfazed, they started preparing for their performance at the Reading Festival at the end of August, as well as making plans for recording their second album.

So *Tempest*, in a way, had come full circle, but there were still plenty of challenges ahead. The first was their appearance at the aforementioned Reading Festival, where they were playing second on the bill to Genesis. The *New Musical Express* review was quite lukewarm, complaining that, though the technique of the band was astonishing, their material was too loose and not played to its best advantage, though he admitted to enjoying their encore — *The Beatles'* song: *Paperback Writer*[2], which he thought used all their talents constructively. He ended on a more positive note, writing: "This particular line-up of *Tempest* is still fairly new, so when they've had a chance to do some more writing, I see no reason why they shouldn't become one of the most exciting bands we've got." *Sounds* was a lot more positive:

"Jon Hiseman played with his never ending drive, though these days he's playing a lot more straight rock than ever he did with *Colosseum. Tempest* is a hundred miles away from *Colosseum* and a whole lot more listenable." Jon remembers feeling very deflated afterwards: "Somehow, once again, I was seeing the writing on the wall." He left quickly, driving to a nearby cinema and losing himself in a long, slow Clint Eastward movie. Things weren't looking too promising for the long-term future of the band.

Meanwhile Barbara was busy gigging again, often taking young Marcus in his carrycot to the nearer venues. She and Jon had to organise their life meticulously during those early days of parenthood. As Jon wryly commented: "We often met on the stairs, one coming in from a gig as the other went out!" In September, Barbara was invited to appear on a Belgian TV show celebrating 100 years of the saxophone. Adolphe Sax can't have had any idea that his invention was destined for such popularity. Barbara remembers: "I was the only jazz player there *and* the only woman. There were all types of saxophones and many classical players. It was a great success. I had written *Blues for Adolphe Sax*, especially for the show's 'outro' music." Later, it became *Paraphernalia*'s 'encore' at gigs. Barbara had no idea how the invitation came about, but it was certainly a great honour.

In October 1973, *Tempest* started recording the new album at Air Studios, with Gerry Bron producing and the in-house sound engineer, Geoff Emerick, who also worked with *The Beatles*; unfortunately, this gave rise to a problem. Before they even started, Gerry Bron got a phone call from Paul McCartney: "He said that he *always* used Geoff Emerick and would I relinquish him. I told him I couldn't do that. Paul said, 'You know we're talking about the next *Wings* album?' I said I didn't care, as I'd booked the time. Looking back it was a terrible thing to say, because what he was going to do was infinitely more important than what *we* were going to do." In the event, McCartney rescheduled his sessions for when Emerick was available again. Jon seems to have been blissfully unaware of all this politicking, which was probably just as well.

Jon thought Gerry Bron provided a very important steadying influence during this period of experimentation: "He never stopped, or altered, our visions, but if he didn't like anything he was, with hindsight, usually right. I was well aware that I was still on a learning curve and I wanted Gerry's goodwill while making this album. I thought we were taking a risk with the trio, because it really was a great live act, but I had my doubts about translating this to vinyl. The best part was that I learnt a lot from Geoff Emerick." They laid the basic tracks down pretty quickly, but Gerry got quite a shock when it came to Ollie's vocals. Though his voice had a great quality 'live', he had problems with pitch in the studio, taking a while to get it right. However, with the album finally in the can, the band went back on the road and in late October, a *Melody Maker* review of their Kingston Polytechnic gig found them in fine form: "With the fast-fingered guitar work of Ollie and powerful vocals, *Tempest* is becoming an exciting band with considerable promise. As they purge themselves of past concepts, so the floodgates will be open for new ideas. It should be interesting to watch them grow."

They played another short UK tour during January 1974 and then took a break. The album was slated for a March release and they wanted to be ready to give it strong promotion. Just before it hit the shops, they played some Italian dates and at one particular gig in Genoa, fans rushed the stage to embrace their heroes. Steve Clarke from the *NME* witnessed the chaos: "The band was pursued by one particularly fun-loving punter who nearly knocked Hiseman over in his keenness to shake his hand." Order was eventually restored and they finished the set with *Paperback Writer*, as usual. Live tapes from the time, show that Ollie was playing a fair amount of Moog synthesiser, while Jon was *really* enjoying himself and is on record as saying that the crowd reactions for *Tempest* were even bigger than those for *Colosseum*.

Living in Fear was released late March 1974 to a very mixed reception from the press. Chris Welch of *Melody Maker* considered it a vast improvement on the first album: "It reflects the way the band has now settled down and stabilised with a happy and productive formula...the band goes all out to entertain." While Chris's review is rather generous, as might be expected, implicitly anticipating the *next* album — *New Musical Express* had a different view: "Overall, *Living in Fear* is an example of just how wrong it is to assume that three good players make for one fine band. *Tempest* may be good musicians, but they are not songwriters or singers." Only *Stargazer* and *Waiting For a Miracle* are singled out for any praise — both penned by Mark Clarke. The main criticism focuses on the weakness of the material, which is a fair point, as it certainly isn't as strong as that on the first album — but *NME* missed one aspect that was picked up by the *Oxford Mail* — it indicated a refreshing resurgence of creative three-piece groups. The *Mail* closed its piece by saying: "...even though it doesn't make a big impression on the first hearing, it is an album that grows on you."

In early April, the band was back in Air Studios recording two Ollie Halsall songs: *Dream Train* and *You and Your Love*, trying for a hit single, but the results were mixed. *Dream Train* had a degree of chart potential, but unfortunately, time was running out for the band. On the surface everything seemed to be going well, but that wasn't in fact the case. After Allan Holdsworth left, Ollie thought his situation would be better, but it didn't work out that way, as he admitted to Allan Jones of *Melody Maker*: "I thought that the trio set-up would be freer, but it was so much more restricted." The problem was that far *more* discipline was required with a trio format, certainly from Ollie. There were musical problems also, as he was surprised at the amount of 'heavy' material they were playing. While *Tempest* was recording *Dream Train*, Kevin Ayers was in the next studio working on his album, *Confessions of Doctor Dream* and invited Ollie to play on one of the tracks. Ollie enjoyed himself so much, he decided to 'de-camp' to the Ayers band, confiding his reasons to *Melody Maker*: "I tried to steer *Tempest* away from heavy music, because I was writing the material and wanted to do more songs, but I don't think they wanted to be drawn in that direction. I was always more interested in writing and singing songs (shades of James Litherland in *Colosseum*), but Jon wanted an instrumental-type band."

It occurred to Jon recently that Ollie's 'off the wall' personality had often stirred up memories of Graham Bond. Both Ollie and Graham were entertainers at heart, who just happened to use their respective instrumental prowess to live their dreams, often to the exclusion of those around them. Though Jon could probably have done with a few more 'entertainers' as sidemen during his career — at this point, he was aware of feeling slightly uncomfortable and maybe Ollie sensed this.

In the midst of all this turmoil, came another bombshell. On the 8th of May, 1974, Graham Bond committed suicide by throwing himself under a tube train at Finsbury Park Station. The man who had played such a big part in Jon Hiseman's early career was gone. Jon had last seen Graham when he'd 'guested' on Dick's solo album and confided to Chris Welch: "It's a terrible thing, but as I said to Dick, after the initial shock, I felt it had been coming for a long time. Nobody could do anything to help him — for me it's the end of an era. It was Mike Taylor that originally introduced me to Graham and now both of them are dead!" Jon felt these deaths on an extremely personal level, as his career had been greatly enriched by them both: "Graham couldn't change himself, but definitely changed those around him — like Miles Davis, he was a real catalyst. He encouraged me...made me believe that my vision was OK — and showed me how not to run a band! I, for one, feel I owe him a very great deal." The *Melody Maker* obituary echoed Jon's sentiments with the headline: 'Bond — Pioneer and Catalyst'.

After his departure from *Tempest*, Ollie confided to Allan Jones of *Melody Maker* that he thought Jon had used him as a 'passport to some intangible commercial utopia'. Jon never ceases to be amazed how musicians see themselves, their endeavours and achievements and feels that Ollie was probably the *least* 'commercial' musician he'd had in any of his bands —

he certainly wasn't writing commercial songs. Moreover, you'd be hard-pressed to find anyone whose art has been less motivated by money than Jon, as he explained to *Sounds*: "I don't want money — I dress as well as I want and don't need private yachts or planes. I wouldn't have time to use them." The truth was that, of all the band's personnel changes, Ollie's was the one that had slipped under Jon's radar. When Allan Holdsworth had said he was leaving, with all those important concerts and broadcasts pending, he had drafted Ollie in order to get *himself* off the hook. Ollie had never really been interested in Jon's musical concept and wouldn't, perhaps couldn't, adapt to it. That being said, Jon loved this trio version of *Tempest* commenting: "It's actually the greatest playing format and when Ollie was on form, I enjoyed it very much, but the audiences were declining — we were out of our time. It was very free and creative on a nightly basis, but the freer and more creative you are, the less reliable the show becomes...listening to it now, it was all a bit desperate...all a bit OTT!"

Jon sensed that life in the music business was about to become more difficult. As he explained on the *Let It Rock* website in 2004: "There was change in the air...the type of music we played, which is quite intricate, was disappearing...I could sense it and I was right, because we were having a really hard time." Neither of *Tempest*'s albums got near the charts, nor did they get the merit they deserved. Though they may not be the best albums that Jon ever made, the band's two brilliant guitarists make both of them worthy of attention. Ultimately though, *Tempest* failed to make a significant impression, as Jon recently summed up: "I think now that the fantastic audience reactions blinded me to our true situation...also, I was enjoying the same kind of musical adventure that I'd had with Graham Bond, but the reality was — we weren't going anywhere!"

Aided by the success of *Uriah Heep* in America, the Bron Organisation had been subsidising *Tempest* for a while, with few grumbles, but faced with yet another personnel change, Jon decided to fold the band — sensing that it had run its course. He felt depressed, but as with *Colosseum* three years earlier, it was mixed with relief. Unable to see any way forward, he was only too aware that he had a family to support, though it has to be said that by now Barbara was earning well, which did relieve the pressure somewhat. Around this time he told *Melody Maker*: "Everywhere I go, people keep mentioning *Colosseum* — record companies, agents and journalists...it's all they want to know about. I've recently been doing a few drum clinics[3] for Rogers and am always being asked when *Colosseum* is going to re-form." However, his memories of *Colosseum* were very mixed and full of contradictions, so at this point, in mid-1974, he wasn't at all sure that this was a course he wanted to take.

FOOTNOTES

1. Harry Isles recalls: "We were travelling from Chicago to Richmond, Virginia that day. I drove the band to O'Hare airport and had it in mind we were flying with United Airlines, so I dropped them at the United terminal, gave them the tickets so they could check-in, then drove off to return the hire car. When I got back, there was no sign of the band and I quickly realised that we were *actually* booked on North Eastern Airlines, but they weren't at the North Eastern check-in either. I had them paged, but no response. North Eastern said they'd not checked-in — then our two roadies arrived with the gear and started to check that in." The flight closed and Harry started to contact other airlines trying to find out where the band was. He eventually discovered they had left 45-minutes earlier on a UA flight. Harry had no alternative but to find another Richmond flight. The earliest one he could get was via Raleigh-Durham, North Carolina. Harry takes up the story: "When the flight touched down in Raleigh-Durham, I was surprised to see what looked like our gear being wheeled across the tarmac. The flight then took off for Richmond. On arrival I took a cab to the hotel and found the band laughing about the whole thing, having had a call from the roadies to say that their flight had been diverted to Raleigh-Durham, due to a storm in the Richmond area and *they* were stuck there till the next morning. The band, having caught the *wrong* flight, had arrived early enough to get into Richmond before the airport closed down. By the time I arrived, on a different flight, the storm had cleared and the airport re-opened! So it *had* been our gear that I'd seen on the tarmac at Raleigh-Durham and the people who didn't make it to Richmond that night were our crew — the *only* guys who'd caught the correct flight!" Confused?

2. There's some speculation about whose idea it was to cover *Paperback Writer*, given that it's an unlikely choice for any band of Jon's, though Jon was a fan of *The Beatles*. Ollie was too, and sometime later, *Monty Python*'s Eric Idle commissioned him to write the music for the spoof *Beatles* film, *The Rutles*, but

Ollie was then disappointed not to be given the role of 'Paul McCartney' in the film — eventually playing the lesser role of Leppo (Stuart Sutcliffe).

3. On 20th May, 1974, Jon gave a drum clinic with Mark Goodwin at Osborne's Music Centre in Banbury. Mark had turned professional at 19 and had worked with Peter Gordeno, Matt Monroe, Tommy Cooper and Lonnie Donegan. The event went on for four hours, attracting many passers-by, possibly intrigued by the noise. All the drum devotees were impressed, especially local bandleader Brownie Lay who admitted: "I went home and looked up the old Gene Krupa drum tutor of 1938 and, after 40 years in the business, began practising again!"

*"I'm proud of this band. Gary Moore
is my partner...my luck was meeting
him and finding that there were things
we both wanted to play."*
JON HISEMAN, 1976

Chapter 15

STRANGE NEW FLESH

AFTER THE DEMISE OF *Tempest*, JON HISEMAN TOOK THINGS EASY FOR A BIT, just doing occasional sessions. In August 1974 he took part in a rock version of Prokofiev's *Peter and the Wolf*, the brainchild of Jack Lancaster and Robin Lumley, who also produced it. Lumley was in *Brand X*, the jazz-rock outfit formed by Phil Collins of *Genesis,* and most of the musicians used on the album were drawn from this band, augmented by Cozy Powell, Bill Bruford, Stephane Grappelli, Alvin Lee and Gary Moore. Earlier in the year, Gary had joined *Thin Lizzy*, replacing the departed founder member, Eric Bell. However, he'd found their music very limiting, plus he hadn't always seen eye-to-eye with bandleader Phil Lynott, so he had left and was now looking for something more challenging. He was well aware of Jon, having seen *Tempest* at the Marquee and been so impressed that he'd gone backstage to actually suggest they should play together. When *Tempest* folded, they met up again and decided to go for it!

As usual, Jon was juggling several projects at the same time; one of which was with Wolfgang Dauner, who Jon first met when *Colosseum* headlined a festival at Heidelberg. In those days, it was quite usual for bands to provide their own PA at the smaller events, but Wolfgang's hadn't turned up and he asked to borrow *Colosseum*'s. Jon's policy was to help other groups wherever and whenever he could, so he gave his crew instructions to make their equipment available to Wolfgang and his band, including lights and PA. Thus, Wolfgang knew Jon to be someone he could work with and later booked Jon for an album and tour with his band *Knasch*. In 1974 Süddeutscher Rundfunk (South German TV) commissioned Werner Schretzmeier to direct a series of shows aimed at the German youth market. It was to be a socio/political mix of discussion, documentaries and interviews, interspersed with music, for transmission on Sundays at 11.30am. Werner asked his good friend Wolfgang to put together a band, choosing anybody he wanted. Jon was Wolfgang's first choice for drums, though he didn't know any of the other members of this illustrious group and wasn't aware that the first session was effectively his audition. The band recorded for a week, four times

278

a year, each time putting enough material 'in the can' for three month's worth of shows. The personnel varied quite a bit to start with, as Wolfgang sought to put together the ideal mix of talents and temperaments, which was later christened *The Band of Bandleaders*. At one point, Wolfgang asked Jon if he knew of a good sax player — it was a question that Jon would hear a few times in the coming years. Jon showed him a photo of Barbara. "If she plays like she looks — invite her for the next session." Nothing sexist there then — and in spite of her looks, she was still with the band 35 years later!

After two years of the television shows, Wolfgang fixed up a live gig for the band to take place one Friday after recording had finished. Nobody had reckoned with the effect of all those TV appearances and when 2,000 people turned up...jaws dropped! The band went on to record and tour for the next three decades as the *United Jazz and Rock Ensemble* (*UJ&RE*). During this period there were many personnel changes, but Barbara, Jon, Ack van Rooyen and Wolfgang remained constant.[1] Jon once brought in Gary Moore as guest guitarist, but he played with such volume that the TV camera signal was affected, distorting the picture! Gary found it very difficult to play with jazz musicians at that stage of his career, as he recalled recently: "I was a wild boy back then and got drunk a lot." Jon was very impressed with Gary's playing, but less so with his drinking and told him, in no uncertain terms, that if he wanted to work with him he'd have to cut it out, though oddly, Jon doesn't recall this conversation.

Jon and Gary started meeting regularly to write material for their new band and invited Mark Clarke to join them. Jon then found a singer, Graham Bell, who'd sung with *Skip Bifferty* and *Every Which Way* (Brian Davison's band), but without a name or any gigs, things drifted for a bit and Mark decided to go to the States with *Uriah Heep*'s Ken Hensley, with whom he had also been working on and off. Finally Bell lost interest and departed. As usual, Jon was walking a commercial tightrope with the style of music he wanted the new band to play. Having obviously

279

learned nothing from his past experiences, he was about to do it all over again, as Gary Moore explained to *New Musical Express*: "We wanted to do something that nobody else was doing — find a hot instrumental based band with strong vocals. You've got people like the *Mahavishnu Orchestra* who do great instrumentals and you've got *Zeppelin* with a good vocalist, but there's no one doing *both*." Gary was also very much into what Bill Connors, the guitarist in Chick Corea's *Return to Forever* was doing on their debut album, *Hymn of the Seventh Galaxy*, but it would certainly be a tall order accommodating vocals within that kind of musical structure. This is probably what attracted Gary to Jon — the project would be quite a challenge and he was looking forward to it. They decided to call the new band *Ghost*.

Gary Moore had been impressed with Jon's playing right from the start. He told *Sounds*: "The first time I played with Jon, I almost fell through the floor. He played everything I've always heard in my head, everything that I thought a drummer should play and a lot more besides. It was just astonishing!" Gary had been looking for someone to work with for a while, but had resolved only to work with the best musicians. Jon played Gary a lot of John Coltrane records and some other examples of jazz, musicians that Gary had never heard before. This was quite a steep learning curve for him, especially as he didn't feel he was all that competent technically, but he learned fast. Gary explained to *Sounds* their method of writing: "Jon gives me the lyrics and I take them home, take them apart and work out the melodies. The good thing about this band is that we've all had a lot of experience in the music business and we're not going to be rushed into any deals...nor are we going to record an album until we've been on the road for at least three months — when we do, it's going to have a very live feel." It was a bold statement...but would it pan out like that?

Around this time, Alan Hewitt, an aspiring band manager, attached himself to the group. Jon can't remember exactly how this came about, since there was certainly no money to pay him on a regular basis — but his enthusiasm for their music and his unswerving belief that they could 'make it', kept the nascent band going through its darkest days. He had come from a stressful career in commerce and was undoubtedly hoping for an alternate lifestyle far removed from the real world; in fact, as he would discover, he had jumped out of the frying pan and straight into the fire.

Jon and Gary continued their search for the right musicians well into 1975. During this depressing period, they rehearsed sporadically with various personnel, in a dank, dark West London basement. Gary always had with him the precious old Les Paul guitar he'd been given by Peter Green, when he became a recluse and divested himself of all worldly goods.[2] Money was very tight during this period and Gary had to survive on the £10 a week he got from Jon. Bassist Andy Pyle[3], formerly of Mick Abraham's *Blodwyn Pig*, joined them for a while and Jon really enjoyed playing with him. Though Andy was in dire financial straits, with a young family to support, he was very enthusiastic about the band. Out of the blue, they were offered a commission to write and record the music for a film, but when they arrived in London's Soho for a meeting with the director, they found themselves at a clandestine screening of a feature-length porno movie! Jon's attitude was, 'why not…if it keeps us going long enough to get on the road'? But, to his surprise Andy and Gary would have nothing to do with it…shortly after this, with no money coming in, Andy just couldn't hang on any longer and left.

They would end up spending the best part of a year looking for a keyboard player, auditioning over 50 hopefuls (amongst them Duncan McKay, of the hit group *Cockney Rebel*). Gary particularly remembers one guy from Germany: "He said he was the man for the job and came in full of confidence. He started playing and it was obvious that he couldn't play at all! We tried not to laugh…it was all so hopeless." Fortunately, soon after this, the multi-talented Don Airey appeared. He'd been in Cozy Powell's band *Hammer*, and the moment they heard him play, they knew he was the right man — and there was a bonus in that Don brought with him *Hammer*'s bass player, Neil Murray. That just left the vocalist slot to be filled.

Alan Hewitt found their man in the most unlikely place...singing in an East End pub! Mike Starrs' history was hardly inspiring — he'd worked with the *Debonaire Show Band* and *Spinning Wheel* — not exactly big names — but he would soon prove to be a worthy addition to the group. Gary Moore explained to *New Musical Express* why it had taken so long to find the right singer: "When I write on guitar, I tend to forget people's limitations and the next thing you know is that I've written notes that no-one can reach..."

After all the problems that Jon and Gary had experienced in the process of getting the right people for the band, they were surprised to find that it took almost another year to get a record deal. Of course, Jon had realised when *Tempest* folded, that the cold winds of change were blowing in the industry and he knew that *this* band's music was not any more commercial, but he hadn't realised just *how* cold those winds actually were. Jon explained to Chris Welch of *Melody Maker*: "What's happening is, there are so many people dependent for their living on the music business, which means organising a profit and loss account, rather than taking a risk. It's a situation where now, few chances are taken." What Jon didn't know, was that this increasing caution would become endemic and result in the least musically creative decade since Elvis Presley first swivelled his hips — the '80s!

At this point, Jon turned to Gerry Bron, whose Bronze record label had gone from strength to strength, spearheaded by *Uriah Heep*, who had, through their many gruelling tours of Europe and the USA, become an international success. Gerry loved the music of Jon's new band, but didn't think he couldn't market it with a name like *Ghost* and suggested resurrecting the *Colosseum* name. (He had, in fact, also suggested this when Jon had formed *Tempest*, so it was no great surprise.) Jon thought

282

about it long and hard and decided to go along with the idea. He explained to *Sounds* the reason for his decision: "*Colosseum* was a name I gave to a basic concept of mine. It's a specific relationship between me and the other musicians. It is too valuable a name to use lightly, plus I have a moral obligation to the guys who gave three years of their lives to the original band." For this reason, he asked all the members of *Colosseum* whether they minded him using the name — and none did.

Jon felt positive about the name change, telling *New Musical Express*: "I think it's valid, calling it *Colosseum II*, because it has this quality about it which makes it different...just as the first *Colosseum* was something totally extraordinary in terms of what we were playing for the time." There was a big difference in terms of their preparation also — *Colosseum II* took a year to get on the road, whereas the old *Colosseum* barely had three months before gigging started!

In spite of Gary Moore's predictions, the band went into the studio to record the first album before making their live debut. It was produced by Jon and engineered by Ashley Howe at Bron's Roundhouse Studio, London. They had plenty of material — including the three tracks already demoed to Gerry Bron (one of which was a scorching version of *Walkin' in the Park*), but, as it turned out, none of these would be used. At this stage, it was only Gary coming up with material, as he recalled recently: "Don and I would clash, because I'd write something on piano and he would say 'you can't do that...it's not harmonically right', but Don didn't actually write any music for the first six months." The album title, *Strange New Flesh*, summed up Jon's new approach, as did the cover design, which depicted the members of the band in a very modern but abstract way and was the work of animator, Ian Emes, soon to work with Mike Oldfield.

Jon was clear about how the band's creative process worked: "Most of the music was created by Gary Moore and Don Airey, who demoed their efforts to the band on their respective instruments. I contributed the lyrics, where appropriate. In other words, nothing was ever written down. We would then meet in a rehearsal studio and gradually develop the arrangements. I also had strong ideas of how a live show should build through the evening, so I had a lot to do with the shapes of the songs and the planning of the concerts."

Listening to the album now, one can hear a definite *Mahavishnu Orchestra* influence on some tracks...Gary Moore readily acknowledges his admiration for John McLaughlin: "I didn't rush out to buy his albums, but any time I heard him, it sank in subconsciously and it started to show in my writing, though I didn't try to copy anything he wrote." Jon told *Artifact* magazine much the same thing: "There's been much innovation in the use of odd time signatures, pioneered by the *Mahavishnu Orchestra*." In truth, the McLaughlin influence is only obvious on the first and last tracks, *Dark Side of the Moog* and *Winds*. It's debatable whether the rest of the album could be classified as jazz-rock at all. Neil Murray has his own theory on who influenced who: "Gary Moore was still young and under the control, or guidance, of Jon Hiseman." Gary commented to *Sounds* that he thought his playing had improved since working with Jon and he was now beginning to forge his own sound: "For the first time in my life, I'm not consciously copying anybody...in fact, when people hear me for the first time, they don't know who to compare me with." Regardless of who influenced who, they were now ready to take their music out on the road.

Their live debut, like *Tempest*'s, was abroad — kicking off with a short Scandinavian tour in September 1975. Jon was pleased with the audience reaction, confiding to *Sounds* that his greatest fear — that they would demand his old numbers — turned out to be unfounded. In fact, the crowd seemed willing to judge the new band on its merits, so Jon could look forward to their UK premiere at Manchester Polytechnic with confidence. There to review it was the same journalist who had witnessed the debut of *Colosseum* Mk.1 in Scarborough back in 1968 — Chris Welch. He claims to have heard at least *one* call for the *Valentyne Suite*, but otherwise the new material was well received. Of course, the difference now was that there were fewer 'names' in this new line-up, so it was heartening to see the audience give them a fair hearing. True, Gary Moore had been in *Thin Lizzy*, but only briefly and well before they found fame with *Whiskey in the Jar*. Chris, nevertheless, was impressed with them all: "The band has a fine singer in Mike Starrs, who looks tough and sings with fire. Alongside him is guitar ace Gary Moore, noted for his speedy technique and on the other side, Don Airey, a keyboard player whose youthful enthusiasm has him leaping from his organ stool — then there is an even younger looking Neil Murray, coping with some impossibly fast tempos on his bass." Chris did note some 'rough edges' though and had some reservations about the Joni Mitchell number, *Down To You*. He also thought that, at times, they were overly complex and a bit too busy, but still considered that the band had potential.

On 7th December, 1975, Barbara gave birth to a daughter, Anna and around the same time, Jon was interviewed by the *Daily Mirror*. The article mentions that their son, Marcus, was already playing the kazoo, so perhaps baby Anna would also have a future in a Hiseman family band? Jon's answer was quite prophetic: "With her lungs, you can say she's our lead singer!" Barbara had worked right up to three weeks before the birth, touring with Neil Ardley's *Kaleidoscope of Rainbows*. She hadn't been too comfortable while travelling, but knew she'd have been bored stiff at home. Soon after Anna was born, Barbara put into action plans to form not just one band, but two! Though she had been a musician for over a decade, she felt she had yet to find her own identity and the only way to do this was to compose, play and record her *own* music, with her *own* band.

Her first group she called *Jubiaba*, which translates as 'Old Voodoo Priest'. It started off as a pub band, playing gigs like the prestigious Bull's Head, Barnes in S.W. London, where, for Barbara, the audience began arriving three hours before the start, to be sure of to getting a seat. The nine-piece line-up was impressive — it included Henry Lowther, Derek Wadsworth,

Kenny Wheeler, Roy Babbington, Peter Lemer, Bill Le Sage and drummer Trevor Tomkins. Jon had depped for Trevor a couple of times and knew him well — in fact, they had both gone to the same school (though several years apart) and he was one of Jon's heroes from the Jazzhouse, Blackheath days. These were all musicians that Barbara knew well, having played on various projects with each of them at one time or another. However, one player in particular would become a very important part of her musical life as Barbara explains: "I came across an album that Jon had made with keyboard player Pete Lemer called *Local Colour*. All the tracks were original compositions and featured incredible players like John Surman. I was really impressed with its freshness and originality, so I immediately contacted Peter, as I wanted him for both bands." However, although he was able to make occasional *Jubiaba* gigs, he just couldn't commit to anything on a more regular basis, as he was wrapped up in his own work at the time. Nevertheless, a creative bond was soon formed between them and Peter remains to this day one of Barbara's closest musical colleagues and his support for her over the years, has been invaluable.

Jubiaba got off to a great start, becoming a very popular draw in the jazz pubs and clubs around London. With everybody contributing compositions and arrangements they quickly built up an enviable repertoire. The band was not, however, without problems, as Barbara recalls: "We did one tour sponsored by the Arts Council and once away from home, the brass section in particular, became lunatics — it was booze for breakfast and 'pot' for tea. Jon came to a few gigs and was quite shocked by the state everyone was in! One gig was at the University of East Anglia and to promote it, I appeared on local TV a couple of days prior. The show's director had apparently been smitten with me and turned up at the gig somewhat 'tired and emotional' — even wheeling his way onto the coach afterwards. However, the band, ever protective, soon 'sussed' what he was up to and threw him off!" They made one album — simply called *JUBIABA*, which was released by MCA in 1978 — it was the first of Barbara's bands to record.

Barbara's other band was completely different, both in size and approach, as she explains: "A lot of jazz musicians who felt very comfortable just playing 'standards' gave me a hard time when I tried to introduce my own compositions." Determined not to be deterred, Barbara set about recruiting musicians who were on her wavelength and understood the kind of music she wanted to play...they were *Jubiaba* bass player, Roy Babbington, drummer Harold Fisher and Colin Dudman on keyboards. She chose the name, *Paraphernalia* ('those things a wife possesses in her own right, which can never become her husband's property'). Three decades later it would still be one of Europe's most successful jazz groups, albeit with several changes of personnel and instrumental line-up. She had, in fact, used the name even earlier, as Jon Hiseman recalls: "Barbara had experimented with different line-ups since the early '70s and had used the name on odd occasions, but it wasn't till 1975 that the personnel stabilised and the band began to appear regularly as *Barbara Thompson's Paraphernalia.*"

At the end of 1975, *Colosseum II* went to Germany to play three festivals at Ludwigshafen, Dusseldorf and Dortmund...their last gigs for a while, before re-grouping in late February for a full tour to promote their first album, due out in March. In the middle of these dates, Jon took off for a solo appearance at the Frankfurt Musical Instrument Fair, demonstrating the Arbiter Autotune drum kit, which was just going into production. Jon explained what was special about the kit in a 1980s interview: "It had a ground-breaking revolving tuning system — the metal rim screwed down onto the fibreglass drum-shell, just like a jam-jar lid, tensioning the head in the process. All the drums, except the snare drum, were single headed and it was a beautiful sounding kit. As any Latin percussionist knows, fibreglass has very interesting acoustic properties. I had more compliments about the sound of that kit than any other I can remember." Jon had planned to use this new kit on the next tour, but production problems meant it wasn't ready in time, so he continued with his trusty maple-shelled Rogers kit.

On 12th March their debut album, *Strange New Flesh*, hit the shops, with press reaction being mixed, but positive overall. *Melody Maker*'s Chris Welch summed it up nicely: "Hiseman has assembled a team of young players whose first consideration is to write, improvise and perform to the best of their ability and create some excitement in the process." He concluding his lengthy review with: "Hiseman can be proud of this band and the band can be proud of an imaginative and exuberant debut album." The *Oxford Mail* suggested that the album was a 'sleeper', saying: "There is much challenging and satisfying music here, largely a result of the contrast between the jazz leanings of Airey and Hiseman and the rock edge of Moore." However, Bob Edmonds from *New Musical Express* was more cautious — while praising the 'hefty pillars' that Jon had assembled around him, he wasn't impressed with Jon's style, arguing that it was outmoded: "Tom-toms explode where hi-hats and snares should shimmer." Maybe he was implying that he should play more like Billy Cobham, but Jon was ever his own man and would continue playing *his* way[4]. Adam Cummings of *Record Mirror* rated *Dark Side of the Moog* the best track, but dismissed the vocals as 'detracting from the musical skill of the band'. Clearly, Cummings would have preferred it to be a more instrumental album and he probably wasn't the only one.

While Jon was nurturing *Colosseum II*'s progress, Dick Heckstall-Smith, reappeared on the musical scene after successfully conquering his back problems and completing his Social Science degree. He joined a new band that already included Tony Edwards, Tony Desborough, Adrian Paton and John Fry. Called *Big Chief*, it would, in time, achieve a legendary status playing jazz-based music fused with elements of rock, but 'with a smile on its face'. Many fine musicians would pass through its ranks, such as Tony Reeves, Henry Lowther, John Etheridge, Pete Lemer and Art Themen. In fact, it was Art, a notable orthopaedic surgeon, who had helped Dick recover from his slipped disc. For the next few years, Dick would make very few personal musical statements, being happy just to gig around. He joined a bebop outfit, *The Tough Tenors*, played on Pete

Brown's 1977 album, *My Last Band,* and on Alexis Korner's 50th birthday *Party Album*, later released on video by Germany's WDR TV, on which Dick later admitted, he'd 'played shit!' After a three-year break, it was only to be expected that it would take a while for him to regain his former fluency and stamina, but most importantly...he was playing again.

Colosseum II was still touring furiously and Geoff Barton from *Sounds* caught their Marquee gig at the end of April. Surprisingly little was played from *Strange New Flesh*, in favour of new songs such as *Sounds Fill My Head*, *Siren Song* and *The Awakening*. Some critics had been accusing them of standing still, but here was evidence to the contrary. There was, however, one 'blast from the past'...the old Graham Bond barnstormer *Walkin' in the Park*. While Geoff Barton remained unconvinced by the album, he made no bones about liking their live act: "Their complex, but infinitely likeable music piles into you with a good deal of forcefulness, so there's no time to stand and contemplate the virtues of its intricacies...and even now Mike Starrs hasn't quite managed to stop posing but, at the same time, you can't help but marvel at his tremendous vocal range."

The band recorded their first BBC session in June, playing only *Dark Side of the Moog* from the album and the two new songs, *Siren Song* and *The Awakening*. A few weeks later, they were in the Roundhouse Studio to 'demo' these two new tracks, together with *Night Creeper*, *Castles*, *The Scorch*, *Rivers* and *Interplanetary Strut*. Don and Gary were clearly 'on a roll' and enjoying a productive run of writing together, with Jon contributing the lyrics. However, the management was becoming increasing unhappy. Jon now admits that, although the band was reasonably successful, they were in dire straits financially and still being kept afloat by Gerry Bron, who therefore was insisting on having more say. He put his wife, Lillian in charge of the group and she immediately started lobbying for the removal of Mike Starrs. Jon remembers her admiring Mike's voice, but never liking his stage presence, finding it too 'cabaret'. The feeling was that, though the first album was good, it fell between two stools, the classy vocals not really meshing with the rougher, tougher instrumental side of the band. So, once again, Jon, unwilling or unable to relinquish his dream and enjoying the adventurous nature of the music, was being interfered with by those holding the purse strings, but he had to admit that Don and Gary were clearly better at writing instrumentals than songs. Though slightly bemused that the management was now coming down on the side of a more instrumental band, Jon reluctantly went along with it and Mike Starrs was out. Mike was of course bitterly disappointed...he'd relished his moment of fame and had performed brilliantly, impressing fans and critics alike. His departure put the band firmly on an instrumental track, but before long came another blow — Neil 'the ace with the bass' Murray also exited the band. Jon remembers this as being about a simple clash of playing styles and Neil just wanting to move on.

Jon Hiseman acted quickly, recruiting rising star John Mole to play bass. He'd been spotted by Barbara Thompson when she was guesting with the local rhythm section at a club in Southend and came home raving about him. "The first time I heard him play, I knew he was going to be special," she said recently. In August 1976, the new line-up played an all-nighter at the Lyceum, London, as a 'dry run' before the Reading Festival. They went on around 3am — drummer Cozy Powell happened to catch them and was very impressed, telling *Melody Maker*: "*Colosseum* should be in America. There isn't a band playing this kind of music anywhere in the world." Chris Welch's review was nothing short of ecstatic, reporting that they premiered a new piece called *South India Line*, as the vehicle for Jon's drum solo. Jon recalls: "*South India Line* was composed by American alto sax player, Charlie Mariano who, though settled in Germany, was a very spiritual person and made frequent trips to India throughout his life. A member of the *UJ&RE*, he introduced the piece during the Schretzmeier TV series on the session that included Gary Moore. The haunting theme, originally played by Barbara on flute, was built on typically Indian multiple-time signatures — two bars of 5/8, a bar of 4/4 followed by a bar of 3/4." Jon took to it like a duck to water, starting off his solo playing the rhythmical cadence before building it into his more usual rhythms and this piece remained his *UJ&RE* drum feature for many years. Some time later, the same cadence would be used by Barbara when composing *Temple Song*, which happened to be at the time Jon was thinking about what to call their joint enterprise. Temple Music seemed to 'ring a bell' with them and thus it became the name of the Company that still represents them to this day.

A few days later, they appeared at a rain-soaked Reading Festival with Rory Gallagher, *Camel*, *AC/DC* and *Brand X* also on the bill. *Colosseum II* played on the Saturday and once again the reviews were somewhat mixed. The *NME* reporter liked them, commenting: "I particularly enjoyed an amusing little hornpipe duet between the guitar and synthesiser as, at the cosmic moment, a gaggle of geese, in a tight Delta formation flew over the stage, heading south." *Melody Maker* was less enthusiastic: "It was only when guitarist Gary Moore took the reins to play a beautiful slow Irish traditional air, followed by a jig that they came to life." It was always important to Jon that the other band members received their fair share of plaudits, which certainly seemed to be happening now and as far as he was concerned, *Colosseum II* had exceeded all of his musical expectations — they couldn't have got off to a better start.

FOOTNOTES

1. The *UJ&RE* met at Süddeutscher Rundfunk TV studios in Stuttgart every three months or so. In addition to the core of the band, the varying line-up included Dave King — bass guitar; Klaus Doldinger — tenor sax; Howard Johnson — tuba; Gary Moore — guitar. When the band settled down as a recording and touring act, the personnel was: Barbara Thompson — saxes & flute; Jon Hiseman — drums; Albert Mangelsdorff — trombone; Eberhard Weber — bass; Volker Kriegel — guitar; Wolfgang Dauner — piano & synth; Charlie Mariano — alto sax & nadaswaram; Ian Carr — trumpet & flugelhorn; Ack van Rooyen — trumpet & flugelhorn. Dauner, Mangelsdorff, Kriegel & van Rooyen formed their own company, Mood Records, when it became apparent that nobody was interested in giving the band a deal. The *UJ&RE* recorded their first album *Live im Schützenhaus* in January 1977, which became Germany's best-selling jazz record ever and Mood, featuring their trademark

black & white cover artwork, continued to be successful into the new millennium. Some time later, the 35-year-old Dave King returned, replacing Eberhard Weber, and Kenny Wheeler joined as lead trumpet, later replaced by Johannes Faber and then Thorsten Benkenstein. Christof Laur took Barbara's tenor sax chair as she replaced Charlie Mariano on alto sax and Peter O'Mara replaced Volker Kriegel on guitar for a couple of tours. Kriegel then returned in 2002 to play what would turn out to be the *UJ&RE*'s final tour. At the time of writing, Volker Kriegel, Albert Manglesdorff, Ian Carr and Charlie Mariano have all passed away. "Barbara and I miss them terribly...but let's face it, their fate awaits us all!"

2. According to Gary Moore, Peter Green bought this vintage 1959 Les Paul Standard guitar for £120 in the mid '60s. Originally he just loaned it to Gary, but subsequently asked him if he wanted to buy it. Gary replied that he was practically broke and couldn't possibly afford it. As Peter's only concern was for the guitar to go to a good home, he suggested Gary sell his Gibson SG and pay him whatever he got for it. Thus, this most famous of all 'bursts' *could* have been Gary's for 160 quid — except that Peter thought that was too much and settled for £110! Its unique sound was the result of the wiring and orientation of the neck pickup being accidentally reversed to create a unique 'out of phase' middle position tone. The Gibson 'Collectors Choice' reproductions of this specific model, currently retail for $12,500! At the time of the *Colosseum II* rehearsals, a near-penniless Gary was afraid to let it out of his sight — very wisely, it seems, as this very same guitar, according to *Guitar Magazine*, would become the 'Holy Grail' for collectors. In 2006, it was sold to an American guitar dealer for something around a million dollars, though this figure is disputed by some. Subsequently, he reportedly offered it for sale for a cool $2,000,000 — or so the story goes.

3. Andy Pyle would go on to have quite a distinguished career in the music business, working with Gary Moore again in 1989 on his album, *Still Got The Blues* and playing on the subsequent tours. Over the years, he worked with many other well-known artists, such as *Savoy Brown*, *Juicy Lucy*, *The Sutherland Brothers* and *Chicken Shack*, as well as individual musicians including Mick Jagger, Ron Wood, Charlie Watts, Otis Rush, Buddy Guy, Pops Staples, Jimmie Rodgers, Albert King, Albert Collins and B.B. King...to name but several!

4. About this time, Jon was inspired by a new drummer on the scene. He heard Stevie Wonder playing drums on his *Talking Book* and *Innervisions* albums, admitting: "It was the most spellbinding experience." In a 1980s interview he elaborated: "Stevie's playing combines for me the naiveté of the beginner with that ultimate of attributes, the ability to create drum parts which sound completely inevitable; as if nothing else could have been played there. It is as if I can hear how every musician would like to have drums played, if all that practice and technocracy wasn't in the way. It is like a vision of beauty unattainable in reality, yet he succeeds — and I love him for it."

"He was very good at putting me on the right path, teaching me about music, integrity and a lot of other stuff — I'll always thank him for that."
Gary Moore on Jon Hiseman

Chapter 16

WAR DANCE

THE YEAR 1976 BROUGHT ABOUT A SEA CHANGE FOR THE BRITISH MUSIC INDUSTRY. A new genre arrived on the scene — 'Punk'. How...or indeed, *why* it met with the success it did has been the subject of debate ever since, but one thing is certain — it was bad news for the current 'regime' of groups. The new movement was spearheaded by the *Sex Pistols* and much of the music media embraced these bands as a welcome change to the established artists, who were now being dismissed as 'dinosaurs'.

With all this in the air, it wasn't a complete surprise when Gerry Bron decided to drop *Colosseum II*, saying he could no longer see a way forward for them. At first, Jon assumed it was related to the band's decision not to replace Mike Starrs with another vocalist, but he'd also felt for a while that the office's enthusiasm was waning and that their interventions had less to do with vision and more to do with desperation. In fact, the quartet of Jon, Gary, Don and John felt very comfortable together, and as the next albums would show, was rapidly finding its 'voice'.

A 'White Knight' soon appeared in the shape of Monty Babson, co-owner of Morgan Studios, who had been responsible for hits with Acker Bilk, as well as producing the pop group, *Blue Mink*. He thought very highly of *Colosseum II* and provided them with studio time to make their second album, which, as executive producer (the money) he subsequently sold on to MCA Records. Considering that the band was now essentially an instrumental quartet, they were fortunate to find another backer so quickly but the decision to 'go' instrumental was probably wise considering Jon's fruitless search for a vocalist who could make sense of his lyrics. He commented recently: "It's not as if I wasn't into vocals — I'm actually very proud of some of the lyrics I contributed, but somehow, singers who were great in other environments rarely felt comfortable in mine. Clem Clempson just never wanted to sing lead and Mark Clarke, who has never really fulfilled his potential, for reasons best known only to him, had the light kind of voice which wouldn't come into vogue until later. Ollie was never a great singer, but always gave it his best shot and on a good night his voice worked well. However, in the more clinical atmosphere of the studio, his pitching was a real problem. Mike Starrs, who sang very well, was deemed by the management to be somehow too polished and they didn't think he fitted with the much heavier image that Gary Moore projected. Gary himself, whose singing I always encouraged, didn't develop vocally until he sang with his own bands later. Chris Farlowe, who has the most powerful set of lungs on earth, was the only vocalist who could and still does, ride over a band in full flight. I've heard him give astonishing performances, but he's such an individualist, even he's an acquired taste."

They were still writing new material for the next album, which was then 'road tested' on gigs. Jon recalls: "The rehearsals were long and hard, as writing 'in the round' is the slowest way to compose, but it does mean that, by the time you get on the road, you really do know the compositions and that leaves you pretty free to be creative. After a tour at the end of 1976, we went straight back into Morgan Studios and recorded *Electric Savage* virtually as you hear it, playing almost all of it live, with just a few overdubs here and there." Produced by Jon, with Dave Harris engineering, some thought it lacked the polish and breadth of *Strange New Flesh*, but it showed Jon the way forward: "I was really satisfied with this album and gained a lot of recording experience. Its success, in my terms, helped me to acknowledge my instrumental roots and learn to live with them."

The Christmas edition of *Melody Maker* carried a rather controversial article from one of its most influential journalists, Richard Williams. Given the musical climate at the time, his hostile diatribe came as a nasty and unwelcome surprise. He argued that by fusing jazz with rock, artists like Miles Davis and *Weather Report* were 'denying the history of their own music'. Furthermore, Williams averred that the rot had set in around 1968 with bands like *Blood Sweat and Tears* and...yes, *Colosseum*. Ironically, Jon Hiseman's favourite musician is cited by Williams as a shining exception, pronouncing that: "We must first take into account the desire of John Coltrane for a music based on folk modes and directed towards the expression of 'spiritual energy' above all else." The scribe went on to claim that drummer Tony Williams was also 'infected with the bacteria of rock'. This type of jazz is a 'bastard child', according to Williams and not worth listening to. This from the man who solemnly 'reviewed' not one, but *two* 'blank' sides of the 4-sided test pressing of John & Yoko's *Wedding Album*; describing the 20 minute 1Khz tone (the test signal used by engineers) as 'rising and falling by as much as a semi-tone'! Reading his scathing remarks today, it seems incredible that such pompous rubbish could ever be taken seriously. Traditionally, musicians have always 'borrowed' from other sources and when creating music of any genre, there have never been any barriers to the mixing of musical styles. A good example is John Coltrane himself, who frequently changed musical direction, searching for what he called the 'mysterious sound', a kind of Holy Grail that he would 'recognise when he heard it'. He was greatly influenced by African tribal music, as well as Middle Eastern and Indian sounds, incorporating them into his playing, which gradually became more and more 'avant-garde'. A similar path had been trodden by Mike Taylor, along with John Stevens, Trevor Watts, Evan Parker and Paul Rutherford et al. So, what Jon and the other 'miscreants' were accused of, was not 'betrayal', but was part of their ongoing musical development.

By January 1977, *Colosseum II*'s lack of popular success and the pressure of their ongoing financial struggle was beginning to take its toll, so when Gary Moore was asked if he wanted to join *Thin Lizzy* on their US tour, depping for guitarist, Brian Robertson (whose hand was damaged in a fight at the Speakeasy), he asked Jon for a leave of absence. *Colosseum II*'s manager, Alan Hewitt, was at pains to stress to all and sundry that Gary would only be helping out for the duration of the tour. With *Colosseum II* now effectively 'grounded', Jon received an interesting offer from an old friend. When *Colosseum* Mk.1 had folded in 1971, Dave Greenslade had formed his own band — *Greenslade*, with Tony Reeves on bass and had recorded four studio albums that all met with a degree of success, especially in Europe. Of late, the band had been in limbo, so Dave had negotiated a solo album deal with Derek Taylor of Warner Brothers and now wanted to promote it with a tour. He asked Jon if he would like to join him — so, in February, half of the original *Colosseum* embarked on short run of UK dates. Dave recalls: "We only played a few gigs, but Jon fitted in brilliantly." Chris Welch saw them at London's New Victoria Theatre and commented: "The result was a fresh, exciting sound, which Dave swears needed barely any rehearsal. These guys are such professionals they don't need to rehearse." It was an enjoyable interlude for Jon and he got a lot of satisfaction from working with his old mates again.[1]

In March, Gary Moore returned from the States and the band left for a European tour. Everything went smoothly until they reached Naples, in the south of Italy. Seven years earlier, Jon had appeared on Italian TV with Frank Zappa, trying to reassure a paranoid 'establishment' that rock music wouldn't bring about the end of civilization. It didn't seem that anything had changed much! The Italian Police were still trigger (and baton) happy whenever large numbers of young people gathered, especially for rock events. A crowd of 4,000 was already inside the Naples Sports Stadium, with half as many again outside demanding free entry. The police then arrived, in full riot gear, predictably enough setting off a riot. The promoters told Jon not to worry, explaining that by 'creating the impression of protecting people from civil disturbances, the status quo was maintained and the power of the State was reaffirmed!'

The backstage area had to be opened up to treat people suffering from the effects of tear gas, then, as predicted, around 10pm the police withdrew — their job done — leaving the fire brigade to douse all the burning vehicles. The band then went on and played until well after midnight, getting a fantastic reception. Jon told Monty Smith of *New Musical Express*: "I was on stage, which was obviously the safest place to be, but at no time did I consider pulling out — it would only have made the situation worse." As it was, the crowd loved their sophisticated style of music and they went down a storm. The next day, *Colosseum II* was on the front pages of all the national papers, just as they were to play to a sell-out crowd in Rome, which included several MCA 'execs' flown in from London. When John Mole was asked by *NME* if he fancied coming back to Italy, he replied pessimistically: "I don't think it's a question of fancying it. It may well be *impossible* to come back here for a few years."

Whenever the band toured in Europe it usually included a visit to Austria, sometimes playing concerts in the most unlikely places, arranged by their Austrian agent 'Pipsi' Fischer[2]. Pipsi knew everybody and the publicity that he managed to drum up was always impressive. He was as thin as a rake and while he was good at ordering food, never seemed very interested in eating it — breakfast for him was usually a glass of red wine and several cigarettes! As with many of his countrymen, he had been an accomplished skier practically from birth and was fond of regaling anyone that would listen with how he and his friends would get very drunk on New Year's Eve, charter a helicopter, fly to a mountain-top all togged up in skiing gear, jump out...and take off! Racing down steep mountainsides, off-piste and by moonlight, he supposedly 'lost' several friends over the years.

About this time, Andrew Lloyd Webber lost a bet with his cello-playing brother Julian over a Leyton Orient football match and as a result was forced to fulfil a long overdue promise to compose a work for him. Called *Variations*, it was a suite of music based on an original theme for violin by Paganini, which Andrew envisaged as a heady fusion of classical music, rock and jazz. He was undecided about which other musicians to use for the project, as he wasn't quite sure whether he could achieve the style he wanted from established session musicians. Then, while visiting his record company, MCA, who were keen to have a follow-up to his previous success *Evita*, he happened to overhear a test-pressing of *Electric Savage* and realised he had found the answer. Soon afterwards, Jon received a phone call. "You won't know me, but my name is Andrew Lloyd Webber — I just heard your new album and wondered if you would like to come to my flat to discuss working together." Jon was intrigued and agreed immediately. After making him welcome, Andrew sat at the piano and played *Variations* to a slightly bemused Jon, who subsequently remembered little of the meeting except Andrew's infectious enthusiasm. He was, however, aware that a couple of the themes were already buzzing around inside his head. Money was still very tight for *Colosseum II* and Jon had a hunch that this project could be interesting and maybe lucrative — now he just had to convince Gary and Don. Jon pointed out that Andrew was with the same record company — so it was all in the family, so to speak, and 10 days' well-paid studio work was not to be sneezed at! As the day of the first run-through drew near, Jon got a phone call from Andrew's manager, David Land, asking if he knew of a saxophonist who could double on flute, play classically *and* improvise. "Absolutely!" replied Jon!

On their arrival at the first rehearsal, Jon introduced Barbara as the wind player *and* his wife, and noticed the look on Andrew's face, as he must have thought...'He's rowed his wife in!' However, as soon as Barbara began playing, Andrew realised that she was the ideal choice. Don Airey was joined on keyboards for these sessions by the gifted keyboard player (and songwriter) Rod Argent who had been brought in by Andrew. This team of Rod, Jon, Barbara and John Mole would, in fact, go on to work with Andrew on many more of his projects over the next 10 years. *Variations* was released early in 1978 and was an immediate success, so much so that presenter Melvin Bragg re-recorded the opening section with Jon and the team for the theme music to his ground-breaking arts programme, *The South Bank Show* and kept it throughout its entire 32-year run.

What really impressed Jon about working with Andrew was that, though he didn't always find it easy to communicate what was in his head, when offered alternatives, Andrew was much clearer about what he wanted. It was a sometimes a little frustrating for the musicians, that he politely ignored most of their ideas or suggestions, but when the album sales went through the roof and they all got gold discs, Jon realised that Andrew knew *something* they didn't!

Colosseum II's second album, *Electric Savage* was eventually released in July '77, with a striking sleeve design featuring a beautiful black woman with electronic circuitry symbols in neon overlaying her naked body. Jon was really impressed and considered it the best of any of the sleeve designs for his albums to date. While most of the reviews were good, Angus McKinnon of *NME* wasn't very impressed it seems: "Fusion music has become just another by-pass system. Its apparently complex niceties are ultimately meaningless." The *Shields Gazette* was positive, in spite of commenting that Jon's drums were loud, writing: "It is worth listening past them, to hear the inventive keyboard of Don Airey and some startling guitar playing by Gary Moore." Pete Makowski of *Sounds* loved the album: "It's strong in content and presents a powerful version of the shape of British jazz/rock fusion." Makowski also singles out Gary Moore for special praise: "he surpasses himself, playing better than he has on any previous record. He can play fast, but every note means something." Makowski observed how well Moore and Airey worked together, but also lauded the new bass player: "John Mole hovers somewhere in between Hiseman's never ending armament of drum-fills and the dual leads of Airey and Moore." In spite of these encouraging comments, the album fared no better than *Strange New Flesh* and failed to chart.

Late in the summer of 1977, the band was back in Morgan studios recording another album. In August, MCA had released *Lament*, a track from *Electric Savage*, as a single, to dire press reaction. Sounds panned it and *NME*'s ace 'punk' supporter, Charles Shaar Murray, cribbing his style from Lester Bangs[3], wrote sarcastically that: "...it would be dangerous to play it on the radio, as it would cause motorists to fall asleep at the wheel." It seemed that the halcyon days of rock bands were over, with plenty of 'pro-punk' journalists ready to offer up a requiem!

The band nevertheless recorded a third album called *Wardance*, produced by Jon Hiseman with Martin Levan as chief engineer. There was abundant new material available and the music exhibits a high level of energy, with the band firing on all cylinders, proving that their constant gigging had moulded them into an impressively tight unit. As well as this, the Arbiter Autotune drum-kit, having overcome all its initial teething problems, was proving a joy to play and record. Jon, however, was keen to point out that he would never cease searching for the ideal drum sound, saying: "There are no rules about tuning drums. I am continually experimenting and changing, but I always seem to return to the system I developed while with the original *Colosseum*."

Wardance certainly fulfilled the promise of *Colosseum II*'s earlier efforts and the decision to take the instrumental path was, by now, surely justified. Their music is variously described as 'jazz-rock' or even 'fusion' and while it is open to debate as to its exact genre, *Wardance* is comparable to other examples of jazz-influenced rock albums, such as *Birds of Fire* by *Mahavishnu Orchestra*, *Romantic Warrior* by *Return to Forever* or *Moroccan Roll* by *Brand X* and must rank as one of Jon Hiseman's finest achievements. This band certainly had one of the most underrated line-ups of the current scene, with Don Airey's musical training bringing a classical influence to the album, while Gary Moore's playing is truly inspirational. Add to the mix Jon's understated drumming, which is both subtle and compelling, together with John Mole's punchy and melodic bass and you have a formidably talented ensemble, which deserved more recognition than it got.

The new album's release date was scheduled for late autumn to coincide with a UK tour. Prior to this, they played some European gigs, including a sprinkling of festivals, one of which was in early September at Scheessel's Speedway Stadium in Northern Germany. The bill was impressive on paper, with big names like *The Byrds*, *Steppenwolf* and *Iron Butterfly*, though the first two were no longer in existence! The promoter was one Jurgen Wiggenhaus, who, due to some very dubious financial calculations, found he'd bitten off more than he could chew. Sensing imminent disaster, he tried to abscond the night before the festival started, but was 'persuaded' by interested parties, among them the Hell's Angels, to stay for the fun. In fact 30,000 people came to see just six bands, two of whom could be filed under the 'never heard of them' category. The better-known names were *Van der Graaf Generator*, *Camel* and headliners *Golden Earring*, whose position as 'top of the bill' resulted in their equipment being destroyed when the stage was burned down at the end of the 'festival'. After picking up the fee for their mid-afternoon performance, *Colosseum II* immediately hi-tailed it for home. Stopped at the German/Belgium border by guards who had got wind of the serious trouble back at the festival, Jon and the other band members assumed their best English manners, charmed the officials and were duly sent on their way. It was clear, however, that foreign festivals were becoming something of a lottery, possibly even dangerous! The band's manager, Alan Hewitt, later described the event to *NME* as a 'total disaster'.

The UK tour kicked off at London's Victoria Palace on the 20th of November, with plenty of music press scribes in attendance, as well as Andrew Lloyd Webber. *Music Week* observed that: "Hiseman himself keeps a low profile, indispensable but unobtrusive. It is Gary Moore who dominates the stage — his antics are pure rock theatre, all slashed sleeves, sequined pants and facial grimaces. His playing was impressive, fast and fluent, full of drama and humour." In some ways, Gary must have appeared oddly out of place, as none of the other 'jazz/rock' bands featured a showman like him — indeed, most of them were renowned for their sobriety! Chris Welch of *Melody Maker* thought a new star had arrived, with the accolade: "Mighty Mole!" Though he was at pains to point out that there were no *stars* in this band. John Gill of *Sounds* was slightly underwhelmed by the show, writing: "They're impeccable musicians make no mistake, but I expected something more original from someone of Hiseman's stature. We BOFs[4] should stick together, but *Colosseum II* exemplifies the unacceptable face of the old wave."

Wardance was by now in the shops, with the mostly positive press reaction helping sales. The Welwyn Times headlined their review: "Where skill is still king." The *Watford Evening Echo* announced: "Another fine album of jazz-rock from a bunch of veterans who know what they are doing." which begs the question, how did Airey, Moore and Mole suddenly become 'veterans'? Interestingly, the *South Yorkshire Times* noted the lack of vocals and deemed the album disappointing. *Melody Maker* and *Sounds* were more enthusiastic, with Hugh Fielder of the latter summing up: "*Brand X* pointed the way, but *Colosseum II* isn't far behind. If they were American they'd probably be getting a lot more attention over here." Seems he hadn't done his homework too well though, as he thought *Wardance* was the band's second album!

The band's next stride forward came early in 1978, with an appearance on *Sight and Sound*, a prestigious joint production between Radio 1 and BBC2 TV. The idea was for the viewer to watch the programme while hearing the sound in stereo, which was achieved by turning the television sound off and listening to the radio broadcast. The show aired on 12th January, just before the band started another run of UK dates. On 16th February they played the Nutz Club in Mumbles, near Swansea, but arrived late, due to some really foul weather, which also deterred a lot of their audience. One fan, Nigel Hobday recalls the night: "When the band eventually did get on stage, there couldn't have been more than 30 people in the place!" The gig aptly ended with *Lament* and the hardy few made their way home in the fast deepening snow. Bad weather notwithstanding, the band could not avoid the fact that their fan base was steadily dwindling.

During the spring, the members of *Colosseum II*, together with Barbara Thompson, were busy playing live concerts with Andrew Lloyd Webber, to promote the *Variations* album, which by March had gone 'Gold'. Gary remembers this as being an awkward time for him: "I didn't read music but, thanks to John Mole, I'd learnt my parts. The rest of them were still reading theirs and I found it all a bit strange, but Andrew was a nice man, though he sometimes had trouble communicating what he wanted." The album was also strongly promoted in the States, so the 'tout ensemble' flew over to play showcase gigs in New York and Los Angeles. While they were quite happy to be in America again, it was quite frustrating for Jon and Gary to be over there but not playing *their* music. Ultimately though, *Variations* didn't make much of an impact in the States, possibly because it was just too 'English'. The overall success of the album (it reached number two in the UK album charts, just failing to knock *ABBA* off the top spot!), combined with Jon & Barbara's other commitment to tour with the *United Jazz & Rock Ensemble*, resulted in a prolonged break for *Colosseum II*.

To illustrate the vagaries of their life on the road, Jon relates this anecdote: "Barbara and I were booked for a European tour with the *UJ&RE*, the final gig of which was in Gdansk on the Polish Baltic coast. Right after contracts were signed, Andrew Lloyd Webber announced that, in response to public demand, *Variations* would play its only London date at the Royal Festival Hall — on the day after the Gdansk concert! I assured Andrew that we would be back in time and he promised to have a car pick us up at Heathrow to get us to the venue for the sound check. 'Fast forward' to Gdansk, where we had checked into a vast crumbling hotel on the beachfront. Barbara had been feeling ill on the journey, which turned out to be a serious bout of flu so on arrival she went straight to bed. Now, at this time in the Eastern Bloc, nothing much worked and services were limited. The hotel menu listed over 100 dishes, but we soon found out, only about five of them were available at any one time. Going hungry, I spent the afternoon trying to get some medicine for Barbara, which involved finding a local doctor ('Sorry, the hotel cannot help') then joining a lengthy queue at the chemists, which went out the door and down the street. The person in front of me turned round and asked me a question, in Polish, naturally. Obviously I didn't understand him and when I replied in English, he proclaimed me to be a foreign visitor and immediately ushered me to the front of the queue. Returning sooner than I expected with the medicine, Barbara then elected not to take it, demanding instead, brandy and soup! I tried room service — no response! I then went down to the hotel restaurant and tried to persuade someone to take a bowl of soup to the room, again without success. Finally I went into the kitchen and started to ladle some out myself, but the cooks and waiters, hanging about sheepishly in the background, were becoming restive and I was beginning to doubt whether I would ever get the soup back to our room. Luckily, at this point, the hotel manager himself intervened and delivered it personally!" Result!

"Next, I had to go to the venue and check out the drums provided by the promoter (it was too risky taking equipment into Poland at this time). The kit was very basic and flimsy, so I asked the stage manager to find a couple of local 'pro' drummers who would let me borrow their gear, so I could make up *one* playable double kit. The stage manager laughed, as my reputation had preceded me and the local drummers were already there in the front row to watch the sound check, as well as the show. With their help, I managed to put together quite a reasonable set. While this was going on, I mentioned to the promoter that Barbara and I really *had* to be on the 9.30am flight from Warsaw to London next morning and asked how reliable was the 8am connecting flight from Gdansk to Warsaw. The answer was a bit worrying; we'd be fine...providing there was no fog! He then recommended that we shouldn't chance it and advised us that he had a taxi-driver friend who, for a fare paid in English pounds, would drive us the 350km to an airport hotel in Warsaw, straight after the gig."

They played the open-air concert, in a chilly drizzle, to a small but enthusiastic crowd, after which Barbara and Jon set off in a distinctly odd sounding taxi. Jon recalls: "Well, I doubt it actually *was* a taxi — it was very small and uncomfortable. My guess is the promoter was doing a friend a favour, probably for a percentage of my English loot. Needless to say after a couple of hours driving, halfway to Warsaw and in the middle of nowhere, the radiator boiled over. Determined to get to the Royal Festival Hall at all costs and with a cold, sick Barbara huddled on the back seat, the driver and I trekked over fields towards the lights of a farmhouse. Returning with two bottles of water, we waited about thirty agonising minutes before risking opening the radiator to top it up. The car just about started and we managed to get underway again, but not having the remotest idea where we were, I was beginning to feel slightly desperate. However, as we were driving through the next town, I spotted a row of relatively modern taxis in front of the train station and realised our best bet would be to 'jump ship'. Ignoring our driver's increasingly shrill protests and with another sizeable sum in English pounds changing hands, we arrived at the airport hotel in the grey light of dawn. After a quick shower and an hour in bed, we headed off to the airport but when we got into the departure lounge, there was the rest of the band, relaxing while waiting for their connecting flight to Frankfurt! Fog — what fog! The story should have ended there, but no — our plane was late taking off from Warsaw and we were re-routed via Amsterdam, resulting in even more delay! By the time we eventually landed at Heathrow, our driver had obviously given up on us and departed. Meanwhile, Andrew, taking no chances (and unbeknown to us) had got 'deps' in for Barbara and me, but though we arrived too late for the sound check, we were in good time for the concert. I ended up feeling like I'd returned from a war zone!"

Back home...and another bombshell! Gary Moore had received a second offer from *Thin Lizzy*, this time to join as a permanent member, which he accepted, telling Jon of his decision after one of the *Variations* gigs. It was all a bit surprising, since he was on record as saying that he didn't get on with Phil Lynott and that *Lizzy*'s music wasn't challenging enough. The likely truth is that Gary thought *Colosseum II* didn't have much of a future now that *Wardance* had bombed. Gary did later confess to *Guitar & Bass* how much he owed to Jon: "He taught me to pull myself together and gave me a kick up the arse...he was very good at putting me on the right path, teaching me about integrity and a lot of other stuff, so I'll always thank him for that. A lot of the music was very demanding though — on some gigs we'd only play six songs because they were so long. You'd come off and have to lie down...with a headache from all the concentration." However, Gary remembers *Colosseum II* as a happy band that bonded well and admits that he had a great time and learned a lot from his time with them.

It looked like *Colosseum II* might be doomed...but no! Even though losing Gary was a blow, Jon determined to carry on. He auditioned many guitarists, eventually (and somewhat surprisingly) settling on Keith Airey, Don's brother, telling *Melody Maker*: "He came down from Leeds Music College and sat in with us. Without hesitation — I offered him the job! He's got such an individual style *and* tremendous power." Jon never understood why Don hadn't suggested him earlier, instead of them wasting time trying to find a Gary Moore clone.

In October 1978, the band played what would turn out to be its final tour, though there are no reports of where they played and nobody seems to be able to recall anything about it — though Jon is fairly sure that they played Spain. On his return, he gave an interview to *Melody Maker* optimistically laying out plans for 1979, based around a world tour, which would include Japan, Australia and the USA, as well as promising a new direction for their next album. There *was* some discussion about going back into Morgan Studios, but nothing came of it and somehow the whole thing just fizzled out.

Recently, Jon had this to say of the band's demise: "Despite its reputation now, *Colosseum II* was always the most dangerous of my bands to lead. John Mole was a sweet guy and though Don and Gary were capable of great writing and playing, they became less and less sure of themselves as the band failed to break through to the public. I had a blind determination not to leave any contracts unfulfilled, but when we got back from that last European tour and we all met with the record company, it was clear that *everyone* had lost faith, most importantly in me and my judgement. I had always trodden a fine line between success and failure, but at that meeting I freely admitted that I couldn't see any way forward. I had the feeling that heavy and technically intricate improvised music had had its day. I wasn't enjoying what we, or other bands of our ilk, were doing. It was over. I had no idea what I would do next, but as *Colosseum II* ground to a halt, I just felt exhausted!"

Jon later revealed just how precarious his own situation became: "There had been some hairy moments along the way. Over the course of the first year I borrowed £7,000 from my bank, just so we could keep rehearsing, auditioning and create the music so we could get a record deal. That was a lot of money in the mid '70s! Then when Gary decided he didn't wish to continue, it put me in big, big trouble. I had to use a lot of persuasion to get him to stay, but the fact that he *did*, saved my bacon and was an important factor in my agreeing to rename the band and get the record deal. Our dire financial situation got even worse, when, out of the blue, the bank wanted the loan repaid. This had to be done, with everybody's agreement, from the band kitty, but it meant that, despite giving our all, we were hardly earning enough to get by. As if all that wasn't enough, I was woken one night with the news that some kind of fracas in a South London pub had resulted in Gary getting his face slashed, which caused me *more* nightmares!"

As well as all this, there were the endless everyday technical problems, some of which required all of Jon's ingenuity: "We trucked a brand new, but, as it turned out, inadequately tested PA to the opening night of our final tour, somewhere in Europe. It was all set up in time for our 4pm sound check, but when it was turned on — nothing but 'roaring silence'. After a cursory investigation by the crew that revealed no obvious cause, I was summoned and informed that the new PA was dead. Rolling up my sleeves, I line-tested the signal chain and discovered that the multi-core cable carrying the microphone lines from the stage to the mixing desk had been incorrectly wired. So I did what any drummer would do under the circumstances — I called for a soldering iron and solder, sat at a makeshift bench for 4 hours and rewired all 32 lines. After that, playing the drums was easy!"

All these shenanigans would have defeated lesser mortals, but in Jon it just reaffirmed his indomitable spirit: "We lurched from crisis to crisis, always keeping faith with the music, but hanging in there by the skin of our teeth. When I looked at our *Sight and Sound* TV show on YouTube recently I was truly overwhelmed — in retrospect, the band sounds fantastic and everything we played made so much more sense to me now than it did back then. Gary, Don and John[5] (R.I.P.) were magnificent. I take my hat off to them. The problem for us lay in the fact that when the record companies aren't making enough money from a band, they start interfering. Now, that may be OK when they're dealing with pop, which was always a shotgun marriage between the creative talent and their business partners — but such a marriage assumes that both are competent and make good decisions. When it comes to art music; jazz, jazz-rock and modern classical music, the business side becomes less and less able to make those decisions because they fall further and further behind the creative momentum."

Recently, Jon somewhat pessimistically summed up the prevailing situation: "In the new millennium, jazz, jazz-rock and modern classical music as musical forms have almost no creative presence that impacts on the public. True you can always hear Mozart, Beethoven etc. being performed in major cities any night of the week, but many of these concerts are aided by arts subsidies, which are also steadily dwindling. The Proms *do* feature the occasional adventurous work, but by and large, dead composer's works are effectively intellectual muzak, however great the performance — or indeed how much the audience enjoys it. Jazz seems to be stuck, re-creating the '50s and '60s...while jazz-rock with its gentler sister, funk, isn't even played in lifts now!"

In spite of the gloomy situation in the UK at that time, Jon Hiseman had no intention of ceasing to play the music he loved. Instead, he formulated a strategy that would maximise the use of his music business experience, based on retaining as much control over his music as possible. He would develop this strategy with increasing success over the next few years — to such an extent that he continued to be a highly productive artist — but from now on, it would be with a new partner!

FOOTNOTES

1. Dave, Jon and Tony had, in fact, been reunited prior to this project. In 1975, Dave was commissioned by the BBC to write the score for a drama series called *Gangsters*, which was set in Birmingham and mirrored the activities of a real life family who dominated the city's nightclub scene. Dave: "This was in the days you could do everything yourself. I was the musical director, wrote all the material and put a band together, which included Jon Hiseman and Tony Reeves, to record it. It was great — and all paid for by the BBC!" Chris Farlowe sang the catchy title song, which was also released as a single which just crept into the UK Top 30. *Gangsters* was later (2006) released on DVD and merits re-visiting, both for the soundtrack and the drama itself.

2. Pipsi Fischer was *Paraphernalia*'s Austrian agent for 20 years, until 1999 when he died of throat cancer. At one stage he teamed up with Norbert Ehrlich who also loved Pipsi dearly and was in many ways, his alter-ego, managing the finances and generally lending a more respectable face to Pipsi's business. Norbert remains Barbara and *Colosseum*'s Austrian agent to this day. On one memorable occasion, Pipsi was put in charge of hundreds of ethnic performers during an African cultural festival promoted by Norbert in Austria. Striding about in an African cloak and wielding a staff, he assumed the mantle of a true 'leader', endearing himself to all and sundry, even signing letters and emails 'Pipsi of Africa'. Jon sums him up succinctly: "after they made him, they broke the mould."

3. Lester Bangs started writing as freelance for *Rolling Stone* magazine in the late '60s. His confrontational and truculent style he got noticed, but unfortunately, his ego frequently got in the way of his work, which often descended into personal attacks and clichés. Several British journalists used a similar approach to attack established bands when punk-rock arrived, which frequently led to them writing histrionic rubbish. In 1982, Bangs died prematurely at the age of 33, after mixing a cold remedy (Darvon) with Valium. In 2000, Cameron Crowe made a film of his life, *Almost Famous*, which featured Philip Seymour Hoffman as Bangs.

4. BOF stands for Boring Old Farts and was an acknowledgement that most journalists perceived punk-rock as the 'main game in town' and a great opportunity to increase circulation by appealing to a 'new wave' of young readers!

5. John Mole died on the 1st of August 2006, after battling cancer for several years. This is part of Jon Hiseman's tribute, which was read at his funeral: "I get the impression that John fought hard these last years and I guess life must have been very tough, both for him and those around him, but as I keep reminding myself, nobody says that life is fair and for most it certainly isn't. John was a quiet, almost reserved character, who often seemed ill at ease with his chosen role, but then when you least expected it; he would step forward, take the obligatory bass solo – and become the life and soul of the party! He played some of the greatest solos that I have had the privilege to accompany and I suspect, on these fleeting occasions, I was seeing the *real* JM. Those moments will be my abiding memory of John — genuine musical outbursts from deep within."

TM Studio

ABOVE: JH in the current TM Control Room, 2009

LEFT: JH's first studio, 1970

BELOW LEFT: TM Studio, 1988

BELOW RIGHT: Stuart Copeland in the TM Studio

LEFT: *ShadowShow* — left-right: Rod Argent, JH, BT, Clem, John Mole

BELOW: *United Jazz & Rock Ensemble* on their only British tour, Octagon Centre, Sheffield — left-right: Ack van Rooyen, Kenny Wheeler, Wolfgang Dauner, Albert Mangelsdorff, Eberhard Weber, Charlie Mariano, Volker Kriegel, Ian Carr, BT, JH

BOTTOM: *UJ&RE* 'Flying United' by Volker Kriegel

UJ&RE

TOO MUCH!

ABOVE: Dill Katz, bass, 1980

ABOVE CENTRE: Peter Hartley, violin, 1981

ABOVE RIGHT: Colin Dudman, keyboards, 1980

RIGHT: BT at Bracknell, 1982

BELOW: *Paraphernalia*, 1983 — left-right: Dave Ball, Bill Worrall, Rod Dorothy, BT, JH

Paraphernalia

313

Paraphernalia

ABOVE: *Paraphernalia, A Cry from the Heart*, 1988 — left-right: Paul Dunne, JH, BT, Phil Mulford, Pete Lemer

RIGHT: JH at NDR, September 1988

BELOW: BT, JH

LEFT: BT, *Breathless*, 1991

BELOW: BT and JH signing

BOTTOM: *Thompson's Tangos*, 2000

315

LEFT TOP: JH, Vienna, February 1990

LEFT CENTRE: BT in 2005; Billy Thompson, violin, 2005

LEFT BELOW: Dave Ball, bass guitar; Miles Ashton, sound engineer; Peter Lemer, keyboards; all 2005

ABOVE: BT on the Harley, Vienna, 2005

RIGHT: JH in Japan, 2007

ABOVE: BT with Marcus and Anna, 1976

BELOW: BT and JH at Lac de Ste Croix, France, near their summer home

THIS PAGE: BT with Humph and Helen Shapiro, London Palladium, 1990s

ABOVE: BT and *The Apollo Saxophone Quartet*, 2003
BELOW: Bandleader, Broadcaster, Author Ian Carr — R.I.P.

"As good as the band is, it would be
nothing without the talents,
both compositional and musical,
of Barbara Thompson."
Chester Chronicle

Chapter 17

WILDE TALES

"Thanks to Jon, I can listen to the albums
today and enjoy them without flinching —
they sound as good as ever. He would
never let anything go and was meticulous
in his role as recording engineer
and producer."
BARBARA THOMPSON

JON HISEMAN AND BARBARA THOMPSON had both led hectic lives since leaving school and forging their careers, but when the children arrived they had to find ways to balance work with their role as parents. Jon, being a 'night owl', didn't function too well in the mornings, but was OK at getting up during the night, so he had been the one on night-feeding duties while Marcus and Anna were babies. On the other hand, Barbara was a morning person and she'd often be up, composing, before the children awoke. All this was fine while they were working at home, but by the late '70s they were both so busy gigging that they could no longer cope without help. Jon told *Arena Theatre*: "It meant buying a much bigger house, one with a flat for the housekeeper that we desperately needed to run the domestic side of things for us — someone who the children could get to know and feel comfortable with. This way, the kids would have all their own things around them, which would give them some measure of stability."

So, at the end of 1977, they bought and moved into an enormous Edwardian eight bedroomed house on the outskirts of South London and hired their first housekeeper (who came with husband and daughter). As Jon and Barbara lay in bed that first night, listening to the creaking of the floorboards from the flat above, they felt they might be losing their precious privacy, but over time they got used to having people around. This first team didn't stay long and after the second round of interviews, Jon determined that young, single girls or childless couples were inherently unsuitable for the role and from then on, they always employed a woman with one or more young children, who was either divorced, or a single parent.

Following the exposure that Barbara received from the *Variations* project, MCA boss Roy Featherstone, obviously impressed by her talent, signed her to a six album deal and in January 1978 she recorded her debut album with *Jubiaba*, produced and engineered by Chris Tsangarides at Morgan Studios. Soon after

322

this came the first album from her main band, *Paraphernalia*, which as Barbara explains, operated on a democratic basis: "I don't treat the other musicians just as backing musicians. Some bandleaders keep the rhythm section firmly behind them, but that has never really turned me on. I like to play *with* the guys — they're just as important as I am, because we all make up the whole, which is what it is all about." She certainly meant what she said...the first track on the album, *Goodtyme Mr Sam*, opens with a drum solo! These first two albums gave Barbara an immense feeling of satisfaction, as she had been a 'side-man' on so many records in the past and now she finally had not one, but two of her own released in quick succession.

The band's first live gigs went very well and included prestigious appearances at the North Sea Jazz Festival in Holland, the Bergen Festival in Norway and another in Paris. The band's line-up varied occasionally, as Barbara explains: "*Paraphernalia* became a quartet with the same line-up as the first album, Colin Dudman on piano and Mini-Moog, Roy Babbington on bass guitar and Harold Fisher on drums. In Colin, I found for the first time someone who naturally understood my music and interpreted it in the right way. Harold was a superb drummer, but more importantly, the person that introduced me to my very first curry!" The band was getting plenty of work and as a result of all the personal publicity she received following the release of her albums, Barbara was chosen by the BBC to represent Great Britain in the European Big-Band Enclave. Each national broadcasting organisation sent one musician to take part and the subsequent concert was broadcast in all the participating countries. Barbara recalls; "It all took place in Barcelona and when I arrived and unpacked my saxophones, the rest of the band stared at me as if they had never seen a female musician before!"

It wasn't long before *Paraphernalia* saw more personnel changes — the first to depart being drummer Harold Fisher. He was building quite a reputation on the session scene and as he had a young family to support, he felt he needed to go where he could earn the most money. Harold, helpfully suggested 17-year-old newcomer Gary Husband, who Jon thought was an extraordinary talent (he would later go on to play with Allan Holdsworth and *Level 42*). However, after he had played a number of gigs with them, Barbara noticed that he had a tendency to play too loud, which was particularly intrusive in the smaller venues and this would occasionally prompt complaints from the audience. On larger stages his playing was more in balance with the band, but as their 'bread and butter' was primarily in the clubs, Barbara began to feel that his playing wasn't sympathetic enough and that he wasn't really right for the band. Maybe she didn't realise it, but the obvious man for the job was right under her nose!

Some nine months after *Colosseum II* folded, Jon gave an interview to *Musicians Only*, which brought forth the revelation that he, Jack Bruce and Allan Holdsworth had formed a new band and had already recorded some demos together. Jon enthused: "Jack is singing and playing better than ever and the idea of Jack and Allan writing together is intriguing. I'm just the drummer in the group, but I'm enjoying every minute!" Jack Bruce was just as enthusiastic: "We're hoping to do some gigs together at the end of the year, after Allan's wife has had her baby." As the music developed though, Jon began to realise that the chances of them getting a deal in the UK were slim, as he was sure there was little commercial interest remaining in progressive music. It would surely make much more sense for them to concentrate on breaking into the American market.

Disappointingly, the project didn't get that far...in fact it didn't progress beyond the demos (which have never seen the light of day), but it did rekindle Jon's desire to get back in the saddle and the obvious move was staring him right in the face...join forces with Barbara! Such a step would bring many benefits — one being that there would be no more long separations — and with his considerable past experience, he could take over the management of the band. In Barbara, Jon would have a proven and prolific composer, but he did realise that this would mean he would no longer have an outlet for his own lyrics: "Actually I felt that any success I'd had with my dream of a workable balance between good lyrics and improvisation had been patchy at best and always hard won. Above all, I was a fan of Barbara's music, so I felt very comfortable with it and felt sure I could help it reach a wider audience, but I think the main incentive came after Barbara's return from a German tour with *Paraphernalia*. It had been a great success; she had been paid in cash every night and on the boat back across the channel, had divided up the spoils with the boys, who were delighted to have finally made some real money. All very nice! However, in due course, all the tour expenses came home to roost on *my* credit card statement — hotels, petrol and food, to say nothing of Barbara's personal shopping!"

So, Jon joined *Paraphernalia* in the summer of 1979, at the same time as Dill Katz replaced Roy Babbington on bass. Soon after this, the band was booked to support Oscar Peterson at Ronnie Scott's Club, in London and Jon found it quite a relief to get away from being the front man and just play drums. He did, however, quickly become aware that every gig they played was packed, but the fee didn't always reflect this. Barbara had never had an agent in the UK and had always negotiated the bookings herself, so Jon's first task was to take over this role — and once again his previous experience at London City Agency back in '65 stood him in good stead. Over the next few months, Jon sorted out the organisation of the band, leaving Barbara to get on with writing the material for the next album. This was quite an ambitious project to which Barbara had given the title, *Wilde Tales*. It featured a concept piece in several movements, called *The Selfish Giant*, based on the Oscar Wilde children's story of the same name with Colin Dudman simulating a very convincing

325

'storm' on his Mini Moog synthesiser.

Looking back to these early albums, Barbara still considers them both strong efforts, but *Wilde Tales* still has a special place in her heart: "*The Selfish Giant* was a great success and I got lots of letters from fans whose children loved it too. Thanks to Jon, I can listen to the albums today and enjoy them without flinching — they sound as good as ever. He would never let anything go and was meticulous in his role as recording engineer and producer, as well as drummer supreme."

Soon after Jon joined *Paraphernalia*, BBC film director Mike Dibb[1] approached him with a view to making a documentary about *Colosseum II*. On learning that the band no longer existed and intrigued by Jon and Barbara's maverick lifestyle, he decided instead to make a film about them. They soon found themselves being followed around by a camera crew for several weeks, which included filming *Paraphernalia*'s appearance at the Bracknell Festival one hot summer afternoon in July '79. The result was *Jazz, Rock and Marriage*, an hour-long programme that aired one Saturday evening on BBC2. Coincidentally, the soundman on the film was Jon's old friend, Mike Savage, who had loaned him his Boys Brigade snare and cymbal back in the '50s and made those first Dave Greenslade Trio recordings in the Eltham Methodist Church Hall. The documentary also included footage of Marcus and Anna, as well as filming *Paraphernalia* recording *Wilde Tales* in Morgan Studios. They also filmed Jon demonstrating drum rudiments — the paradiddle, single and double-stroke rolls and the flam and he also explained, with the help of a video recording, what he thought had been wrong with his drumming back in the *Colosseum* days and admitted that, at times, when he couldn't hear the monitors he could easily lose touch with the other musicians. During the editing, director Mike Dibb came up against a familiar dilemma — the film was about the life of two musicians, but in telling their story, not much space had been left for music. When the 'powers that be' at the BBC saw a 'rough cut' of the film, they must have been impressed, because they scheduled 40 minutes of *Paraphernalia*'s performance at the Bracknell Festival appearance to be shown as a separate programme the following Monday, thus solving Mike's problem.

The two *Paraphernalia* albums, together with the TV documentary and the televised festival appearance, all contributed to Barbara's growing reputation and boosted her confidence. They also attracted much media attention, which probably contributed to *The Observer* nominating her as one of the artists most likely to become a star in the coming decade in an article entitled: *Eighty for the '80s*.

Barbara was gradually becoming aware of the need for some stagecraft to improve the band's live appearances, explaining in one interview: "A lot of jazz musicians, literally or metaphorically, turn their backs on the audience, but I know that audiences prefer you to acknowledge them, talk to them and let them know what's going on." *Paraphernalia*'s audiences covered a wide range of age groups and professions, but they all recognised the individuality of her music and appreciated her friendly and chatty stage announcements. Barbara then tried to describe the music they played, but found it quite difficult: "*Paraphernalia* is partly an electric band, but there are no guitars, so it's not overpowering. I suppose you could say we are in the same general area as *Weather Report*, though our sound is completely different." Coincidentally, it was when Jon saw a *Weather Report* concert that an important idea struck him. This legendary American group turned up at the Rainbow in North London with an obviously deaf sound engineer. The band's volume was so loud that after about 30 minutes, people were leaving in droves. Jon realised that with the very small PAs being used in the early '70s, most music, especially instrumental, hadn't been very loud. Considering the size of some of *Colosseum*'s audiences, their PA had been tiny. Three guitars, drums and a singer, all playing the same simple riffs, could be appreciated even at deafening levels, but the layered, complex, interactive playing of *Paraphernalia* had to be presented at a listenable volume and with great clarity. Most touring groups had a continuous battle with the acoustics of the different venues, but at least you stood a chance if you had a high quality PA, with the volume set well below maximum.

Paraphernalia's musical style was unquestionably an eclectic mix, but the fact is that Barbara, drawing on all her musical experiences and earlier influences, had finally found her own unique voice. While she was beginning to regard herself as a composer who just happened to play saxophones, at the same she was developing a unique voice on her instruments. Skating over the top of the rhythm section, always responding to what her fellow musicians were playing, using her ear rather than her technical knowledge and ignoring the limitations of her instruments, she developed a melodic style which connected directly with her audience. Most importantly, the audiences could never tell where the writing stopped and the improvisation began and listening back to live performances, recorded for radio and TV, neither could the band.

Early in 1980, Jon and Barbara were invited to work on another Andrew Lloyd Webber project. It was a musical called *Tell Me on a Sunday*, featuring singer Marti Webb and, as well as playing on the record, they also appeared in the TV special. This sort of gig was always scary for Jon as he still didn't sight-read music and relied on memorising his part after playing it through a couple of times. Jon remembers one particular example of Andrew being absolutely clear about the kind of sound he wanted to achieve: "We went into the studio to record *Take That Look Off Your Face* and during the rather cursory run through, Andrew told me to play 'massively', as if I was on a Phil Spector session. Listening back in the control room, I began to plan changes to my part for the second take. However, there was no second take — Andrew decided that we had played exactly what he wanted the first time and wasn't about to have it interfered with. He was right as usual and it was a great success, reaching number three in the UK singles charts. At the subsequent *Top of the Pops* recording session, Jon was playing his 'massive' drum part, when the producer asked him to play *louder*. The other musicians fell about laughing...*no-one* ever asks a drummer to play louder! Jon also assumed this to be sarcasm, until Andrew assured him in the headphones, that they did indeed require more volume. Jon obligingly went into overdrive!

Things were also busy on the *Paraphernalia* front, with a live double-album recorded at the Queen's Theatre, Hornchurch. Proving that they weren't resting on their laurels, they unveiled three new pieces — *Summer Madness*, *Scrummage* and the lengthy Peter Lemer composition, *Allyah*, featuring the second of Jon's recorded drum solos. The *Chester Chronicle*'s review got straight to the point: "As good as the band is, it would be nothing without the talents, both compositional and musical, of Barbara Thompson. She contributed six of the eight titles, which vary from the hauntingly melodic to the kind of outgoing disco/jazz usually associated with *The Crusaders*...and she takes risks in her playing — on *From Nowhere*, which changes tempo several times, she plays four instruments: tenor, alto, soprano saxophones and flute, in succession."

Any band recording a live album with a fair amount of new material on it, lets you know they are in good shape. In fact, this album would prove to be the most successful of Barbara's released by MCA and probably did more than any other to put her firmly on the map. In the modern vernacular, the band was now 'hot' and when they turned up for a gig at the 100 Club, Oxford St., towards the end of 1980, they were astonished to find that the queue stretched around the block.

Though the quartet format was serving them well, Barbara felt that adding another 'front line' musician would enable her to become more adventurous with her writing. However, she was wary of adding an overtly 'jazzy' instrument like trumpet or trombone. Then when Barbara and Jon were judging a jazz band competition in London in the early autumn of 1980, a violin solo played by a young Pete Hartley caught their ears. "I immediately realised that violin would be an the ideal partner for the saxophone and with its enormous range, would enable me to write more interesting and complex themes — and the band would become more 'orchestral' which of course, was in my background anyway."

So, they promptly recruited him and within 6 months he was also playing in an 'offshoot band' *20th Century Blues*, formed by *Paraphernalia* members Colin Dudman and Dill Katz, which featured the funky jazz drumming of Nick France. The band released one well-received album and the two bands, sharing personnel, coexisted amicably and even played on the same bill together a few times, but as Pete reminisced recently: "The difference was, I got paid for the gigs with *Paraphernalia!*" Perhaps Colin and Dill were discovering that it wasn't as easy to run a band as Jon & Barbara made it look.

In November, *Paraphernalia* played the Band on the Wall club in Manchester and to quote the effusive reviewer from the local *Evening News*: "They rarely fell short of breathtaking!" continuing: "The heavily accented rhythms give the music a vibrant physicality and provided sturdy underpinning. Dill Katz's propulsive bass guitar and Jon Hiseman's high-energy drumming meshed perfectly." Though the band was now taking off in England, it was still lagging behind their status in Europe, as Barbara told *New Musical Express*: "I've done so much television in Europe, but hardly any here. It's ridiculous. All the European festivals are filmed for television and I'm inundated with offers of work in Germany, but because of the lack of media interest here, you don't stand a chance." *Paraphernalia* was now so busy that Barbara decided to call time on her larger pub band, *Jubiaba*. Some of the guys borrowed the band's 'pad'[2] and did try to keep it going — but it didn't last long without her.

Paraphernalia had got a powerful head start in Germany, courtesy of the original *Colosseum* and the *United Rock & Jazz Ensemble*. The latter had become very big in Europe, having followed up their original live album with two further offerings: *Teamwork* and *The Break Even Point*, so now they were playing much bigger venues, which in turn was great promotion for Barbara. Jon remembers *Paraphernalia*'s first trip to Germany with him in the drum chair: "We had been booked into smallish clubs and they were so packed it was dangerous. We often encountered the exact same publicity stunt that had dogged *Tempest* and *Colosseum II*...the posters for the gig had JON HISEMAN emblazoned across them, several times the size of the band's name. Some of the venues, though, were arts centres and I quickly realised that they were perfect for us, as their capacity ranged from 200 — 1000 seats. We gradually built our following over several years, to the point where we could fill the larger venues, or play two to three nights in the smaller ones, thus making routing much easier. On that first tour, we had the use of a Bose PA system for the first couple of gigs, but then the Bose execs became so enamoured of the band that they stayed with us the rest of the tour, setting up their system at every venue. I was so impressed with the sound and portability, that on our return to the UK, I purchased 12 cabinets and amps, which we used for the next 10 years or so. I recall, after two very successful shows at the Capitol Theatre in Mannheim, collecting our fee and asking the manager who was doing the best business for him. He smiled and replied: 'Miles Davis, the *UJ&RE* and *Paraphernalia*,' which was music to my ears!"

Sometime later, at a *UJ&RE* concert in Munich, a very significant meeting took place. Trumpeter Ian Carr introduced

Jon to Eckart Rahn, a former bass player, who had set up a record company that had single-handedly been responsible for the birth of New Age Music[3]. He had recorded Paul Horn playing solo flute, quite literally *Inside the Great Pyramid*, then followed up its phenomenal success with *Inside the Taj Mahal*. It was the first attempt to marry simple, spiritual music to an external vision, producing something far greater than the sum of its parts. Eckart also had the innovative idea of licensing early classical recordings from the Decca catalogue, assembling all the slow movements onto one LP and calling it *Andante*. He then did the same with the fast movements (*Presto*), thus creating the unthinkable...classical music compilation albums!

In 1979, Rahn heard about the new and exotic style of contemporary music emerging in Brazil. After several trips to Rio de Janeiro and Sao Paulo, he recorded some examples of it for release on his Black Sun label, which he launched to promote the music of important musicians such as Egberto Gismonti and Marcio Montarroyos. He later suggested that Jon record with some of them and so, in January 1981, Jon flew to Rio de Janeiro and made his first solo album. One impressed reviewer wrote of it: "This is a departure from *Colosseum* and *Colosseum II*, but with a nod to *Paraphernalia*, in that Hiseman has more of a support role. The album has a Latin feel running through it, with greater emphasis on groove from Hiseman, which could be down to the influence of producer Marcio Montarroyos, who, in the past, has played trumpet with Stevie Wonder, Ella Fitzgerald and Carlos Santana." Jon called the album *A Night in the Sun* and he recorded his parts in about nine hours spread over two nights, interrupted occasionally by power cuts. Sadly, this first solo work remains a well kept secret — now a rare collector's item on vinyl, it has, to date, never been released on CD.

Meanwhile, Barbara was writing several new compositions, but finding it difficult to tell whether a piece would work until the rehearsal stage, admitting in an interview with *Arena Theatre*:

"It's quite a blow to the ego to take something to rehearsal and find that it sounds terrible. I usually end up crossing bits of it out; but this is something you must be prepared to do — and accept criticism gracefully. In the jazz environment everyone's a composer in a sense, because you improvise all the time and things change from night to night." She realised that the process of writing music required a long apprenticeship, though she had benefited from the help and advice she received from Neil Ardley back in the *NJO* days. This had certainly brought results, as she had already been commissioned to write works, both jazz and classical, for BBC Radio 3.

In April 1981, Jon and Barbara, together with Rod Argent and John Mole, joined yet another Andrew Lloyd Webber project, *Cats*. They spent a few weeks rehearsing with Andrew, developing their parts, before opening with the show at the New London Theatre and staying on for two weeks to record the London Cast Album at Olympic Studios. Jon worked throughout from his own skeletal drum parts and from memory, mostly playing what was in his head. A couple of days before the theatre's pit musicians were due to take over, Jon was handed a set of drum parts which Andrew had arranged to be transcribed from the cast recording and was shocked to see what it looked like written down. He felt sure that he wouldn't have got beyond the first few bars sight-reading, but when the new young drummer Graham Ward[4] arrived, he read it straight through, playing brilliantly.

As soon as he was finished with Cats, Jon received an invitation from *Focus* guitarist Jan Akkerman, to join him for some European dates with his group, *Special Edition*, which included a marvellous Danish keyboard player, Kenneth Knudsen. When Jon arrived at Copenhagen Airport, wearing only a light leather jacket, in sub–zero temperatures, Kenneth offered a gem of Scandinavian logic, delivered in perfect English: "There is no such thing as inclement weather — only inadequate clothing!" Jon didn't really enjoy the gig, as he felt he had entered a time-warp, playing with a very loud, very fast guitarist who seemed to have lost his empathy with the music, merely using it as a vehicle to impose his will and show off his technique. Moreover, Jon never had a clear idea of what was required of him and found it very difficult to 'jam' over the endless modal grooves and — bottom line — wasn't really interested in finding out.

A few months later, Barbara and Rod Argent went into Morgan Studios to record a joint project, an idea that had been mooted while rehearsing *Cats*. On the occasions they had worked together with Andrew Lloyd Webber, Barbara and Rod had formed a 'mutual admiration society' and agreed to share the writing on the album. Jon was to produce and, of course, play drums...John Mole on bass, Keith Airey (from *Colosseum II*) on guitar and Robin Jones on percussion. The music was a lot more laid back than anything Barbara had done before and featured a lot of gentle flute playing: "I think the title track worked really well, with a great drum feel, ghostly piano phrases and echoing alto flute, which made it very mysterious but funky at the same time. It nearly made it into the charts, as we had MCA behind us, but unfortunately I wasn't sufficiently 'single' oriented." MCA did release a 12" cut aimed at the disco/club market, which became a minor hit but, despite encouragement from the record company, Jon decided that it would be better to concentrate on what they had achieved with their own music, rather than start diversifying into another genre. The *Ghosts* album was eventually released in early 1982, with Rod and Barbara appearing on BBC's *Old Grey Whistle Test* to promote it, but it wasn't long before they returned to *Paraphernalia* business.

Paraphernalia's next album should have been the sixth and final one under Barbara's MCA contract. Once again, though, Jon sensed a sea change in the air, a growing awareness that major record companies were no longer prepared to support jazz and/or rock-based instrumental music. However, Jon had been developing a completely revolutionary plan which would enable them to play their chosen music and make a decent living. Back in 1979, he had been approached by ITV schools director, Peter Tabern, who needed soundtrack music for a children's educational drama called *The Shadow Cage*. This turned out to be a series of percussion-based 'sound-scapes', synched with the film's action, all of which were very well received. Over the next couple of years, Barbara wrote the soundtrack music for several shows, with Jon producing and he soon began to realise that, rather than paying expensive fees to other studios, he ought to build his own. Not only would they be able to record TV & film music between tours, but it would free them from their financial dependence on major record companies. More importantly, they could retain copyright control, both mechanical and publishing. Jon recalls: "Times, they were a-changing and I realised that no longer would any major record company be prepared to give me £100,000 for a three album deal, spread over a couple of years. That was the old days — and they were gone. A whole new management team had taken over at MCA, with their own way of doing things and I felt that unless we could record and deliver the master tapes with our own resources, we wouldn't be able to work to the standard I was used to. For a year I read up on studio design and acoustics, while searching for an old church to convert, but I began to realise that if this was to be set up on a proper business model, I would have to forget playing and become a studio manager, in order to hustle enough business to pay the overheads. Then it dawned on me...our big Edwardian house had a large L-shaped garden and all I would have to do was drain the pond (a nasty thing inherited from the previous owner) and build the studio onto the side of the house. I calculated that using the available space, the studio would be big enough to easily accommodate 10 musicians, plus a grand piano and a drummer, with a control room adjacent which would be bigger than the one I was used to at Morgan. If I used it primarily for our own projects, but also made it available for selected projects from friends, I could simply walk away and leave it when we went on tour. Thus, we would have our own means of production and could become good Marxist-Leninists!"

So, Jon went to see the new regime at MCA and suggested that they might prefer not to continue with an instrumental group that had such limited market potential. The 'new brooms' were visibly relieved and agreed to release Barbara forthwith, thus clearing the way for Jon to sign a deal with veraBra Records[5] in Cologne, a small but efficient record label run by their friend and European agent, Vera Brandes. Jon agreed to license the master-tapes to her free of charge and in return the record company would supply records (later CDs) for sale on the tours at a healthy discount, plus the artists would receive 20% of the dealer price as their royalty. This way, accounting would be straightforward, as no advance payments would be made and royalties would be paid from the first record sold, with veraBra covering all the up-front costs — sleeve design, initial pressing and publicity. It was a good deal for all, but most importantly, Jon and Barbara would be completely free from interference.

1981 had also been a good year for Dick Heckstall-Smith fans, as he had finally returned to playing music full-time. After getting his degree in 1976, he continued studying on and off for the next few years to obtain his PhD, but never managed to complete the course. While this was going on, he kept body and soul together by playing itinerant gigs. His son, Arthur, recalls his return to playing was somewhat tentative: "I think he might have been working with Julian Bahula's *Electric Dream* around then, possibly doing the occasional one-off jazz and poetry gig. I also remember him doing a few studio sessions with various people, including one all-nighter with Ginger Baker." The first major project Dick got involved with was the *Famous Blues Blasters*, a band featuring ex-*Thin Lizzy* guitarist Eric Bell, which got some good crowd reaction. They later changed their name to *Mainsqueeze*, recorded an album and toured Europe with considerable success. The album was called The *International Blues Rock Review*, and was quite well received, but they then accepted an offer to be the legendary Bo Diddley's backing group for a year. Arthur recalls: "It was really a comedy act and great fun. Bo had this box-shaped homemade guitar with strings that never snapped, they would just fall off the guitar!" During this period, it would seem that Dick was up for anything, as his involvement with the German band, the *Django Rheinhardts*, illustrated. It was not his kind of music at all, but he quite enjoyed playing with them. Jon's view was typically acerbic: "Actually, Dick was being used by off-the-wall anarchic groups — even comedy groups — because he looked the part and could play as 'out' as anyone. Sadly, he seemed incapable of making critical judgments about what he got involved in. It was all about living for the moment." Dick also started a couple of his own bands, *3-Space* and *Matt Black*, but they made little impression. Undeterred, he continued to apply his 'have saxophone — will travel' philosophy, in one way or another, for the rest of his life.

Arthur is quite clear about what drove his father during this period: "He enjoyed the idea of being back in those heady, early days...pre-Bond even, when he would turn up for a gig, not knowing what was going to happen. He wasn't nostalgic for *Colosseum* or anything else and never got emotional about such things. He did however, have one special memory; he had jammed with Hendrix during an American tour with Mayall."

Footnotes

1. Mike Dibb has been producing and directing films for television for almost 40 years, on subjects ranging from cinema and jazz to art, sport, literature and popular culture. Apart from *Jazz Rock & Marriage*, other music-related films include, *What's Cuba Playing At?* (BBC *Arena* 1985 — on the Afro-Spanish roots of Cuban music), *The Miles Davis Story*, a two hour special for Channel 4 about the legendary jazz trumpeter (which won an International 'Emmy' in 2001 for Arts Documentary of the Year), *Tango Maestro — the Life and Music of Astor Piazzolla* (BBC) and *Keith Jarrett — the Art of Improvisation* (Channel 4).

2. The 'pad' is what musicians call the collection of music that makes up a band's repertoire. Sometimes, as with *Colosseum*, the 'pad' is kept in the head, or scribbled down as chord sequences on odd scraps of paper! Jon always thought a gig should slowly "open like a flower" and considered that Clem had a good 'nose' for the shape of a show.

3. Eckart Rahn maintains that it was the record industry's inability to keep up with new developments in music that opened the door for him to found *Kuckuck Schallplatten* in 1969. Such was his success with groundbreaking artists like Paul Horn and Japanese artist Kitaro, that by 1980 the company was turning over a million dollars a year.

4. Graham Ward claims on his website to be the original drummer in *Cats* — he wasn't (check out the original London Cast Album), but he *is* a very successful session drummer whose other credits include work with Paul McCartney, Tom Jones, Jimmy Page, Jon Anderson, Donna Summer, Mark Knopfler, Ray Charles, Dionne Warwick, The Bee Gees, Lulu, The Supremes, Judy Collins, Ben E. King and Johnny Mathis. Jon and Graham have in common Jimmy Page, Lulu, José Carreras, Placido Domingo, Sarah Brightman, Elaine Page and *The Royal Philharmonic Orchestra*!

5. veraBra Records later changed its name to Intuition and was eventually sold to the Schott Group, a long established music publishing company with offices in a castle located in the centre of Mainz, Germany. When Jon and Barbara had occasion to visit there, they were introduced to the boss, who proudly admitted to being a big *Colosseum* fan in his youth. Schott was the original publisher for Beethoven and Mozart's music during their lifetimes and while there, J&B were shown original manuscripts from both composers. Beethoven's was full of corrections and rewrites, but Mozart's was pristine and appeared to have been written from left to right as the music came into his head

"I have never played jazz professionally in my life."
JON HISEMAN

Chapter 18

TEMPLE MUSIC

IN THE SUMMER OF 1982, Barbara was again invited to play at the Bracknell Jazz Festival, but this time, instead of *Paraphernalia*, they wanted a special project. In association with the Arts Council of Great Britain, they commissioned a new work for an augmented line-up, which Barbara christened *Serendipity*, after the Sanskrit name for Sri Lanka (Serendip). After meticulous research using the BBC archives and with help from the Sri Lankan Embassy, who provided her with tapes of ethnic music, she composed a suite of five movements, *In Search of Serendip*, based on Sri Lankan folk music. Unfortunately, Jon had been so busy supervising the construction of their recording studio[1], that when he finally came to set up his kit onstage at Bracknell, he was totally exhausted. He hadn't thought about drums or even picked up his drumsticks for over three months and having been involved in some of the physical work equipping the studio, he went on stage feeling as though he was wearing boxing gloves! On his own admission, he played like an amateur that night and got a deservedly bad review for some insensitive playing.

The studio was ready for action by August — albeit with unfinished décor and Barbara, having already written the music for the next album months ago in expectation of it being released through MCA, was also ready to go. With a UK and continental tour being booked for the spring, *Paraphernalia* began recording the day after the new mixing desk was commissioned.

Pete Hartley had been with the band for just a year, but at the end of the summer, he had left to make his own way in the world. Determined that the new album would reflect the changes in her writing brought about by the addition of a violin, Barbara immediately began looking around the local scene for another violinist but eventually stumbled upon the ideal replacement by pure chance, as she recalls: "Jon and I were in Cologne, on tour with the *UJ&RE* and were out strolling near the Cathedral, when we heard this incredible violinist playing. He was actually playing a kind of jazzy improvised folk and this immediately resonated with me." The busker had drawn a huge crowd and they waited patiently to talk to him, only to discover that he was English! This twist of fate led to Anthony Aldridge joining *Paraphernalia* for the recording of *Mother Earth*, which turned out to be a most impressive album.

Barbara's writing had really blossomed with the three movements of the *Mother Earth Suite*: *City Lights*, *Country Dance*[2] and *The Adventures of Water*. Jon's playing comes across as if he had finally found his *niche*, sounding more relaxed and content to let others set the pace. In fact, behind the scenes, Jon was, of course, anything *but* relaxed, as he was playing drums and producing at the same time as learning all he could about the workings of the new studio. With Martin Levan having recorded the tracks, Jon spent some time mixing the album as he grew accustomed to the sound of the new control room's huge Urei monitors. With all that under his belt, he and Barbara moved on to do a couple of short TV music projects, while impatiently awaiting the release of *Mother Earth*.

When they moved into their 14-room Edwardian house in 1977, they had a mortgage of just £13,000. In order to fund the building of the studio in 1982, Jon had upped this to £90,000 (and remember...during the '80s, mortgage interest rates rose to 15%!). Oddly enough, Jon doesn't remember feeling that this was any kind of gamble at the time, since he had absolute faith in Barbara as a composer, performer and artistic personality. Recalling the release of *Mother Earth*, Jon says, with pride: "This was our first, entirely owned and funded, in-house recording project — released on our own label and upon which all our hopes for the future were pinned!" It eventually hit the shops in March 1983, to coincide with their tour and proved to be a great commercial and artistic success: "...especially considering that it was only instrumental music *and* tainted with 'jazz!'" adds Jon.

Jon and Barbara were now much in demand, with an impressive work schedule that included several important TV appearances with Andrew Lloyd Webber. It was an incredibly exciting period, as Jon told Dmitry Epstein recently: "One minute I'm working with stars like Placido Domingo, José Carreras and Sarah Brightman, playing with a big symphony orchestra, when the drummer's approach has to be completely different because they are always playing much later than you, so you really have to learn to play inside it. Then, the next minute, I'm playing with the *United Jazz & Rock Ensemble*, where every musician is a bandleader in his own right and, as a drummer I have to get into each writer's head. To be honest, I'm not too happy with a lot of my playing on the *UJ&RE* records, because we tended to record live, after just a few days' rehearsal — and before I had a real understanding of how each piece worked."

Following their extensive tours of Germany and the UK on the back of the *Mother Earth* LP, *Paraphernalia* took a break and Barbara and Jon, with the studio available, took the opportunity to reunite with Rod Argent, John Mole and Clem Clempson in a band they called *Shadowshow*. It was a happy time for Clem: "I remember it was great fun working with Jon and Barbara again, especially with the luxury of having Jon's studio at our disposal. I really enjoyed the sessions, but one in particular stood out for me — when we recorded a song I'd written with David Sancious and Gary Bell, called *Manhattan Midnight*. I asked David (who happed to be touring the UK with Billy Cobham) to play keyboards on the track and he came up with the most stunning, effortless solo — on the first take!" Barbara recalls: "It was a nice album to make, but maybe it was a mistake making it half instrumental and half vocal. It *was* quite commercial, though and we did get offered a slot on one of the top TV shows, though unfortunately, this had to be cancelled, as I went down with flu. In fact, the band only ever played one gig and made one TV appearance on an arts programme in Bristol. We did, however, release a single, *Secure in You*, with a great Rod Argent vocal, that one Radio 2 DJ really loved and played to death. We nearly got it into the charts — but, in the end, the money we spent on promotion was all to no avail!"

This ill-starred project did, however, highlight several issues for Jon. Owning his own studio, he assumed that they could record whatever they liked and release it to an eagerly awaiting public. He now realised that making the records was the easy bit; the question was — how would they finance the marketing and promotion? Unless you produced commercial records, ('product', as the suits liked to call it) no major company would ever be interested — but *they* were the only ones with the money *and* the promotional 'clout'. One way was to concentrate their efforts on the free publicity that came with playing lengthy tours, i.e. name the tour after the album and hit as many European towns as possible, ensuring that the posters featuring the album sleeve were plastered everywhere they played. This, together with local press and radio interviews, plus the odd TV appearance, would ensure that they reached their fan-base...a policy that worked remarkably well. Playing with both the *UJ&RE* and *Paraphernalia* virtually exclusively, enabled them to focus their creative output and concentrate on building the Barbara Thompson name, but the downside was that they would no longer be able to get involved with any odd projects or artists whenever they fancied.

While Jon and Barbara were moonlighting in *Shadowshow*, Colin Dudman and Dill Katz, decided to leave *Paraphernalia* in order to concentrate on their own group, *20th Century Blues*, and Anthony Aldridge took the opportunity to move on as well. At first, Barbara was quite shocked and found herself feeling bereft: "This incident brought about the first real low in my musical life, as up to then everything had been getting better and better, scaling new heights and winning audiences wherever we played. I viewed *Paraphernalia* as very strong unit — especially with Colin on keyboards and Dill on bass...and I missed them."

However, Barbara is never one to rest on her laurels and she and Jon immediately decided to re-form *Paraphernalia* and record the five *Serendipity* pieces she'd written for the Bracknell Jazz Festival as the backbone of the next album. The new line-up comprised Jon, Dave Ball on bass, Rod Dorothy on violin, Bill Worrall[3] on keyboards and, of course, Barbara, who planned to play her old school recorders on some tracks, to add a touch of ethnicity. Of the three new guys, only Dave had auditioned — the others had all come recommended. Jon had already spent two days listening to numerous bass players and was exhausted. He was actually sitting in the studio toilet, when Dave plugged in to an amp and started to warm up on *Country Dance*. "I didn't need to play with him — I just knew at once we were on the same wavelength," recalls Jon — and although Dave left for 10 years to pursue a heavy rock career, he is still with *Paraphernalia* at the time of writing.

After more than 15 years on the road, Jon had certainly developed a deft touch with 'managing' musicians. Finding 'simpatico' sidemen for a band that, of necessity, has to spend several months a year together in close proximity is never easy. As a 'tough young man amongst tough young men', Jon had learned quite early on how to get along with some pretty awkward characters and about the difficulty of living and working with artists who are self-absorbed, egocentric and, in many cases insecure — until the moment they walk on stage! Most performers have dual personalities — the onstage and offstage personas, with very little correlation between the two. However, in Jon's experience, almost without exception, the best performers were also the nicest people, probably because they had the 'goods on them' and were aware of it. So, whenever Jon auditioned, he always made sure he looked at *both* sides of a player.

Less than a year after fitting out the studio, it was time for the first upgrade. With early (and very expensive) CD players just coming onto the market, Jon realised that the vinyl LP was on its way out, so before work started on the new album, he purchased the groundbreaking Sony F1 digital recording system, using Betamax video tapes as the audio recording media. Thus, instead of making a conventional 24-track recording, requiring overdubbing and mixdown, Jon, with this new technology, intended to make a direct-to-digital *stereo* recording for subsequent release on LP *and* CD. The musicians would be recorded playing live together in the studio, so any 'cock-ups' meant they would have to re-start each number. Since Jon was playing drums, his favourite engineer, Martyn Webster was brought in to man the control desk and carry out the live mix. However, there was a minor incident that threatened the project on the very first morning, as Barbara recalls: "I had a French friend, Pascale, living down the road and she decided that we should go for a jog around the block every morning. We wore these silver boiler suits that stopped the traffic every time! Anyway, the morning we were due to start recording, we set off — but a hundred yards down the road, I tripped over an uneven bit of pavement and fell headlong. I was OK, except I totally skinned my palms and had bits of gravel stuck in the flesh. However, the other musicians were waiting and 'the show must go on', as they say. Having finished the day's recording wearing gloves, Jon drove me to our local A&E, where they had to pull the skin back to swab out the gravel — which was very painful." In the event, since the band was so well rehearsed and with Barbara playing through the pain, the album took only four days to record.

It's interesting to note that Martyn Webster's mix for this album puts Jon's drums more to the fore than on previous *Paraphernalia* recordings; also there seems to be a greater musical contrast than hitherto, making it difficult to classify. Although there's a great deal of improvisation, it's not really jazz — with its contrasting styles it comes closer to what later became known as 'world music'. The album, called *Pure Fantasy*, was released in the late spring of 1984 and Jon believes that it was the first all-digital recording (DDD) of a pop, rock or jazz album to be manufactured and released on CD in the UK. It was re-released in the 1990s, when the title was changed to *Nightwatch*.

The European tour that followed was one of their longest and most successful so far, but the Hiseman children, now approaching their teens, required more and more attention. Fortunately, the studio was now very busy with a myriad of projects helping to underpin their finances, which meant for a few years, they could cut out the longer tours and work for shorter periods, closer to home. During this time, Jon was asked to represent the Paiste cymbal company, as part of their International Drummer Service which, though it didn't bring in much extra income, did give him the opportunity to spend some very pleasant evenings, talking drums with some of the world's finest players.

At this point, Jon and Barbara got involved in one of the strangest projects ever. They filmed a 'commercial' for the Electricity Generating Board, called *Busy Kitchens*. Jon got a call from Tom Parkinson (the producer of *Supershow*, back in 1969) who asked him if he wanted to take part in an advert, playing drums — and, by the way, did he happen to know a female 'trumpet' player (echoes of *Variations*!). A deal was quickly done and they soon found themselves in a film studio, set up like a suburban home. The scenario was that, after a busy day for the 'domestic' couple and their children (not Marcus and Anna!), the 'electric' dishwasher did all the dishes, while they relaxed with their favourite pastime — her blowing 'electrifying' sax and him playing 'electric' drums. Jon was intrigued to discover that Trading Standards required that, before you show an open dishwasher with all the contents sparkling, it really *did* have to wash a load of dirty plates and glasses that had actually been used by the cast on screen. Given that it was their first attempt at anything like this, it was all going very well and after the initial takes, while they were finding their feet, the crew and director took them for granted. The soundtrack had been pre-recorded at Jon's studio, so they could mime to the playback. While they were waiting around, he and Barbara had a little 'jam' and one surprised crew member shouted down from the lighting rig: "Wow! You actually play them?" Jon answered "Yes, we're musicians." "Blimey — we thought you were professional actors and wondered how come we'd never seen you before!" It had been a prerequisite that they join the actor's union, Equity, for the two days of the shoot, but that was the start *and* the finish of the Hiseman/Thompson TV soap opera.

Back in Sutton, the Temple Music office was now being expertly managed by Diane Cuthbert, an extremely able and efficient lady. She originally joined Temple Music on a part-time basis, working just a few hours a week. Ten years later she was booking all the UK gigs, managing all the publishing and record company accounts and generally running Jon and Barbara's lives. In truth there were times when Jon felt he had lost touch with where the money came from — and disappeared to, because she took care of it all. Diane's taking over all the admin work, gave both J&B the freedom to concentrate on their music *and* spend more time with the children. Finally she fell in love with a studio client and after staying on long enough to teach Jon the business and help him to computerise the office, she rode off into the sunset.

When they were not on the road, Jon and Barbara were becoming increasingly involved in writing and producing film and TV soundtracks, which occasionally featured Jon's experimental simulations of orchestral ensembles, using a combination of synths and live instruments. They decided to adapt this technique for some of the tracks on Barbara's solo album, *Heavenly Bodies*, recorded over the summer of 1986, the inspiration for which came from Jon and Barbara seeing five 'pop-art' paintings by Swiss artist Dominique Appia in Berlin. Barbara had been struck by the stories they conveyed and felt they would work well musically. So, when she was in Switzerland for a few concerts, Barbara visited Appia in Geneva and asked permission to reproduce his paintings for the CD booklet. When writing the suite, she didn't restrict herself to a specific line-up, but took a more classical approach, varying the instrumentation to suit each piece. The second half of the album comprised a reworking of some of the themes Barbara had created for film and TV projects and in keeping with the spirit of the music, Jon played mostly percussion — which included a pair of tympani, bought especially for the occasion. Making his debut on *Heavenly Bodies*, following the departure of violinist Rod Dorothy, was new young guitarist, Paul Dunne, who, interestingly, had first been inspired to take up guitar after seeing an early incarnation of *Paraphernalia* playing at The Tramshed in Lewisham. This album, which was never toured as such, provoked the least reaction of any of their releases and Jon has always counted it as something of a failure. He was sure the music would never adapt to live performance, but Barbara was made of sterner stuff and over time roughly half the album found its way into *Paraphernalia*'s show, albeit substantially re-arranged.

Considering that they now had their own studio, their own projects hadn't exactly been prolific since its inception — just the two *Paraphernalia* albums, *Mother Earth* and *Pure Fantasy*, plus the ill-fated *Shadowshow* project and Barbara's solo album Heavenly Bodies. By the mid '80s there were, however, many others who wanted to use the studio facilities and Jon, as house producer/engineer was once again, on a learning curve. One of the first 'outsider' projects had been a fifty-minute film documentary, *The Challenge* — about Peter de Savary's attempt to win the America's Cup yacht race. Later, in 1986, the film's editor was working on an ITV cop series called *Cats Eyes* and recommended J&B for the soundtrack music. Barbara wrote the theme (which featured Jon playing Simmons drums, the first ever viable electric drum kit) and they subsequently created the incidental music for over 20 episodes. Producers and Directors of TV drama series were well aware of how the right music could enhance a scene — indeed, many scenes shot in haste under TV's ruthless production schedules had to be rescued by the soundtrack music. But, by the same token, its powerful influence was feared by many directors for the havoc it *might* wreak on their project. As Jon explains: "The script would have been argued over for months, then the assigned director would have spent about six weeks prepping, six weeks shooting and six weeks editing, only for a team of 'musos' to arrive and mess with their baby at the last minute! Those few directors who *did* understand the power of music — who knew the contribution it could make and filmed with this in mind, were a joy to work with."[4]

Everything seemed to be going so well now — but they were both about to get the fright of their lives. Jon hadn't been feeling quite right for some months, but had shrugged it off it as the effects of overwork. They both set off for yet another *UJ&RE* tour, but at the first rehearsal in Stuttgart, Jon began to feel extremely unwell. At first he thought the ache in his shoulders and neck was due to lugging heavy suitcases around, but his condition worsened during the night. He was initially checked over by a sport chiropractor, who noticed that Jon's blood pressure was abnormally high and immediately gave him pills to bring it down — a few minutes later, Jon threw up all over his carpet. Determined to keep playing, Jon, slept in the back of the band coach on the way to Frankfurt and somehow got through the next gig, but when he awoke the following morning, he knew something was seriously amiss. He took himself to Accident and Emergency at the Goethe University Hospital and described his symptoms. After waiting for an hour or so, he was shown to a cubicle where his blood pressure was taken again — and all hell broke loose — it was now going through the roof and fifteen minutes later, after a blood test, he was diagnosed with acute kidney failure! Jon tried to get off the bed, declaring: "I've got a gig to do!" "You, my friend, are not going anywhere," the doctor told him, pushing him back down firmly. Later that evening, he slipped into a coma, but before that happened, determined to tough it out alone, he told Barbara there was nothing she could do...and to rejoin the tour.

Jon spent the next five weeks in hospital, where it was discovered that he had only *one* kidney and the blood supply to it was partially blocked. Barbara returned to the hospital when the tour was over, sat around for a day, but Jon then dispatched her back home to the UK, where the children *and* a deadline for a new TV theme awaited her. Staying in touch by phone, she feared the worst and began to prepare for a life with Jon on dialysis. For his part, Jon, with a lot to live for, simply never contemplated that this could be the end of the road. However, the hardest part came when, following the discovery that his only kidney was not functioning, he had to lie motionless for two days so the incision in his leg, where a catheter had been inserted, could heal. At this point, a nurse brought him a telegram from Keef Hartley: "Stop messing about — need the belt-sander now!" Unable to move for fear of re-opening his wound, two nurses had to hold him still while he shook with silent laughter...and gratitude for being bought back to the real world. This telegram, now framed, occupies pride of place on the wall of the TM studio toilet! After a three week battle to find the right cocktail of drugs to control his elevated blood pressure, the surgeon who had performed Germany's first heart and lung transplant a few weeks before, cut Jon nearly in two, piled his innards on the table beside him, took a piece of vein from his leg and joined his kidney to his aorta — rather like repairing a drum kit, as Jon liked to say later. Coming round from the anaesthetic in intensive care with a large tube inserted down his throat, a nurse arrived and started giving instructions to Jon — in German! Not understanding what he was supposed to do and unable to respond, the nurse assumed Jon had suffered brain damage and pressed the panic button! He was immediately surrounded by a team of medics, trying to assess the nature of his problem. With great presence of mind, he slowly raised his hands and mimed writing on a piece of paper. A pad and pen were promptly thrust at him and he wrote in large letters — 'ENGLISH'! The team immediately realised what the problem was and showed Jon his chart...his name was spelt: 'HEISMANN'!

He arrived home barely able to walk and very underweight. When he went for a check-up at his local NHS hospital, the specialist read the notes provided by the German doctors and remarked that it looked like someone had been getting their own back! "We wouldn't have treated your problem this way," Jon was told, "We would have dealt with it medically." Jon: "Would I have been able to work during the treatment?" Specialist: "No, I don't think so; not for a couple of years!" Eight weeks later Jon was back rehearsing...in another four he was back on the road and the old war wound hasn't troubled him since!

In early 1987, Jon and Barbara appeared on the *UJ&RE* album, *Round Seven*, with Barbara contributing one track, *Voices Behind Locked Doors* (which *Paraphernalia* later also recorded on their second live album). The ensuing *UJ&RE* tour was, as usual, a great success and it seems that J&B's musical life had now settled into a pattern of tours and albums, with the *UJ&RE* and *Paraphernalia* alternating, though always ensuring that they didn't both tour in the same year. *Paraphernalia* always drew a lot of interest wherever they played in Europe, helped, of course, by their frequent personal appearances on local television and radio. Indeed, Barbara, whose physical image hardly changed throughout her career, was quite often recognised on the street in Germany, Austria and Switzerland — quite a contrast to her relative anonymity in the UK.

Ever active, Barbara was already writing furiously for her next album and at this point, keyboard player Peter Lemer finally joined *Paraphernalia*. Throughout the years since Barbara was at college and Jon was semi-pro, they had always stayed in touch with Peter and he had been Barbara's first choice back when she had originally formed the band, so things had kind of come full circle — it also meant that Jon would be working with his old friend again. Barbara recalls: "Peter always played to such a high standard, rising to whatever challenge I gave him, however difficult. We've played some interesting gigs in the past — I remember one at a lawyer's convention in Windsor Park, which my dad had fixed for us through his Law Court connections, where they were debating the pros and cons of Britain joining the EU — needless to say Peter joined in vociferously. The students were really impressed with our music too; begging us to play some more...and one young female lawyer came up to me afterwards and said that she'd never been so moved!" It seems Barbara often affected people this way, as Dave Gelly confirms: "My next-door-neighbour also plays saxophone and I remember him saying that it was seeing *Paraphernalia* when he was a teenager that influenced him to take up music."

Back in England, *Paraphernalia* prepared for their autumn 1987 UK tour. The line-up was now Jon and Peter Lemer, with Paul Dunne on guitar and a wonderful young bass player, Phil Mulford. The plan was to record a live double album toward the end of the tour at a suitable London venue, but this turned out to be fraught with problems. Jon had heard that the BBC Riverside Studios in Hammersmith had recently been converted to an Arts Centre and that it still had all the original soundstage acoustic treatment[5] on its walls, so he went along to check it out. He was quite impressed and thought it would be ideal for the live recording. Riverside were happy to promote two consecutive nights with the band and Jon decided to play the same show twice each night, giving them four recordings of each piece to choose from.

Jon had, for a while, been researching 24-track tape machines, as the one he had bought cheaply in 1982 was showing signs of age and becoming noisy. The background noise or 'hiss' that accompanies recording on tape had become a real problem with the advent of CDs, because they, unlike the LP, reproduced the music cleanly, with no extraneous noise. At one point he had four machines on test in the control room, recording the same things onto each simultaneously and then comparing the playback quality. Dolby, now famous for its movie 'surround-sound' system, had recently introduced Dolby SR, a new 6-band tape-noise reduction system (costing £14,000 *back then*!) and it became terrifyingly clear to Jon that if the recorder did not replay *exactly* what it recorded, the Dolby system seriously screwed with the sound. Of these four machines, three failed the test and one was far and away the best — the MCI, based on the original classic Ampex design. Having purchased one, Jon, with the upcoming live album in mind, set about finding a mobile recording unit that used these machines. He was eventually successful and booked it for three months' time, but when he arrived on the afternoon of the first concert, was shocked to discover that they had replaced the MCI with the Otari MX80 — the worst sounding machine of the four he had tested.

Despite these problems, the album was expertly recorded by Martyn Webster, mixed by Jon over the Christmas period and released in the spring of 1988. The band treated the audience to a well-structured programme, providing plenty of dynamics, with, in Jon's view, Peter Lemer's keyboard playing excelling. On *Eastern Western Promise* he managed to convey a unique insight into an ethnic world that, as the son of a mid-European Jewish immigrant, was obviously embedded deep in his psyche. His performance that night touched a chord with both Barbara and Jon and in the years since, he has contributed many stunning ethnic accompaniments to Barbara's and his own compositions and now — some 22 years later, is still an integral part of *Paraphernalia*. As far as Jon and Barbara are concerned, it is inconceivable that the band could exist without him.

For Jon, this album is also notable for finally ridding him of one of his demons. He'd always been nagged by the fact that, when he heard himself on records, his playing never sounded as he'd intended, something that had bugged him from the very early days. Jon: "I was always experimenting...pushing myself. I now realise this wasn't always good for the band I was playing in. I didn't get it under control until the late '80s, when, for the first time on *A Cry from the Heart*, I heard recorded, what it was that I had intended to play."

This second live *Paraphernalia* album was very well received and for the next couple of years the band continued to tour successfully. It also brought a welcome bonus for Jon, who was delighted to be able to make the decision that it would be the last of their albums released on vinyl and cassette. It also marked another watershed — it was ten years since Jon had left the rock world behind and looking back, he felt that it had been a much happier and more creative time. Not only had he laid a lot of ghosts, he had also developed a number of additional skills...now he and Barbara could view the future with optimism. Jon felt that he had learnt his lessons well: "The success of the *Paraphernalia* albums albeit interspersed with the failures of *Shadowshow* and of *Heavenly Bodies*, had taught me that an album was, in reality, a snapshot of a given moment in time and not a continuing event. So for it to be an artistic and commercial success, it was necessary to get every element right — the title, the music, the players, the sleeve design and, in our case, the promotional aspects of a well-planned tour. Those early days when anything new was given a hearing were gone. By the '90s every artistic endeavour had to be more focused than ever to succeed — so Barbara and I spent more and more time planning a project, before a note of music was written, let alone played. I was never under the illusion that playing purely instrumentally would bring in the big bucks, but I always felt completely at home with the wonderfully inventive music that seemed to flow out of Barbara. She was a composer who could respond creatively to any vision, whether evoked by a well-expressed idea or an imaginative title. Of course, I abandoned my grand design of trying to fuse complex rock rhythms, intelligent lyrics and heavy instrumental improvisation, which, as I was happy to admit, had finally 'died in sight of day.'"

In 1990 Barbara and Jon visited the 12th century Abbaye du Thoronet in Provence, near to their summer home. They were both impressed by the fantastic acoustics and thought that the enormous vaulted space, with its natural seven second reverberation, would be perfect for recording a solo saxophone album. After much thought Jon came up with the title *Songs From the Centre of the Earth*, which helped shape the music Barbara would write. She researched ethnic folk songs from several different countries, finding a wealth of material, including a work composed by the 16th century monarch Henry VIII, who, it turns out, was a prolific writer of ballads. It then took about 18 months of correspondence between their good friend Werner Viertmann and the French Historical Monument department, obtaining permission to set up a digital recorder in the Abbaye. Then, because it was open to visitors, they were only allowed to record between the hours of 9pm and 3am, which was a trifle eerie. Barbara said she could even hear bats squeaking in the darkness above while she played...but with a couple of bottles of cool rosé wine and some tasty French cheese, the two pleasantly warm summer nights passed by in a flash — and another album was in the can.

Songs From the Centre of the Earth included some haunting songs, the most famous of which would probably be *The Fanaid Grove* — an Irish ballad telling a sad tale of lost love. The extent to which some of these traditional songs had been forgotten was evidenced on *Paraphernalia*'s next tour when they played Belfast and Barbara introduced *The Fanaid Grove* to the audience as 'here's one you'll know' — but nobody did!

In the early '90s, Pip Burley, the producer of the TV series *A Touch of Frost*, who knew of Jon and Barbara through his daughter, as she had been to school with Anna Hiseman, gave a copy of the CD to the editors of the pilot episode for them to use as incidental music. Barbara and Jon were then commissioned to compose and perform the music for the whole series and the original Abbaye recording of *The Fanaid Grove*, with additional orchestral backing, became the show's title music. The series, starring David Jason, was an immediate success, getting tremendous ratings and continued for many years, with Jon and Barbara recording the music for the first 22 episodes of the show before having to bow out due to pressure of their other work.

Very little mention has yet been made, so far, about Jon's music publishing business. In the early '80s, with their own studio enabling them to keep control of their copyrights, the next logical step was to add a publishing arm to Temple Music. Starting with all of Barbara's compositions, Jon then managed to take over *Colosseum*'s publishing from the failing Bron Organisation. About the same time, Eckart Rahn, the German owner of specialist New Age music label Celestial Harmonies, who had bankrolled *A Night in the Sun*, suggested that Jon become his UK sub-publisher and track licensing manager. This deal brought TM nearly 6,000 titles, including many jazz classics from giants like Benny Golson, Cecil Taylor and Ornette Coleman. A long association with Eckart followed, during which he released two of the Barbara Thompson 'specialist' albums, *Songs From the Centre of the Earth* in 1991 and *Three Quartets* (featuring the *Apollo Saxophone Quartet*) in 2006.

By the late '80s, Jon had become involved in importing and marketing the complete Celestial Harmonies catalogue, in partnership with Laurence Aston[6]. Laurence also managed Mike and Kate Westbrook, who at that time were planning to record a concept album, *Goodbye Peter Lorre*, at Jon's studio. This project would also give Jon an opportunity to create some sound-scapes to complement the songs. The Westbrooks got on famously with Jon, as he instinctively understood what these two highly creative and individual mavericks were trying to achieve. Mike, a gifted composer and arranger with a love of the more esoteric chordal possibilities and Kate, writing and singing in the Art/Cabaret tradition in several languages, had the ability to create glorious musical chaos by combining unlikely genres — all the while retaining a hard core of jazz improvisation. Over the next 20 years, they would throw a series of off-the-wall albums at Jon to engineer and mix, many of which he rated as his most challenging projects.[7]

Back on the *Paraphernalia* front, 1991 saw them in the studio again, recording what would turn out to be one of their finest albums. The band now comprised a core of three musicians — Peter Lemer, Barbara and Jon and joining them this time was Malcolm McFarlane on guitar, with Phil Mulford once again on bass. Called *Breathless*, it has a feel-good atmosphere permeating throughout and is packed with inventive and strong material. One track, *Sax Rap*, which had taken Jon six weeks to record, began turning up on radio stations all over Europe, either as a theme tune or station ident.

Around this time, Miles Ashton joined the *Paraphernalia* fold as sound engineer. Miles was the son of Bill Ashton, founder and leader of *The National Youth Jazz Orchestra* and he proved to have fantastic 'ears' for mixing in the most difficult environments. The audio team from AKG, who had supported Jon since the *Colosseum II* days, supplying all the mics for the studio and tours, often turned up to gigs in Vienna and they were always most complimentary about the sound balance that Miles achieved. High praise indeed! Eventually, Miles set up his own studio, but often returned to TM when recording larger ensembles.

As usual, *Paraphernalia* went on the road promoting their new album. Ron Atkins of *The Guardian* caught them at Ronnie Scott's early in 1992 and praised the eclectic range of their music: "The set opened with *Jaunty*, an old-fashioned blues from their current album and went on to cover a broad musical terrain from Greek to Irish. The upbeat closing number *Sax Rap* featured a blazing solo from Thompson, kicked along by Hiseman, commandeering throughout, from behind his forest of cymbals." The tour continued on into Germany, where they played to ever bigger and ever more adulatory crowds, often breaking the house records. *Paraphernalia* now only toured when they had a new album out, so to keep their hands in between times, they decided to form an acoustic group. Jon was aware that there were many venues around the UK that couldn't afford, or weren't suitable for *Paraphernalia* and the *Jon Hiseman Quartet* (*JHQ*) would fill that gap perfectly. The nucleus of the band was, of course Jon, Barbara and Pete Lemer, plus whoever played bass for *Paraphernalia* at the time. They travelled light, with little gear, playing acoustic versions of some *Paraphernalia* numbers and various other jazz pieces. About this time, Barbara was asked by Jazz Services[8] to come up with something special for a tour, so she used the opportunity to invite several European musicians and put together a band she called *Sans Frontiere*, which provided her with an opportunity to air material that wasn't suitable for *Paraphernalia*. Almost simultaneously, she and Jon formed another band, this time with 19 musicians, called *Moving Parts*, where they were able to work alongside some of Britain's most talented young musicians, playing expanded versions of *Paraphernalia* material, as well as 'custom' arrangements.

For quite a while, Barbara had also been running music workshops at a number of schools, usually during *Paraphernalia*'s UK tours and had won herself something of a reputation in this field. The idea was for young musicians to rehearse the simpler of Barbara's big band charts over several days and then perform them, together with *Paraphernalia*, in concert. Barbara outlined how it worked: "Usually I would go along on my own to work with the bands and their conductor/teacher, ironing out any problems before the rest of *Paraphernalia* arrived. It was so successful that we often played with the same big band on several occasions. The kids loved playing with Jon's drumming behind them and it was a great experience for us, as well as them." One gig in Birmingham was particularly memorable: "We played at the prestigious Cannon Hill Park Summer Festival, in front of 90,000 people, kicking off with the local school big-band and finishing with a set from *Paraphernalia*. As we came off, who should be there applauding us, but the members of the *City of Birmingham Symphony Orchestra*, together with conductor Simon Rattle, who were about to go on and close the concert — accompanied by an impressive firework display!"

Come the spring of 1993, it was time for *Paraphernalia*'s next album. Called *Everlasting Flame*, it would be the first to feature one of their children, Anna Hiseman (a.k.a. Ana Gracey) singing lead on one track, *So Near, So Far,* and backing vocals on three others. This was a new departure in itself, but the album is also of interest for other reasons. Barbara increased her already extensive range of instruments to include clarinet, wooden flutes, recorder and tin whistle. The longest cut on the album, Barbara's, *Ode to Sappho*, is based on a rare fragment of Greek music surviving from the era of the iconic poetess. The album is truly a team effort, as every member of the band contributes to the writing, including guitarist Malcolm MacFarlane, who composed the track, *The Night Before Culloden*. The album ends with Barbara and Pete Lemer playing a gentle duet version of *The Fanaid Grove*, reprised from *Songs From the Centre of the Earth*. Though perhaps more varied than most of their previous efforts, *Everlasting Flame* proved that *Paraphernalia* was still 'pushing the envelope'.

It was now 22 years since the demise of the original *Colosseum*, but the pressure to re-form the band, both from the fans and from the original members, was unrelenting. Over the years, they had all played frequent tours of Europe, largely courtesy of their *Colosseum* credentials and every one of them had been asked constantly if the band was ever going to get back together again. From Jon's point of view, it wasn't a very attractive proposition, as he was already fully committed to two great bands and had plenty of studio work as well — he was just about as busy as he wanted to be. He also felt that all he had to show for those days was a load of painful memories — and in any case, *who* would want to come and see *Colosseum* now?

Little did Jon realise...the clock was ticking and all that was needed was a little more time for sufficient momentum to build up. A dastardly plan was being hatched by the other members of *Colosseum* to inveigle Jon into a reunion, a plan that would be neatly carried out at a certain founder member's upcoming birthday party!

FOOTNOTES

1. The TM studio was truly a daunting project and as he sat in the moonlight on the bathroom loo at 4am the night before the build commenced, Jon really did wonder what the hell he was letting himself in for.

It would be extremely complicated, since, rather than a conversion, he'd decided to build a fully-floating, isolated structure from the ground up. First an external, cavern-like edifice was built, which included a layered roof filled with seven tons of silver sand, to isolate the studio from overhead planes and the odd helicopter. The internal 'room within a room' structure for both the studio and control room rested on mineral-wool quilts. With no parallel walls and the ceiling at angles to the floor, the finished studio provided a completely insular environment with a light, bright and clean sound.

Jeff Atter, head of tech services at the famous Townhouse Studios in Chiswick, advised Jon to invest his money in quality wiring, on the basis that, though *equipment* purchased now would eventually become obsolete, good wiring would accommodate any future changes. Great advice, as it turned out. Jeff would show Jon how to do the wiring for each stage in the process then leave him for several days while he completed the job. With over 2 km of wire and

360

hundreds of connections, Jon realised that the worst thing would be to run a studio not understanding how all the elements in the recording chain physically linked together. By literally wiring the studio himself, he was always able to 'tech' the inevitable problems.

The local building inspector, who had given the builders a hard time from day one, after some final horse-trading with Jon about the external appearance, signed off the studio a week before the Bracknell Festival. Shaking hands with Jon, the inspector remarked with a smile how much he was looking forward to seeing Barbara's performance there the following Sunday!

2. London's Capital Radio adopted *Country Dance* as their station ident. It replaced *Birdland*, written by Joe Zawinul who led the band that many compared to *Paraphernalia — Weather Report*. However, Jon is on record as saying that he watched many musicians dilute their own talent by taking too much notice of what others were doing. Jon and Barbara always tried to avoid listening to bands that were too close to home, preferring to keep their heads clear.

3. Keyboard player, Bill Worral, who plays so well on *Pure Fantasy*, would go on to become a respected session player on the London scene. Unfortunately, he became afflicted with Parkinson's in the late '90s and at the time of writing, is still battling his worsening neurological condition.

4. Don Leaver, who won a BAFTA award for the original *Prime Suspect* series in 1991, was the line producer on *Frost*. He was also the director of four episodes and was always very clear about the kind of music he wanted to enhance a scene. Jon recalls: "A couple of times he rang to congratulate us after those episodes were put to bed...which made me feel that we had risen to the occasion. Dave Greenslade also composed music for several of his other projects and Don thought very highly of him...'I can always tell a Greenslade score' he told me."

5. Most TV, film and recording studios use absorbent materials to soak up and control the sound waves generated by performers. This enables a clean pick-up of the sound by the microphones and allows the engineer to add a combination of reverberation and delay electronically, to simulate whatever space is deemed correct for the music or scene. This type of artificial reverb is mainly used in pop, rock and jazz, whereas classical music is often recorded in a natural space like a concert hall or church, so that little or no artificial reverb is needed.

6. Laurence Aston was, at the time, a record marketing consultant and music adviser. In addition to these roles, he was co-founder (with John L. Walters) of Unknown Public, described as, 'a journal and a compilation CD, a creative music festival for the front room.' Nowadays, he is primarily a manager of film music composers.

7. The Westbrooks' projects, with Jon at the controls, included: *Goodbye*

Peter Lorre (1991); *Good Friday 1663* (1993); *Cuff Clout* (2001); *L'Ascenseur/The Lift* (2002); *Chanson Irresponsable* (2002); *Turner in Uri*, for Swiss TV — J&B performed on and Jon mixed (2003); *Art Wolf* (2005); *The Nijinska Chamber* (2006); *Waxeyworks Show* (2007); *Tamar River*, film promo music (2007); *Allsorts* (2009); *Fine 'n' Yellow* (2009) — on which Jon also plays drums.

8. Jazz Services is the leading national jazz organisation in the UK, providing a voice for jazz and promoting its growth and development, by offering such services as: information, education, touring, communications, marketing and publishing.

*"Dave, Dick, Clem and Chris ganged
up on me."*
JON HISEMAN'S TAKE on how
Colosseum re-formed

*"When the band started up again, there
was this feeling of 'Why did we split up
in the first place?'"*
MARK CLARKE

Chapter 19

THE GRASS IS ALWAYS GREENER

THE 18TH OF JANUARY, 1994, WAS DAVE GREENSLADE'S 50TH BIRTHDAY and his wife Jan decided to organise a small surprise party, but it turned out to be a much bigger event than she had anticipated. Dave recalls: "I got whisked away for a meal, but someone suggested we stop at the Black Horse for a beer first. When we got there, these velvet curtains were hanging across part of the bar and hiding behind them was Jon Hiseman, Dick Heckstall-Smith, Clem Clempson, Chris Farlowe, Barbara Thompson, Colin Richardson and Francis van Staden. It was fantastic!" The line-up was almost complete; Mark Clarke lived in America and couldn't make it. The early part of the evening was spent reminiscing about the old days — then, after a few more beers, someone spotted that there was a piano in the corner and the evening turned musical, with Dave playing *Stormy Monday Blues*. Jon takes up the story: "Although some of the boys had written to me about the pressure they had been getting from the fans to re-form *Colosseum*, I never seriously considered it. I was living a 366-day year and anyway, I never was one for looking back. However, as the evening wore on it became quite clear that there was a concerted effort to get me to make some kind of commitment to doing it all again. I can remember Dave playing the piano, Chris singing and Clem sitting down next to me and saying: 'Listen to that — great isn't it?' One by one, throughout the evening, the boys sidled up to me and started a seemingly casual conversation on the same topic."

Jon already had some idea of what the prospects of a reunion might be, since he regularly computed and paid out the publishing royalties and knew by the sales of the re-mastered CDs that there was a resurgence of interest. But to go on the road in the style he had become used to with Barbara and *United Jazz & Rock Ensemble*, they would have to fill 1,000 seat venues on a regular basis. Was there *that* level of interest? Other groups had tried, with varying degrees of success — some on the club circuit and others in concert halls and occasionally even bigger venues but on the other hand, Jon knew that *their* situation was almost unique, in that all the original members of their final *Live* album had kept in great shape by constant playing. So, having been put on the spot by the others, he agreed to give it some serious thought and by the end of the evening it seemed there was a good chance that *Colosseum* would be re-born. It would be necessary to sort out everyone's schedules and get Mark Clarke on board. It was his old friend Clem who phoned him to ask if he was interested. Mark's reply was succinct: "Are you kidding? Just tell me where and when and I'll be there!" It was actually pretty much a foregone conclusion, as Mark had made his position clear in a letter to Jon written from New York, in February 1979: "If you *do* ever decide to reform *Colosseum* and you don't ask me — I'll be pissed off. I owe you so much with regard to my playing and I will never forget that." Clem had a slightly more practical view of the reunion: "I was really excited about having the chance to play some of this great music again, especially as we would be performing it after more than 20 years of technological advances in live sound reproduction."

When Dick Heckstall-Smith attended Dave's party, he was in much better health than he had been for a couple of years. Early in 1992, he had been hospitalised after complaining of shortness of breath and when the surgeon opened him up, they discovered that he needed a triple heart-bypass. During the operation, he suffered not one, but two strokes! Arthur Heckstall-Smith recalls: "I wasn't in touch that much at that time, as I was working in Brussels. I flew in just after his operation and when I saw him, I was shocked — he seemed like a vegetable and didn't recognise me. However, after a day or two he did remember who I was." Dick was by no means out of the woods though, as two months later his left lung collapsed and filled with fluid, requiring the removal of part of his lung. Fortunately his doctor was a bit of a fan and suggested he try playing his sax briefly each day as part of his rehabilitation. Arthur recalls what bad shape he was in: "He had lost the ability to read and had to re-learn how. I remember him telling me, with great delight, what was happening to him. He had tunnel vision and had to concentrate on one word at a time, but he seemed to take great pleasure in learning to read again." He also recited nursery rhymes and other basic ways a child learned to read. When word of his condition got around, no fewer than five benefit gigs were arranged by his fellow musicians and Dick admitted to being 'stunned and humbled' by it all. He spent many of the ensuing months at Pete Brown's house convalescing and a year before Dave Greenslade's birthday party, he was well enough to play again.

Soon the rumours of *Colosseum* re-forming started to fly and though Jon felt reasonably committed to it happening, the question was — when and where? It was now that fate took a hand. While Jon was on the road with *Paraphernalia*, he developed a persistent and severe sore throat. Jon explains: "We were on tour in Germany and following a gig in Freiburg, I visited Dr Alexander Heisler[1] for treatment. We had known each other for some time, since both *Paraphernalia* and the *UJ&RE* had performed at the Freiburg Zelt Musik Festival, of which he was founder and artistic director. He was aware of the rumours and persuaded me, as only he could, that the festival would be the ideal occasion for our debut reunion appearance. He's a 'one-off' — a man of enormous enthusiasm and drive, laced with a sense of chaotic informality and I immediately felt that, though it was a somewhat daunting undertaking, it would go well under his patronage." They agreed an informal deal and, on his return, Jon contacted the rest of the band, discussed a set-list...and sent them all the relevant *Colosseum* CDs to help them re-learn their parts. The band then re-convened at Jon's studio: "We met up on 17th June 1994...I counted them in for *Those About to Die* and we played as if the band had never been apart! When Chris followed that with a fantastic performance of *Skellington*, I realised this was for real!" Mark Clarke, who had flown over from the States to be there, had similar feelings: "When the whole band started up, I couldn't help thinking — why did we split up in the first place?" The depressing memory of those final days in 1971 was suddenly replaced with a sense of euphoria!

So...it came about that, on the 24th of June 1994, surrounded by the beautiful Black Forest scenery, *Colosseum* rose 'phoenix-like from the ashes' to a tumultuous reception. The concert was a sell-out and outside the site, on the nearby hillside, sat hundreds of ticketless fans trying to catch a glimpse of this momentous occasion. The band rattled through their set and the clock was well and truly turned back. Apart from the *Colosseum Live* tracks, there was a welcome return of *Valentyne Suite* and *Theme for an Imaginary Western*, as well as James Litherland's *Elegy* — its first ever live performance. Of course, Jon's drum solo was a main feature and just as before, tagged onto *The Machine Demands a Sacrifice*. In keeping with the spirit of the original performance on *Colosseum Live*, the one unrehearsed piece they played was *Stormy Monday Blues*. The gig was an unqualified success and the autograph hunters came out in force. The band signed countless numbers of albums, including some rare bootleg items they'd never seen before.

Miles Ashton was the crew manager and sound-mixer for the re-born *Colosseum*. He had already become indispensable to Jon and Barbara, who had come to trust his judgement absolutely. Seemingly unflappable and undaunted by any problem, he is still in charge at the time of writing. His speciality is recording every show to digital multi-track, as well as mixing the live sound. As a result, Jon has archived most of *Paraphernalia* and *Colosseum*'s performances since the late '90s.

Jon was totally blown away by the band's performance — it was if the intervening years had honed everybody's ability to play the music they'd created more than a quarter of a century earlier. Now Jon was being pressed by the guys to think about touring, so he got in touch with *Paraphernalia*'s German agent Gerd Schultz-Pilath and asked: "If *Colosseum* got together next year, could we do four or five dates?" Gerd's response was cool: "I'll check it out." Secretly delighted, he contacted his list of promoters, many of whom had been *Colosseum* fans in their youth but had never seen them 'live'. Within a few days, he had over 60 positive replies. Perhaps, deep down, this was the response that Jon had anticipated. After all, having played such a blinding reunion gig, they couldn't possibly just leave it there. The key to this enthusiastic response, Jon believed, was the fact that he was presenting the complete and original *Colosseum Live* line-up. Jon is on record as saying at the time: "...one of the tricks of the business is having a nose for when it's right to do something. It was right when I formed *Colosseum* and it was right when it finished. Now it's the right time, in 1994, to resurrect it."

Gerd also proposed the idea of a TV special — to be filmed before a live audience, by WDR's Peter Sommer, and Jon immediately negotiated, on behalf of *Colosseum*, to buy the worldwide video and CD rights. So, on the 28th of October, at the E-Werk in Cologne, the second *Colosseum* reunion concert was captured on video, before a wildly enthusiastic audience. It took two days for Jon and Peter Sommer to edit the video for transmission on the WDR show, *Rockpalast*, then another 10 days re-editing it for the Temple Music video. Since Jon had arranged for the sound to be recorded on multi-track, the tapes were then brought back to the Temple Music studio to mix and get in sync with the pictures. With over £130,000 of hired video equipment, Jon was again on a massive learning curve, hooked this time by the possibilities of the 'flickering image'. Timed to coincide with the Reunion tour, the band released its first album in nearly 25 years...aptly called *Colosseum Lives — The Reunion Concerts 1994*. Mixed by Jon and Dave, it contained eight cuts, two from their Freiburg show and six from the Cologne TV concert. It came out on *Paraphernalia*'s record label, Intuition, and the highlight of the album turned out to be a powerful reprise of the *Valentyne Suite*, featuring a searing and emotional soprano sax solo from Dick on *February's Search* (the video footage of Dave Greenslade's reaction speaks volumes). The press reviews and subsequent sales of the *Colosseum LiveS* video and CD, financially underpinned the next couple of tours, with a DVD version being released in 2003.

The TV show aired in Germany, Austria and Switzerland at the beginning of March 1995, just as the band commenced its first tour of Germany in 24 years, followed by concerts in Italy, Austria and the Czech Republic — all of which were huge successes. *Colosseum* was back with a vengeance!

368

As the tour progressed, they began thinking about recording a new studio album. Jon remembers that it didn't take long for new material to appear: "Riding high in our coach, crisscrossing Europe, Dave Greenslade played us demos of songs he had written which soon began turning up at our sound checks." Before long, Clem and Dick also began writing, as Clem recalls: "After enjoying the reunion so much, we just wanted to keep going and the logical way to do that was a new album. While it was important to recognise that we'd all moved on since the '60s, we knew we shouldn't lose sight of what our audiences loved about *Colosseum*'s music."

By the end of 1995, the band had played over 100 shows, mostly to full houses — their fans, it seems, had returned in droves. Mark Clarke: "I wasn't surprised that we were selling out the shows. I would have been disappointed if we hadn't!" Clem adds: "It was wonderful to discover how many people wanted to hear us play again...and very moving to hear how much the band had meant to them — especially in Eastern Europe, where we heard stories of a single, precious bootleg album being passed around from fan to fan. How impossible it must have seemed to those people at the time, that they would ever have the chance to hear us in concert."

It was good to see Dick and in such great form, though noticeably changed. His son, Arthur remembers: "The stroke removed a lot of his inhibitions and his 'ears' were now on another level. It may have affected his ability to play the way he once did, but judged purely in artistic terms, he was in wonderful form — though now seemingly unconcerned about what people thought of his playing. The band appreciated what he had been through and let him know how well they thought he was doing. *Colosseum* helped him a lot, as it imposed a discipline on him...Jon in particular was very encouraging and supportive. It also increased his income dramatically, helping him to feel more secure." Dick was undoubtedly very proud of the band and when he wasn't blowing, he would adopt a schoolmasterly stance, with a look on his face that implied: 'Look how good my pupils are!' His onstage presence was certainly just as imposing and compelling as ever.

Jon's drumming on *Solo Colonia* shows how much he had matured, though he *did* resurrect his stick juggling routine, which now climaxed with him rotating three sticks between hands and mouth! In some interviews around this time, Jon is on record as saying that he thought *Colosseum* was playing far better than in the old days. Of course, in some ways this was only to be expected, as they all had another 20-odd years of musical experience under their belts — but how did the other members of the band feel about this claim? Dave Greenslade's perspective is slightly different. Commenting on a live taping of the *Valentyne Suite* recorded on the 1969 USA tour, he said: "It sounds like we were fearless. We were young and there was nothing we couldn't do. Nowadays, we tend to be more analytical and view things more maturely. Of course, our technique is better now because we are all more experienced." Mark Clarke adds: "I wouldn't say we played badly in the '70s, but we sound better now — 20 years of playing certainly increases confidence in your ability." Comparing the live albums of 1971 and 1995, one is struck by how raw the earlier performance sounds, bearing out Dave's comment about 'having no fear'. The later album does come over as much more polished but, understandably perhaps, it cannot match the energy levels of six young men in their twenties.

While Jon was away touring with *Colosseum*, Barbara was working as hard as ever. She had been invited to write a composition for and perform on, a George Martin produced album with the *Medici String Quartet*, which was sponsored by Classic *f*M radio. Having befriended the quartet's leader, Paul Robertson, who greatly admired her improvising skills, she searched for an album project on which they could collaborate. Her old friend Neil Ardley offered to write an arrangement of the Kurt Weill composition *Barbara Song*[2] and Barbara immediately saw that as a terrific album title. She quickly commissioned several of her favourite contemporary composers[3] to arrange other Weill compositions for the project, which was recorded in a church in Kent by Jon, who then licensed the master to Virgin Classics for release. Barbara later recalled: "I became so involved with promotion and concerts for the *Barbara Song* album, that, for the first time in years, Jon and I were back to passing each other on the stairs again."

As if this was not enough, Barbara was also working on two new commissions. The first was from Pam Reekie (director the Norwich Arts Centre, a regular *Paraphernalia* venue) who asked her to write a piece for the well-known percussionist Evelyn Glennie. It was to be performed at the Theatre Royal, Norwich in April 1995, just as Jon commenced the *Colosseum* reunion tour. The second came from BBC Radio, ostensibly for a jazz piece to be broadcast live in November '95 from the Queen Elizabeth Hall London, as part of the London Jazz Festival. However, having written a semi-classical work for Evelyn Glennie, Barbara elected to compose a 50-minute long crossover piece based on the poems of Philip Larkin, which she called *Love Songs In Age*. It was scored for an expanded musical combination featuring the 24 voices of the BBC Singers, the *Medici String Quartet*, *Paraphernalia* members Peter Lemer and bassist Paul Westwood, together with percussionist Simone Rebello, while Barbara featured prominently on a range of reed instruments. The first half of the concert featured *Barbara Song*, prompting Chris Parker of the London Times, to write: "The collaboration between composer/saxophonist Barbara Thompson, the *Medici String Quartet* and the BBC Singers, exploring the music of Kurt Weill and the poetry of the late Philip Larkin, proved genuinely uplifting. Thompson has a round, pure tone on all the saxophones, particularly well suited to blending with strings. The arrangements of the Weill material, from Geoffrey Burgon's suitably melancholic *Surabaya Johnny* to the stunningly adventurous version of Mike Westbrook's *September Song*, were wonderfully rich."

That same year, Barbara was awarded the MBE for Services to Music, but, as luck would have it, the date of the investiture fell on the day after a gig in Plymouth, so Barbara and Jon had to suffer a cramped cold compartment on an overnight train in order to make it to the ceremony at Buckingham Palace. As only two extra guests were allowed, each took their mother. Prior to the ceremony, Barbara had filled in a questionnaire, which included a section for any comments, so Barbara mentioned that she had played at a surprise concert celebrating the Queen's birthday some years before, held in the chapel at Windsor Castle: "We secretly rehearsed there all week — to perform a short musical called *Cricket*, written specially for the occasion by Andrew Lloyd Webber and Tim Rice. Jon was playing drums, Rod Argent keyboards and John Mole bass. I remember the Queen being very interested in Jon's drumming and they had a good old chat. She told him that, at dinner a day or so previously, she was sure she could hear music (the rehearsals), but that the Duke had said she was imagining it. When I reminded the Queen of the occasion, I think she was quite intrigued — the pictures certainly show us both smiling a lot!" Barbara rarely, if ever, mentions her award — but privately she is, of course, extremely proud of it.

Barbara and Jon were now spending two months of the year recording the soundtrack music for *A Touch of Frost*, but not everything they produced got used. For instance, in episode 2, there was a scene involving two Porsche cars roaring around country roads, before screeching to a halt in a gravel courtyard. Barbara wrote a 40 second cue, which was dropped because the director preferred the sound of the engines! One of the vagaries of writing music for film or TV is that the composer is never sure how their efforts will be received — even powerful passages of music will be discarded if they don't match the director's vision. There was, however, something about this particular piece that haunted Jon and he persuaded Barbara to expand it — the strangely Eastern flavour, he thought, would suit the next *Paraphernalia* album. He and Pete Lemer spent several days in the studio, trying to create an intro for it, but with their next tour looming, there was insufficient time to do it justice, so Jon decided to put it on the back burner. Though they didn't know it then, the foundations had been laid for what would be *Paraphernalia*'s strongest album in a decade.

Meanwhile, they still needed a new CD for the upcoming tour. Jon brought back Martyn Webster to engineer and Barbara started gathering some of her favourite ballads...including some by Duke Ellington, Paul Simon and Stevie Wonder, plus a couple of her own and one Pete Lemer composition. By this time she was describing Pete as the 'cornerstone' of the band and after guitarist Malcolm McFarlane left to return to Scotland, Barbara decided she didn't want the hassle of replacing him and kept the band as a quartet, which was apposite, because the material was primarily based on timeless melodies and has a much more laid-back feel. The opening track, *In Memory*, is dedicated to Barbara's father who had recently passed away. Barbara: "He was a devoted, loving father and a charming man who everybody liked and who loved music, especially *my* music — he used to come to all my concerts in the London area, often bringing colleagues from the Law Courts, where he had been Master of the Queens Court of Criminal Appeal. I played at his memorial service held at the chapel in Lincolns Inn Fields, where protocol required that the bell be tolled."

The fact that the saxophone was now the sole front-line instrument offered some interesting musical opportunities, as it put Barbara even more to the fore and this is reflected in the title of the album, *Lady Saxophone* (some venues were already advertising her thus, so it was an apt choice). The album contains some of her most reflective playing ever, while still giving plenty of opportunity to the other musicians. Barbara recalls: "Paul Westwood, on bass guitar, was a joy to work with. The quartet format gave him plenty of scope and he played some incredible bass lines and solos. I've been so lucky to have had some great bass players playing with the band."

Meanwhile, Clem, Dick and Dave had all been busy writing new material for *Colosseum*. The band felt they really had a point to prove and knew that they needed to produce music that was relevant for the time. Jon describes how they went about it: "We met several times through 1996, writing, rehearsing and recording demos. Songs changed, floated away for a time, then returned, disguised, in typical *Colosseum* fashion. By March 1997 we were ready to record the 11 titles that survived." Arthur Heckstall-Smith recalls that Dick was, "...perhaps a little disappointed they didn't use more of his stuff." But as Jon recalls, "Dave and Clem were providing finished demos, which meant that decisions could be quickly made about what was likely to work. If anyone had a serious objection to a song, we didn't do it. Typically, Dick brought sketches and fragments, some with Pete Brown lyrics and if we liked any of it, Dave or Clem would then work it up into something we could use."

Recording had hardly started when there came a ring at the front door and Dave answered it. A diminutive 80-year-old lady stood there, greeted him by name and asked for Jon. "Dave fetched me from the control room and she greeted me warmly — like an old friend. Intrigued, I asked who she was and what she wanted. 'My name's Maria and I've come to see *Colosseum*!' she announced matter-of-factly and then proceeded to relate a tale that was so bizarre; she couldn't have made it up. In the end, I invited her to lunch, then made arrangements to put her up in a local hotel and she stayed for several days." Her story, which verged on the unbelievable, went as follows: She lived alone in an apartment on the Austrian border and, unable to sleep one night, had turned on her TV, which happened to be showing the WDR *Colosseum* reunion concert. The band in full flight, made such an impression on her that she had contacted the TV station and they had referred her to *Colosseum*'s German agent. He had apparently sent her a video of the Cologne concert, which she watched many times. Sometime later, a family visit planned for Easter was cancelled at short notice, due to illness and rather than spend the holiday alone, she had decided on a whim, to go visit *Colosseum*! So how did she manage to find her way to the studio? Well, it seems the video's lyric booklet listed Temple Music's PO Box address in Surrey, so after catching a flight from Munich to Gatwick, she took a train to Croydon and then on to Sutton, where she hired a cab on a hunch that a local taxi driver might just know the whereabouts of Temple Music. As luck would have it, she picked the very minicab firm that Jon used all the time and the driver kindly dropped her on Jon's doorstep! Mark remembers her visit: "She told us how much she loved our music, explaining that she too was an artist — and turned up for several years at our concerts, giving us all rather intense abstract paintings. Then, just as suddenly as she had appeared, she vanished." The incredible coincidence of her arriving when the whole band was in the studio was never satisfactorily explained, but it meant that she reaped the additional reward of seeing *Colosseum* recording their comeback album, *Bread & Circuses*.

It's hard to say what *Colosseum*'s fans expected from their first album of new material. Some must have hoped for more epics like the *Valentyne Suite*, but as Jon wrote in the sleeve notes, they should not expect a *Son of Valentyne Suite*. Not that the band made a conscious decision — they didn't have to. The fact was, they had all evolved since 1971 and their writing reflected that. The songs were shorter, but still jazz and blues biased and none lasted longer than six minutes, though still packed with as many ideas as possible. There was less time for long solos to showcase their individual talents, but that wasn't so important now — and they *could* all stretch out more when performing them live. Dave Greenslade was, as usual, the main contributor, writing more than half the album. He revealed how he felt in an interview at the time: "We've all enjoyed having our own bands at one time or another, but there's just something about *Colosseum*; even more so this time around. There's something about the combination, the chemistry — everyone in the band is very different; each character has his own unique musical contribution to make. It's been a fascinating evolution."

It was during the recording of *Bread & Circuses* that Barbara revealed some shattering news to Jon. Sometime back in 1994, while playing a *Variations* charity concert, she had noticed that one of her intricate flute passages hadn't come off very well, which she put down to lack of practice. However, over the next couple of years, her increasing inability to play repetitive phrases, together with lower-back pain, neck-ache and stiffness, led to her making an appointment with a specialist. On her return home, during a studio break, she broke the news to Jon that she had been diagnosed as being in the early stages of Parkinson's Disease.[4] Jon's immediate, but tongue-in-cheek reaction was typical: "Great — a female saxophonist in a wheelchair...could be good for business!" He was ready to cancel recording for that day to discuss the situation, but Barbara was quite adamant that life should continue as normal, thus setting the tone for the way she intended to fight the condition. She was determined to carry on working as before and be just as productive — an attitude which she maintains to this day, as she continues driving herself from one project to the next.

They immediately set about researching all the literature on Parkinson's, which they found quite disturbing. For a while though, they weren't even certain that the diagnosis was accurate, as an extensive course of homeopathic remedies, together with vitamin supplements, seemed to bring some improvement, but then a top neurologist at King's College Hospital confirmed the original diagnosis. Though Barbara was worried and frightened, it was mainly a fear of the unknown and she quickly developed a strategy to cope with this, as she recalls: "Most of the time, when I am concentrating on what I am doing, I don't even think about PD. Negative thoughts like 'Why me?' are rejected instantly. Firstly because they don't help the situation and, secondly, this suggests that you would rather someone else had it than you, which again, is negative thinking." Jon's research into Parkinson's privately caused him to be quite pessimistic at first, especially the accounts on the Internet of others' experiences. But, as time passed and Barbara's condition didn't worsen as rapidly as predicted, he realised that, although life *would* have to change, it would be at a rate they could both cope with. As if to thumb her nose at the situation, the first thing Barbara did after her diagnosis was to write the saxophone arrangement for *No Pleasin'* on *Bread & Circuses*!

Finally, the album that *Colosseum* fans had been waiting for, but never expected to see, was released. The title echoed that of their first album, with its Roman connotations, but there's very little of the 'in your face' jazz-rock of that era, though there are plenty of subtly clever moments. Clem isn't too sure of how he sees the album after a decade or so, but rates *Big Deal* and *I Could Tell You Tales* quite highly. Jon also picks out *Big Deal* as an example of what the new band could do and considers the album on a par with the *Daughter of Time*. Dave also says that the band made a conscious decision not to try to recreate the live glories of old, though his track *No Pleasin'* turned into a rocking jam that surprised everyone and later became a staple of the live show. A lengthy promotional tour of Germany and Italy was scheduled for June 1997 immediately following the album's release. Obviously the new material would be unveiled on the tour, but they couldn't exclude *all* the old favourites like *Valentyne Suite* and *Lost Angeles* — the question was…just how would the fans react to the new stuff?

The *Badische Zeitung* reported: "Even when Hiseman plays the clown during his drum solo (juggling) or when his used drumsticks are being sold outside — people never see this as ersatz friendliness or overt commercialism. The songs from their new album *Bread & Circuses* do not reheat old dishes, but lend the sound completely new elements. It is amazing how Chris Farlowe is still in good voice; darting about the stage like a little gnome…with the greatest of ease he still reaches all the right notes — a great concert!"

The European dates were followed by several appearances in the UK, giving the home fans a taste of the new *Colosseum*. Just like before, as the tour progressed, each new song took on an identity of its own…evidence that the band had successfully re-invented itself. The new material integrated seamlessly with the old and if the crowd reactions were anything to go by, the fans were delighted with what they heard.

Following the success of the *Reunion* and *Bread & Circuses* tours, Jon began to get offers from many of the European festivals. The problem was that it was only economically viable to do these intermittent festivals on equipment rented by the promoters and Jon always felt it was ironic having to play the biggest and therefore most important gigs without their own gear. Although the odd guitar could always be flown in a flight case, saxes had to be carried in the cabin, since their sensitive 'balanced action' could be seriously impaired by any knocks. Dick always had two saxes on the road and Barbara currently takes three or four. Try getting those past your average flight attendant! Clem used a variety of guitars, together with an array of special effects to create the many rhythm and lead sounds he coaxed from his amps. He always found it especially difficult to relax and get into the music if he was fighting with the sound from the hired gear. Jon had similar problems; if the snare drum, bass drum and cymbals didn't sound right, he simply felt powerless — as if he couldn't play at all. Often he would get two single drum kits and have to 'marry' them together in order to get his normal seven-drum set-up — and finding somewhere quiet at a festival where he could tune the unfamiliar kits was nigh on impossible.

However, tempted by some very lucrative offers, the band decided to throw caution to the winds and undertake an eight-gig festival tour of Europe, including a first ever visit to Istanbul and finishing up in Italy. *Colosseum* dubbed these 'fly-by-night gigs', as they travelled from one venue to the next by plane, carrying excess baggage at a cost of around £300 a flight, which comprised their specialist gear, carried in the hope that it would make the hired equipment feel more like their own.

The promoter of the Italian festival was Francesco Sanavio, who they knew from the original *Colosseum* days, as well as *Tempest* and *Colosseum II*. He had come out of the woodwork to offer them a date in Naples. In all their years of touring, Jon and Barbara only ever had problems getting paid by Italian promoters — in fact, Barbara is still owed money from one jazz tour! *Tempest* once had their entire tour fee confiscated by Italian customs and Jon never got paid for his guest appearance at a Pistoia festival, back in the late '80s. However, Jon feels it's important to make it clear at the outset of this story, that their current Italian agents, Blue Sky Promotion of Cesena, are a fantastic team, with whom they've never had any problems.

Sanavio's offer was a good one and Jon had no reason to suspect that things would be any different this time. All the airfares were to be paid upfront, plus excess luggage costs, hotels and transport, with all the sound equipment supplied exactly as specified. The festival bill looked exciting too — according to the poster sent to Jon, Chick Corea was also appearing.

The deadline for the arrival of the money to buy their air tickets came and went. Jon discussed this with the band and it was decided to purchase them anyway, hoping against hope that it would all be all right on the night. The truth of the matter was that the band quite fancied a couple of days of Italian sunshine and hospitality, at the end of what would be quite a gruelling tour.

On arrival at Naples airport, after the usual hugging reunion with their old promoter friend, they were taken to a 4-star hotel, where Jon was introduced to 'the money' in the shape of the town's financial agent. Everything seemed to shaping up nicely! After a lot of hanging about, fairly typical of Italian gigs, they were taken on a somewhat tortuous drive through the seedy backstreets of Naples to the festival site...a small sports stadium in a pretty bad state of repair. The stage was still in the process of being built — the electricity supply was intermittent and the local crew was bemoaning the fact that, against their better judgement, they had once again got involved with this promoter. As the band struggled with the inadequate gear provided for them, Jon began to suspect that nothing was as it seemed. Finally, it was 'showtime'...to an audience of about 350 people — and not another band in sight! Whether any other bands *had* ever been booked is a moot point, as was the question of whether any proper promotion had been done. Jon doubted it, but come next morning — all would be revealed.

Jon had been promised that the fee and the airfares would be paid in cash that morning, at the hotel. The 'man from the ministry' eventually turned up, without cash, but with a large chequebook. Both Jon and Sanavio were furious, although Jon suspected that one of them was acting! It was obvious that no cash would be forthcoming, so Jon had no choice but to take the cheque, accompanied by sincere assurances as to its validity.

With an hour or so to go before their transport to the airport arrived, Jon had a bright idea. He asked the hotel reception the whereabouts of the bank upon which the cheque had been written. As it was only a couple of blocks away, he hurried there to ask if they would cash the cheque, explaining that it was the fee for a concert they had played the previous evening and they were returning immediately to London. He was politely ushered to a small office, where a young man examined the cheque and tapped something on his computer keyboard. Avoiding eye contact, he informed Jon, in low tones and out of the side of his mouth, that their client held two accounts with the bank, one of which had a sizeable sum of money in it and a second that was virtually empty. You can guess which one Jon's cheque had been drawn on! It was obvious that the client was 'well-known' there and the bank had clearly bent the rules in giving Jon this information, but they regretted that they couldn't be of any further help.

On his return to the UK, Jon deposited the cheque which, after about four weeks, unsurprisingly bounced. So, who exactly had perpetrated the scam? Had the town of Naples paid for a festival that never existed? And had *Colosseum* called their bluff, by buying their own flight tickets and actually having the effrontery to turn up? It's doubtful that anyone will ever know, although Sanavio maintains to this day that *he* didn't receive a penny either. However, despite the outcome, the band enjoyed their first visit to Italy in nearly thirty years — and thanks to the enthusiasm of the admittedly small crowd, they did not 'see Naples and die'!

In the summer of 1998, *Paraphernalia* returned to the studio to start recording their next album, the first since Barbara's diagnosis. Jon dug out the multi-track of the Eastern-flavoured *Touch of Frost* cue that he and Peter had worked on a couple of years before. Amazed at how good it sounded, he immediately saw how to take it forward. He got Barbara to write another couple of passages, divided it all up into sections that could then be linked with solos. He then had Peter create what they called 'snakes' --- long, sinuous, melodic lines to underpin the solos. While Barbara had been writing the album, she and Jon had decided that sax and violin made an ideal front-line combination and had put the word out that they were looking for a good violin player. They received several tapes, some from very fine players, but all pretty conventional stuff. Then, when Barbara was judging a jazz competition with Ronnie Scott, she saw Billy Thompson playing in a pick-up jazz group and suggested he send in a demo tape. Jon recalls: "We put Billy's tape on and, after about 30 seconds, I turned to Barbara and said — 'If this is for real...if he *really* is playing that stuff and it's not some kind of studio hocus-pocus, then he's our man!' It wasn't so much his violin playing, as such...you could hear that he was just on a different planet...and we'd already spent a lot of time there!"

So, with Billy Thompson on board, his sinuous violin playing helping to emphasise the Eastern influence, Jon tried to ensure, as producer, that the music wasn't too conventionally structured or symmetrical. As he explains when introducing the piece on stage: "...*Shifting Sands* — because nothing, *nothing* is ever as it seems..."

The 20-minute title track portrays an epic adventure, with the music creating a labyrinth of sound, twisting and turning — imbued with a seductive Middle-Eastern ambience. Barbara explains: "It was an extended piece featuring everyone in the band, with passages and bridges linking the solos and a major theme that floats in and out. It seems that I had unwittingly based the original *Frost* cue on Eastern scales and that's what Jon picked up on." It certainly rates as one of *Paraphernalia*'s most interesting albums and is also the one that Jon would pick as his favourite. Barbara was very keen to pay tribute to all of the other musicians, a sentiment which at least one reviewer echoed...Jack Massarik, writing for *What's On*, was fulsome in his praise: "Pete Lemer and young violinist Billy Thompson are unpredictable, un-hackneyed improvisers, while Hiseman and Paul Westwood adapt to each mood and keep everything moving." Barbara describes the ensuing tour as 'the best ever' — with special mention of their week-long headlining appearance at Ronnie Scott's, when the reception was nothing short of incredible. If Barbara had suffered from nerves prior to the tour, it hadn't taken long to dispel them and PD or not, she was playing better than ever!

The sad reality was, however, that Barbara's condition was slowly deteriorating. To combat this and to enable her to play, she had to inject her medication 30 minutes before each set and then lie down for 20 minutes to alleviate the nausea it brought on. The timing was critical, as the beneficial effect only lasted about an hour, so if their set was delayed, the medication would wear off before the end. The road-crew took to carrying a massage table with them, to ensure that there was always somewhere close to the stage for her to lie down. Both band and crew were amazed at her fortitude, not to say bravery, but Jon, who knew her so well, wasn't surprised: "Iron lady? Margaret Thatcher's got nothing on Barbara!" As her condition worsened, Barbara found the best course of action was to keep mentally, if not physically, active and decided to return to her first love — classical music and composition, in order to continue to be musically creative. Jon soon realised that all those years of working with highly talented and innovative musicians had given her an understanding of, and feeling for, the rhythmic and textual complexities that would become the trademark of her new compositions.

When the *Shifting Sands* tour was over, Jon moved his focus back to *Colosseum*. It was now 1999 and the new millennium was fast approaching. So far, the reunion had been a joy and everyone felt positive about the future. They had now been successfully touring for five years (two years longer than the first time around) and they all believed that there was still plenty of life left in the band. Now, with everybody older and wiser, they were determined to enjoy what they had while they could, though the future, as always, had a few surprises in store for them...unfortunately, not all of them pleasant.

FOOTNOTES

1. Dr. Alex Heisler, artistic director of the Freiburg Zelt Musik Festival, was mentioned by Jon in the CD booklet notes for *Colosseum LiveS* as being the catalyst that finally brought about the reunion concert. Incredibly, he was 'shopped' by a medical colleague and fined 1,000 Deutschmarks by his peers for 'publicity seeking'. After the hearing, the several members of the committee asked him for tickets to events at his next festival!!!

2. *Barbara Song* was Jon's last brush with a major record label and it proved a salutary lesson that vindicated his earlier decision to go it alone. By now Virgin Classics was part of EMI, but specialised in the modern/crossover field. When Jon presented the finished master of *Barbara Song*, he was amazed by the A&R department's fulsome praise of the concept, performances and recording. The one sticking point in the deal was that he wanted to license the tracks for a maximum of 10 years, but Virgin wanted to buy the copyright, which would mean Temple Music losing the rights forever and having no control over subsequent availability. The deal was finally agreed by their 'legal eagle' (with a twinkle in his eye) inserting a clause agreeing that, if the album wasn't made available in any territory for 3 consecutive years, the rights for that territory would revert to TM. Just as the CD was being shipped, the whole of the London office of Virgin Classics was closed down, its personnel sacked and the catalogue moved to EMI France. The CD was released, but caught in the fallout and, given no publicity, sank without trace. The only promotion the album received was from Barbara's European tour with *The Medici*, receiving little or no support from any of the affiliate record companies. When conceding the reversion rights to the master, an unheard of deviation from accepted practice, the folk at Virgin Classics probably sensed what was coming.

3. The other composers who contributed arrangements of Weill songs were: Neil Ardley, Geoffrey Burgon, Richard Rodney Bennett, John Dankworth, Mike Gibbs, Barry Guy, Gary Schneider and Mike Westbrook, while Barbara arranged the tracks *Mack the Knife* and *Je ne t'aime pas*. It is hoped to re-release this album in the near future.

4. Parkinson's Disease is not, in fact, a disease — it's a condition. Basically, as a result of damage to several tiny areas of the brain, the production of the chemical dopamine decreases, resulting in muscles being unable to respond to messages from the brain. Some medications help to conserve the naturally produced dopamine, while others add it to the system, albeit inefficiently. With

the correct drug dosage, the sufferer, or 'Parky', can appear virtually normal (often called the *On* state), though, after 10 years, there is no true 'normal.' The *Off* state varies from person to person, but Barbara becomes so stiff she can hardly move — "an active brain in a cadaver" is how she describes it. The switch between *On* and *Off* can take as little as a couple of minutes and happen several times a day and thus, life for Parkinson sufferers and their carers becomes progressively less predictable. The main hope for an eventual cure seems to lie in stem-cell research, but it's more realistic to hope that major breakthroughs in treatment, with alleviation of the symptoms, will be made within the next decade.

"*You live the life you invent for yourself.*"
PETE BROWN'S LYRICS from *Big Deal*

"*There's nothing after...nowhere to go...
so we had better damn well enjoy
it while we're here!*"
DICK HECKSTALL-SMITH

Chapter 20

AND THE BANDS PLAYED ON...

IN OCTOBER 1999, *Colosseum* WERE ABOUT TO START A SHORT UK TOUR, when, with just six weeks to go, Chris Farlowe got an offer he felt he couldn't refuse...Van Morrison wanted him to 'guest' on a series of shows and Chris was sure that this would be good for his career. Jon, however, was furious, partly because he knew very little about Van Morrison: "He was just one of many artists who, as a result of always being busy in my own world, had passed me by." Maybe it *was* a good thing for Chris, but Jon, having always worked on a 'first come, first served' basis, didn't see it that way. Chris and his manager, however, were adamant, so rather than pull the tour (something he had never done before) Jon needed to find a 'dep' and fast! He decided to bring in Paul Williams, who had so nearly joined *Colosseum* back in 1970 and who had later been *Tempest*'s lead vocalist. Jon's explanatory announcement at each of the shows made reference to 'leprechauns stealing singers away in the dead of night'. In fact, when *Colosseum* had re-formed in 1994, Chris had stated: "I'm a vocalist who needs to be stretched — and I love being able to do things that others can't do." It was never likely that Van Morrison's material *would* stretch him and whatever the benefits to his career, he knew he had let Jon and the band down. It was an awkward time and Chris may have had some doubts about returning to *Colosseum*, but Jon always knew that this was *the* line-up for him and Chris was a crucial member of it. In the end it was all shrugged off and when the band next got together, they really enjoyed hearing about Chris's experiences with 'Van, the Man'.

Meanwhile, two years after *Shifting Sands* was recorded, *Paraphernalia* were back in the TM studio laying down tracks for their next album. Barbara was always searching for new and different concepts to inspire her writing and now she had found one. The working title for the new album was *Tangos* and Barbara explains how it happened: "I got the idea from seeing Sally Potter's film *The Tango Lesson*. The tango is such an unbelievably inspirational form of music...mysterious, untouchable and with a slightly threatening quality." Jon remembers being quite shocked on hearing her computer demo of the first Tango: "I thought that she had it absolutely right, but I also realised that the drum parts I would have to create would be quite a challenge. However, the title of the album had become quite obvious to me — *Thompson's Tangos*!" More than any other *Paraphernalia* album, this one emphasised the importance of Peter Lemer, both as a soloist and accompanist — his quirky, melodic accompanying lines confirm Barbara's opinion that the tango has 'an air of mystery' about it.

The four very different tangos all complement each other well and provide ample scope for Billy Thompson to show off his burgeoning talent on violin. His playing on *Shifting Sands* had dovetailed into a perfect partnership with Barbara and this is clearly evident on the new album. The fourth Tango was re-arranged by Barbara for the *UJ&RE*, when it became the vehicle for Jon's drum solo and was recorded for their tenth album, *X* in 1999.

It was clear that Barbara's condition, however, was growing steadily worse. Up till then her medication had been directed at prolonging her brain's ability to produce dopamine — but now she would have to start taking a different drug, levodopa. She had begun getting 'stuck' in one position — for example, while standing at the kitchen sink — when Jon would have to pull her slightly off balance for her to regain control over her movements. Jon and Barbara's life had always hinged on deadlines — planes, ferries, trains and performances all part of their normal schedule. Now Barbara would have to contend with alternating between the 'on' and the 'off' state that was symptomatic of Parkinson's. With levodopa, the 'on' phase enabled her to appear quite normal and even play better than ever. However, the 'off' phase could recur suddenly and without warning, causing her to become uncoordinated, or worse...'seize up' completely. As the new drug's effectiveness was altered by the food in her stomach, it was all a bit 'hit or miss' and the stress of timing her 'on' state to coincide with the duration of a live gig — up to two hours — was becoming ever more difficult and preoccupied them both. Taking the levodopa tablets for the first time had produced a miraculous mitigation of her symptoms. However, from everything they had learned, they would be lucky to get more than a few years' respite before the crippling side-effects of this new medication would begin to show.

Just prior to the *Tango* tour and against Jon's advice, Barbara announced that, due to the worsening of her condition, these dates would be her final live appearances. In spite of the encouraging advances in research indicating that a cure might be found in the not-too-distant future, Barbara had made up her mind: "I decided that it would be better for me to concentrate on composing and to give up live concerts for the time being." The tour culminated with a week at Ronnie Scott's — to wide critical acclaim. Nina Caplan of *Metro* was there and wrote: "The band as a whole is disciplined, executing breaks with perfect co-ordination. Thompson's inventive eclecticism will be a loss to live jazz in Britain." Fellow musician and old friend Ian Carr paid this tribute: "She will be in the thoughts of all her friends and fans in Britain, Europe and elsewhere. Hopefully her indomitable spirit may yet see her through to improved health." Her mentor from the *New Jazz Orchestra* days, Neil Ardley, also expressed his great faith in her: "With her considerable powers of musical expression now concentrated on composition and with her mind open as ever to all musical possibilities, I'm sure there is much more to come!" Indeed, there were already several commissions in the pipeline, including one from the Norwich Festival for a 100-voice choir called *Big Sky* and another for the *Apollo Saxophone Quartet*. One thing was certain — it wouldn't be the last they heard of Barbara Thompson!

Things also gradually came to an end for *The United Jazz and Rock Ensemble* with the tragic death, in June 2003, of Volker Kriegel, followed two years later by Albert Manglesdorff. Volker had been a distinguished cartoonist, animator and broadcaster, as well as a great guitarist, who never 'turned his amp up to 11' or succumbed to the bombast of many of his contemporaries. His compositional skills were crucial to the *UJ&RE*, indeed *Circus Gambet*, from their first album, had remained its encore to the end. Albert was one of the most accredited and innovative trombonists in modern jazz, garnering many accolades for his distinctive technique of playing multi-phonics. Trumpeter Ian Carr had already been unable to play for a couple of years, due to his failing health. A first-class musician for over 40 years, his career had also included roles as author, broadcaster and enthusiastic leader of his own groups like *Nucleus*. Back in the '60s he had also championed many up and coming younger players like Mike Taylor, Barbara Thompson and Jon Hiseman. Jon fondly remembers spending many an hour with Ian on tour, putting the world to rights over a meal and a glass or two of wine.

Colosseum however, now with an enthusiastic new agent in Germany, Gert Lange (no mean guitarist and singer himself), continued touring well into the new millennium enjoying great success and going from strength to strength. Their album *Bread & Circuses* had undoubtedly given the band a new lease of life, though that was now five years ago. So, following a gig at the Spring Rock Festival, Rotherham in April 2002, they fell to discussing their next album and the direction it should take. The overall feeling was that it should be simple and bluesy, but still recognisably *Colosseum*. The band's main songwriters, Dave Greenslade and Clem Clempson, were all fired up and promptly set about writing material for it. Of course, the new *Colosseum* operated differently to the old days when the band was in almost daily contact and they could get instant feedback on their ideas. Now it could take weeks or months before songs were presented and accepted by the band. By the time they finally convened at Jon's studio in January 2003, they were hoping to make this album a lot quicker than *Bread & Circuses*, but by July they still hadn't got enough material to complete it. The intensity of writing and recording was summed up by Clem who thought this might be the last album they would ever make, confessing: "We're all getting a bit old for this kind of thing! It's just very time-consuming, because we're such perfectionists. We set out thinking we'll make an album in two or three weeks and six months later — we're still trying to finish it." When the band started its European tour, the album was still unfinished and a long, slow and tragic drama was about to play itself out, one that would result in a fundamental change for the band.

Dick, usually quite a prolific writer, only contributed one song to the new album, but there was a good reason for this. Unbeknown to anyone, least of all himself, he was terminally ill. A few months earlier, his son Arthur met up with him for lunch during a short visit to the UK. Arthur recalls: "I took one look at him and pleaded with him to see a doctor as soon as possible. He told me about a number of problems and said that he'd been waiting to see a specialist for months. It turned out he had a serious liver condition." Arthur had been living and working abroad since 1991, but returned in the summer of 2003 and rented the Old Parsonage, near Totnes in Devon, which was where he had grown up and where he and his father had spent many happy times together. He tried to organise a family reunion there, but, as Arthur explains, "Dick went in to the Royal Free Hospital and, except for the odd week, never really came out. He needed a liver transplant, but he was already too weak — the operation would have killed him. He was crumbling inside — his whole system was too fragile and all his problems were interconnected."

Jon recalls the final sessions with his old friend: "The recording of *Tomorrow's Blues* started off well, but with Dick tiring quite quickly. As it dragged on, he became more and more debilitated, until he could do little more than play his solos — seated. I really knew something was seriously wrong when he asked to stay over, but instead of going up to one of the guest rooms, he wanted to crash out on the lounge sofa in front of the TV. Something was not right and it turned out, he didn't think he could get up the stairs. Dick desperately wanted to do the upcoming tour and was doing his best to hide his problems from me. I told him we should go to my local A&E, but he insisted that he had an appointment with a specialist the very next morning — who took one look at him and shipped him straight to hospital."

When it was eventually finished, *Tomorrow's Blues* turned out to be quite distinct from *Bread & Circuses*. Many of the songs seemed to be more reflective and somewhat downbeat. Clem was quite positive though: "I'm very proud of *Tomorrow's Blues* — both the album and the track, which is probably the best song I've ever written...plus I wrote most of the lyrics. Although we had fun recording that album, my enduring memory is that the sessions were Dick's last...but he still played incredibly well. I love his solos on *Tomorrow's Blues* and *Hard Times Rising*." Dick also felt good about it: "The great thing about the new album is that, like all the *Colosseum* albums, it's different. They all represented our progress and this one does too — we are not repeating what we've done before and I'm proud of that." The album certainly sounds fresher than *Bread & Circuses*, with several tracks being first takes, including *In the Heat of the Night* and *Leisure Complex Blues*. During recording a worried Barbara Thompson had watched Dick's condition deteriorate, unaware that fate was leading her toward a crucial role in *Colosseum* — one that she would never have thought possible!

A tour was scheduled following the release of *Tomorrow's Blues*, but Dick's health was worsening. His ex-wife Gary was with him a lot during this period: "I was there when the doctor told him he couldn't go on tour. He said 'I must go' and the doctor replied 'If you do, you'll die!' So I phoned Jon to tell him." With the European tour due to start in five days and an important TV date just two days in, Jon knew he had no choice but to find someone to fill in for Dick and although he knew Barbara was the logical choice, he wasn't sure it was wise for her to return to doing live gigs. Not certain what to do and running out of time, he first approached another sax player, Chris Biscoe, whose work he had admired in some of the Westbrook projects and whose playing had a similar anarchic quality to Dick's. Biscoe recalled recently: "Jon's request came out of the blue and I was already committed to a bunch of other gigs. I've always tried to avoid pulling out of things I've agreed to do, though I must say I regretted not being able to accept Jon's tour." Although this effectively decided matters for him, Jon sat for a while weighing things up. He knew how much Barbara was missing playing live, being on the road and meeting the fans, plus she had just started new medication that held great promise. So — decision made! Barbara was the one...but she was away at their house in France, where she was taking a yoga course with some friends! Barbara recalls how fast things moved: "I had a day's notice. I had just settled down to my first relaxing yoga session, when the telephone rang and it was Jon saying: 'Sorry, but you have to come home — NOW!'"

As there were no written parts for *Colosseum*'s music which Barbara was to play, Jon had to find someone to transcribe all of Dick's saxophone parts from the CDs to sheet music...literally overnight. Jon kept up the fiction that somehow his old friend would survive, so the arrangement was that Barbara would fill in for the first few gigs of the tour while they waited for news of Dick's condition. Dick, of course, was still living in hope and to keep that alive Jon booked a seat for him on every plane, a room in every hotel and sent him all the date sheets and tour info. At any given time on the tour, Dick was just a few steps from the stage — in fact, they would sometimes phone him during the show and relay messages to and from the audience. But, sadly, every time it looked like Dick was going to make it, complications set in. When they came off the road and started preparing for their next UK tour in January 2004, Jon hatched another plan to keep Dick in the loop and living in hope. His idea was that Barbara and Dick would share the gig, as it was clear he would never be able to do the whole show. With some trepidation, Jon put the idea to Dick who, after a short pause for reflection, accepted the inevitable and pronounced himself happy with the arrangement. So, for a couple of days, Dick, now out of hospital, joined Jon and Barbara at the Temple Music Studio to work out the arrangements. In spite of his frail condition, he seemed in a very positive frame of mind, obviously trying to convince Jon that he could make it back. Jon thought that, if he did, the contrasting styles of the two saxophonists would add yet another dimension to the band. Unfortunately, Dick then suffered further complications and the idea had to be abandoned.

On the UK tour, as a kind of homage to Dick, they played *Hard*

Times Rising to a click-track[1] with his solo synced in. Some of the band already began to feel it might be the end of an era. Clem recalls: "I can't say it came as a shock that Dick didn't make the tour, but I suppose that when we took the mid-tour break and Dick *still* wasn't well enough to join us, we finally accepted the grim reality of the situation." They were very lucky that Barbara was willing and able to help them out, because although there were some great saxophonists around, replacing someone as special and so dearly loved by their fans as Dick, was nigh on impossible. Fortunately, Barbara had always been part of the *Colosseum* family, which made the situation more acceptable, both for the band and the audiences.

It must be said that Barbara's joining was never likely to be straightforward, even though some of the band had played with her before and knew how good she was. Neither was Barbara under any illusion that the transition could be made seamlessly — Dick's legacy made that unlikely, if not impossible. Barbara recalls: "When I arrived for the first *Colosseum* rehearsal, no decision had been made — the band was still divided as to whether I was the right choice. Only Jon and Clem had worked with me before and knew my capabilities. Dave, Chris and Mark had little idea of what I could do...but it only took one number to convince them. Jon, of course, always felt sure it was the right move. If you think about it, everything had come full circle — he joined *Paraphernalia* all those years ago — now I've joined *Colosseum*." Jon quips: "She's Mrs Hiseman when she's in my band — and I'm Mr Thompson when I'm in hers!" The third gig into the tour was the major German TV show *Rockpalast*, which she had dreaded and with good reason. The band looked pretty grim-faced throughout — maybe an indication of the pressure they were all under. Jon certainly wouldn't mind if those TV tapes are lost without trace! However, when the band played the Jazz Café on their return to the UK after the European tour, the London *Evening Standard*'s critic wrote: "The unexpected appearance of Barbara Thompson was touching and very welcome. Though diagnosed with Parkinson's and officially retired, she played beautifully. Her elegant, dazzling soprano-sax solos and Greenslade's deft Hammond organ touches supplied the jazz input while Clempson, Clarke and Hiseman were the rockers."

Over the summer of 2004, *Colosseum* played nine UK dates, with Barbara looking more and more like a permanent member. When the band appeared at Wavendon Stables, Milton Keynes, Dick surprised everybody by turning up to see the show and was photographed with them afterwards. He looked very frail, but got up and took a bow on stage, telling the audience he would be back playing with the band sometime soon. Sadly, though, this would prove to be the last time the classic *Colosseum* line-up would stand shoulder to shoulder.

As the year passed, Dick stayed in his hospital bed, sleeping more and more of the time. In late autumn, Jon and Barbara went to visit him and found his son Arthur there. He was very glad to see them and together, they managed to give Dick the sort of morale boost that only they could. The conversation between Jon and Dick inevitably took on a necessary air of fantasy...talk of how and when Dick would join the tour — and much laughter when stories of the old days were recounted. Jon remembers: "As the light began to fail outside, I realised that I was probably saying goodbye. Suddenly Dick sat up, turned to me very earnestly and said, 'Jon...we have a problem.' 'How so, Dick?' 'What will happen to *Colosseum*...because I can't walk.' 'Don't worry about the walking, Dick...if you can blow the saxophones, we'll get you onto the stage...come to think of it, we'll all get onto the aircraft first if you're in a wheelchair...we've been trying to achieve that for years!' And we had a good laugh...sadly, the last of many."

Arthur was truly grateful for Jon and Barbara's unwavering support: "They brought a feeling of optimism and revitalised his spirits in a way which I found difficult to do. It was wonderful to witness their loving affection for him." It's hard to imagine how sad that moment must have been for all concerned.

On the 16th of December, 2004, the Hisemans flew to Rome for a few days break. Barbara had organised the trip as a surprise for Jon, who had no idea where they were going till they got to the airport. They both loved the Eternal City, but hadn't been there except to perform since the children were little. On the afternoon of the 18th, they decided to finish the day's sightseeing at the Colosseum. Stopping off at a café on the way, they arrived just before 4pm and found it closed. After strolling around it, they took one last look and as they turned to leave, it started to rain. Then Jon's mobile phone rang...it was Clem.

Jon: "It's Dick, isn't it?"
"Yes," came the muted reply.
Jon: "When?"
Clem: "Yesterday..."
Jon catches Barbara's eye and shakes his head. After so many years together, so many ups and downs, musical and otherwise...Dick had finally gone. Jon stood there, with the Colosseum behind him...how could this possibly be just a coincidence?

It was indeed 'a story ended'. The world of music lost one of its most unique characters — a bald, bespectacled giant, whose style was without barriers, encompassing blues, jazz and rock. A visionary who had seized his every opportunity...who 'jumped ship' from jazz to the fledgling British blues scene alongside Graham Bond, Ginger Baker and Jack Bruce...blazing a trail against the odds. The many obituaries were fulsome in their praise, noting the significance of Dick's passing. The *Daily Express* even tracked down Mick Jagger, who recalled the time they were both in *Blues Incorporated*: "I remember him well, because in the middle of a blues number, he'd come up with a fantastic jazz solo which was really out of left-field at the time...he was a true great and an excellent role model for all the saxophonists who followed him."

In truth, Dick Heckstall-Smith was much more than a musician. In 1989 he had written his autobiography, *The Safest Place in the World* and included a chapter headed *Race & Racism in*

Music. The fact that jazz has its roots in the African-American culture is undeniable and some white musicians have felt vaguely uncomfortable with this. Dick summed it up thus: "Unlike white classical musicians and black jazz musicians, I have nothing and no one behind me. I represent no one but myself...To reduce this to its ultimate racist absurdity — if I play well, it's because I've learned to copy a music that is intrinsically not my own — and if I play badly, well then it's not surprising, because I am white and it's no more than expected."

Dick Heckstall-Smith was cremated in January 2005 and his ashes buried at Oakfield Wood, Wrabness, Essex on Tuesday 10th May. At his memorial service, Pete Brown read the lyrics to *Crabs* from Dick's first solo album, *A Story Ended*. The onerous task of clearing his flat fell to ex-wife Gary and she relates how difficult it was: "He had lived there since the early '70s, hardly ever throwing anything away, so it was stuffed to the rafters; one room was piled high with newspaper cuttings and articles on every subject under the sun, all horded for future reference. However, most of it had not been disturbed for years and going through it all was both interesting and heartbreaking." Dick had over 2,000 books — most of which had to be thrown away, but the majority of his own music and tapes were salvaged and eventually archived.[2]

It was clear that Dick's passing had to be marked with some kind of memorial event and, as it turned out, three were held. The first was at Bryanston School, Blandford Forum in Dorset on 6th March 2005, which featured the *Barrelhouse Blues Orchestra*, Andy Shepherd, John Etheridge, Art Themen, Pete Brown, Chris Jagger, Johnny Mars, Ben Walters and James Litherland. James recalls the event: "It was quite strange for me, as I hadn't been in the limelight for many years. I went with Pete Brown and we were about two hours late. When I got out of the car and walked toward the hall, I heard a band, with a brass section, playing *Walkin' in the Park*. As I reached the stage, they stopped; the vocalist apologised for singing it and asked me to take over. I also sang *Backwater Blues* and afterwards everyone was kind of bowing to me and treating me like a superstar, which felt very odd." The second event, at the end of May, featured *Colosseum* and was held at the Fabrik Club Hamburg, where Dick had played many times, not only with them, but also with *The Hamburg Blues Band* and his own band *DHSS* with John Etheridge.

The final tribute concert was at the Astoria[3], London, on the 6th of June, aptly titled *A Story Ended*. It boasted an all star line-up which included Jack Bruce, Gary Moore and *Colosseum*, with original members Tony Reeves and James Litherland joining in. The event was organised by Dick's son Arthur, 'with a little help from friends'. The MC for the evening was Pete Brown, who reminisced: "Dick was one of my closest friends — I was there with him after his heart operation in 1992, when he came to my house and learned to play again. I shared in a very productive part of his life, writing the *Celtic Steppes* and *Blues & Beyond* albums with him. If he had stopped drinking he would still be with us, but he only gave up smoking. It was the worst thing I've ever seen — he was in complete denial about his drinking."

Jon had been friends with Dick since 1966: "He was an original in every sense of the word, at once difficult, charming, vague, focused, vain, gifted, insightful and obsessed — with his music, the Sunday papers, his current 'read' and with his search for the ultimate saxophone mouthpiece; his personal Holy Grail. His ultimate obsession, however, was with alcohol and although I never saw him drunk, it was, of course, alcohol that eventually killed him — but, as he once said to me during one of our 'philosophical' discussions, 'There's nothing after...nowhere to go — so we had better damn well enjoy it while we're here!' Amen to that!"

In the summer of that year, Barbara and Jon went into their studio to record what would be, for Barbara, the most challenging *Paraphernalia* album yet. It had been four years since she had announced her retirement and she was now four years further down the slippery slope that is Parkinson's, so the title,

Never Say Goodbye, was both defiant and apt. The main work was a suite, *Living in the Fast Lane*, which featured some rather special guests. Back in 2001, Barbara had been commissioned to write some music for the *Apollo Saxophone Quartet* to perform at the Brighton Festival. They had been delighted with the work and Barbara, inspired by their playing, had written two further Quartets — enough music for an album. Logically called *Three Quartets*, it was recorded in late 2003, with Jon producing. Now as luck would have it, Barbara heard that two of the quartet's members, Rob Buckland and Andy Scott, were playing in the vicinity, so she invited them to dinner, telling them to bring their saxophones, as there was something she wanted them to try out. One thing led to another and by 3am they had recorded all the saxophone parts for *Living in the Fast Lane*. Barbara was very impressed: "It was a mammoth achievement — particularly as they'd never seen the parts before!"

Barbara wrote in the CD liner-notes that the album 'lays many ghosts.' By this she meant that it included several pieces she had written or arranged in the past that hadn't, for one reason or another, ever been recorded. For instance, *Living in the Fast Lane* had already been performed live as a tuba concerto with a jazz orchestra — as Barbara had originally intended. Jon wanted to include it on the album, as he feared it might otherwise never see the light of day as a recorded piece[4] — and he never liked letting anything go that he really believed in. So this album was, as he put it: 'literally to tidy up', though it did include some new material — the title track, *Never Say Goodbye,* and *Son of a Gun*. Barbara really felt that something about the making of this album was different: "There was an inner strength and confidence — a belief in the quality of what we were trying to do which transcended our individual efforts — and the result was one of our best albums ever." Actually, for Jon the recording was quite tricky, because Barbara's medication, levodopa, was by this time inducing a lot of involuntary movement, the clinical term for which is dyskinesia. After trying several different ways to keep her in front of a single microphone, he resorted to using four mics so that he wouldn't miss a single note!

Following the success of the *Colosseum* DVD and realising that time was running out for Barbara, Jon decided to film one of the *Never Say Goodbye* tour gigs, opting for the Theaterhaus in Stuttgart, spiritual home of the *UJ&RE*. Mike Dibb, who had filmed the *Jazz, Rock and Marriage* documentary, was co-opted to help with the planning and logistics for *Para Live '05* as well as being lead cameraman. Since he was also about to start making a film about Barbara's ongoing battle with Parkinson's (called *Playing Against Time*), the footage of the concert could also be useful for that documentary. Jon was determined to use this opportunity to build on his previous experience and get into digital video editing properly. Now, some five years later, the *Paraphernalia* DVD is expected to be released in the spring of 2011. Jon: "I consider this video to be an important part of our legacy — there's something really special about everyone's contribution." However, like the guys in *Colosseum* after the first *Live* recording, none of the band felt sure that they had given of their best in first half of the concert and Barbara had been quite upset in the interval. This was partly due to the fact that, four days before, Jon had been informed that they wouldn't be able to get into the venue until late in the afternoon, which meant that they would have very limited time to carry out their complicated sound and light check. With so much to do, in so little time, they just about managed to finish and get offstage as the audience came in. In the half hour or so remaining, Barbara had little chance to relax and then, with minutes to go, 'Mr. Parkinson' arrived and delivered a massive 'down' — right before show time! It seems that her natural apprehension induced by the occasion interacted with her medication and for the first few numbers, left her feeling quite 'powerless'. Jon: "Incredibly, none of this is at all apparent in the finished video — indeed, situations like this probably just heighten everyone's senses, giving their performance that extra edge. I remember thinking at the time, 'not to worry — I've been here before — it's just history repeating itself!'"

Meanwhile, *Colosseum*'s touring schedule continued apace, with Barbara now established as a full-time member of the band.

Taking Dick Heckstall-Smith's place was an achievement in itself, but she soon stamped her own personality on the band's sound: "Dick was the ultimate jazz/blues saxophonist — I'm more of a catalyst — my musical experience covers the whole spectrum, which I think reflects in my playing. I pick up on what I hear around me and adapt accordingly, whereas Dick had definite ideas of what he wanted to play and stuck to it. Though Dick's approach was totally different to mine, occasionally I find myself playing in the same areas, especially on tenor. I think it's because the music at its most intense level demands a raunchy sound and there's no other way of doing it. People have said that I have changed *Colosseum*'s sound and that they now play with more light and shade." Mark Clarke gives his take on what Barbara brings to the band: "Often, when I hear something she plays, I get chills up my spine, kind of lose my concentration and find myself just listening to her. She's added so much to the band." It seemed that *Colosseum*, traditionally quite a masculine band...big and punchy, now had a feminine touch, which seems to have brought an inner strength to the music.

During 2006 the band revisited Italy for a short tour and it felt wonderful being back in such a hospitable country, where they had been so rapturously received the first time around. Then in February of 2007, they visited Japan for the first time, playing two concerts in Tokyo. They had been warned to expect a fairly cool reception from the audience, but in fact, the fans were ecstatic, queuing for over an hour afterwards to meet, exchange a few words with the band and get their autographs...several of them crying with emotion! It had only taken 39 years for their heroes to get there! Furthermore, Barbara was astonished to realise how many of them were aware of *Paraphernalia*, who they would also get to see just a year or so later, when they followed in *Colosseum*'s footsteps

Later that year *Colosseum* released a 2-CD set, *Live'05* — timed to coincide with yet another European tour. This new album showed just how the band had changed since Barbara joined and Dave Greenslade, for one, is convinced it's the best yet. Although some songs came from the recent studio albums, they were now given a new lease of life. *Valentyne Suite*, for example, sounds fantastically fresh! Barbara comments: "The end of *January's Search*, when I duet with Dave and the alto solo in *February's Valentyne* alongside Mark's fantastic vocals are delights. I have had such a great time playing with these guys — they're such good musicians *and* nice people. Though I've known them all since I was 22 years old, it was never from the musical side of things and now we have formed a really strong musical relationship. I love working with Chris — he is such good fun, always with a twinkle in his eye and...*what* a voice! Clem is fantastic; his guitar playing never ceases to amaze me...while Dave is the rock upon which everything is built. I suppose I should have also mentioned Jon — but you know all about him!"

The 2007 tour of Europe was a great success and the new album sold very well. In fact, as early as the third gig, Jon had to order more for the later dates. Most of the tour was sold out and at the Bochum concert, the merchandising man, Andre, enterprisingly took copies of the new CD outside and sold them to those people who hadn't been able to get tickets! The band had decided to bring back the old favourite, *Skellington*, for the tour, as well as introducing a new song, *Morning Story*[5], by the band's favourite writers Jack Bruce and Pete Brown, from Jack's album *Harmony Row*. Indeed, some shows included as many as three of the talented duo's songs. As Jon often informed the audiences, it wasn't Lennon and McCartney who were *their* muses, but Jack and Pete. *Morning Story* was an excellent choice for the band, as it has an epic quality to it and was an ideal vehicle for Barbara and Clem's solos, as well as great lyrics for Chris. Mark Clarke was by now something of an 'unsung hero' in *Colosseum*, having developed his stage presence and by physically giving 100% every performance. One of the show's highlights was Clem and Mark improvising together, swapping riffs over the end of *Lost Angeles*. The tour certainly proved that *Colosseum* still had bags of energy — and the desire to continue playing, recording and touring.

Jon invited me, as the author of this book, to spend several days with the band during this tour and on 31st March 2007, I was at the sound check in the Music Hall, Worpswede. It was fascinating to see them still tinkering with bits of the show, with Mark and Clem working on a smoother transition for the *Theme for an Imaginary Western/Walking in the Park/Stormy Monday Blues* medley, then honing Jack Bruce's *Morning Story*...which, as a new addition to the set, still had few rough edges. The Music Hall was an intimate venue with lots of character, as well as great acoustics...in fact the band had recorded *Rope Ladder* from *Live'05* there on the previous tour. Actually, it was clear that the material changed subtly every time they played and it was interesting to hear how much Clem's guitar intro to *Tomorrow's Blues* on his old purple Stratocaster, varied from earlier versions.

Colosseum is pretty relaxed on tour these days and they have the look of a band that is very comfortable with how they go about their business. Jon always refers to them as a family and it's easy to understand why — after all these years they have grown very close. However, on the tour's occasional rest days, they don't necessarily hang out with each other. Minor disagreements still crop up from time to time and Dave is as forthright as ever — Clem and Mark a little less so, though still making their voices heard. Jon generally tends to let everyone have their say and only then does he voice *his* opinion, though it wasn't always like that, as Chris Farlowe remembers: "In the old days I thought he was like a schoolmaster, always giving orders, but now he has chilled out and is a different person...much more relaxed." Nowadays touring isn't as stressful, as they go by luxury coach and stay in four-star hotels, very different from the early days. There is definitely a feeling that they have finally arrived, but are totally aware that their time might be limited, so they fully intend to carry on for as long as they can. Mark Clarke: "*Colosseum* has been put more and more on the front-burner by all of us over the last 10 years. I think it's more precious to us now than it ever was."

Speaking in 2009, Jon had this to say about the nuts-and-bolts of *Colosseum*, its history and its legacy: "I had started playing the shift from the jazz beat to the rock feel with the *Wes Minster Five* back in the early '60s, but the rock element was solely used in a blues context. *Colosseum* was arguably the first jazz-based band in the UK to start the shift to rock. We took that rhythm and linked it to improvised solos, not the American way, but the kind of improvisation that came naturally to us. Dave, Dick, Tony and I were very influenced by classical music and all of us were proud of our European roots — I am proudest of *Colosseum* when it sounds European — because therein lies its uniqueness."

Clambering on his soapbox, Jon continued: "As long as there are people out there wanting to see us and we are fit enough, we will continue to play. I think there will always be an audience for the original bands of the '60s, but I do fear for today's young musicians. We have only been able to enjoy our musical endeavors, because we made enough money to bring up families and have a decent lifestyle. When physical media such as CDs, DVDs and the old LP, was the only way to own a creative work, the revenue stream was easy to control and channel back to the artists. 'Free Music' campaigns, started by the anti-capitalist idealists in 1968, never really caught on and had all but fizzled out within a decade. Now, 25 years later nearly everyone thinks music should be free, or at least cheap, especially when their favourite movie or album is only a click away. Up to the mid '90s, individuals or companies invested money in creative work with a fair chance of getting a return that would enable them to make a profit and reinvest in the next project. Now, with the ubiquitous free downloading of movies and music, the revenue stream is drying up. By and large, today's artist royalties are pitiful and none of the young musicians I come into contact with can earn enough to support a career. I suppose we had all better get used to the idea of music becoming the domain of amateurs operating in their spare time, who have 'proper' jobs in order to pay the mortgage — I'm seeing it happening already. I know that there's some very good music being created out there, against the odds — I just wish people were prepared to pay for it. However, it's heartening to remember that the only thing you can't reproduce is us playing live on stage...*yet*!!!"

From the point when the TM studio was built in the early '80s and their flirtation with Andrew Lloyd Webber's music was over, Jon and Barbara had divided their time between *Paraphernalia* and the *UJ&RE*. From 1994 on, the reunited *Colosseum* was added to the mix and until 'Mr Parkinson' arrived to spoil the party, they enjoyed a thrilling roller-coaster ride. For both of them, there is nothing quite like the feeling they have when coming off stage exhausted...the applause of the audience ringing in their ears. It's a source of pride for Jon that the audience is still applauding them and the music they create. As instrumentalists, it would have been so easy just to work for others as 'guns for hire', but something drove them both to tread their own path and gain recognition for doing their own thing.

Today, Barbara continues to write classical compositions and, while her creativity is boundless, her energy levels are not — which she finds increasingly frustrating. At the time of writing, apart from the *Three Quartets* and the choral work *Journey to a Destination Unknown* she has completed two concertos for saxophone quartet and string ensemble, a flute concerto, a piano concerto and an orchestral tone-poem for symphony orchestra, *The Crossing*. Nowadays, the 14 tablets she needed to swallow down daily have been replaced by a subcutaneous 10 mm needle and transfusion line, connected to a small waistband pump, delivering apomorphine 17 hours a day. Jon, with typical irony, says: "I've been sticking metaphorical needles in her for years — now each morning, I get to do it for real!"

As the 'noughties' fade and the new millennium enters its second decade, Jon and Barbara are still touring, all the while fighting Parkinson's, hoping against hope that a cure will be found before it's too late.

On reading this book in its final draft, Jon summed up: "It's been quite a journey but the real success has been my family life with Barbara and our two children, Marcus and Anna. Of course, we lived all the usual soap-opera stuff, but always set against the uplifting soundtrack of our many concerts and albums. I, like so

404

many of the musicians who appear in these pages, got the bug when I was in my teens and just went for it — seldom looking left or right, *never* looking down and just 'playing the band.' Life seemed pretty simple to me, in that every decision was made with the sole purpose of getting the current project brought home to a successful conclusion...then moving on to the next idea, which was already taking shape in my fevered brain.

Ultimately, though, I guess this book is about what I did in my life, or appeared to do, as others saw it...not so much about what I *thought*. Thank God my thoughts always have been my own!"

THE END.

FOOTNOTES

1. With the advent of small laptop computers and multi-track audio programs, playing to backing tracks on live performances became very easy. Using a click-track, Jon could keep the whole band in time and DHS's solo track from *Hard Times Rising* could be heard at the appropriate moments in the song. When the lighting team dimmed the lights and started the glitter-ball high above the audience, Jon always felt as if there was a friendly hand on his shoulder.

2. Arthur describes how Dick's tapes came to be archived: "Paul Wilson of the British Library Sound Archive took a couple of sports bags stuffed full of Betamax PCM-F1 and cassette tapes to be digitised and transferred to optical storage by the British Library back at the beginning of 2005, which is still in progress, as far as I am aware. There are still a couple of very large cardboard boxes full of cassettes, which I am slowly sorting through — even after throwing away the majority of the hundreds he had accumulated over the years."

3. The Astoria was packed...*Big Chief*, a band that included Tony Reeves on bass, and with whom Dick had played for about five years, got things off to a rousing start. They were followed onstage by blues guitarist Eddie Martin and then Pete Brown played three songs with *his* band. Next on was John O'Leary and after him came ex-*Rolling Stone* Mick Taylor. Jack Bruce had put together an impressive trio especially for the concert, featuring Gary Moore and Gary

Husband and they played a fine set, which included two *Cream* numbers, *I Feel Free* and *Sunshine of Your Love*, to a cheering audience. It was only fitting that *Colosseum* should close the concert, but before they did, Barbara Thompson and James Litherland played a beautiful acoustic duo piece. *Colosseum's* poignant and moving finale brought Tony Reeves and James Litherland back on stage for the aptly named *Elegy*. Then, Barbara's solo on the very apposite *Theme from an Imaginary Western*, brought the house down! Arthur Heckstall-Smith had compiled a 7-minute personal video tribute to his father for screening on the night. It was set to an atmospheric piece of music: *La Muerte de un Trompetista (Death of a Trumpet Player)* by a relatively little-known group called *El Columpio Asesino* from Pamplona in northern Spain. Arthur chose this recording because it was the last piece of new music he had shared with his father, a month or so before his death. Towards the end of the concert, Arthur went on stage with his children to thank the crowd for coming to celebrate Dick's life in such an impressive manner. He later thanked the other contributors: "I had a lot of organisational help from agent Don Mackay, and technical help from the *Colosseum* guys who were fantastic — Jon Hiseman and Miles Ashton were great, their experience and judgement was crucial and the gig would never have been as good without them." Everyone agreed that it was, without doubt, a most fitting tribute to Dick, his music and his legacy.

4. In fact, Barbara's *Tuba Concerto* has been recorded in an arrangement for *Foden's Brass Band*, featuring two of the world's greatest tuba players, James Gourlay and Les Neish. The album, entitled *Double Trouble*, showcases the compositions of Barbara and Andy Scott and is released on the Egon label.

5. When rehearsing *Morning Story*, Jon suddenly got a sense of *déjà vu*. He realised that he didn't need to learn it — he already knew it...but couldn't think how. It was only later that he recalled that he had played it with *Colosseum II* back in the '70s.

ABOVE: *Colosseum* after Reunion Concert, 1994 — Mark, JH, Alex Heissler, Clem, Chris, DHS, Dave

LEFT: *Bread & Circuses* unused booklet cover

RIGHT AND BELOW: *Bread & Circuses* promo pics

ABOVE: DHS and Clem, Vienna, 2000

LEFT: *And Not Forgetting...*

BELOW LEFT: JH... "Where *did* I put that stick?"

BELOW: Chris, Vienna, 2000

ABOVE: DHS records his last *Colosseum* solo

ABOVE RIGHT: Dave drives us home at the end of the tour

RIGHT: BT and DHS work on sharing the show, 2004

BELOW: DHS's Last Stand, The Stables, Wavendon, Summer '04

ABOVE: The Last *Colosseum* Line-up

RIGHT: BT in Rome with *Colosseum*

BELOW: After hours — Dave, Clem, BT, with Gert Lange, our German Agent

OPPOSITE ABOVE: *Colosseum* in Moscow

OPPOSITE BELOW: Chris finds Moscow's only cake shop

TOP: BT on Tour — still composing

ABOVE: JH... *"Where's my computer?"*

LEFT: Mark Clarke sings on the *Valentyne Suite* in Japan

APPENDICES

Playing the ~~Band~~ Drums...

So far, not much has been said in this book about the actual business of drumming, so here, finally, is the 'drummy' bit.

It's *not* a tutorial as such — just a collection of ideas I've developed over the years that have helped me master this 'darkest of arts'. My rules are mainly intended for those starting out — the exercise at the end is for those drummers who want to move onto a higher plane. Everybody else can run for cover!

Rule One:

Learn to play the piano — *I'm not kidding*!

For the first couple of years, spend longer at the piano than you do on the kit — you won't regret it. It is far easier to learn how to read music on the piano than it is on the drums. It also teaches you how to follow other instrumental parts and interpret them for the drums, as well as helping you to learn the language that all the other musicians will be speaking. Finally, it will teach you that you are different...because you are a DRUMMER.

If you can find a drum teacher who understands how and what you want to play, by all means have drum lessons too, but keep an open mind about what you are being taught, as there could well be better ways to do things than the teacher's — don't be afraid to experiment.

You might even end up settling for the piano, which will probably come as a great relief to your parents or 'better half...'

414

Rule Two:

Record yourself playing as often as possible — preferably with other musicians, but, if necessary, on your own. Listen to other drummers and learn to compare what they are doing with what you are doing. Does what you play sound as you intended it to? In the same way that actors have to know how they look to an audience, or how they appear on camera, learn how you sound to the listener. Buy a cheap drum machine and practise to it — it'll help your timing...and, as is mentioned elsewhere in this book...timing is everything!

Rule Three:

Play with a band. It's important to realise that, with the exception of the odd drum solo moment, the drums are only really useful when played inside the music, as part of a band. Drummers who spend years practising on their own can find it difficult to play in a band situation. So, finding people to play with early on is important, whatever standard you, or they, have attained. There are many clips on the Internet of what I call 'Exercise Drummers' — their antics are great for keeping your weight down, but that's about all and you don't want to become one of *those* — do you?

Rule Four:

Never practise what you already know you can play.

Performing as much as I have over the years, I had to develop a way to advance my playing by snatching just a few moments practise, every so often. The best method is never to practise what you can already do well...practise the things you can't do, or those that you didn't get right on the last gig. Most players develop the ability to screw-up and get out of it gracefully, so that no one notices. Remember those moments, reproduce them in practise, break them down into their component parts and then work them back up. NEVER try to incorporate them into your playing at the next gig. When the move is ready, it will turn up of its own accord at the appropriate moment.

RULE FIVE:

Try to develop a split personality...again, I'm not kidding!

The drums, like no other instrument, can lend themselves solely to technical accomplishment, with the music getting lost along the way. Don't let it be said of you: "he plays a lot of drums, but very little music!" Make a conscious division between practise and performance. Give your fellow musicians a 'magic carpet ride'! Don't speed up...don't slow down — just groove along and you'll find that both the band and the audience will love you for it.

RULE SIX:

Bless the drum kit.

Have you ever noticed that a good drummer appears to be taking part in a 'laying on of hands' ceremony? The sticks appear to be in charge and the whole movement is a fluid one, from your trunk via the upper arms, lower arms, wrists to the fingers and ultimately to the sticks. What follows is how you can best achieve that. It starts with a discussion about 'Loud and Soft'.

Whatever the size of your drum kit, you really only have loud and soft beats to make your drumming move people. Listen to your favourite drummers and check out which beats they play loudly and which quietly. Then, as I said earlier, record yourself and listen to whether your accented hits are really standing out from the ones you meant to be quiet? Not making a big enough difference between loud and soft beats, is the most frequent single fault I hear in young drummers.

Finally, here is a killer exercise for players who are already playing in bands and who want to improve their natural technical ability.

This routine will increase your power and speed, at the same time, giving you greater control over loud and soft.

If you are a beginner and don't know what a Paradiddle is — DON'T try this exercise until you have read a good drum tutor that includes some exercises based on 'Rudiments', and specifically, the Paradiddle.

Rudiments are the 'scales' of drumming. Almost all of them have loud and soft beats (accents and taps) and, though they are not used much in today's rock drumming, jazz drummers certainly still do. I recommend that every drummer should practise rudiments, as they improve the technique, touch and feel, whatever kind of music is played.

This exercise involves the Paradiddle, one of the basic standard 26 American rudiments. However, it can be applied to any of the rudiments. I was taught this routine by Eric George, of the US Air Force, at 'Drum City' in London's Soho, back in the late '60s and to whom I say a big 'thank you'. After three months practising it, I never worried about my technique again...it was always better than I was!

The Paradiddle — consists of four strokes: the first one accented — RLRR. The complete Paradiddle cycle consists of eight strokes, with the first and fifth accented — RLRRLRLL. The

Paradiddle is often taught and practised without an accent. It's the accent that makes it really useful.

<u>The Exercise — 'Idle hand high'</u>

RH = Right Hand
LH = Left Hand

There are two positions: Accent and Tap. The accent should be played considerably louder than the tap and on a snare drum you could use a rim-shot.

Start with the tip of the RH stick at eye level (accent position) and the tip of the LH stick 15 cm above the centre of the drumhead (tap position).

1. RH plays accent and returns directly to 15 cm above the centre of the drumhead. Tap position — level with waiting LH.

2. LH plays tap and returns directly with the tip of stick at eye level. Accent position is now ready and waiting to play the next accent.

3. RH plays tap then returns to Tap position.

4. RH plays tap, then returns to Tap position.
   First Paradiddle is now completed, the hands are reversed and in position to start the next Paradiddle, with the left hand accent.

5. LH plays accent and returns directly to 15 cm above centre of drumhead. Tap position — level with waiting RH.

6. RH plays tap and returns directly with tip of stick at eye level. Accent position now waiting to play the next accent.

7. LH plays tap returning to Tap position.

8. LH plays tap returning to Tap position.

Start 'out of time' — in front of a mirror, checking the hand positions after each stroke. When you are sure your hand positions are correct, play to a metronome or drum machine, but VERY, VERY SLOWLY — continuing to check hand positions. Very gradually, increase your speed. As you get faster the stick positions will get closer to the drum. When you are pretty fast and fluid with the Paradiddle, any other rudiment that involves accents and taps can be practised with this method.

Carry out this practise for 30 minutes each day. Then forget it...and I mean forget it — and practise normally. What you learn from this exercise will be absorbed into your playing naturally, over time.

Finally...always remember, when you leave the practise room — *'don't play the drums...play the band!'*

That's all we know!

Jon Hiseman

BLOODY COMPUTERS!

JON'S RELATIONSHIP WITH PERSONAL COMPUTERS began almost at their inception. In 1980, while on tour with *Paraphernalia*, he saw an advert for the *Sinclair ZX80*. Jon read the blurb and immediately realised that it could help him calculate his VAT returns and decided to get one. Using the built in BASIC language, it took him just a couple of days to write a program that did everything he wanted except provide a final total — because he had already exhausted the 1k of memory! He sold the *ZX80* the very next day and bought from Radio Shack, a *Tandy TRS-80* that had 4k of memory, which he upped, within days, to 16k. His program, converted for the *Tandy*, ran beautifully. Using the manuals that came with it, which were brilliantly written as computer primers, Jon absorbed all he could — and even joined a local *Tandy* enthusiasts club.

So that's how it all started. Then, after being driven crazy by the desperate attempts on the part of the various manufacturers to improve the reliability and power of their desktop computers, all of which were, with hindsight, more trouble than they were worth, Jon was recommended the first *Macintosh* computer in 1984. *Macintosh*, in this context, does not refer to an item of rainwear, but to the *Macintosh* variety of *Apple*! This machine proved to be a revelation, but, initially, was restricted to office tasks. With software in its infancy, Jon quickly gravitated towards *4th Dimension*, the first graphical relational database on the market — written in France for the leading computer of the day...the *Apple Mac*.

Learning to program, using the first version of this software, he quickly built applications to compute and effect payment of the publishing and recording royalties, look after the equipment insurance lists and create the paperwork for the Customs Carnet required to take the band's equipment across Europe's borders. Formulating such programs became virtually the only hobby he had — and while he certainly found great satisfaction in writing elegant code, the finished product was always music-biz related.

By the mid '80s, Jon was using the BBC *Micro* in the studio, running a 16 MIDI channel UMI music sequencer in sync with the 24-track tape machine. For the first time ever, a keyboard player could record a performance which could subsequently be manipulated — for example, by altering the octave, changing the synth sound or even moving notes around. In fact, *Queen* used a UMI on their hit album, *A Kind of Magic*. In time, MIDI would allow computers, synthesizers, sound cards, samplers and drum machines to control one another, thus spawning much of today's synth and sample-based TV, film and pop music.

The first comprehensive MIDI music sequencer was *C-Lab*'s *Creator* software, running on the *Atari ST* computer. The program later became *C-Lab Notator*, which included the ability to print out music scores and parts, which immediately got Barbara's interest. Then in 1992, *C-Lab* became *Emagic*, when they re-wrote their program for the *Mac* and called it *Logic*. Some ten years later, this was purchased by *Apple*, who wanted the technology for its *Garage Band* and for *Final Cut Pro*, its film-editing software.

Looking back on this era evokes painful memories for Jon: "As artists, we always need reliable systems, working well within the current technological capabilities, so that we can just concentrate on the music. In fact, the claims made by the companies regarding their computers' abilities were always way behind the software designers' ideas about what was *theoretically* possible. In the real world, there were endless delays caused by problems that were never satisfactorily nailed. To be creative in a studio during the mid-'90s, you had to have the patience of a saint. It was literally like working in glue for days at a time. The problems did eventually go away, but only after you bought and installed the next generation of hardware. Trouble was, in always hoping for 'fixes' and by continually updating the software, we were locked in a vicious circle. Throughout this long and difficult period, you just didn't know who to blame for the problems — and of course, there was always that nagging feeling that they might just be down to your own incompetence!"

What made everything worse was that, as more and more rival manufacturers each brought their competing software to market, a 'features war' started and the programs became 'heavier and heavier', until you could hear them creaking. The designers didn't help matters either, as they never went back and fixed the earlier problems, which were just left to fester. Jon again: "The *Emagic Logic* notation program is a good case in point. Barbara became quite expert in creating big orchestral scores with this software, in spite of being endlessly frustrated by relatively simple problems that never got sorted. Finally, at my instigation, she gave up on *Emagic* and switched to *Sibelius*. It can't compete with *Emagic*'s quick manipulation of MIDI and its audio capabilities are very limited, but as a composer's tool, it is relatively transparent and when you finally have the notes on the screen...WYSIWYG when printing them out. In the end I had to ban *Logic* from the studio, because I couldn't cope with having to work around the endless problems. Indeed, there were some really awful days, when Barbara, Pete Lemer and I were trying to work in the studio, but just couldn't achieve anything creative. It's a good job that Pete is virtually family, so I could still let off steam if he was around — otherwise I might well have had several serious heart attacks! Because I always have a clear vision of how I want things to be played or to sound — working in such circumstances was just too frustrating. Listening to those CDs now...well, I just don't know how we did it, but — somehow we did."

When Jon installed *Digidesign*'s *Pro Tools* in 1999, it came as a blessed relief to work in the rarified atmosphere of well-designed, robust and professional software. However, *Digidesign* was bought-out by *Avid* and the corporate suits are now busy 'rebranding' and Jon fears for its future: "With competition increasing and as more facilities than ever are 'bolted on', I just hope the designers are allowed to stay on the case. My love-hate relationship with computers continues...but I am very pleased to have lived through their developmental years, always trying to stay at the sharp end. I willingly confess that they have become completely central to my life and I will, of course, continue to push them to their limit; but it *would* be nice to meet up with my old friend, the drummer...just occasionally!"

JON HISEMAN & BARBARA THOMPSON
Selected Discography

EARLY DAYS

1965   *The New Jazz Orchestra — Western Reunion* (DECCA)
*Big P, Shades Of Blue, So What, If You Could See Me Now,
Tiny's Blues, Milestones, Django, Maria, Western Reunion*

1966   Mike Taylor — *Pendulum* (EMI)
*But Not For Me, Exactly Like You, A Night In Tunisia,
Pendulum, To Segovia, Leeway*

       Peter Lemer Quintet — Local Colour (ESP)
Ictus, City, Frowville, In The Out, Carmen, Enahenado

       Mike Taylor — *Trio* (EMI)
*All The Things You Are, Just A Blue, While My Lady Sleeps,
The End of The Love Affair, Two Autumns, Guru, Stella By
Starlight, Abena*

1967   Howard Riley — *Discussions*
*Sweet & Lovely, Romance, Nardis, Sunflower, Children At
Play, What's New, Folk Theme No.1*

1968   *John Mayall & The Bluesbreakers — Bare Wires*
*Bare Wires Suite: Bare Wires – Where Did I Belong – Start
Walking – Open A New Door – Fire – I Know Now – Look
In The Mirror, I'm A Stranger, No Reply, Hartley Quits,
Killing Time, She's Too Young, Sandy*

1969   *The New Jazz Orchestra — Le Déjeuner sur l'Herbe*
*Le Déjeuner sur l'Herbe, Naïma, Angle, Ballad, Dusk Fire,
Nardis, Study, Rebirth*

424

Jack Bruce — *Songs For A Tailor* (POLYDOR)
Never Tell Your Mother She's Out Of Tune, Theme From An Imaginary Western, Tickets To Waterfalls, Weird Of Hermiston, Rope Ladder To The Moon (JH is not on this track), *The Ministry Of Bag, He The Richmond, Boston Ball Game 1967, To Isengard, The Clearout*

1970 *Graham Bond ORGANisation — Solid Bond* (WARNER BROS)
(Rec. 1966) *Green Onions, Springtime In The City, Can't Stand It, Only Sixteen, Last Night, Long Legged Baby, Walking In The Park, It's Not Goodbye, Neighbour Neighbour*

Jack Bruce — *Things We Like* (POLYDOR)
(Rec. 1968) *Over The Cliff, Statues, Sam Enchanted Dick/Sam's Sack/Rill's Thrills, Born To Be Blue, HCKHH Blues, Ballad For Arthur, Things We Like*

COLOSSEUM

1969 *Those Who Are About To Die Salute You* (FONTANA)
Walking In The Park, Plenty Hard Luck, Mandarin, Debut, Beware The Ides Of March, The Road She Walked Before, Backwater Blues, Those About To Die

Walking In The Park/*Those Who Are About To Die* (Single)

Valentyne Suite (VERTIGO)
The Kettle, Elegy, Butty's Blues, The Machine Demands A Sacrifice, The Valentyne Suite; Theme One – January's Search,

425

Theme Two – February's Valentyne, Theme Three – The Grass Is Always Greener

1970 **Daughter Of Time** (VERTIGO)
Three Score And Ten, Amen, Time Lament, Take Me Back To Doomsday, The Daughter Of Time, Theme For An Imaginary Western, Bring Out Your Dead, Downhill & Shadows, The Time Machine (live)

1971 **Colosseum Live** (BRONZE)
Rope Ladder To The Moon, Walking In The Park, Skellington, Tanglewood '63, Encore: Stormy Monday Blues, Lost Angeles

1972 **Collectors Colosseum** (BRONZE)
Jumping Off The Sun, Lost Angeles, Elegy, Butty's Blues, Rope Ladder To The Moon, Bolero, The Machine Demands A Sacrifice, The Grass Is Always Greener

1995 **The Reunion Concerts** (INTUITION)
Those About To Die, Elegy, The Valentyne Suite, Theme From An Imaginary Western, The Machine Demands A Sacrifice, Solo Colonia, Lost Angeles, Stormy Monday Blues

1997 **Bread & Circuses** (INTUITION)
Watching Your Every Move, Bread & Circuses, Wherever I Go, High Time, Big Deal, The Playground, No Pleasin, I Could Tell You Tales, Storms Behind The Breeze, The One That Got Away, The Other Side Of The Sky

2003 **Colosseum LiveS** (DVD) (ANGEL AIR)
Those About To Die, Skellington, Elegy, Tanglewood '63, The Valentyne Suite, Rope Ladder To The Moon, Theme For An Imaginary Western, The Machine Demands Another Sacrifice, Solo Colonia, Lost Angeles, Stormy Monday Blues, Walking In The Park
Bonus Documentary

426

Tomorrow's Blues (Rious Music)
Tomorrow's Blues, Come Right Back, In The Heat Of The Night, Hard Times Rising, Arena In The Sun, Thief In The Night, Take The Dark Times With The Sun, The Net Man, Leisure Complex Blues, No Demons

2004 **Those Who Are About To Die Salute You** — Reissue (Sanctuary)
Walking In The Park, Plenty Hard Luck, Mandarin, Debut, Beware The Ides Of March, The Road She Walked Before, Backwater Blues, Those About To Die; Bonus tracks: *I Can't Live Without You (Studio Outtake), A Whiter Spade Than Mayall (BBC), Walking In The Park (BBC), Beware The Ides Of March (BBC), Plenty Hard Luck (BBC), Walking In The Park (Top Of The Pops, BBC)*

Valentyne Suite — Reissue (Sanctuary)
Disc 1: *The Kettle, Elegy, Butty's Blues, The Machine Demands A Sacrifice, The Valentyne Suite; Theme One – January's Search, Theme Two – February's Valentyne, Theme Three – The Grass Is Always Greener* Bonus Tracks: *Arthur's Moustache (BBC session), Lost Angeles (BBC session)*
Disc 2 (Second USA album): *The Grass Is Greener – Jumping Off The Sun, Lost Angeles, Elegy, Butty's Blues, Rope Ladder To The Moon, Bolero, The Machine Demands A Sacrifice, The Grass Is Always Greener*

Daughter Of Time — Reissue (Sanctuary)
Three Score And Ten Amen, Time Lament, Take Me Back To Doomsday, The Daughter Of Time, Theme For An Imaginary Western, Bring Out Your Dead, Downhill & Shadows, The Time Machine (live)
Bonus Track: *Jumping Off The Sun*

Colosseum Live — Reissue (Sanctuary)
Rope Ladder To The Moon, Walking In The Park, Skellington, Tanglewood '63, Encore; Stormy Monday Blues,

Lost Angeles
Bonus Track: *I Can't Live Without You*

2006 *The Reunion Concerts* — Reissue (SANCTUARY)
Those About To Die, Elegy, The Valentyne Suite, Theme From An Imaginary Western, The Machine Demands A Sacrifice, Solo Colonia, Lost Angeles, Stormy Monday Blues

Bread & Circuses — Reissue (SANCTUARY)
Watching Your Every Move, Bread & Circuses, Wherever I Go, High Time, Big Deal, The Playground, No Pleasin, I Could Tell You Tales, Storms Behind The Breeze, The One That Got Away, The Other Side Of The Sky

Tomorrow's Blues — Reissue (SANCTUARY)
Tomorrow's Blues, Come Right Back, In The Heat Of The Night, Hard Times Rising, Arena In The Sun, Thief In The Night, Take The Dark Times With The Sun, The Net Man, Leisure Complex Blues, No Demons

2008 *Colosseum & The New Jazz Orchestra Live at the Camden Festival* (DUSK FIRE)
(Rec. 1970) *Stratusfunk, Tanglewood '63, Shades Of Blue, Rope Ladder to the Moon, Dusk Fire, Naima, Nardis, Sturdy, Rebirth, Ballad, Le Déjeuner sur l'Herbe, National Anthem & Tango*

2009 *Colosseum: Morituri Te Salutant* (4CD Box Set) (SANCTUARY)
Disc 1: *In The Studio 1968-1969:*
Walking In The Park, Mandarin, Beware The Ides Of March, Debut, The Road She Walked Before, Backwater Blues, I Can't Live Without You, In The Heat Of The Night*, Those About To Die*, Tell Me Now*, The Kettle, Elegy, The Machine Demands A Sacrifice, The Valentyne Suite: January's Search – February's Valentyne – The Grass Is Always Greener
Disc 2: *In The Studio 1970-1971:*

428

Jumping Off The Sun, Rope Ladder To The Moon, Bolero, The Grass Is Always Greener, Three Score And Ten, Amen, Time Lament, Take Me Back To Doomsday, The Daughter Of Time, Theme For An Imaginary Western, Bring Out Your Dead*, Downhill And Shadows, Jumping Off The Sun, The Pirate's Dream*
Disc 3: **Rope Ladder To The Moon (live sessions):**
Rope Ladder To The Moon*, Skellington*, I Can't Live Without You*, The Time Machine, The Machine Demands A Sacrifice, Stormy Monday Blues*The Valentyne Suite*
Disc 4: **Walking In The Park:**
Butty's Blues (live in Boston), The Machine Demands A Sacrifice (live in Boston), Beware The Ides Of March**, Walking In The Park**, Plenty Hard Luck**), Arthur's Moustache**, Lost Angeles**, Same Old Thing, Dark Side Of The Moog (Colosseum II), Tomorrow's Blues (Post-reunion), Those About To Die (Post-reunion) *Previously unreleased, **BBC session

JON HISEMAN SESSIONS

1968 *The Crazy World of Arthur Brown — Fire/Give Him a Flower* (Single) (TRACK)

1976 Keith Emerson — *Honky Tonk Train Blues* (Single) (MANTICORE)

2003 Dave Cousins — *Two Weeks Last Summer* (Rec. 1972) *Two Weeks Last Summer, October To May, Blue Angel, That's The Way It Ends (including The World), The Actor, When You Were A Child, Ways And Means, We'll Meet Again Sometime, Going Home*

Wolfgang Dauner — *Et Cetera* (Rec. 1972) *The Really Great Escape, Sun, Yan, Tuning Spread, Yin*

2005 *Keef Hartley Band — Overdog*
(Rec. 1970) *You Can Choose, Plain Talkin', Theme Song, En Route, Theme Song Reprise, Overdog, Roundabout, Imitations from Home, We Are All The Same*
Bonus tracks: *Roundabout (Part 1), Roundabout (Part 2)*

2007 Mike Taylor — *Remembered* (DUSK FIRE)
(Rec. 1973) *Half Blue, Pendulum, I See You, Son of Red Blues – Brown Thursday, Song of Love, Folk Dance No.2, Summer Sounds, Land of Rhyme in Time, Timewind, Jumping Off The Sun, Black & White Raga*

TEMPEST

1973 *Tempest* (BRONZE)
Gorgon, Foyers Of Fun, Dark House, Brothers, Up & On, Grey & Black, Strangeher, Upon Tomorrow

1974 *Living In Fear* (BRONZE)
Funeral Empire, Paperback Writer, Stargazer, Dance To My Tune, Living In Fear, Yeah-Yeah-Yeah, Waiting For A Miracle, Turn Around

2005 *Under The Blossom — The Anthology* (SANCTUARY)
Disc 1: *Gorgon, Foyers Of Fun, Dark House, Brothers, Up & On, Grey & Black, Strangeher, Upon Tomorrow, Funeral Empire, Paperback Writer, Stargazer, Dance To My Tune, Living In Fear, Yeah-Yeah-Yeah, Waiting For A Miracle, Turn Around*
Disc 2: *You & Your Love*, Dream Train*, Foyers Of Fun**, Gorgon**, Up & On**, Grey & Black**, Brothers**, Drums Away**, Strangeher*** **Previously unreleased,* **BBC session

COLOSSEUM II

1975 *Strange New Flesh* (Bronze)
*Dark Side Of The Moog, Down To You, Gemini & Leo,
Secret Palaces, On Second Thoughts, Winds*

1976 *Electric Savage* (MCA)
*Put It This Way, All Skin & Bone, Rivers, The Scorch, Lament,
Desperado, Am I, Intergalatic Strut*

1977 *Wardance* (MCA)
*War Dance, Major Keys, Put It That Way, Castles, Fighting
Talk, The Inquisition, Star Maiden/Mysterioso/Quasar,
Last Exit*

2005 *Strange New Flesh* — Reissue (Sanctuary)
Disc 1: *Dark Side Of The Moog, Down To You, Gemini &
Leo, Secret Palaces, On Second Thoughts, Winds;*
Bonus tracks: *Castles (version 1), Gary's Lament, Walking In
The Park*
Disc 2: *Night Creeper, The Awakening, Siren Song, Castles
(version 2), The Scorch, Rivers, Interplanetary Slut, Dark Side
Of The Moog (live), Siren Song (live), The Awakening (live)*

DICK HECKSTALL-SMITH

1972 *A Story Ended* (Bronze)
*Future Song, Crabs, Moses In The Bullrushourses, The Pirate's
Dream, Same*

2001 *Blues & Beyond* (Blue Storm Music)
*Rollin & Tumblin, Millennium Blues, Watching Your Every
Move, Cruel Contradictions, Angie Baby, Grind, Glitch and
Snit, Spooky But Nice, Hidden Agenda, Twilight Shuffle, (Dix
WWW) Swamp, Big Deal, If You Know You Don't Love Me*

Why In The World Don't You Leave Me Be?

2004 *A Story Ended* — Reissue (SANCTUARY)
Future Song, Crabs, Moses In The Bullrushourses, The Pirate's Dream, Same Old Thing; Bonus Tracks: *Moses In The Bullrushourses (live), The Pirate's Dream (live), No Amount Of Loving (live), I'll Go Back To Venus, I Can't Get It*

ANDREW LLOYD WEBBER

1978 *Variations* (MCA)
Introduction, Theme & Variations 1 to 4, Theme 7, Theme 8, Theme 9, Theme 10, Theme 11 to 15, Theme 16, Theme 14 to 15, Theme 17, Theme 18, Theme 19 to 20 & 6 (varied), Theme 21 to 22, Theme 23

1979 *Tell Me On A Sunday* (MCA)
Capped Teeth And Caesar Salad, Come Back With The Same Look In Your Eyes, I'm Very You You're Very Me, It's Not The End Of The World (If He's Married/If He's Younger/If I Lose Him), Let Me Finish, Let's Talk About You, Letter Home To England, Nothing Like You've Ever Known, Second Letter Home, Sheldon Bloom, Take That Look Off Your Face, Tell Me On A Sunday, You Made Me Think You Were In Love

1981 *Cats* (MCA)
Disc 1: *Jellicle Songs For Jellicle Cats (Act 1), The Naming Of Cats (Act 1), The Invitation To The Jellicle Ball (Act 1), The Old Gumbie Cat (Act 1), The Rum Tum Tugger (Act 1), Grizabella, The Glamour Cat (Act 1), Bustopher Jones (Act 1), Mungojerrie And The Rumpelteazer (Act 1), Mungojerrie And The Rumpelteazer (Act 1), Old Deuteronomy (Act 1)*
Disc 2: *The Moments Of Happiness(Act 2), Gus: The Theatre Cat (Act 2), "Growltiger's Last Stand" including "The Ballad*

432

Of Billy McCaw" (Act 2), Skimbleshanks (Act 2), Macavity
(Act 2), Mr. Mistoffelees (Act 2), Memory (Act 2),
Journey To The Heaviside Layer (Act 2)

BARBARA THOMPSON

1978 *Barbara Thompson's Jubiaba* (MCA) (Trevor Tomkins — Drums)
*The Funky Flunky, Seega, Helena, Cuban Thing, Black Pearl,
Touch of Blue, Slum Goddess*

1986 *Heavenly Bodies* (veraBra)
*Le Grand Voyage, Extreme Jonction, Requiem pour Deux
Pilotes, Entre Les Trous de La Memoire, Les-Barricades
Mysterieuses, Heavenly Bodies, Love on the Edge of the Life,
Elysian Fields, Flights of Fancy, Tibetan Sunrise, Horizons New*

1991 *Songs from the Center of the Earth* (BT Solo Saxophone)
(Black Sun)
*The Fanaid Grove, Nobilis Humilis, Chanterai Por Mon
Coraige, Al Ya Zane, Cancion De Cuna, Toriad Y Dydd,
Suspira Coracao Triste, Whereto Should I Express Estilo,
O My Love How Long, Winder Wie Ist No Dein Kraft, I
Can't Stay In Egypt Lan' De Ribber Ben Come Dung, Down
By The Sally Gardens*

BARBARA THOMPSON & PARAPHERNALIA

1978 *Paraphernalia* (MCA) (Harold Fisher — Drums)
*Goodtyme Mr Sam, Study to be Quiet, La Tranquillite D'ame,
Spanish Memories, Sicilian Sting, Next Spring, Temple Song,
Stairways*

1979 *Wilde Tales* (MCA)
Playtime, The Giant, The North Wind, The Linnet, The Child,

*Spring Song, Garden of Paradise, Late Again, Pipe Dream,
Frankfurt Fayre, Cacion Sin Nombre*

1980 **Live In Concert** (MCA)
*Summer Madness, Frilly Bolero, From Nowhere, Scrummage,
Little Annie-ooh, The Blues, Sunset, Aliyah*

1982 **Mother Earth** (VERABRA)
*Aspects of Mother Earth, City Lights, Country Dance,
The Adventures of Water, Fear of Spiders, Humaira, Castles in
the Air*

1984 **Pure Fantasy** (later released as **Nightwatch**) (VERABRA)
*Field of Flowers, The Coconut Hurling Game, Dusk,
Nightwatch, Kafferinya, Chapter and Verse, To Ceres, Listen
to the Planets, Pure Fantasy, Firefly*

1988 **A Cry From The Heart (Live in London)** (VERABRA)
*Joyride, L'Extrême Jonction, A Cry From The Heart, Entre
Les Trous De La Mémoire, Out To Lunch, Close To The Edge,
Voices Behind Locked Doors, Eastern Western Promise (Part I
& II)*

1991 **Breathless** (VERABRA)
*Breathless, Sax Rap, Jauntry, You Must Be Jokin', Squiffy, Bad
Blues, Cheeky, Gracy, Breathless (short cut), Sax Rap (short
cut), Cheeky (short cut)*

1993 **Everlasting Flame** (VERABRA)
*Everlasting Flame, The Eye of a Storm, Emerald Dusky
Maiden, Unity Hymn, So Near So Far, Tatami, Ode to Sappho,
The Night Before Culloden, Ancient Voices, The Fanaid Glove*

1996 **Nightwatch** (previously released as **Pure Fantasy**) (INTUITION)
*Field of Flowers, The Coconut Hurling Game, Dusk,
Nightwatch, Kafferinya, Chapter and Verse, To Ceres, Listen
to the Planets, Pure Fantasy, Firefly*

434

Lady Saxophone (VERABRA)
In Memory, All in Love Is Fair, Falling Stars, I Do It for Your Love, Reuben, Reuben, Out on a Limb, Waterlands, Waiting for the Rain, What Am I Here for, Lady S

1998 **Shifting Sands** (INTUITION)
Shifting Sands, In the Shadows of the Moon, Guardians of the Deep, The Whisper in the Spell, The Wave Police, Sun Shapes, Head in the Sand

2000 *Thompson's Tangos* (INTUITION)
Tango 1, Tango 2, Tango 3, Tango 4, Naima, Regga Ragga, Smokey Embrace, The Slider, The Real Softshoe

2005 *Never Say Goodbye* (INTUITION)
On The Wings Of A Prayer, Still Waters, Living In The Fast Lane, Never Say Goodbye, Giant Steps, Son Of A Gun, Are You Real

2011 *Para Live05* (DVD)
Close to the Edge, Are You Real, Smokey Embrace, On The Wings Of A Prayer, Still Waters, Living In The Fast Lane, Breathless, Son of a Gun, Shifting Sands, Nightwatch, Kafferynia

UNITED JAZZ & ROCK ENSEMBLE

1977 *Live In Schutzenhaus* (MOOD)
Circus Gambet, Hey Day, Steps of M C Escher, South Indian Line, Hypnotic Pignose, The Love That Cannot Speak Its Name, BeBop-Rock

1978 *Teamwork* (MOOD)
Gone With The Weed, Stumbling Henry's Divorce March, Sicilian Steal, Pale Smile, Albert's Song, Yin, To An Elfin Princess, Wart G'schwind

435

1979   *The Break Even Point* (Mood)
Boorcet, Chateau Sentimental, Sparrhärmlingslied, Alfred Schmack, Sidewalk (Carr), Amber, Song With No Name, One Sin A While

1981   *Live In Berlin* (Mood)
Ausgeschlafen, Red Room (Mariano), Storyboard, Out Of The Long Dark, Freibad Süd, Des'sch Too Much, Simply This, Tranz Tanz, South Indian Line

1984   *United Live Opus Sechs* (Mood)
Garberville, Wendekreis des Steinbocks, Rip Off, Die Wiederkehr, Some Time In Silence, Lady Bountiful

1987   *Round Seven* (Mood)
Suite in 3 Movements: Feuerwerxmusik – Ouvertüre – Funk – African Dance, Seriously Deep, Raga Yagapriya, Balance, Voices Behind Locked Doors, Midnight Oil, Raving Raven, Randy – Late Night Mix Live, Ganz schön heiß man

1992   *Na Endlich!* (Mood)
Don't Follow The 'Follow Me' Sign, Capriccio Funky, Ode To Sappho, Ansage Albert Mangelsdorff, Meise Vorm Fenster, Plum Island, Be Bop Scat, Echoes Of Harlem

1996   *Die Neunte Von United* (Mood)
Double Blind, The Worm's Turn, Postcard For F W Bernstein, Drachenburg Für R, Lie In Wait, In Memory, Midday Noon, Wounded Love, Eongate

The UJRE Plays Albert Mangelsdorff (Mood)
Wart G'schwind, Raving Raven, Ansage Albert, Meise Vorm Fenster, Midday Noon, Elongate, Rip Off, Sparrhärmlingslied, Ganz Schön Heiss Man

436

1999   *X — Live At The Cotton Club* (Mood)
*United Funk, Flying Carpets, S'a Wahnsinn, Things Past,
Tribute, Autumn Bugle, Burn Up, SWR 2, Thompson's Tango*

The UJRE Plays Wolfgang Dauner (Mood)
*Ausgeschlafen, Feuerwerxsmusik (Dauner), Tranz Tanz,
The Love That Cannot Speak Its Name, Capriccio Funky,
Wendekreis Des Steinbocks, Boorcet, Yin, Bebop Cat,
80er Jahre*

The UJRE Plays Volker Kriegel (Mood)
*Double Bind, Balance, Chateau Sentimental, Circus Gambet,
Freibad Süd, Garberville, Don't Follow The 'Follow Me' Sign,
Hypnotic Pignose, Postcard For FW Bernstein, Stumbling
Henry's Divorce*

2002   *The UJRE Plays Barbara Thompson* (Mood)
*Die Wiederkehr, Echoes Of Harlem, Sicilian Steel, Ode
To Sappho, In Memory, Voices Behind Locked Doors,
Thompson's Tango*

MISCELLANEOUS

1981   Barbara Thompson & Rod Argent — *Ghosts* (MCA)
*Poltergeist, With You, Secret Soul, All Alone, Ghosts,
Little Girl, Falling Stars, Moving On, Sweet Spirit*

1983   Barbara Thompson & Rod Argent — *Shadowshow* (TM)
*Secure in You, Down On Your Luck, Sleepwalker – Siren,
Manhattan Midnite, It's Over, Echoes, Moving In The
Morning Sun, Doing What Must Be Done, Midday Riser,
Times Past*

Rod Argent & John Dankworth — *Metro*
*Bang Bang, Sea Dreams, City Streets, Sultry Sundeck,
Dinosaur's Fandango, No.1, Bad Talk, Meanwhile*

2010 Kate & Mike Westbrook — *Fine 'n' Yellow* (GONZO)
Fine and Mellow, Yellow Dog, Dollarbird, My Lover's Coat, Yellow Fig Leaf, Through the Dark, Yellow Tracery, My Lover's Heart, What I Like

JON HISEMAN

1982 *A Night In The Sun* (KUCKUCK)
Topeiro, The Hearts of Carnival & Sunroof, A Night In The Sun, Eunice, Makenna, Beach & Walking on Air

1991 *About Time Too!* (INTUITION)
Solo Berlin – The Metropol, Granz Schon Heiss Man – Big, Granz Schon Heiss Man – Mannheim, Solo Hannover – The Pavilion, Solo Hamburg – The Road To Berlin

ANA GRACEY

2003 *Innocence* (TM)
Lay Me Down, Redeemable, Dream, She Wants, Jimmy, Tonight, Seven, You Rain Down, Innocence, You Got Me Wrong, Mo Lah Du Say o

438

INDEX